CW00665986

FORGOTTEN WAR

FORGOTTEN WAR

The British Empire and Commonwealth's Epic Struggle
Against Imperial Japan, 1941–1945

BRIAN E. WALTER

CASEMATE

Philadelphia & Oxford

Published in the United States of America and Great Britain in 2023 by
CASEMATE PUBLISHERS
1950 Lawrence Road, Havertown, PA 19083, USA
and
The Old Music Hall, 106–108 Cowley Road, Oxford OX4 1JE, UK

Copyright 2023 © Brian E. Walter

Hardback Edition: ISBN 978-1-63624-357-3
Digital Edition: ISBN 978-1-63624-358-0

A CIP record for this book is available from the British Library

All rights reserved. No part of this book may be reproduced or transmitted in any form or by any
means, electronic or mechanical including photocopying, recording or by any information storage
and retrieval system, without permission from the publisher in writing.

Printed and bound in the United Kingdom by CPI Group (UK) Ltd, Croydon, CR0 4YY

Typeset in India by Lapiz Digital Services, Chennai.

For a complete list of Casemate titles, please contact:

CASEMATE PUBLISHERS (US)
Telephone (610) 853-9131
Fax (610) 853-9146
Email: casemate@casematepublishers.com
www.casematepublishers.com

CASEMATE PUBLISHERS (UK)
Telephone (0)1226 734350
Email: casemate-uk@casematepublishers.co.uk
www.casematepublishers.co.uk

Cover images, from top: Hawker Hurricane Mk II. (Royal Air Force, public domain); The Japanese 33rd
Army surrendering to 17 Indian Division. (Chris Turner, public domain); Australian assault on pillbox,
Buna, January 1943. (Australian War Memorial, copyright expired, public domain, image 014001);
HMS *Illustrious*, 1944. (U.S. Navy National Museum of Naval Aviation, photo No. 1977.031.085.071)

*The book is dedicated to my immediate family: Debi, Kaleigh
and Ashley. Thank you for your many years of unwavering
support as I pursued my dream of becoming an author.*

*The book is also dedicated to the men and women who served
in the armed forces of the British Empire and Commonwealth during
World War II with particular emphasis to those who served in the Asia/Pacific war.*

Contents

Introduction

Even before the first rays of sunlight emerged from the distant horizon on the morning of 9 August 1945, the flight deck of HMS *Formidable* was alive with activity as men and machines prepared to commence the day's flying routine against the Japanese home islands. An *Illustrious*-class aircraft carrier, *Formidable* was a veteran warship having conducted a myriad of operations against the Italians, Germans, Vichy French and now the Japanese in four different theatres of the war. *Formidable*'s combat debut occurred some four and a half years earlier in February 1941 when its aircraft carried out a strike against Axis shipping in Italian-controlled Massawa resulting in the destruction of the 5,723-ton Italian merchant ship *Moncalieri*. One month later, *Formidable* participated in the battle of Cape Matapan where its aircraft damaged Italian warships thus directly leading to a night surface engagement that resulted in the destruction of three Italian heavy cruisers and two destroyers for no British loss. Still, *Formidable*'s fortunes were not always positive, and in May 1941 it suffered heavy damage from German bombing while supporting operations off Crete. This would not be the last time *Formidable* sustained damage, but thanks to its stout construction and armoured flight deck, the venerable warship was always able to carry on. Some highlights of its subsequent service included participation in the invasions of North Africa, Sicily and Salerno, launching air strikes against German shipping off Norway, operations against the Japanese at Sakishima Gunto in support of the invasion of Okinawa and now its current actions against Japan itself.

Accompanying *Formidable* in this current endeavour—the carrier strikes against Japan—were three other British aircraft carriers, *Victorious*, *Indefatigable* and *Implacable*. Like *Formidable*, *Victorious* was an *Illustrious*-class aircraft carrier whereas the other two were of similar design, but had greater hangar capacity thus giving them the ability to operate more aircraft. Also like *Formidable*, all three aircraft carriers were veterans in their own right having engaged in considerable previous combat. In terms of *Victorious* and *Indefatigable*, this included recent service with *Formidable* off Okinawa where all three ships had endured the Kamikaze onslaught and still carried the scars from previous Kamikaze hits. *Implacable* had arrived in the theatre too late to participate in this action, and other than a training strike against the isolated Japanese naval base at Truk, was now on its first series of operations against the Japanese. Still, if *Implacable* lacked recent participation in the Pacific

The flightdeck of the aircraft carrier *Formidable* during operations off Norway in the summer of 1944. The aircraft in the foreground are Chance Vaught F4U Corsair fighter-bombers. (Hudson, F. A. (Lt), Royal Navy official photographer, public domain)

war, it was no stranger to combat. In the closing months of 1944 *Implacable* had conducted a series of attacks against German shipping off Norway resulting in the destruction of a fleet minesweeper and seven merchant ships/auxiliary vessels worth 12,927 tons and damage to a further 11 vessels worth 13,800 tons.[1] Also during these strikes *Implacable's* aircraft severely damaged and forced the grounding of a German U-boat, *U1060*, which was subsequently destroyed by the Royal Air Force.

While most attention focussed on these four British aircraft carriers, they were just part of a far greater force operating in the Japanese home waters. From the British perspective, the main combat element involved in this was Task Force 37, which consisted of these four aircraft carriers, the battleship *King George V*, six cruisers and 15 destroyers. In turn, this represented just the tip of the spear as the entire British Pacific Fleet possessed over 270 assorted vessels including a substantial fleet train to keep the forward deployed warships adequately supported. The British maintained a similar number of ships in the Indian Ocean where they served under the auspices of the East Indies Fleet. Task Force 37 had begun strike operations against the Japanese home islands on 17 July where it served alongside the much larger American Task Force 38, which was also conducting concurrent air strikes. While the make-up of Task Force 37 and the British Pacific fleet was predominately British, various elements also came from the Commonwealth. For instance, three of the attending cruisers at the start of this strike period were HMCS *Uganda*, HMNZS *Achilles* and HMNZS *Gambia* from Canada and New Zealand respectively. Likewise, two of the attending destroyers, HMAS *Quiberon* and HMAS *Quickmatch*, were from Australia. All of these vessels were British-built, but had been turned over to the respective Commonwealth navies as part of the collective relationship that personified much of the combined British/Commonwealth war effort.

To this latter point, when Britain went to war against Germany some six years earlier, it did so as the head of a great global empire and Commonwealth of Nations and not simply as the United Kingdom. In the hours and days immediately following Britain's wartime declaration; Australia, New Zealand, South Africa and Canada had each followed suit with their own declarations of war. Then as the conflict expanded into a multi-theatre contest with Italy and Japan joining the Axis cause, these same Commonwealth nations reacted in kind as part of a collective British response to the expanded threat. In doing so, the Empire and Commonwealth became an integral part of the British war effort. This was not simply an alliance of like-minded nations. Instead, Imperial and Commonwealth forces integrated directly into the British command structure and order of battle. Often times, these formations were indistinguishable from their British counterparts in terms of the uniforms they wore, the equipment they used or the practices they followed. This collective relationship was particularly prevalent in the European and Mediterranean theatres where Imperial and Commonwealth formations served almost exclusively within the context of the greater British war effort and command structure. The situation in the Pacific was somewhat different as sizeable Commonwealth formations operated in an independent manner or in conjunction with the Americans, but even here they still maintained a strong connection to their British lineage.

Another example of this collective war effort was the fact that beyond dedicated units, tens of thousands of men from all over the Empire and Commonwealth directly served on British warships and merchant vessels or within various British air and ground units. This was certainly the case with Task Force 37 and the greater British Pacific Fleet. One such man was Lieutenant Robert Hampton 'Hammy' Gray, a pilot assigned to *Formidable*. The son of a jeweller, Gray was born in Trail, British Columbia, Canada, on 2 November 1917. After attending the University of British Columbia, he joined the Royal Canadian Naval Volunteer Reserve (RCNVR) in 1940, and was soon selected to undergo officer and pilot training. Over the next few years Gray carried out a number of assignments including a two-year stint in Africa before joining *Formidable*'s 1841 Naval Air Squadron flying Chance Vaught F4U Corsair fighter-bombers in 1944. In August of that year, Gray participated in strikes against the German battleship *Tirpitz* and other warships off Norway where he earned mentions in dispatches for his bravery. Later, when *Formidable* deployed to the Pacific in 1945, Gray was in attendance and participated in a number of strikes against Japanese targets. A highlight of this occurred in July when he was credited with sinking a Japanese destroyer thus earning him a Distinguished Service Cross.

Known as 'Hammy' to his friends and associates, Lieutenant Gray was well liked and respected amongst his shipmates. Part of this was indicative of the bonds that these men shared. Among other things, no matter where they were from, be that the United Kingdom, Canada, Australia or any other part of the English-speaking world, they all shared a common reality of being a long way from home. Beyond this, they also shared common hardships. Duty on a deployed warship was not easy as life was overwhelmingly defined by long hours, hard work, limited physical comforts, boredom, tedious watches and routines and the ever-present spectre of impending danger. Of course, the pilots and aircrews were most susceptible to this latter threat, but as the Kamikaze onslaught off Okinawa had demonstrated, none of the ship's crew was immune to the potential wrath of the enemy. At any time, an unnoticed Kamikaze might crash into the flight deck or a torpedo fired from a lurking Japanese submarine slam into the hull, bringing about death and mayhem. It had been some time since the last such event had occurred, but the threat of these dangers was always present.

Perhaps another bond these men shared was the sad reality that their sacrifices and exploits largely went unnoticed in their home countries. Much of this obscurity stemmed from the Eurocentric nature of the war in which Britain had devoted most of its energy and attention to the defeat of Germany. This view was perfectly reasonable given Germany's proximity to Britain and the threat it had posed to British independence. Among other things, this contest had directly impacted the entire British nation, which had endured bombing, blockade and an invasion threat. Given these factors, any part of the war not directly related to the contest against Germany was viewed as a secondary matter. One reflection of this was the fact that the British Fourteenth Army, which had just liberated much of Burma from the clutches of the Japanese, commonly referred to itself as the 'Forgotten Army'. Of course, by this time the war in Europe was now over, but this development brought little attention to events in the Far East. After almost six years of conflict, the British people were war weary and ready to put the whole matter behind them. Now, as the nation took its first tentative steps into the new post-war world, which included the first general election in ten years, people were aware that there was still an ongoing conflict in the Far East, but this was hardly front and centre in their minds. After all, this conflict was literally on the other side of the world and had little direct impact on their personal lives.

Still, notwithstanding this lack of popular exposure, the British war effort in the Far East was actually quite extensive with the activities of Task Force 37 only representing a minute portion of this undertaking. Over a vast area stretching from India in the west to the Solomon Islands in the east and Australia in the south to the waters off Japan in the north, a massive British and Commonwealth force of upwards of two million men waged direct war against the Japanese or supported this endeavour. Actions currently underway during the second week in August included the activities of the recently formed British Twelfth Army, which was conducting mopping-up operations against the remnants of three Japanese armies in Burma. At the same time, sizeable Australian formations confronted isolated Japanese garrisons across the South Pacific including at Bougainville, New Britain, Borneo and along the northern coast of New Guinea. Meanwhile, throughout the region British and Commonwealth air and naval units conducted ongoing operations against the Japanese. In terms of the latter, this included the activities of British submarines, which claimed the destruction of at least 21 assorted Japanese vessels (of mostly minor tonnage) during the first week in August alone.[2] Likewise, this also included the actions of the British East Indies Fleet, which was in the midst of preparing for an upcoming British invasion of Malaya, codenamed Operation *Zipper*. As part of this process, the fleet had recently carried out three preparatory operations off Sumatra in Indonesia to clear mines, perform photo reconnaissance and weaken Japanese defences.

Nor was this the extent of the proposed British war effort within the region. Instead, preparations were underway to vastly expand this presence. Already, sizeable reinforcements had arrived, or were in the process of arriving, to substantially bolster the size and striking power of the British Pacific Fleet. Most prevalent among the new vessels joining this force were the light fleet aircraft carriers *Colossus*, *Glory*, *Venerable* and *Vengeance* and the battleships *Duke of York* and *Anson*. In terms of the former, these light carriers essentially doubled the number of British strike carriers available for future operations against Japan. Meanwhile, in terms of air reinforcements, preparations were underway for the formation and deployment of a heavy bomber unit, known as Tiger Force, containing a proposed 11 British, eight Canadian, one New Zealand and two Australian squadrons. Flying a combination of Lancaster, Lincoln, Liberator and Mosquito bombers, Tiger Force was earmarked to operate from Okinawa as part of the aerial support for the anticipated invasion of Japan. Finally, beyond the proposed British invasion of Malaya, which was scheduled for October, discussions were underway to create a British/Commonwealth corps that would also participate in the invasion of Japan with a likely deployment date sometime in 1946.

Of course, these theatre-wide activities and preparations were of little consequence to Lieutenant Gray and his shipmates on *Formidable*. For them, the focus centred upon the daily routines of the ship and the continuation of strike operations against Japan. These operations had begun some three and a half weeks earlier and generally consisted of two strike days followed by intermediate replenishment periods. Thus far, the British had executed three such cycles during which their aircraft had inflicted heavy damage against Japanese air and naval assets in southern and central Japan. A highpoint in these earlier operations included attacks carried out by all four British carriers that hit and sank the Japanese auxiliary escort carrier *Shimane Maru* off Shido Bay in the Inland Sea on 24 July. After a particularly long delay following the last series of strikes carried out on 28 and 30 July, the fleet was once again poised to hit targets in northern Japan. Attacks had been scheduled the day before, but severe weather had forced the postponement of these operations. Now on the 9th, the weather was substantially better, and flying operations commenced on *Formidable* at 0410 hours with the launching of the first strike of 12 Corsair fighter-bombers followed an hour later by a second foray of Avenger bombers.

By mid-morning it was Lieutenant Gray's turn to join the fray. Leading a force of eight Corsairs, Gray took off from *Formidable* at 0810 hours and set course for the Japanese coastline. Split into two flights of four aircraft each, these Corsairs were armed with two 500-pound bombs and six wing-mounted .50 machine guns. Their proposed target was Matsushima airfield, but just before leaving *Formidable*, Gray was informed that Japanese warships were reportedly in nearby Onagawa Bay. Accompanying Gray on the strike were six pilots from the United Kingdom and one from Norway. Three of these pilots were recent replacements on their first combat missions. Making landfall north of Kinkasan Point at approximately 0920 hours, Gray turned his aircraft southward and followed the coastline to the target area. En route, the force flew past Onagawa Bay, where Gray confirmed the presence of warships including two that appeared to be destroyers. Proceeding to nearby Matsushima, Gray determined that the airfield had already been heavily damaged due to an earlier raid and decided that Onagawa was a better target for his strike force.

This proved to be a prudent decision as Onagawa Bay contained more than a dozen naval vessels within its confined waters. Most of these were auxiliaries and minor craft, but they included a handful of purpose-built warships. Of the latter, the largest was the 2,560-ton escort ship *Ōhama*. Although possessing the size, speed and appearance of a destroyer, *Ōhama* actually started life as a fast target ship. However, during its construction, the Japanese converted *Ōhama* into a bona fide warship by substantially increasing its armament to help compensate for their recent heavy destroyer losses. As such, *Ōhama* was armed with two 4.7-inch guns, 32 25mm anti-aircraft guns and 36 depth charges. Another powerful warship present in Onagawa Bay was the *Etorofu*-class escort *Amakusa*. This vessel fell into a category of warships referred to as Kaibōkans (sea defence or coastal defence ships) that were roughly equivalent to frigates or escort destroyers in the British and American navies. In the case of *Amakusa*, the ship displaced 870 tons and had an armament consisting of three 4.7-inch guns along with lighter anti-aircraft guns and up to 60 depth charges. A similar vessel was the converted escort *W33*. Originally built as a minesweeper, the Japanese had converted *W33* to fulfil an escort role by removing its minesweeping gear and replacing that with depth charges. In this configuration, the 648-ton *W33* possessed a main armament of three 4.7-inch guns and 36 depth charges. Finally, the last notable warship in the bay was the 420-ton sub-chaser *CH42*, which carried a 3-inch gun and 36 depth charges.

Attacking these vessels would not be an easy task. The target area was a confined inlet measuring about a mile in length and 500 metres across surrounded by steep hills on three sides. Most of the vessels present within the bay were located around its exterior with some positioned parallel to the shoreline thus making them more difficult to attack given their close proximity to the surrounding hills. The sole exception to this was *Amakusa*, which was located in the centre of the bay perpendicular to the shoreline. This position made it an obvious target. In attacking the bay, the British could expect heavy opposition from the large number of anti-aircraft guns installed on the various warships as well as additional guns located in the surrounding hills. Given the morning's earlier activities including the raid against nearby Matsushima airfield, Lieutenant Gray could expect the Japanese defenders to be fully alert. Approaching from the northwest, he opted to make a diving attack through an adjacent valley that emptied out into the bay thus minimising his exposure to enemy observation and providing an unobstructed egress to the sea. It was hoped his aircraft would be in and out of the bay before the Japanese were fully able to react to their presence with the full duration of their attack run lasting no more than 30 seconds.

Commencing their attack from 10,000 feet, the eight Corsair fighter-bombers made a high-speed dive into the valley with Gray in the lead. Flying low through the surrounding hills, the Corsairs abruptly emerged over the open bay where they immediately encountered a heavy barrage of anti-aircraft fire. Much of this fire seemed to concentrate on the lead aircraft piloted by Gray as he made an attack run towards the exposed *Amakusa*. Almost immediately, Gray's aircraft was hit and appeared to catch fire. Likewise, one of the 500-pound bombs he was carrying was shot off the aircraft and seen to fall away. Yet, despite his obvious distress, Gray continued his attack run levelling out at about 50 feet above the water. Japanese witnesses would later state that Gray's aircraft was flying so low that they could clearly see his face in the cockpit. At the last moment, Gray dropped his remaining bomb, which struck *Amakusa* on the port side below its No. 2 gun platform. The bomb penetrated the engine room and detonated a nearby ammunition magazine. This caused an immense explosion that blew out a large section of the starboard side of the ship. The stricken escort destroyer immediately took a heavy list to starboard and began to sink. In just a few minutes, the vessel was gone, taking 71 members of its crew with it.

If Lieutenant Gray was ever aware of the success he had just achieved, we will never know. His burning aircraft flew on for about another mile, and then abruptly rolled over and plunged into the sea. No remains of Lieutenant Gray were ever found, and the obvious speculation is that he probably died on impact. As this event occurred, one of the remaining pilots announced over the radio, 'There goes Gray'.[3] This seemingly indifferent statement was reflective of the cruel reality these men lived. One minute you were alive; the next minute you were dead. It could happen in the blink of an eye or through a more prolonged, agonizing process. For the men that remained, they just had to carry on. Still, if this statement seemed to indicate a callousness to the plight of their leader, that was not the case. Instead, clearly angry and distressed, the men took the unusual decision to carry out two more attack runs against the remaining warships at Onagawa Bay. This action was contrary to standing guidance that limited attacks to a single pass to minimise danger to the aircrews. Fortunately, this brash action did not result in any further loss to the remaining aircraft. Against this, the strike meted out heavy damage against the surviving Japanese ships leaving some on fire or sinking. This damage, plus that from follow-up strikes, would eventually result in the destruction of *Ōhama*, *W33* and *CH42* along with most of the smaller vessels in the bay. Their vengeance satisfied; the remaining British aircraft returned to *Formidable* absent their leader. In doing so, one of the Corsairs crashed upon landing due to a hydraulic failure that caused its landing gear to collapse upon touchdown.

Formidable and the other British aircraft carriers continued strike operations for the remainder of the day. Beyond the havoc wreaked upon the shipping at Onagawa Bay, these attacks claimed the destruction of 45 Japanese aircraft with 22 more damaged. British losses in return amounted to seven aircraft including the one piloted by Lieutenant Gray. From a strictly military point of view, this represented a very favourable exchange rate, but this practical consideration could not entirely allay the grief of the day's losses. While each of the men killed on this day represented a tragic development, none gained more notice than Lieutenant Robert Hampton 'Hammy' Gray, who later received a posthumous Victoria Cross, Britain's highest military honour, for his demonstrated valour during the attack. For the men of Task Force 37, this was just another day in a war that had already cost the British and Commonwealth forces confronting the Japanese over 250,000 combat casualties in terms of men killed, wounded or captured. This was a very heavy toll for a conflict that garnered little attention back home. If this was a forgotten war, it was also an extremely costly one.

How much longer this forgotten war would last was anyone's guess. One thing plainly certain was that the Allies were winning. That point was obvious to commanding admirals and generals down to the lowest enlisted ranks. Among other things, the activities of Task Force 37 clearly indicated the decisive edge the Allies had gained as British warships were able to operate on Japan's very doorstep while no Japanese warships could conceivably operate anywhere near the British Isles. In fairness, it was the Americans who had predominantly brought about this situation, but British and Commonwealth forces had also contributed. Still, if the Allies were winning, that did not mean the war was won. Despite the distressed nature of its situation, Japan still controlled large swathes of Asian territory where tens of millions of people suffered under the yoke of Japanese occupation. Likewise, tens of thousands of Allied prisoners languished under harsh and often criminal conditions within a variety of Japanese prisoner of war camps spread throughout the region. To relieve this suffering, it was imperative to end the war quickly. However, given the intransigent nature of the Japanese leadership and their seeming indifference to the suffering of their own people, the war might continue on for months or even years. The only things certain for the men of Task Force 37 was that another series of air strikes was scheduled for the coming morning and that more men would almost certainly die.

Maps

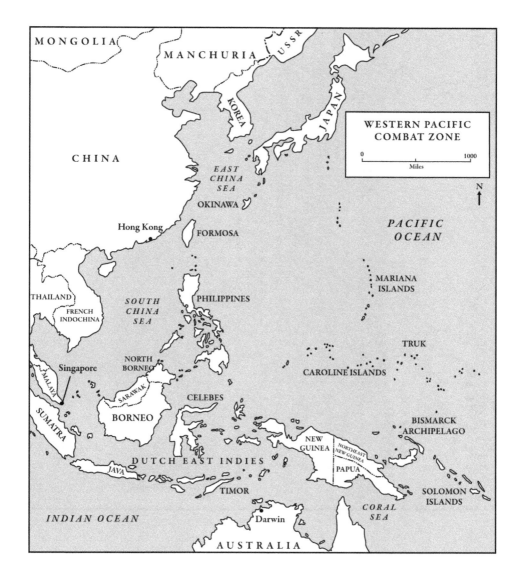

MONGOLIA
MANCHURIA
USSR
CHINA
KOREA
JAPAN
EAST
CHINA
SEA
OKINAWA
Hong Kong
FORMOSA

WESTERN PACIFIC
COMBAT ZONE

0   1000
Miles

N

PACIFIC
OCEAN

THAILAND
FRENCH
INDOCHINA
SOUTH
CHINA
SEA
PHILIPPINES

MARIANA
ISLANDS

TRUK

Singapore
NORTH
BORNEO
CAROLINE ISLANDS

MALAYA
SARAWAK
CELEBES
BORNEO

BISMARCK
ARCHIPELAGO

SUMATRA

NEW
GUINEA
NORTHEAST
NEW GUINEA

DUTCH EAST INDIES
JAVA
PAPUA

SOLOMON
ISLANDS

TIMOR

CORAL
SEA

INDIAN OCEAN
Darwin

AUSTRALIA

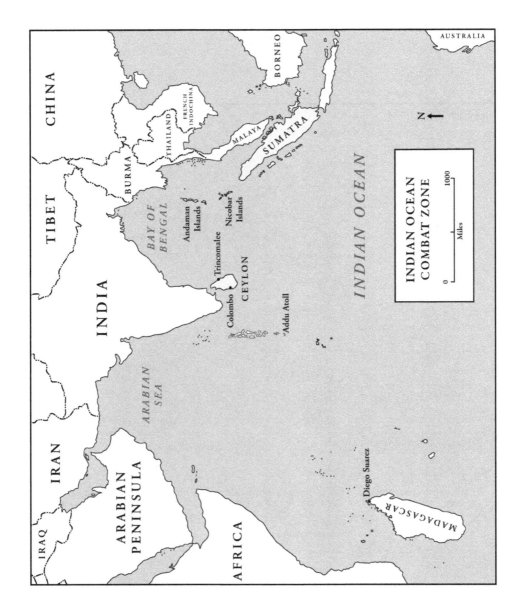

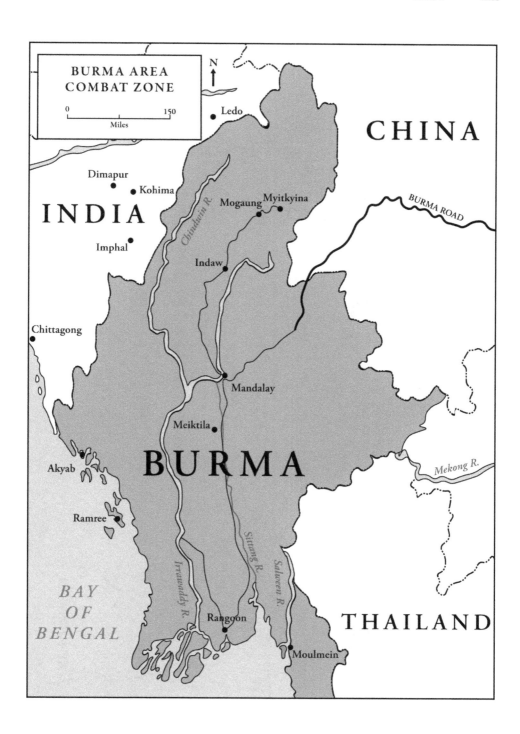

BURMA AREA
COMBAT ZONE

0   150
        Miles

N

CHINA

Ledo

INDIA

Dimapur
Kohima
Imphal

Mogaung Myitkyina

Chindwin R.

BURMA ROAD

Indaw

Chittagong

Mandalay

Meiktila

BURMA

Akyab

Mekong R.

Ramree

Irrawaddy R.

Sittang R.

Salween R.

BAY
OF
BENGAL

Rangoon

Moulmein

THAILAND

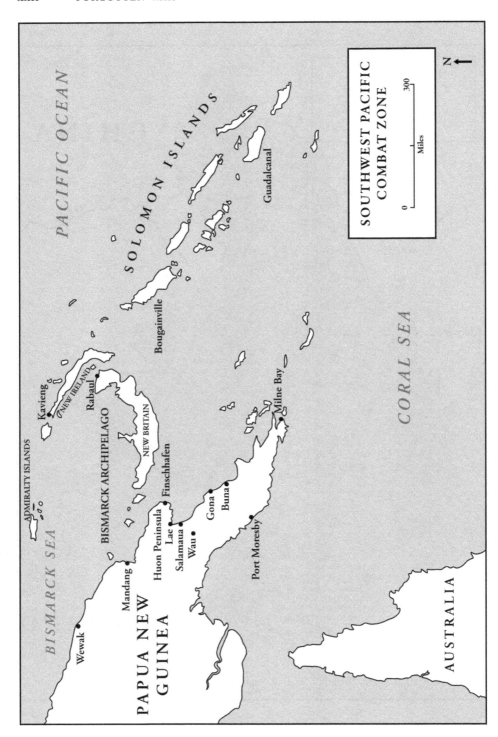

CHAPTER I

The Long Road to War

On the eleventh hour of the eleventh day of the eleventh month in the year 1918, the guns in Europe fell silent as the conflict later known as World War I drew to an abrupt and unceremonious end. After 51 months of unprecedented warfare and bloody carnage that had ravaged Europe as well as much of the rest of the world, Britain and its Entente partners finally stood triumphant over Germany and the Central Powers. This had been a war of unparalleled proportions in terms of its scope and intensity far exceeding anything previously experienced in all of human history. Some 15 years earlier, Europe had emerged from an era of relative peace and stability to begin a period of growing tension and rivalry between the continent's major powers. As tensions mounted, the various European nations grouped off into differing alliances to counter their perceived adversaries. In August 1914 war finally erupted on the European continent and quickly escalated into an immense conflict initially pitting the Entente Powers consisting of the British Empire, France and Russia against the Central Powers of the German, Austro-Hungarian and Ottoman Empires. Although primarily centred in Europe, the war quickly spread to other parts of the world thus transforming it into a truly global endeavour. By 1918 Russia had bowed out of the conflict, but its departure was counterbalanced by the entry of the Kingdom of Italy and the United States, which both joined the war on the side of the Entente Powers. In a contest of brute force against brute force, the combined strength of the Entente nations finally brought Germany and the other Central Powers to the brink of collapse, and in November 1918 they sued for peace thus ending the war.

While this development brought a great sense of relief and pride to the British nation, many Britons shared an underlying sense of distress and frustration regarding the war's conduct and outcome. More than anything else, this discontent was fuelled by the high cost the war had inflicted upon the nation. In a little over four years of combat, Britain and its Imperial and Commonwealth allies had suffered 3,428,535 total casualties including 947,023 fatalities.[1] The fact that these casualties were substantially lower than those suffered by Germany, France, Russia and the

Table 1.1. World War I Personnel and Materiel Losses for the Major Powers.

	Total military casualties	Military fatalities	Financial costs in billions	Major warship losses*	Merchant tonnage lost**
Major Entente Powers					
British Empire	3,428,535	947,023	£10.395	162	7,759,090
French Empire	6,220,800	1,397,800	£9.975	32	891,000
Russian Empire	9,300,000	1,600,000+	£5.121	47	183,000
Kingdom of Italy	2,197,000	680,000	£3.629	22	872,341
United States	325,236	116,708	£6.464	4	531,000
Major Central Powers					
Germany	7,209,413	1,808,555	£11.614	592	4,900,000
Austro-Hungarian Empire	4,650,200	1,496,200	£4.921	70	1,100,000
Ottoman Empire	1,965,000+	550,000+	£0.689	4	61,470

Source: Randal Gray and Christopher Argyle, *Chronicle of the First World War, Volume II: 1917–1921* (New York: Oxford, Facts on File, 1990); Arthur J. Marder, *From Dreadnought to Scapa Flow, Volume V: Victory and Aftermath (January 1918 – June 1919)* (London: Oxford University Press, 1990); Henry Newbolt, *History of the Great War, Naval Operations, Volume V* (London: Longmans, Green and Co., 1931); and C. Ernest Fayle, *Seaborne Trade, Volume III: The Period of Unrestricted Submarine Warfare* (London: John Murray, 1924).

* Major warships listed in this category consist of vessels classified as battleships, battlecruisers, cruisers, destroyers and submarines. German and Austro-Hungarian figures include wartime losses and vessels surrendered or seized after the Armistice.

** German and Austro-Hungarian merchant casualty figures include wartime losses and tonnage surrendered or seized after the Armistice.

Austro-Hungarian Empire during the conflict did little to console a grieving population. The navy and merchant marine's portion of this butcher's bill was mercifully small, but their materiel losses had been tremendous. The Royal Navy's casualty list included 2 dreadnought battleships, 11 pre-dreadnought battleships, 3 battlecruisers, 13 cruisers, 12 light cruisers, 67 destroyers and 54 submarines sunk during the conflict.[2] The British merchant fleet's losses had been even higher with 2,479 vessels worth 7,759,090 tons having been sunk.[3] Finally, the war's financial costs had exacted a staggering toll on the British Treasury and economy amounting to some £7.852 billion for the United Kingdom and £10.395 billion for the British Empire as a whole.[4]

Still, while many Britons reviled these heavy losses, no informed observer could dispute the immense and indispensable role that the nation's armed forces had played in bringing about the demise of the Central Powers. Nowhere was this British contribution more critical than in the war at sea. This triumph centred upon the achievement of two fundamental and overriding objectives: the British had maintained control of the oceans while denying the same to their enemies.

As such, British maritime power made four vital contributions to the Allied war effort as defined by the Admiralty in 1917:

1. The protection of the Sea Communications of the Allied armies, more particularly in France, where the main offensive lies.
2. Prevention of enemy trade as a means of handicapping his military operations and exerting pressure on the mass of his people.
3. Protection of British and Allied Trade, on which depends the supply of munitions and food to the Allied armies and people.
4. Resistance to Invasion and Raids.[5]

The Navy's success in deterring invasion was self-evident, but what of its other contributions? First and foremost, the Royal Navy and merchant marine sustained vital seaborne trade that fulfilled the material needs of the British population, industry and military. This was absolutely essential since Britain lacked sufficient quantities of several key strategic resources and required large inflows of imports to sustain its population and economy. Likewise, the key Allied nations of France and Italy were also dependent upon maritime trade to compensate for their own resource shortfalls. This was particularly true regarding the importation of British coal, which was indispensable in keeping both countries in the war. In maintaining this vital seaborne trade, the Royal Navy and merchant marine provided the very means by which the British nation and its allies survived and prosecuted the war. To be sure, this success came at a very high cost and was often accompanied by periods of great anxiety within the British government and Admiralty. Nevertheless, enough ships and supplies invariably got through to sustain these nations and support their collective war efforts.

By comparison, the Royal Navy swept all hostile commerce from the oceans and imposed a long and debilitating blockade against Germany and the other Central Powers. This physical blockade, coupled with economic and political pressure, slowly isolated the Central Powers and deprived them of a number of key strategic resources. Paramount amongst these was a severe reduction in the importation of foodstuffs and fertilizer. By 1918 agricultural production and food availability was so adversely impacted by this blockade that large segments of the German population suffered from acute malnutrition. This, in turn, made many people more susceptible to disease. In 1918 the civilian death rate in Germany was 37 percent higher than it had been before the war, and a post-war analysis estimated that the blockade had directly or indirectly contributed to some 760,000 German civilian deaths during the period of 1915 through 1918.[6] The situation was even worse for the Austro-Hungarian Empire where privations were more widespread and severe. Meanwhile, the armed forces were generally better off than the population as a whole, but food rationing was still prohibitive. Eventually, the blockade wrecked the German and Austro-Hungarian economies, undermined the morale and confidence of their populations and fostered mutiny and revolution within their armed forces. These conditions were far worse than anything the Germans were able to inflict upon the British and played a major role in eroding the Central Powers' will and ability to continue the war.

At a more direct level, the British effectively used maritime power to support their military operations in Europe, the Middle East and Africa while denying the same to the Central Powers. This was particularly vital in Northwest Europe where the British successfully deployed and maintained an expeditionary force that eventually comprised five field armies containing over sixty divisions. Likewise, British mastery of the seas set the conditions and means by which the two million-strong American Expeditionary Force deployed to Europe. The volume of war-related traffic traversing the English Channel amply demonstrated the magnitude of these undertakings. During the duration of the war, 147,674 ships crossed the Dover Straits to deliver 1,250,000 tons of materiel, including 650,000 tons of ammunition, and transport some 16 million soldiers to and from the continent.[7] This application of maritime power helped foster victories on the battlefield that, along with the blockade, eventually persuaded Germany and its allies to sue for peace.

A final major achievement stemming from Britain's maritime success was the surrender of the German fleet. As part of the armistice bringing about the end of the war, Germany agreed to surrender most of its formidable High Seas Fleet and all of its submarine force to the Allies. On 20 November 1918 the first German U-boats (submarines) arrived off Harwich, England to surrender to Rear-Admiral Reginald Tyrwhitt. Early the next day the British Grand Fleet weighed anchor and silently slipped out of Rosyth in Scotland. By mid-morning this massive force, which consisted of some 370 warships including Dominion, American and French contingents, rendezvoused with the German High Seas Fleet and escorted it into captivity. With this and subsequent capitulations, the British and their allies eventually interned a total of 11 battleships, five battlecruisers, eight light cruisers, 50 destroyers and 176 U-boats. In doing so, they eliminated all vestiges of offensive German naval power and achieved what is arguably a victory unparalleled in the annals of maritime history.

For its part, the British army also made substantial and vital contributions to the Allied war effort. The maintenance of large standing armies was not part of the British military tradition. Instead, Britain had generally depended upon the Royal Navy to be its senior service while maintaining a smaller, but highly professional army to police the Empire and engage in selected campaigns as needed. This was certainly the case at the beginning of World War I when the regular army only numbered about 255,000 men rising to a total mobilised strength of 713,514 men when reservists were added in. By comparison, Austria, Germany, France and Russia all possessed armies numbering in the millions.[8] Yet, despite this disparity in size, the British straightaway dispatched an expeditionary force consisting of six divisions to France at the opening of the conflict. This force immediately came into action and fought major engagements at Mons, Le Cateau, the Aisne and Ypres that largely exhausted its strength by the end of 1914. Still, through these actions the British Expeditionary Force made important contributions in blunting the initial German offensive and helped derail their plans for an early victory.

With the strength of the pre-war regular army now largely expended, the British began a major mobilisation effort that would see the British army expand to a size never before attained in its history. Eventually, this army, bolstered by contributions from the Empire and Commonwealth, expanded to a peak strength of some four million men of which half were deployed with the British Expeditionary Force in France and Belgium. Beyond this, large contingents of British and Commonwealth troops also saw service in other battlegrounds including at Salonika in Greece, the Dardanelles in Turkey, Italy, East Africa and the Middle East. In turn, over the next three years these forces engaged in a series of major battles involving hundreds of thousands of men including at Gallipoli and Loos in 1915, the Somme in 1916 and Passchendaele and Cambrai in 1917. None of these battles resulted in meaningful victories but could better be described as part of an extended war of attrition in which both sides suffered heavy losses. In this, the British and Commonwealth forces held their own and generally inflicted comparable casualties upon their adversaries as they themselves suffered.

This situation changed in 1918. The first half of the year was dominated by a major series of German offensives on the Western Front designed to knock the Allies out of the war before the American Expeditionary Force could arrive in Europe to tilt the balance of power in the Allies' favour. Many of these blows fell upon British forces, which were forced to give ground, but did not break. Eventually, the Allies halted this offensive thus shattering Germany's final bid for victory. Thereafter, the Allies seized the initiative and scored a series of decisive victories during the latter half of the year that facilitated the precipitous demise of the Central Powers. British and Commonwealth forces were at the forefront of many of these operations. This included a spectacular British victory in Palestine that was the primary impetus behind the collapse of the Ottoman Empire. British participation in the battle of Vittorio Veneto in Italy helped attain a similar outcome against the Austro-Hungarians. Of most importance, on the Western Front the British army played the pivotal role in the series of counterattacks known as the Hundred Days Offensive that finally vanquished the German army. This latter contribution was highlighted by the fact that the British, who only made up about 30 percent of the available Allied forces, accounted for 49 and 43 percent of the prisoners and guns seized during this offensive (188,700 of the 385,500 prisoners and 2,840 of the 6,615 guns).[9]

Summarising these accomplishments, during a period of a little more than four years, the British army expanded from a small regular force primarily designed to police the Empire to an immense modern army that eventually proved itself equal or superior to that of its vaunted German adversary. In the process of doing so, the British adopted many new innovations including the development and use of tanks in ground warfare. Likewise, by war's end the army had become very adept at using artillery including counterbattery fire and precision targeting. Unlike the Royal Navy, which dominated the maritime conflict, the British army never attained a senior numerical position within the Allied hierarchy, but it was at the forefront of many of the war's key ground actions and arguably emerged from the conflict as the most competent and accomplished of the various Allied armies. An example of its effectiveness was the fact that the British Expeditionary Force was responsible for 41 percent of all German prisoners taken on the Western Front during the duration of the conflict (319,138 out of 774,000).[10] Added to this British bag were another 100,657 Turkish prisoners taken in Palestine and Mesopotamia and 34,046 Austrian prisoners taken at Vittorio Veneto during 1918 alone.[11]

Finally, beyond the vast contributions made by the navy and army, the war also instituted the rise of a new service in Britain's military establishment. In the previous

Each of the British armed forces made substantial contributions to the defeat of the Central Powers during World War I. Pictured here are British troops during the Hundred Days Offensive. (John Warwick Brooke, public domain)

55 years there had been limited use of stationary balloons to perform reconnaissance, but World War I saw military aviation become an integral component in the execution of national warfare. The primary instrument in this new military revolution was the heavier-than-air airplane, which had only been in existence for 11 years at the start of the war. Not surprisingly, these early aircraft were extremely primitive and initially only used in a reconnaissance role. However, within a matter of months the various combatants began incorporating a progressive series of technical improvements to their aircraft designs while expanding their uses into a variety of functions including tactical air support, strategic bombing, aerial combat and maritime support. By war's end, all the major combatants possessed sizeable 'air forces' to carry out this new form of warfare. Of these, none was larger or more capable than Britain's Royal Air Force (RAF), which was officially formed on 1 April 1918 and became the first such service to gain independent status from its naval and army counterparts. In turn, the RAF played an important role in bringing about the demise of the Central Powers.

Given the size and strength of these combined services, Britain was arguably the strongest military power in the world at the end of 1918, but the nation was exhausted after four years of warfare and earnestly sought to return to a semblance of peacetime normality. Accordingly, the nation underwent a massive demobilisation. At war's end the Royal Navy boasted a strength of some 415,000 officers and men operating a fleet of 1,300 war vessels totalling 3,250,000 tons. This immense force included 42 dreadnought battleships and battlecruisers, 109 cruisers, 13 aircraft carriers, 527 destroyers and torpedo boats and 137 submarines.[12] Within weeks of the Armistice, the British began an aggressive plan to draw down the navy. By the middle of June 1919, the Admiralty had released no fewer than 13,600 officers and 202,000 men from naval service.[13] This trend continued into the new decade with corresponding reductions in fleet sizes and naval expenditures. In 1920–21 naval spending fell to £92,505,000 compared to £334,091,000 just two years before.[14] The situation was much the same for the army and air force, which underwent similar budget and force reductions. Particularly hard hit was the army, which went from an active strength of 3.5 million men in November 1918 to just 370,000 in November 1920 and 231,000 by 1923.[15] The government justified these large reductions by the adoption of a 'ten-year rule' stating there would be no major wars in the next ten years thus eliminating the need for large standing forces.

Yet, even as these demobilisation efforts progressed, the spectre of a new threat materialised in the Pacific with the rise of a new potential enemy. This emerging danger had been a long time in coming, and yet the fact of its very existence was nothing short of miraculous. Seventy years before, Japan had been a primitive, isolated, semi-feudal state run by Shogun warlords and a warrior samurai caste. In 1869 a new reform-minded emperor consolidated control over the warlords and began an immense push to modernise his nation. In the decades that followed, the Japanese underwent an incredible period of industrialisation and expansion that transformed their nation into a major economic and military power. Ironically, much of this meteoric rise was bolstered by British assistance. This was particularly true regarding the fledgling Imperial Japanese Navy, which sought to emulate the long-standing prowess of the British Royal Navy. Accordingly, the Japanese brokered an agreement with Britain in which the latter provided materiel and advisory support to the Japanese. With this, Japan soon acquired a British-trained officer corps and a fleet made up of modern European warship designs.

The Japanese were quick to exploit this newly acquired power for external gain. Much of this centred upon the use of gunboat diplomacy and military coercion to exact concessions from their weaker and fragmented Chinese and Korean neighbours. This included a temporary deployment of military forces to Formosa in 1874 that later gave the Japanese justification to assume sovereignty over the Ryukyu Islands. A year and a half later a Japanese naval squadron arrived off Seoul and forced the Korean Regent to sign the Treaty of Kanghwa, which gave Japan access to Korea for the purpose of trade and economic exploitation. Over the next several years Japan extended its influence over Korea, which caused ongoing tensions with China. Finally, in August 1894 these tensions boiled over into armed conflict between Japan and China. A major event in this short war was the battle of the Yalu River in which a fleet of Japanese warships decisively defeated a Chinese naval force of similar size. This victory gave Japan dominance over the Yellow Sea, which allowed them to lay siege and capture the key Chinese ports of Port Arthur and Weiheiwei. In April 1895 the fighting ended, and with the signing of the Treaty of Shimonoseki, China recognised Korea's independence and ceded Formosa and the Penghu Islands to Japan.

With China now subdued, the Japanese next turned their ire against a European opponent. Vexed by growing Russian influence in the region as well as diplomatic manoeuvring that had granted Russia access to Port Arthur in Manchuria, the Japanese opted to use military force to address their grievances. On the night of 8/9 February 1904 and without the legitimacy of a formal declaration of war, Japan launched a surprise attack against the Russian Asiatic Fleet at Port Arthur. During this attack and the various actions that followed, the Japanese largely destroyed or captured the majority of Russian warships present in the area. Thereafter, the Japanese captured Port Arthur on 2 January 1905 following a long siege. While this was underway, the Russians hastily readied and dispatched a second fleet from the Baltic to proceed to the Far East. Upon its arrival in the Korean Straits in May 1905, the Japanese promptly engaged this fleet off Tsushima Island and decisively defeated it in one of the most lopsided victories in naval history. With the elimination of two separate fleets, the Russians opted to enter into peace negotiations, which resulted in the Treaty of Portsmouth on 5 September 1905. With this, Russia recognised Japanese claims to Korea and ceded Port Arthur and South Sakhalin to Japan. Five years later Japan annexed Korea thus formalising their control over the neighbouring nation.

Thus far, everything had gone largely in Japan's favour, and this trend continued with the advent of World War I. Early in the conflict the Japanese joined the war on the side of the Allies, but they did very little actual fighting against the Central Powers. The most significant event in Japan's wartime participation was the siege and capture of the German settlement of Tsingtao in China along with its 4,000-man garrison. Beyond this, Japan's contributions were minimal. Nevertheless, the Japanese used this time, when the world was preoccupied with events in Europe, to expand their influence in China and force the latter to sign a treaty granting Japan rights and leases in Manchuria and Mongolia. Then, at the conclusion of hostilities, Japan received control over Germany's former Pacific island colonies north of the equator including the Caroline and Marianas groups and the Palau Islands. Thus, for the minor cost of 13,245 wartime casualties (compared to the millions suffered by the major combatants), Japan emerged from the war practically unscathed and in a greatly enhanced position.[16]

This fact was not lost upon the British, who viewed Japan with growing trepidation. On one hand, Japan was still technically a British ally, but the British clearly recognised it as an ambitious, rising power that was intent on further expansion throughout the region. Making matters worse, the Japanese had yet to experience a serious reversal or heavy cost in their recent belligerent activities that might tend to temper their nationalistic ambitions. This made Japan an obvious threat to British interests in the Far East, which included extensive colonial holdings as well as strong political, economic and cultural ties to the Commonwealth nations of Australia and New Zealand. Recognising that any major conflict in the Pacific would be naval-centric, in 1919 the Admiralty directed Admiral John Jellicoe, the former commander of the British Grand Fleet, to assess the region's defensive needs. In response, Jellicoe recommended the stationing of a permanent British fleet in the Pacific containing a minimum of 16 battleships and battlecruisers with the costs of such being split between the British, Australian and New Zealand governments at a ratio of 75, 20 and 5 percent respectively.[17]

This proposal garnered little enthusiasm from British officials who were primarily concerned with the restoration of a peacetime economy and had limited resources available to fund such an undertaking. Making matters worse from a financial point of view, the British soon faced the prospect of a new naval arms race as both the United States and Japan conveyed aspirations to challenge Britain's naval supremacy. By the beginning of 1921 the United States was already well underway in constructing four new 32,600-ton battleships armed with eight 16-inch guns and had begun laying the keels of six additional 43,000-ton battleships armed with twelve 16-inch guns.[18] At the same time, Japan was pursuing its own building programme that proposed the construction of eight new battleships and eight new battlecruisers by 1927. Given their tight post-war budgets, the British were averse to spending limited resources on a new building programme. Nevertheless, the government and navy realised the potential threat posed by this challenge, and both resolved to respond in kind if necessary.

Fortunately, the initial impetus behind this threat quickly subsided as pacifistic movements and fiscal realities took hold across the world. It soon became apparent that none of the major powers, including the United States and Japan, had much stomach for a renewed naval arms race. Instead, the various governments increasingly turned to diplomacy, negotiations and treaties as a means to advance their national agendas and security arrangements. For the Japanese, this apparent reversal was largely a calculated recognition of economic reality. Despite its recent industrial transformation, Japan still lagged behind both the United States and Britain in terms of national wealth and economic power. As such, the Japanese knew they lacked the means to effectively compete against either nation in an all-out arms race. For the British, this development represented a welcome opportunity to avoid a costly shipbuilding programme as they hoped to capitalise upon the burgeoning idea of international arms control as an inexpensive means to solidify their prominent naval position.

To this end, in November 1921 Britain joined the other major powers and convened a conference in Washington to discuss naval disarmament and other security issues. After weeks of negotiations Britain, the United States, Japan, France and Italy concluded the Five-Power Naval Limitation Treaty, also known as the Washington Treaty. The main provision of this treaty set limits on the total capital ship tonnage allowed to each nation. Based upon a ratio of 5, 5, 3, 1.75 and 1.75, the treaty allocated 525,000 tons of battleships and battlecruisers to Britain and the United States compared to 315,000 tons for Japan and 175,000 tons for France and Italy. A similar arrangement covered aircraft carriers with Britain and the United States allotted 135,000 tons compared to 81,000 tons for Japan and 60,000 tons for France and Italy. The treaty also established limits on the size and armaments allowed for various classes of warships with battleships limited to 35,000 tons and 16-inch guns and cruisers to 10,000 tons and 8-inch guns. In terms of aircraft carriers, the treaty allowed each nation to build two at 33,000 tons with all other carriers limited to 27,000 tons and 8-inch guns.

One of the treaties more controversial provisions was an American-proposed ten-year moratorium on new battleship construction. The British delegation initially objected to this proposal arguing that it would put the Royal Navy at a qualitative disadvantage as compared to its American and Japanese rivals. Other than the battlecruiser *Hood*, commissioned in 1920, the British had not laid down any new capital ships since 1914. Likewise, the largest calibre armaments carried on British ships were 15-inch guns. By comparison, both the United States and Japan had constructed newer battleships including some armed with 16-inch guns. The British feared the moratorium would freeze the Royal Navy into a position of inferiority if implemented in its original form. Therefore, the British delegation proposed the scrapping of the most modern American and Japanese battleships as a condition for agreement. Eventually the delegates reached an alternate compromise that allowed the British to build two new 16-inch gunned battleships to match the three 16-inch gunned battleships retained by the United States and the two 16-inch gunned battleships retained by Japan.[19]

Britain's recent nemesis, Germany, was not a party to these negotiations, but still figured into the disarmament equation. While not directly addressed in the Washington Treaty, German naval strength was restricted by the provisions set forth in the Treaty of Versailles, which had been concluded in 1919 to officially end World War I. In particular, the Treaty of Versailles limited the German Navy to six pre-dreadnought battleships, six light cruisers, 12 destroyers and 12 torpedo boats. New German construction was limited to the replacement of these units after attaining certain age requirements—20 years for battleships and cruisers and 15 years for destroyers and torpedo boats. Likewise, replacement tonnage was limited to 10,000 tons for battleships, 6,000 tons for cruisers, 800 tons for destroyers and 200 tons for torpedo boats. The treaty strictly prohibited the Germans from possessing U-boats, aircraft carriers and naval aircraft. Finally, German naval staffing was limited to 15,000 total personnel including 1,500 officers and warrant officers.

On 6 February 1922 Britain and the other participating powers signed the Washington Treaty thus determining the Royal Navy's size and structure into the next decade. In doing so, the British government avoided the threat of a new naval arms race and freed itself to engage in a more moderate building programme commensurate with its limited treasury resources. On 28 December 1922 the British began construction on the two battleships authorised under the treaty. These ships, named *Nelson* and *Rodney*, were completed in 1927. Both vessels displaced 33,313 tons and mounted nine 16-inch guns. The British further authorised the construction of 17 cruisers, 34 destroyers, 14 sloops, 22 submarines and a minelayer from 1922 through the end of 1930.[20] During the same period the British completed construction or conversion projects already underway on the aircraft carriers *Furious*, *Hermes*, *Eagle*, *Courageous* and *Glorious*. However, these additions only partially replaced the multitude of worn-out and obsolete vessels decommissioned after the war, and the fleet's overall size continued to shrink. In keeping with this, the government stabilised naval expenditures and staffing at a significantly reduced level. During the period of 1922–23 through 1930–31 annual naval expenditures averaged approximately £56,435,000 while staffing levels averaged some 100,470 personnel.[21]

Sadly, while the Washington Treaty succeeded in easing pressure on the British Treasury, it did little to address the growing threat that Japan posed to British interests in the Pacific. To the contrary, in some respects the treaty actually made the problem worse. While Britain retained a substantially larger navy than Japan, this navy was required to fulfil a number of global commitments including home defence and the maintenance of vital sea lanes in the Atlantic, Mediterranean and

Constrained by limited finances and arms control agreements, the Royal Navy underwent a major contraction during the inter-war years. Pictured here is the battleship *Nelson*, one of just two new British battleships completed during this period. (Unknown photographer, public domain)

Indian Oceans. By comparison, the Japanese were free to concentrate the entirety of their navy in the Pacific. This made it virtually impossible for the British to match Japan's regional naval strength while still maintaining their other commitments. The limitations imposed by the Washington Treaty formalised this reality and ensured that Britain now lacked adequate resources to permanently station a sizeable fleet in the Pacific even assuming there was a political will to do so.

The British solution to this problem was twofold. First, they looked to the United States as an agent to help check Japanese aggression. While not formalised in a treaty or through direct coordination, the Americans maintained a sizeable Pacific fleet and had their own reasons for wanting to contain Japan. Thus, the British were content to let the United States serve as the primary bulwark against the Japanese while they themselves only deployed sufficient forces to ensure trade protection and the maintenance of national authority. To this end, in 1921 the British acquiesced to American pressure and declined to renew the defensive alliance they had with the Japanese. They did this to gain favour with the Americans and to avoid involvement if war broke out between the United States and Japan. Meanwhile, in a more direct measure, they also decided to build a large naval base at Singapore in southern Malaya that would be capable of handling the main British fleet if authorities decided to dispatch it to the region. Formally approved in 1923, the British started construction on the base that same year, but changing governments and funding constraints caused frequent pauses and delays to the programme. By decade's end, the base was still little more than a concept as Britain's defensive aspirations suffered from ongoing political and financial paralysis.

Two overriding factors facilitated this stagnant situation. The first was economic. Despite the best efforts of consecutive British governments, the country remained mired in a persistent and debilitating economic slump. This situation was only made worse in 1929 when an American stock market crash plunged the world into a global recession. The British government responded to this deepening crisis by seeking additional spending cuts. This resulted in three consecutive declines in annual naval expenditures culminating in a post-war low of £50,164,000 in 1932–33.[22] The army underwent a similar decrease with its budget reduced every year going from just over £43,500,000 in 1923 to less than £36,000,000 in 1932 while staffing levels fell from 231,000 to 207,000 during the same period.[23] Accompanying these economic constraints was a widespread pacifistic movement prevalent throughout the nation. This prevailing mood was largely a repudiation of the carnage and waste brought about by World War I. Many Britons adopted a 'never again' mentality as they strove to advance disarmament and internationalism as a means to supplant war. The primary vehicle for this effort was the League of Nations; an association of nation states created in 1919 to maintain the peace through collective security and conflict arbitration.

Given these same budgetary and pacifistic sentiments, in 1930 the British government took another crack at international arms control when it hosted a new round of naval disarmament negotiations in London. The resulting agreement, signed by Britain, the United States and Japan and commonly referred to as the London Treaty, extended the moratorium on new battleship construction through the end of 1936 and mandated the disposal of several obsolete capital ships. The treaty also set limitations on the size, armament and replacement intervals for cruisers, destroyers and submarines and set total tonnage caps for these vessels to be implemented by the end of 1936. The Admiralty opposed these cruiser and destroyer reductions arguing they jeopardized imperial security and trade protection. Nevertheless, the government overruled these objections and signed the treaty on 22 April 1930 thus further subordinating Britain's practical defensive requirements to a dubious notion of international cooperation.

Unfortunately, despite these noble intentions, the facade of internationalism slowly unravelled as new dangers arose in Asia and Europe. Already understood was the potential hazard posed by Japan, but in the early 1930s this threat increased due to political developments within that nation. Japan's phenomenal rise as a world class power did not come without its costs. Throughout this period Japanese society struggled to keep up with and adapt to the industrial and political transformations underway. In the 1920s Japan experienced intense political strife as various elements in the government and society struggled to win the hearts and minds of the Japanese people. At one end of this ideological battle were labour unions, leftists and liberal

Table 1.2. London Treaty Tonnage Caps to be Implemented by 31 December 1936.

	United Kingdom	United States	Japan
Heavy cruisers with guns of more than 6.1-inch calibre	146,800	180,000	108,400
Light cruisers with guns of 6.1-inch calibre or less	192,200	143,500	100,450
Destroyers not exceeding 1,850 tons and 5.1-inch guns	150,000	150,000	105,500
Submarines	52,700	52,700	52,700

Source: Articles 15 and 16 of the International Treaty for the Limitation and Reduction of Naval Armaments.

Note: All figures represent tons allocated for each warship classification.

politicians who pushed the nation to embrace policies of liberalism, democracy and openness. On the other end were conservatives, militarists and ultranationalists who argued for a more traditional form of government and society based upon total obedience to the emperor. Aided by the near collapse of the Japanese economy due to the worldwide depression begun in 1929, these latter forces increasingly won the political argument, and in the early 1930s the conservatives, with support from the military, crushed all political and social opposition and gained firm control over the Japanese government.

Sadly, this new leadership embraced a form of racial nationalism and military fanaticism that would eventually prove to be every bit as extreme as that practiced by the Nazis in Europe. These leaders believed that Japan's future prosperity and prestige depended upon a programme of military and territorial expansion. In particular, they hoped to establish an Asian empire that would supply Japan with the natural resources and land necessary to sustain a growing economy and population. Up to this point, Japan had proven itself to be an ambitious and aggressive nation, but with the rise of this new leadership, Japan now posed an even greater threat to the balance of power within the region. With the majority of worthwhile Asian territory already under European or American control, it was inevitable that Japan would eventually have to encroach upon one or more of these existing powers to fully achieve its imperial designs. In the meantime, the Japanese contented themselves with attacking lesser opponents.

In September 1931 the Japanese set their expansionist plans into motion. Using a staged bombing incident in Mukden as a pretext, the Japanese launched a military invasion into Manchuria in Northeast China. Brushing aside ineffective Chinese resistance, the Japanese quickly overran Manchuria and transformed it into the puppet state of Manchukuo. Britain and the rest of the world responded to this blatant aggression with diplomatic protests and a weak and ineffective resolution through the League of Nations. Emboldened by this tepid response, the Japanese continued their expansionist and confrontational posture. Over the next six years Japan bombed and occupied the important Chinese city of Shanghai, forced the Chinese to accept a humiliating truce, undermined Chinese rule in the country's northern provinces, withdrew from the League of Nations and denounced the provisions of the Washington and London Treaties. Once again, Britain and the rest of the world did little to counter these provocations, although the British did accelerate construction on their Singapore naval base.

A major impetus behind this limited response was the fact that Britain was preoccupied with more pressing matters closer to home. The most ominous of these was the rise of Adolf Hitler and Nazism in Germany. After years of political and economic turmoil following World War I, Hitler and his fledgling Nazi party were able to seize control over the German government in 1933. Immediately upon taking office, Hitler began efforts to restore German power and prestige. That same year Germany withdrew from the League of Nations characterising the latter as an instrument for maintaining the territorial and arms limitation provisions of the Treaty of Versailles. Hitler then began a series of actions to rearm Germany. At first these actions were limited and covert, but as time went on, Hitler became increasingly brazen and openly expressed his rearmament ambitions. In the preceding years Germany had built three new 12,000-ton armoured cruisers and a handful of light cruisers and destroyers that nominally complied with the Treaty of Versailles. Now in 1934 Germany cast the treaty aside and ordered the construction of two new battlecruisers, the *Gneisenau* and *Scharnhorst*, which would each eventually displace 31,850 tons. During the same year the Germans began construction on prefabricated submarine sections for U-boat assembly. Finally, in March 1935 Hitler announced the creation of a German air force (the Luftwaffe) and began conscription for the German army with a stated goal of staffing 36 divisions with some 550,000 men.[24]

Tragically, these provocations failed to elicit an effective response from the Allies. Many of Germany's rearmament actions were clear violations of the Treaty of Versailles. Nevertheless, neither Britain nor France was willing to confront these violations and take decisive actions to enforce the treaty. Instead, the British government opted for negotiations to limit Germany's rearmament efforts. In June 1935 the British concluded the Anglo-German Naval Agreement allowing Germany to build up to 35 percent of the Royal Navy's total tonnage and 45 percent of its submarine tonnage. The agreement further granted Germany the option to build up to 100 percent of Britain's total submarine tonnage if a situation arose warranting this action.[25] The Germans wasted little time in exercising their tonnage allotments and on 9 July 1935 announced a new building programme comprising two battleships, two heavy cruisers, 16 destroyers and 28 submarines.[26]

A few months later a new crisis arose to further complicate Britain's defensive posture. In October 1935 Italy, under the direction of the Fascist dictator Benito Mussolini, invaded the independent African nation of Abyssinia (present day Ethiopia). Since both Italy and Abyssinia were members of the League of Nations, this invasion was a clear violation of the League's covenant and obligated members to impose sanctions or take other appropriate actions to curb this aggression. A sizeable portion of British society sympathised with the Abyssinians, and many people supported the implementation of strong sanctions up to and including the use of military force. Others advocated the avoidance of war for strategic or philosophical reasons. In the end the British government chose a middle ground. Under British and French guidance, the League of Nations imposed economic sanctions on a variety of commodities and materials, but declined to restrict strategically important resources such as oil. In doing so, they caused Italy a degree of economic distress, but failed to seriously undermine its ability to wage aggressive war. Accordingly, in May 1936 Italy completed its conquest of Abyssinia, and the League terminated the sanctions shortly thereafter.

The Abyssinian Crisis produced a number of strategic consequences for Britain. First and most serious, it drove a wedge between Italy and the Western Allies thus transforming a former ally into a potential adversary. From this point on, Italy would increasingly align itself with Germany, and Britain would find itself confronted by three potential threats coming from differing quarters in the form of Germany, Italy and Japan. This represented a startling deterioration in Britain's strategic situation as the country increasingly moved away from the naive assurances of its ten-year rule to a nightmare scenario where it might have to confront multiple foes on disparate fronts. Second, the crisis clearly demonstrated the limitations of collective security as Britain and France were the only nations truly inclined and capable of deterring Italian aggression. In keeping with this, the crisis thoroughly discredited the League of Nations as an instrument for conflict resolution. Although the League continued for a few more years, its effectiveness as a peacekeeping organisation was severely diminished. Finally, Britain's failure to effectively counter this aggression demonstrated weakness and a lack of resolve that only promised to encourage more aggression. Unfortunately, the British government would require more time to fully learn this lesson.

This latter point was amply demonstrated in March 1936 when Hitler dispatched military forces to reoccupy the Rhineland in western Germany. This action was another clear violation of the Treaty of Versailles, which prohibited the establishment of German military forces and fortifications on the left bank of the Rhine River to within fifty kilometres of the right bank. At the time Germany was still in the early stages of its rearmament programme and would have been very hard pressed to resist a forceful French and British response to this violation. Nevertheless, Hitler gambled that the Allies would vacillate and wither in the face of this latest challenge, which is precisely what happened as both France and Britain declined to take effective action to counter the German provocation. In doing so, they granted Hitler an immense strategic and political victory at virtually no cost to himself.

Based upon these events and the growing threat posed by three potential adversaries, the British government finally awoke from its pacifistic slumber and began a series of rearmament initiatives. This first began with an enlargement of the RAF in 1935, but extended to the Royal Navy and army in 1936. In terms of the former, in 1934 the RAF maintained some 560 aircraft in the United Kingdom with another 160 overseas. In May 1935 the government approved a plan, designated Scheme C, to triple the size of the home-based RAF to 123 squadrons and 1,512 first-line aircraft by 31 March 1937.[27] In February 1936 the government modified this plan and adopted Scheme F calling for 124 home-based squadrons containing 1,736 first-line aircraft, 37 overseas squadrons containing 468 first-line aircraft and 26 Fleet Air Arm (FAA) squadrons with 312 aircraft by 31 March 1939. In addition, Scheme F significantly increased the number of reserve aircraft available to the RAF and FAA to 225 percent and 210 percent of their respective front-line strengths. Likewise, the plan increased reserves for both air and ground crew personnel. Finally, Scheme F improved the striking power of the RAF by eliminating its light bomber squadrons and replacing them with medium and medium-heavy bombers.[28]

In terms of the navy, in February 1936 the government authorised a large-scale ship building programme. At its core, the programme called for the initial construction of five new 35,000-ton *King George V*-class battleships armed with twelve, later reduced to ten, 14-inch guns and six new 23,000-ton armoured aircraft carriers of the *Illustrious* and *Implacable* classes. During the next three years naval expenditures rose to £80,976,000, £78,259,000 and £96,396,000 respectively as the British began construction on these new capital ships as well as 21 new cruisers, 34 destroyers, 12 sloops, 18 submarines and three minelayers.[29] Coinciding with this materiel expansion, the British also increased naval staffing to meet the needs of their growing fleet. In 1932–33 the navy's average personnel strength had fallen to a post-war low of only 89,667 officers and men. By 1935–36 this average had increased to 94,259, but was still insufficient in meeting the navy's future needs.[30] Over the next three years the British added some 25,000 additional personnel to this total, and by 1 January 1939 the Royal Navy's staffing strength stood at some 10,000 officers and 109,000 enlisted personnel plus a further 12,400 officers and men in the Royal Marines.[31]

The efforts to revitalize the army were far less pronounced as it was last in priority for funding compared to the other two British services. Not only did this dearth of funds prevent the army from undergoing any significant expansion, but it severely restricted its modernisation efforts. From 1926 through 1934 the army never received more than £1,000,000 per annum for the purchase of new equipment.[32] In November 1933 the government established a Defence Requirements Committee

Table 1.3. British Naval Expenditures, Staffing and New Construction between the Wars.

Year	Naval expenditures	Average naval staffing	New warships ordered				
			Battleships/ battlecruisers	Aircraft carriers	Cruisers/ minelayers	Destroyers/ escorts	Submarines
1919	£154,084,000	176,087	–	–	–	–	–
1920	£92,505,000	124,009	–	–	–	–	–
1921	£75,896,000	127,180	–	–	–	–	1
1922	£57,492,000	107,782	2	–	1	–	–
1923	£54,064,000	99,107	–	–	–	–	–
1924	£55,694,000	99,453	–	–	5	2	–
1925	£60,005,000	100,284	–	–	4	–	–
1926	£57,143,000	100,791	–	–	3	–	6
1927	£58,123,000	101,916	–	–	1	11	6
1928	£57,139,000	100,680	–	–	–	13	4
1929	£55,988,000	99,300	–	–	1	9	3
1930	£52,274,000	94,921	–	–	3	13	3
1931	£51,015,000	92,449	–	–	3	13	3
1932	£50,164,000	89,667	–	–	3	13	3
1933	£53,444,000	89,863	–	–	3	14	3
1934	£56,616,000	91,351	–	1	4	15	3
1935	£64,888,000	94,259	–	–	3	13	3
1936	£80,976,000	99,886	2	2	7	24	8
1937	£78,259,000	107,040	3	2	7	22	7
1938	£96,396,000	118,167	–	1	10	–	3
1939	£99,429,000	120,000	–	1	3	94	–

Source: Stephen Roskill, *Naval Policy Between the Wars, Volume I: The Period of Anglo-American Antagonism 1919–1929* (New York: Walker and Company, 1968).

Note: The 1939 data only reflects figures accrued prior to the outbreak of the war.

(DRC) to study the readiness deficiencies in each of the armed services and make recommendations on spending priorities to remedy these issues. Over the next two years the DRC issued three reports to the government in which it recommended the allocation of £40,000,000 to the army to address capacity shortfalls. The government halved this recommendation and allocated just £20,000,000 to the army, but directed that much of this additional funding be earmarked to improve home defence.[33] Still, this was enough to allow the army to begin a fledgling modernisation effort including the acquisition of new armour and artillery weapons.

As the British implemented these new rearmament programmes, the strategic and diplomatic situation continued to deteriorate. In July 1936 civil war broke out in Spain as Nationalist forces under General Francisco Franco revolted against the left-leaning Republican government. While Britain and France remained neutral, both Germany and Italy quickly dispatched troops, weapons, aircraft and naval units to support the Nationalist forces. This assistance eventually helped the Nationalists prevail over their Republican rivals and provided Germany and Italy with an ideal proving ground to test their weapons and tactics under combat conditions. Meanwhile, in October 1936 Germany and Italy concluded a loose diplomatic pact known as the Rome-Berlin Axis. One month later Germany and Japan made similar inroads when they signed the Anti-Comintern Pact aimed at countering international Communism. Finally, in March 1938 Hitler scored his greatest coup to date when he sent troops into neighbouring Austria and annexed the small nation into his greater German Reich.

The situation in the Far East was equally bleak. In July 1937 Japan launched a full-scale invasion into China following a minor boarder clash on the Marco Polo Bridge near Peking. This began a long, drawn-out struggle in which the Japanese gained control over most of eastern China, but encountered persistent resistance in the interior of the country. A notorious attribute of this fighting was the immense brutality the Japanese practiced against the Chinese population as highlighted by the infamous Rape of Nanking. During a six-week period following the capture of the city of Nanking in 1937, the Japanese army indulged itself in an orgy of killing, raping, looting and arson against the city's inhabitants. Estimates of the number of Chinese murdered range from 30,000 to 250,000 while an estimated 8,000 to 20,000 Chinese women were raped.[34] Even Nazi observers expressed shock at this level of brutality. Meanwhile, that same year Japan began construction on the first of three new super battleships. Displacing a staggering 64,000 tons and armed with nine 18.1-inch guns, these new *Yamato*-class battleships proposed to be the most powerful surface combatants ever built and far exceeded anything present or projected in the British and American fleets. Sadly, there was little the British could do to counter this aggression. Even though their base at Singapore was now almost complete, the British no longer had a fleet readily available to dispatch to the Pacific. Instead, the British were compelled to retain the vast bulk of their naval forces in the Atlantic and Mediterranean to confront the growing threats posed by Germany and Italy.

To this end, in 1938 the situation in Europe reached a crisis point. With the annexation of Austria, German territory now bordered the western portion of Czechoslovakia on three sides. This border area, known as the Sudetenland, contained some three million ethnic Germans. Under Nazi orchestration, these Sudeten Germans soon clamoured for unification with Germany as Hitler for-mulated plans to seize the Sudetenland through the use of intimidation or force. Despite German posturing, the Czech government remained defiant and resolved to defend its territory if attacked. They were not alone in this regard. France was obligated by treaty to come to Czechoslovakia's defence while the Russians had good relations with the Czech government and also offered their support. Britain was not obligated by treaty to intervene, but reluctantly resolved to stand with France in the event of war.

As tensions mounted the British Prime Minister, Neville Chamberlain, initiated a series of diplomatic efforts to peacefully resolve the crisis. This included pressure put upon the Czech government to make concessions and appeals to Hitler to act with restraint. Finally, in late September 1938 the leaders of Britain, France, Germany and Italy met in Munich to parley their differences in a last-ditch effort to avoid war. During these negotiations Chamberlain and the French Premier Edouard Daladier finally agreed to transfer the Sudetenland to Germany upon assurances from Hitler that he would take no further action against Czechoslovakia and that this was his last territorial claim in Europe. In a follow-up meeting Hitler also signed a joint declaration with Chamberlain espousing a mutual desire to avoid war and promising consultation as a means to resolve future differences. With this, an imminent outbreak of war was avoided, and Chamberlain returned home proclaiming the achievement of 'peace for our time'.

Yet, few were taken in by this hopeful sentiment. Instead, the major powers continued their preparations for war as many concluded the agreement had only bought additional time before the coming onslaught. In Britain, rearmament proceeded with an increased sense of urgency as the Munich Crisis had clearly demonstrated significant deficiencies in British defence preparations. Unfortunately, time to complete these rearmament efforts was quickly running out as Europe's slide towards war continued unabated. In March 1939 Hitler cast aside his Munich assurances and sent troops to occupy the rest of Czechoslovakia. During the same period Hitler also began making territorial demands on Poland. With these developments, few observers, including Chamberlain, could deny the true nature of Hitler or the abject futility in attempting to appease him. Instead, many Britons resigned themselves to the inevitability of war as the British and French governments made assurances to help defend Polish independence.

With this, the government accelerated plans to bring the nation to a state of wartime readiness, and British military expenditures reached £367,000,000 in the year 1939–40.[35] In March the government adopted a plan to increase the Territorial Army's establishment from 165,000 to 170,000 and then doubled it to 340,000.[36] One month later the government reintroduced conscription and shortly thereafter the navy called up 15,000 reservists. During the same period the Admiralty brought its Operational Intelligence Centre and corresponding radio tracking stations to a high state of readiness to monitor German signal traffic and naval movements. In June the navy mobilised the Reserve Fleet and began preparations to assume control over and arm the Merchant Navy. Both the army and the RAF underwent similar measures to bring themselves to a wartime footing as the former prepared to send the first four divisions of a British Expeditionary Force (BEF) to Europe to stand with their French allies while the latter prepared to support this endeavour and defend the United Kingdom against expected German air attacks.

Undeterred by these developments, Hitler continued to pursue his territorial demands against the Poles. In April he denounced the provisions of the 1934 German-Polish Non-Aggression Pact and the 1935 Anglo-German Naval Agreement. During the same month Germany began massing troops along the Polish border, and in the months that followed Hitler made preparations for a full-scale invasion of that country. In doing so, he again gambled that the Allies would wither in the face of this latest provocation and do nothing just as they had done during his encroachments into the Rhineland, Austria and Czechoslovakia. Similarly, to avoid interference from the Soviet Union, he entered into secret negotiations with the Soviet government resulting in a non-aggression pact signed on 23 August 1939. With this pact, the German and Soviet governments agreed to a secret provision prescribing their joint dismemberment of the Polish nation. Two days later, Hitler formalised his plans and set an invasion date for 1 September. After 21 years of often turbulent peace, Europe once again braced itself for war.

CHAPTER 2

The Storm in Europe

Early on the morning of Friday, 1 September 1939, the German battleship *Schleswig-Holstein*, which was in Danzig under the guise of a ceremonial visit, slipped its moorings and began a point-blank bombardment of the Polish naval depot and garrison at Westeplatte. These were the opening shots in what quickly became a crescendo of thundering fury as German forces launched a full-scale invasion across the length and breadth of the Polish frontier. Two days later, after the issuance of various unanswered ultimatums, the British and French governments honoured their commitments to Poland and declared war on Germany. In the hours and days immediately following these declarations, Australia, New Zealand, South Africa and Canada each followed suit and dutifully issued their own declarations of war against the German nation. With this, Britain and its Commonwealth partners embarked upon a war they had neither sought nor desired. Yet, despite past hesitancies and trepidations, the British resolved themselves to the task at hand and went forward with newfound determination against the German aggressor.

Sadly, there was little the British could do to provide immediate assistance to the beleaguered Poles. Much of this was due to the overwhelming force the Germans employed against Poland as well as the great speed in which they overran the country. Attacking Poland with five field armies containing over 1.5 million men along three different avenues of approach (out of the north from Prussia, out of the west from Germany and out of the south from Slovakia), the Germans made strong advances against the brave, but ultimately ineffective Polish resistance. A key factor in this success was a new German tactical doctrine, referred to as *blitzkrieg* (lightning war), that emphasised speed and mobility to bypass and overcome the less dynamic Polish formations. To the majority of military and political observers schooled in the static trench style warfare of World War I, *blitzkrieg* came as a severe shock. Within a matter of days, Poland's position became untenable as German spearheads converged upon Warsaw. The coup de grace occurred on 17 September when the Soviet Union launched a major invasion into eastern Poland. This action was in accordance with the recently signed non-aggression pact between Germany and the Soviet Union and signalled the end of the Polish nation. Over the next several days, the Germans eliminated the last major bastions of organised Polish resistance at Warsaw and Modlin while other German and Soviet forces partitioned the country. By 6 October, all significant resistance ended thus culminating the brief but decisive Polish campaign.

For Poland, the war was over; for Britain, the war had just begun. At its onset, the British depended upon three substantial bulwarks to help defend their island nation. The first of these was geography as the nations of France, Belgium and the Netherlands provided a geopolitical barrier that shielded Britain from the prospects of direct German assault. Even assuming the Germans were able to compromise or bypass these intermediate nations, the North Sea and English Channel provided an immense physical obstacle to any offensive ambitions imperilling the United Kingdom. The second bulwark was Britain's alliance with France, which reputedly possessed the most powerful army in Europe containing almost five million men with the call up of reserves at the beginning of the conflict. Bolstering this powerful army was a recently built series of strong defensive positions, collectively known as the Maginot Line, along France's eastern border with Germany that proposed to deter or stymie German offensive options. The final bulwark was the Royal Navy, which had served as Britain's senior service and primary defender of the realm for the past four hundred years. Now with the onset of this new conflict, despite two decades of general neglect and downsizing, the Royal Navy still constituted the largest navy in the world far exceeding that of its German rival, the Kriegsmarine.

Reviewing this naval balance further, by the beginning of September 1939 the Royal Navy's fighting strength included 12 battleships, three battlecruisers, seven aircraft carriers, 13 heavy cruisers, 45 light and anti-aircraft cruisers, 157 destroyers, 69 submarines and 51 sloops and escort vessels.[1] The Commonwealth added a further six cruisers and 11 destroyers to this total while the British had dozens of new warships under construction including five battleships, six aircraft carriers, 19 cruisers and 32 destroyers.[2] Finally, beyond their own internal assets, the British could also call upon support from the powerful French navy, which possessed five battleships, two battlecruisers, one aircraft carrier, seven heavy cruisers, 12 light cruisers, 70 assorted destroyers and 77 submarines at the beginning of the war.[3] Against this, the Kriegsmarine possessed or was about to take possession of two old battleships, two battlecruisers, three armoured cruisers, two heavy cruisers, six light cruisers, 22 destroyers, 11 torpedo boats (small destroyers) and 57 U-boats.[4] In terms of the latter, many of these U-boats were small coastal or experimental types that left the Germans with an effective strength of just 25 ocean-going U-boats at the beginning of the conflict, which was one-twelfth the stated number they projected as necessary to effectively combat the Royal Navy. Of course, the Germans also had a number of warships under construction (including two battleships and an aircraft carrier), but these numbers paled against that of the British building programme.

Table 2.1. Comparative Fleet Strengths for the Major Combatants in September 1939.

	British Empire	France	Germany
Battleships/battlecruisers ·	15	7	7*
Aircraft carriers	7	1	–
Cruisers	64	19	8
Destroyers and torpedo boats	168	70	33
Submarines	69	77	57
Escort vessels and sloops	53	24	10

*Includes the three armoured cruisers.

Compared to the navy, the status of the British army was far less advantageous. Among its many deficiencies, the most obvious was numerical as the British army was far smaller than its German or French counterparts. Even with the implementation of limited conscription four months earlier, the British army could only muster a full strength of 892,697 men in September 1939. Of these, only about 224,000 were regular army personnel with the balance coming from the reserves or the part-time Territorial Army.[5] This left the British with a force that was less than one-fourth the size of its German counterpart, which in 1939 possessed some 3.75 million men with a main combat strength consisting of 106 divisions.[6] Unfortunately, this was just the beginning of the army's shortcomings as none of the territorial units were ready for immediate deployment while most of the reserve personnel required substantial training. Of the regular army personnel, roughly 40 percent were deployed overseas on garrison duties including a substantial portion stationed in India where they served alongside native troops to form the British Indian Army. This left the British with just four infantry divisions that were immediately ready to deploy to France with further divisions that would be deployed as they became available.

In terms of manpower, the British could also call upon inputs from the Empire and Commonwealth. In this regard, the largest force available was the aforementioned British Indian Army, which on 1 October 1939 possessed 194,373 men. Beyond this, another 109,000 men were spread across local auxiliary and territorial formations and the Indian State Force.[7] However, most of these Indian troops were earmarked to perform internal security, and few were immediately available to assist in the European war. The same was true of the various Commonwealth contingents, which possessed far smaller armies and generally limited their contributions to the European war to volunteers. An example of the former was the Australian army, which at the outbreak of the war numbered just 3,500 permanent personnel and 70,000 part-time militia.[8] An example of the latter was Canada, which adopted a policy of limited liability that called for the initial creation of two divisions for service in Europe made up entirely of volunteers. This garnered an initial volunteer force of 54,844 men in September 1939, but expansion went slowly thereafter with fewer than 35,000 men volunteering over the next eight months.[9] The situation was much the same with the other Dominion nations. Eventually, the Empire and Commonwealth would provide substantial forces to the European war, but it would take many months, if not more than a year, before any of these forces could arrive in any meaningful strength. Until then, the British army would have to depend entirely upon its own resources to confront the Germans.

Another major deficiency was that of materiel readiness as the army was woefully short on several categories of modern weapons. One glaring example of this was a lack of tanks and other armoured fighting vehicles. The British army had pioneered tank warfare in World War I, but by the onset of World War II, it was shockingly weak in this regard. Against seven Panzer divisions immediately available for service in the German army, the British had two mobile divisions (the 1st and the 7th) that were in the process of forming up, but neither would be fully ready for several months if not longer. Of the tanks available to the British, most were of poor quality compared to their German counterparts. An exception to this was the new Infantry Mark II Matilda tank that was just coming into service, but only two of these were on hand at the beginning of the war. In another example of materiel deficiencies, the four regular army divisions that were earmarked for immediate deployment to France only possessed about 50 percent of their allotted anti-tank and anti-aircraft guns and about 30 percent of their ammunition on the eve of the conflict.[10] As bad as this was, the materiel shortages were far worse in the territorial formations, which in some cases were almost totally devoid of heavy equipment.

For the Royal Air Force, the situation was only marginally better. In 1939 the Luftwaffe was some 677,000 men strong, possessing a strength of 2,564 operational aircraft spread across 302 squadrons.[11] Overwhelmingly, these aircraft were of high quality including the Messerschmitt Bf 109 single-engine fighter, the Junkers Ju 87B dive-bomber and the Heinkel He 111 medium bomber. Against this formidable force, the RAF was roughly half its size with a staffing strength of just 11,753 officers and 163,939 other ranks and an air strength of 1,660 frontline aircraft spread across 139 squadrons.[12] Aircraft types in the RAF ranged from excellent to obsolete with the Hawker Hurricane and Supermarine Spitfire fighters, Vickers Wellington medium bomber and Short Sunderland flying boat being in the former category while the Gloster Gladiator biplane fighter, Fairey Battle light bomber and Avro Anson maritime reconnaissance aircraft were in the latter.

Excluding overseas contingents, the Royal Air Force primarily broke down into seven subordinate commands of which three were operational flying commands. In terms of the latter, the largest was Bomber Command, which at the beginning of the war possessed a nominal strength of 55 squadrons with 920 aircraft. However, by the end of September, this number was whittled down to just 33 frontline squadrons containing 480 aircraft as several squadrons were transferred to perform other duties or were put into non-mobilisable status to serve as replacement and training units.[13] Meanwhile, the aerial defence of the United Kingdom was primarily entrusted to

Table 2.2. Characteristics of Selected German and British Aircraft in 1939.

	Roles	Top speed (mph)	Armament
German			
Messerschmitt Bf. 109E-1	Fighter	342	2 × 7.92mm MGs, 2 × 20mm CANs
Messerschmitt Bf. 110C-1	Fighter	336	5 × 7.92mm MGs, 2 × 20mm CANs
Junkers Ju. 87	Dive-bomber	238	1,100lbs of bombs, 3 × 7.92mm MGs
Dornier Do. 17	Light bomber	270	2,210lbs of bombs, 6 × 7.92mm MGs
Heinkel He. 111	Medium bomber	252	5,501lbs of bombs, 6 × 7.92mm MGs
British			
Hawker Hurricane Mk I	Fighter	320	8 × .303 MGs
Supermarine Spitfire Mk I	Fighter	355	8 × .303 MGs
Fairey Battle	Light bomber	241	1,000lbs of bombs, 2 × .303 MGs
Vickers Wellington Mk I	Medium bomber	235	4,500lbs of bombs, 6 × .303 MGs
Avro Anson MK I	Maritime patrol	188	360lbs of bombs, 2 × .303 MGs
Short Sunderland	Maritime patrol	210	2,000lbs of bombs, 7 × .303 MGs

Fighter Command, which possessed 35 squadrons at the beginning of the conflict of which 22 were equipped with Hurricanes or Spitfires. Rounding out this operational force was Coastal Command, which possessed 19 squadrons consisting of mostly obsolete types to perform maritime reconnaissance and strike duties.[14] Finally, in addition to these established air commands, the British immediately dispatched ten Battle light bomber squadrons to Europe as part of the Advanced Air Striking Force. This would be followed by additional squadrons as time went on.

At the onset of hostilities, the Allies primarily assumed a defensive posture as they hoped to contain Germany and slowly strangle it through economic blockade. In this, they were generally accommodated by the Germans, who initially declined to take any major offensive actions against the western regions of Europe. This development came as a welcome relief to British leaders who had previously anticipated that the Germans would open the war with a major bombing campaign targeting British cities. Instead, no attacks materialised, and the RAF encountered minimal German air activity in the proximity of Britain. Meanwhile in Europe, in the six months following the conquest of Poland, both sides assumed a static posture that was so devoid of action that the press dubbed it the Phoney War or Twilight War. This description was generally true for the British army and RAF as the former did little more than deploy its expeditionary force to Europe while the latter primarily occupied itself with the execution of a number of ineffective bombing raids against German surface warships and the dropping of propaganda leaflets to sway German public opinion.

Still, if this was a Phoney War on land and in the air, that was not the case at sea. Beginning on the first day of hostilities with the loss of one British and three

German merchant ships and continuing thereafter, both sides commenced competing campaigns to attack the other's shipping. For the British Admiralty, the first order of business was to secure maritime lines of communication to ensure a steady flow of life-sustaining imports to the United Kingdom. The impetus behind this was the fact that Britain lacked self-sufficiency in a number of key resources and commodities such as oil and foodstuffs and had to depend upon seaborne commerce to make up the difference. In 1938 total imports into the United Kingdom had amounted to 68 million tons, and although British authorities realised they could reduce this number through rationing and increased domestic production, they still determined that a minimum annual requirement of 27 million import tons was absolutely essential in meeting the nation's basic needs.

Of course, the Germans were also aware of this British vulnerability, and they immediately commenced operations to attack British and Allied maritime trade. Utilising a combination of surface warships, mines, aircraft and most notably U-boats, the Germans managed to sink 1,303,672 tons of British, Allied and neutral merchant shipping during the first seven months of the war of which 683,800 tons were British.[15] Beyond this, the Germans also sank a handful of British warships including the aircraft carrier *Courageous* and the battleship *Royal Oak*. While this toll appeared impressive, these losses were not considered unduly heavy given the size of the British merchant fleet and the number of trips made during this period. In fact, the British merchant fleet actually expanded during this time going from a combined strength of 17,784,000 tons on 3 September 1939 to 18,200,000 tons by 31 March 1940.[16] Likewise, imports into the United Kingdom amounted to 30,779,000 tons over the seven-month period, which equated to almost 53 million tons on an annual basis or almost double the minimum threshold established by the British government.[17] Thus, despite their losses, the British effectively held their own during this period. Further bolstering this relative British success was the infliction of some heavy losses upon the German navy during this time, which included the destruction of the surface raider *Graf Spee* and 17 U-boats.

While these defensive efforts were underway, the British concurrently executed a second major tenet of their naval strategy by implementing a maritime blockade against Germany. As a continental power, Germany was not as reliant upon seaborne imports as was Britain to support its social and economic needs, but it still derived significant benefit from this trade. As demonstrated during World War I, Germany was susceptible to the gradual withering of a prolonged and effective blockade, and the British eventually hoped to inflict decisive damage against the German war effort through this endeavour. Accordingly, at the onset of hostilities, the British enacted a series of measures to blockade Germany and sever its access to the Atlantic Ocean. For the next seven months, British and French warships drove the vast bulk of German merchant shipping from the world's sea lanes. In doing so, they captured 26 German commercial vessels worth 107,530 tons and sank or forced the scuttling of 30 more merchant ships worth 181,601 tons.[18] Beyond this, the British also implemented maritime cordons to intercept and confiscate contraband cargo bound for Germany in neutral vessels. Using these resources, the British seized 529,471 tons of contraband by 1 January 1940, which represented a greater volume of cargo lost to the Germans than the comparable British losses during the same timeframe.[19]

Finally, the British used the Phoney War period to execute a third tenet of their maritime strategy by successfully transporting the British Expeditionary Force to Europe and subsequently maintaining its logistical needs. On 9 September 1939 the first troopships departed Southampton for Cherbourg, and by 7 October the initial four divisions of the expeditionary force were safely in France consisting of some 161,000 soldiers, 24,000 vehicles and 140,000 tons of stores.[20] Despite the scale of this early success, these deployments only represented the beginning of a long and continuous process as the British dispatched a steady stream of ships to reinforce and support their deployed formations. Then from December 1939 through April 1940, the British transported another nine divisions to France, bringing the total size of their expeditionary force to nearly a half million men and some 89,000 vehicles by June. This represented a major undertaking as Portsmouth Command alone administered the sailing of 731 transports and 304 laden convoys during the opening months of the war.[21] Meanwhile, the newly arrived British formations fell in alongside their French Allies, where they diligently prepared to meet an ever-anticipated German offensive.

In this, their fears were finally met. In the spring of 1940, the relative tranquillity of the Phoney War abruptly vanished when the Germans unleashed their *blitzkrieg* war machine against the West. This started in April when German forces occupied Denmark and launched a bold seaborne invasion of Norway. British authorities had long planned to draw the Kriegsmarine into a battle around Norway, but the speed and timing of the German invasion caught the British by surprise. As such, the British were always in a reactive mode and were never able to gain a decisive advantage during the subsequent fighting, which saw the Germans quickly secure control over southern Norway while gaining firm footholds in the central and northern portions of the country. A major factor facilitating this was the dominance of the Luftwaffe, which quickly established superiority over Norwegian airspace and severely impeded Allied naval and ground operations. During the initial fighting, the British were able to inflict some heavy losses upon the Kriegsmarine, which included the destruction of two cruisers and ten destroyers while Norwegian forces sank a third cruiser, but this was not enough to reverse the growing dominance the Germans were gaining over the country. By the end of April, the British were forced to abandoned their recently occupied positions in central Norway, and the long-term prognosis for retention of the north became increasingly dire.

A key factor in this deteriorating situation was the fact that British attention was soon consumed by events closer to home. On 10 May the Germans launched a massive offensive utilising 136 divisions with some 2,350,000 men and 2,700 tanks against the Low Countries and northern France. Employing the same *blitzkrieg* tactics used so successfully against Poland, the Germans launched a sweeping attack through the neutral countries of Luxembourg, Belgium and the Netherlands thus avoiding the strongest French defences along the formidable Maginot Line. The Allies countered this incursion with 136 divisions of their own, including the ten divisions of the British Expeditionary Force, along with some 2,862,000 men and 3,000 tanks.[22] Yet, only a fraction of these Allied forces were in position to counter the main thrusts of the German offensive, and the Germans were generally able to attain local superiority at selected points on the battlefield. This, plus qualitative advantages in leadership, training and mobility, allowed the Germans to make immediate and sustained progress against the Allied coalition. Picking off the weakest members first, the Germans overran Luxembourg in a single day while the Netherlands surrendered on the 14th. Meanwhile, powerful German spearheads smashed into Belgian and French forces sending them reeling back under a heavy onslaught of speed and firepower.

On 14 May the British Expeditionary Force, which held positions along the Dyle River south of Brussels, came into its first substantial contact with the Germans and held its ground against a series of German attacks. Despite this initial success, the British were soon compelled to withdraw due to a growing disintegration of Belgian and French forces on their left and right flanks. Over the next several days the British made additional phased withdrawals as the overall Allied situation continued to worsen. This deterioration was particularly true on the right flank where strong German forces broke through the French Ninth Army at Sedan and began a headlong drive to the coast against negligible opposition. On 20 May German forces reached the Channel coast near Abbeville thus isolating the British Expeditionary Force and other Allied formations from the bulk of the French army in the south. Despite this event, the British did not immediately retreat back towards the Channel. Instead, on 21 May the British launched a limited counter-attack near Arras that achieved a fair degree of local success and threw the German command into a temporary panic. However, this triumph was short lived as the overall situation continued to deteriorate. On 22 May, German forces began moving northward up the French coastline thus threatening to sever the expeditionary force from the sea, and on the 25th the British began a general withdrawal back towards the French port of Dunkirk.

The next evening, British authorities acknowledged the hopelessness of their situation and ordered a full-scale evacuation from Dunkirk. Beginning the next day under the designation Operation *Dynamo*, the British initially hoped to evacuate some 45,000 men over a two-day period. Instead, Operation *Dynamo* attained a scope and level of success far exceeding all expectations. During a nine-day period culminating on 4 June, an armada of British and Allied ships of all sizes successfully evacuated 338,226 soldiers from the Dunkirk perimeter of which 308,888 were transported on British vessels.[23] When combined with 27,936 rear echelon personnel evacuated during the week preceding *Dynamo*, the total number of rescued soldiers increased to 366,162. Of this total, roughly 224,000 were British representing almost the entirety of the trapped British Expeditionary Force while the remainders were overwhelmingly French.[24] In all, 848 Allied vessels participated in Operation *Dynamo* of which 72 were lost due to enemy action (mostly from Luftwaffe bombing) while 163 more were lost to accidents, groundings and other maritime causes.[25] The vast majority of these losses came from the ranks of the minor vessels used, but six British and three French destroyers were also included in these numbers. Nor was this entirely a maritime affair. The RAF, operating mostly from Britain, contributed 2,739 Fighter Command, 651 Bomber Command and 171 Coastal Command sorties in support of Operation *Dynamo*. This support cost the home-based RAF 145 aircraft including 99 fighters while the Luftwaffe lost 132 aircraft in opposition to the evacuation.[26]

Unfortunately, the spectacular success of Operation *Dynamo* was attained against the backdrop of an ongoing disaster. Even as *Dynamo* was underway, Belgium surrendered, and on 5 June the Germans launched a massive offensive with 140 divisions against France's northern flank. The French, now largely devoid of Allied support and severely weakened by the previous four weeks of fighting, were unable to hold back this onslaught, and within a few days the French defences disintegrated. On 14 June the Germans occupied Paris, and eight days later the French surrendered. These actions compelled the British to evacuate their remaining forces from France, which still consisted of some 150,000 men. During the period of 10–23 June, the British carried out a series of seaborne evacuations from St. Valéry-en-Caux, Le Havre, Cherbourg, St Malo, Brest, St Nazaire, Nantes, La Pallice, Bayonne and St-Jean-de-Luz. Despite fog that impeded operations at St. Valéry-en-Caux resulting in the surrender of some 6,000 men from the British 51st Division and the destruction of the liner *Lancastria* off St Nazaire that caused a heavy loss of life, these operations were highly successful eventually securing the evacuation of 191,870 military personnel of which 144,171 were British, 24,352 were Poles, 18,246 were French, 4,938 were Czech and 163 were Belgian.[27] Meanwhile, given the unfolding disaster in France, the British decided to evacuate their remaining forces from Norway, which they accomplished in June with a minimum loss to army personnel, but at a cost to the navy of the aircraft carrier *Glorious* and two destroyers that were intercepted and sunk by German warships.

By the end of June, Germany controlled most of Western Europe, and the British were now exiled from the continent. This put the British in an extremely precarious situation. Ten months before, Britain had entered the war as part of an alliance confronting a single adversary. Now with the events just described, Britain abruptly found itself devoid of European allies and confronted by two powerful assailants. The latter was true because on 10 June Mussolini opportunistically declared war on

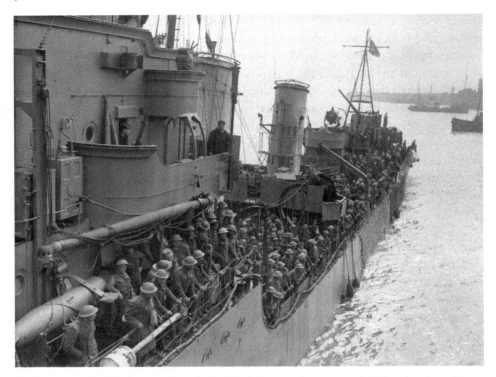

In the spring of 1940, Germany launched a *blitzkrieg* campaign against the West that drove France out of the war and forced Britain to evacuate the continent. Pictured here is a troop-laden destroyer arriving at Dover during the Dunkirk evacuation. (Puttnam (Mr) and Malindine (Mr), War Office official photographer, public domain)

Britain and an already collapsing France. While this was of little consequence to the French, Italy's entry into the conflict meant that Britain now faced the reality of a two-front war with one front focused in Northwest Europe and the Atlantic while the other centred upon the Mediterranean and Middle East. Of these fronts, the former was by far the most important. Having lost two of its defensive bulwarks and with the third heavily strained, for the first time in 135 years, Britain now faced a realistic prospect of invasion and conquest. In fact, many informed observers openly wondered if Britain would offer any resistance at all or bow to the inevitability of its situation. This was certainly true in the case of Adolf Hitler, who publicly anticipated that the British government would quickly recognise the hopelessness of its position and agree to a negotiated settlement.

Fortunately, under the indomitable leadership of Prime Minister Winston Churchill, who had recently replaced Neville Chamberlain, the British opted to fight on and defend their island nation. This point was made abundantly clear on 3 July when a British naval force attacked the French fleet at Mers-el-Kebir and destroyed one French battleship with two more disabled. During concurrent operations in Britain, Alexandria and Dakar, the British seized or immobilised numerous other French warships including four more battleships. The purpose of these actions was to prevent the possibility of Germany gaining control over these vessels, which would have altered the balance of naval power in the Atlantic. With the French fleet now secured, the British turned to the task of deterring or defeating an expected German invasion. In this, they were bolstered by the knowledge that the Royal Navy still maintained a sizeable strength advantage over the German Kriegsmarine, which had been made worse by the heavy naval losses the Germans had suffered off Norway. Given this naval disparity, it quickly became apparent to both sides that an essential factor in any German invasion would be the attainment of air superiority over the Royal Air Force. It was only under the protective umbrella of the Luftwaffe that the Kriegsmarine could possibly hope to contend with the Royal Navy's vastly superior numbers.

To this end, beginning in July and increasing through August and early September, the Germans launched a concerted air campaign with an initial force of some 2,600 aircraft to destroy the RAF and prepare the way for a proposed invasion, designated Operation *Seelöwe* (Sea Lion). On a nearly daily basis (weather permitting), sizeable formations of German bombers and fighters set out to attack a variety of targets in and around Britain with the goal of drawing out and wearing down the British fighter force, which consisted of a frontline strength of 644 aircraft in Fighter Command as of 7 July.[28] Despite being outnumbered by a factor of roughly four to one, the British proved far more resilient to these attacks than the Germans had anticipated, and Fighter Command was able to hold its own and inflict heavier losses upon the Germans than it itself suffered. While this was underway, British bombers and naval forces carried out numerous attacks against the occupied ports of northern France to disrupt the ongoing German invasion preparations. This offensive exacted a modest, but growing toll against the would-be German invasion fleet and made it abundantly clear that both the RAF and Royal Navy remained potent adversaries to any German invasion attempt. These results, along with Fighter Command's continued success over Britain, convinced Hitler that Germany had failed to gain the prerequisite ascendancy over the RAF, and on 17 September he postponed the invasion indefinitely. Although air attacks would continue against Britain well into the next year, the invasion threat was now over, and Germany tasted its first instance of strategic failure.

On a less positive note, while the British were able to stave off invasion, their vital maritime lines of communication came under increasingly heavy attack. In the first ten months of the war, the British held their shipping losses to a tolerable level, but in the next year, from 1 July 1940 through 30 June 1941, these losses more than tripled. The main perpetrator of this was Germany's U-boat arm, but other assailants included surface warships, auxiliary cruisers, mines and aircraft. There were three major factors that contributed to this upswing. First, on 17 August 1940 Hitler

Table 2.3. Key Statistics regarding the Battle of Britain.

	RAF Fighter Command aircraft losses	Luftwaffe aircraft losses	British civilian casualties from bombing killed/wounded	German naval losses in Channel area due to bombing and naval action sunk/dam
10–31 Jul 1940	69	155	258/321	.
01–31 Aug 1940	359	653	1,075/1,261	.
01–30 Sep 1940	364	553	6,954/10,615	126/153
01–31 Oct 1940	144	318	6,334/8,695	16/0
TOTAL	936	1,679	14,621/20,892	142/153

Source: Richard Hough and Denis Richards, *The Battle of Britain, the Greatest Air Battle of World War II* (London: W. W. Norton & Company, 1989), pp. 357–370; Frank K. Mason, Battle over Britain (New York: Doubleday & Company, Inc., 1969) p. 615 and ADM 199/2447, German Ships: Losses and Damage in NW European Waters, 1939–1945.

Note: German shipping losses overwhelmingly consisted of barges and other minor vessels of limited tonnage.

declared a total blockade of Britain thus giving his forces greater freedom to attack vessels in the adjacent waters without warning. Second, with the seizure of French, Belgian and Dutch territory, the Germans possessed far better bases to reach into the Atlantic and attack British maritime traffic from both the sea and the air. This was particularly true regarding the basing of German and Italian submarines in the French Biscay ports, which greatly extended their ability to operate into the Atlantic with far shorter turnaround times. Finally, the British lacked sufficient numbers of escort vessels to counter this onslaught. Part of this was due to recent heavy losses sustained off Norway and Northwest Europe as well as the need to maintain sizeable forces in Britain to counter the expected German invasion. As such, German U-boat crews dubbed this period the 'happy time' as they were often able to operate with near impunity from British countermeasures.

Fortunately, as bad as this was, British shipping losses never reached a level that was truly prohibitive, and by the spring of 1941 things began to improve. The first evidence of this occurred during a two-and-a-half-week period in March when British forces sank four German U-boats while a fifth U-boat was lost to unknown causes. This loss of five U-boats during a relatively short period signalled an end to the 'happy time'. Thereafter, the Germans would continue menacing British maritime traffic, but would encounter increasingly heavy resistance in the process. Two months later the British scored a second important victory when the Home Fleet chased down and destroyed the German battleship *Bismarck*. With this and the subsequent destruction or seizure of several German supply vessels that had been pre-positioned in the Atlantic to support *Bismarck*'s sortie, Germany ceased major surface raider operations for the remainder of the war. At the same time, the

Following the Battle of Britain, the British engaged in a multi-year campaign to secure vital maritime lines of communication. Pictured here is an aerial view of a British convoy. (Priest, L. C. (Lt), Royal Navy official photographer, public domain)

Germans also withdrew the majority of their Luftwaffe assets to prepare for their pending invasion of the Soviet Union. In doing so, they significantly reduced the number of attacks and mining operations launched against British maritime targets. Finally, over a period of several months culminating in the summer of 1941, the British broke key German naval codes that rendered the vast majority of signals transmitted to or from their U-boats accessible to British decryption. This invaluable intelligence, which the British referred to as Ultra, allowed the Admiralty to route numerous convoys away from U-boat concentrations and/or reinforce threatened convoys thus significantly reducing shipping losses.

While this was underway in the Atlantic and home waters, the British remained fully engaged in the Mediterranean as well. Despite being heavily outnumbered by Italian forces on sea, land and in the air at the onset of the Mediterranean conflict, the British immediately assumed an aggressive posture that quickly stymied Italian efforts to make appreciable gains. In naval terms, the Italians started the war with a strength of six battleships, one old armoured cruiser, seven heavy cruisers, 12 light cruisers, 61 destroyers, 69 torpedo boats and 115 submarines either on hand or about to enter service. The British countered this with an initial strength of just four battleships, one aircraft carrier, nine light cruisers, 21 destroyers and six submarines present within the theatre.[29] Undeterred by this imbalance, the British utilised various surface warships and naval aircraft to win a series of minor naval victories during the opening months of the war. While this was underway, a steady stream of reinforcements arrived to bolster their forces. Then in November 1940 the British scored their greatest success to date when aircraft from the carrier *Illustrious* attacked the naval base at Taranto and sank the Italian battleship *Conte Di Cavour* while two other battleships were temporarily disabled. This action altered the balance of power in the Mediterranean and firmly solidified the Royal Navy's growing ascendancy in the area.

The British matched this success at sea with similar successes on land as they engaged the Italians for control of North and East Africa. Operating from Libya, Eritrea, Abyssinia and Italian Somaliland, the Italians initially possessed a force of some 540,000 men in Africa against a regional British strength of just 83,500 men.[30] Despite being outnumbered by a factor of better than six to one, the British launched a series of raids and aggressive patrols that kept their superior Italian foes frozen in place for the first two months of the conflict. This changed in August when Italian forces from East Africa launched a successful invasion of neighbouring British Somaliland. Heavily outnumbered, the British quickly realised they had no viable prospect of holding the impoverished colony and instead conducted a skilful fighting retreat inflicting 2,052 casualties on the invading force for the cost of 260 casualties to themselves.[31] One month later an Italian army some 100,000 men strong launched an invasion into western Egypt from Libya. Once again, the British were too weak to directly contest this incursion, and instead yielded ground while conducting minor harassing operations. As it was, the Italians only advanced some 60 miles into Egypt before halting at Sidi Barrani on the coast. From there, they built up their logistics and made plans to continue their advance towards Mersa Matruh,

Unfortunately for the Italians, this pause gave the British time to bring in reinforcements, and in December the British launched a limited counter-attack, designated Operation *Compass*, against the forward Italian position at Sidi Barrani. Although initially envisioned as a large-scale raid lasting no more than four days, the British were completely successful in this assault capturing the stronghold and taking 38,300 prisoners for the loss of just 624 casualties to themselves.[32] Thereafter, the British were able to continue their offensive using captured Italian equipment and supplies to launch a series of attacks against Italian positions at Bardia, Tobruk and Beda Fomm. The result: over a ten-week period, a British force, which never exceeded more than two under-strength divisions, advanced some 500 miles, drove the Italians out of Egypt and conquered Cyrenaica (eastern Libya). In doing so, the British destroyed an Italian army of ten divisions, took some 130,000 prisoners and destroyed or captured over 380 tanks and 845 guns. British casualties for the operation amounted to just 500 dead, 1,373 wounded and 55 missing.[33] The breakdown of losses in the air was equally lopsided as the British destroyed 58 Italian aircraft in aerial combat, captured 91 more intact and found no fewer than 1,100 wrecked or disabled aircraft on the ground for the loss of just 26 aircraft to themselves.[34] Finally, Italian naval losses included the armoured cruiser *San Giorgio*, which was scuttled in Tobruk harbour along with several merchant ships and auxiliaries.

By the beginning of 1941, the British appeared poised to continue their growing success over the Italians, but a German intervention into the theatre quickly complicated this proposition. The first example of this occurred on 10 January when German dive-bombers heavily damaged the aircraft carrier *Illustrious* off Malta thus putting it out of action for several months. The German army soon joined this effort when a small expeditionary force arrived in North Africa to bolster the hard-pressed Italians. In March this force, led by General Erwin Rommel, launched a counter-attack that caught the British off guard after the latter had sent a 58,000-man expeditionary force to Greece to bolster that country after it had been attacked by Italy. This deployment left the British with just two understrength divisions immediately available to defend Cyrenaica. Attacked by one German and three Italian divisions, these overextended formations were unable to mount a coherent defence and immediately gave ground. Thankfully, this loss of territory was not matched by a high casualty rate as the British units were generally able to extricate themselves intact. Still, in less than a month, the British were forced to abandon most of the territory they had recently captured in Cyrenaica. The sole exception to this was the port of Tobruk, which the British retained with a strong garrison built around the Australian 9th Division. In April and May, Rommel launched two major attempts to capture Tobruk, but both were repulsed, and thereafter both sides settled in for a long siege.

Meanwhile, to the north the situation was equally difficult. In March the British Mediterranean Fleet won a spectacular victory off Cape Matapan where it destroyed three Italian heavy cruisers and two destroyers for no loss to itself. One month later, the British attained a similar success off Kerkenah Bank when a force of four destroyers sank a five-ship German convoy and two attending Italian destroyers for the loss of one British destroyer. Sadly, these actions proved to be highlights in what was otherwise a bleak period. In particular, on 6 April, Germany declared war on Yugoslavia and Greece, and launched large-scale invasions into both countries. In results reminiscent of the fighting in France the year before, Yugoslavia fell almost immediately while the Greeks, who had previously held their own against the Italians, were unable to stem this German onslaught. In turn, this compelled the British to first withdraw their expeditionary force from Greece and then later carry out a similar evacuation from Crete. During the process of the latter, German bombers exacted a heavy toll against the British naval units carrying out the evacuation including the destruction of three cruisers and six destroyers with several other warships damaged to varying degrees. Meanwhile, British personnel casualties for the short campaign numbered over 30,000 including 25,793 men taken prisoner in Greece and Crete.[35] Given these losses, the British emerged from the operation in a highly weakened state.

While the loss of Cyrenaica, Greece and Crete represented severe setbacks for the British, they were able to partially mitigate this with the execution of a highly successful campaign in East Africa. In January 1941, the British launched concurrent invasions into Italian East Africa from both north and south using a combined force of five Imperial and Commonwealth divisions supported by British naval and air assets. The first of these was an offensive out of Sudan by the 4th and 5th Indian Divisions against Italian-controlled Eritrea. After making initial good progress in the northern part of the country, the British encountered stout Italian resistance at Keren on the Asmara Plateau that took eight weeks to overcome. For the cost of 536 dead and 3,229 wounded, the British finally broke through the Italian defences on 27 March thus breaking the back of the Italian resistance.[36] Thereafter, the British captured the rest of Eritrea with little difficulty including the important Italian naval base at Massawa on the Red Sea. Meanwhile, a thousand miles to the south, the British carried out their second offensive using the 1st South African and the 11th and 12th African Divisions to attack Italian Somaliland from Kenya. Despite harsh terrain and climatic conditions, this offensive made good progress against largely indifferent Italian opposition and quickly captured the important Somali port cities of Kismayu and Mogadishu. The British then drove northward into eastern Abyssinia where they again overcame ineffective Italian resistance and seized the capital of Addis Ababa on 6 April. Concurrently, they also executed a seaborne landing that secured the liberation of British Somaliland.

By the middle of April, the British controlled Eritrea, Italian Somaliland, and most of Abyssinia along with their regained colony of British Somaliland. This concluded the offensive's major objectives, although substantial mopping-up operations continued in some of the northern and interior portions of Abyssinia until November. With this, the East Africa campaign ended, and the British celebrated their first complete offensive victory of the war. During a ten-month period culminating in November 1941, the British eliminated Italy's East African Empire, conquered some 700,000 square miles of territory, secured vital lines of communication and removed a force of some 290,000 men from the Italian order of battle including an estimated 15,211 Italian servicemen killed and over 200,000 taken prisoner.[37] Italian materiel losses included some 450 artillery pieces, 400 aircraft, 126 armoured cars and 60 tanks.[38] Finally, related Italian maritime losses included seven destroyers, two torpedo boats, four submarines, a minelayer and 43 assorted ocean-going merchant ships (both Italian and German) worth 255,239 tons that were sunk or seized in the waters around East Africa.[39] The cost in attaining this great victory was about 6,000 combat casualties and no warship losses for the participating British forces.[40]

As spectacular as this was, on 22 June Britain received news of far greater consequence when Germany launched a full-scale invasion of the Soviet Union. With this act, Germany dramatically altered the strategic realities of the war and gave Britain a new and powerful ally in the form of the colossal continental nation.

No longer would Britain (in conjunction with its Commonwealth partners) have to stand alone or bear the brunt of Germany's military effort. Instead, for the rest of the war, Britain benefitted from the tremendous diversion of resources the Germans were required to expend in their struggle against the Soviets. In the summer of 1941, this included the overwhelming majority of the German army and Luftwaffe as only the Kriegsmarine remained focused on Britain. While many years of hard fighting remained ahead, the British could now realistically look past the prospect of simply defying Axis domination to a future where outright victory was truly possible.

To this end, the British continued their struggle focusing their efforts on three primary campaigns during the second half of 1941. The first of these was the battle of the Atlantic, which was the decisive campaign in the West. As discussed earlier in the chapter, the beginning of 1941 saw the British particularly hard pressed in this maritime effort, but their fortunes substantially improved during the second half of the year. A number of factors contributed to this upturn including the availability of more escort vessels thus allowing the British to run fully defended convoys across the Atlantic and the aforementioned Ultra intelligence gained by the breaking of the German naval codes. As a result of these and other improvements, Allied shipping losses in the Atlantic and waters around Britain declined by almost two-thirds during the latter half of 1941 compared to the first half of the year. Meanwhile, German U-boat losses nearly doubled during the same timeframe. This latter point was highlighted in December when the Germans lost an unprecedented ten U-boats, which represented their highest monthly loss to date.

Together, these factors provided an important respite to the hard-pressed British Merchant Navy and corresponding supply effort. In terms of the former, despite heavy losses, Britain's available shipping pool largely remained constant during the year and actually expanded compared to its size at the beginning of the war thanks to new construction and the use of foreign flag time-charters. To this point, at the end of 1941 the British had 3,616 merchant ships worth 20,693,000 tons available for use compared to just 2,999 such vessels worth 17,784,000 tons in September 1939.[41] Together, these merchant ships delivered some 44,586,000 tons of total imports into the United Kingdom during 1941.[42] While less than prewar import levels, this inflow of seaborne trade satisfied Britain's basic needs thus ensuring the nation's survival and ability to fight on. In turn, these results effectively eliminated any prospect of an outright German victory in this critical naval conflict.

The second campaign involved British activities in the Middle East. In the spring and summer of 1941, the British engaged in a series of successful peripheral operations that reaffirmed or brought Iraq, Syria, Lebanon and Iran firmly within the Allied camp. As previously mentioned, this period also saw the conclusion of mopping up operations in East Africa that eliminated the last vestiges of Italian power within the region. Things were less active in the north where the British largely contented themselves with building up their forces in Egypt for a proposed future offensive.

Table 2.4. Key Performance Indices from the Battle of the Atlantic.

	Total Allied merchant shipping tonnage lost due to submarine attacks	Total Allied merchant shipping tonnage lost due to other military means	Merchant shipping under British control at the end of each period (in gross tons)*	Total import tons delivered to the United Kingdom**	U-boat losses***
Sep–Dec 1939	421,156	334,081	17,772,000	16,234,000	9
Jan–Jun 1940	715,770	864,840	20,477,000	30,890,000	15
Jul–Dec 1940	1,470,388	940,643	20,854,000	24,119,000	7
Jan–Jun 1941	1,451,595	1,432,712	20,131,000	20,646,000	12
Jul–Dec 1941	720,159	724,092	20,693,000	24,604,000	23

Source: The Central Statistical Office, *Statistical Digest of the War* (London: Her Majesty's Stationery Office, 1975), pp. 174, 184 and S. W. Roskill, *The War at Sea 1939–1945, Volume I* (London: Her Majesty's Stationery Office, 1954), pp. 615–616.

Note: Loss figures are compiled from all theatres of the war.

*Only covers ships of 1,600 gross tons or greater.

**These import figures are based upon estimated weights included in the Trade and Navigation Accounts for each month and are unadjusted for subsequent minor revisions.

***The U-boats Losses column only covers German losses. Italian submarine losses are not included due to the limited role these boats played in the overall tonnage battle.

While this was underway, the British also conducted extensive supply operations to maintain their garrisons at Tobruk, the only significant piece of Libyan territory still under their control, as well as the island fortress of Malta located in the central Mediterranean. In terms of the latter, Malta served as an important base for British interdiction operations against Axis supply movements to North Africa, and in the second half of 1941 Malta-based forces, which consisted of aircraft, submarines and occasional surface warships, took a heavy toll on this crucial Axis merchant traffic. In turn, these interdiction successes contributed to an ever-precarious logistical situation plaguing the German and Italian forces in Cyrenaica.

The culmination of these various efforts occurred in November when the newly formed British Eighth Army, which was some 118,000-men strong, launched an offensive out of Egypt and engaged a local German/Italian army of roughly equal size. After a month-long battle in which the momentum swayed back and forth, the British finally prevailed in this action, which was designated Operation *Crusader*, thus forcing the Germans and Italians to retreat. In doing so, the Axis were forced to abandon some isolated garrisons along the coastline, which later surrendered to the British. Including these capitulations, total Axis casualties for the battle numbered some 38,300 men of which roughly three-quarters were taken prisoner compared to 17,700 casualties for the British.[43] A major factor in this outcome was the continued deterioration of the Axis supply situation. Much of this was brought about by

In the opening years of the war British forces scored a number of spectacular victories against the Italians but struggled to attain similar results against the Germans. Pictured here are South African troops at Moyale in East Africa. (Unknown author, public domain)

British maritime successes, which in November and December included two Italian cruisers, two destroyers and 11 merchant ships sunk by British warships, a destroyer and 11 merchant ships sunk by British submarines and 12 merchant ships sunk by British aircraft. As a result of these losses and other affiliated disruptions, the Axis only succeeded in delivering 68,905 tons out of 126,888 tons of supplies dispatched to North Africa during this period.[44] This amount was wholly inadequate in meeting the Axis needs, and by the end of December the British controlled Cyrenaica once again. Yet despite this success, sizeable Axis forces still remained in western Libya thus ensuring that the fighting would continue in the upcoming year.

The final major component in Britain's operational efforts encompassed their various activities to take the war to Germany. The most prevalent of these was the fledgling strategic bombing campaign, which sought to undermine Germany's ability and willingness to wage war. Unfortunately, at this early stage in the conflict, this effort was hampered by inadequate numbers of bombers, aircraft of limited ranges and bombloads, insufficient navigational aids and inexperienced crews. As such, most

British raids during this period garnered few tangible results and constituted little more than defiant gestures. Nevertheless, improvements were underway to remedy each of these deficiencies, and it was only a matter of time before this bombing campaign netted major strategic benefit. In particular, German cities, industry and infrastructure would soon come under ever-increasing attacks that would disrupt the German economy and compel their armed forces to divert substantial resources to defend the homeland.

In concurrent operations, the British also set about to destroy German seaborne trade by attacking the German merchant fleet. As discussed earlier in the chapter, Germany was not as dependent upon maritime trade as was Britain, but the Germans still benefitted from the importation of certain key commodities including rubber, tin and tungsten from the Far East and phosphorus-rich iron ore, molybdenum and nickel from Scandinavia. In terms of the former, from the beginning of the conflict the British were successful in sweeping the vast bulk of German merchant shipping from the world's oceans. Yet, despite this near-complete embargo, the Germans still tried to run occasional merchant ships through the British blockade to bring in rare products or provide logistical support to their own raiders at sea. In 1941 British naval units destroyed, captured or forced the scuttling of no fewer than 25 German and German-affiliated merchant ships in the North and South Atlantic and waters around South America. Meanwhile, a further nine Axis merchant ships were captured or forced to scuttle when British forces occupied the Iranian ports of Bandar Shapur and Bandar Abbas in August of that same year. Finally, British forces seized 13 Vichy French ships during this period, some of which were engaged in blockade running.

In terms of the latter, Britain's interdiction options were far more limited given its restricted access to the Baltic Sea and the close proximity of Scandinavia to German-controlled ports. As such, the British adopted a strategy of attacking German-controlled shipping anywhere they could to cause continuous attrition that would strain the overall German shipping situation and eventually degrade operations everywhere. In this, the British used a number of weapons including sea and air-laid mines, RAF strike and bomber aircraft, submarines, surface warships and even occasional carrier air strikes to attack German shipping. In 1941 these various agents accounted for more than 200 German and German-affiliated vessels sunk in the waters off Northwest Europe. When attrition from other sources such as accidents and Soviet actions were added into this tally, total German losses within the region increased to some 320 vessels worth over a half a million tons during this time. Many additional ships were laid up for repairs or maintenance due to combat damage or normal operational wear. By comparison, new construction and additional shipping attained from the occupied nations failed to keep pace with losses. As such, these shortfalls along with other related disruptions reduced Germany's cargo carrying efficiency by an estimated 19 percent from 1940 to 1942 thus validating Britain's overall strategy in this area.[45]

The final component of Britain's offensive effort was the use of naval and specialised ground forces to launch commando raids against selected coastal targets in occupied Europe. The first of these, Operation *Claymore*, occurred on 4 March when British forces successfully destroyed a number of industrial and maritime targets in the Lofoten Islands in northern Norway. Nine months later the British followed this up with two concurrent raids, Operations *Anklet* and *Archery*, against the Lofoten and Vaagsö Islands that netted similar results. In the grand scheme of things, these actions caused little appreciable damage, but they forced the Germans to deploy proportionally larger forces to defend the vast coastlines of occupied Europe against the prospect of additional raids. Meanwhile, these incursions served as great morale boosters for the British and gave them a means to maintain an offensive posture during a time when more substantial operations were impractical. Finally, they provided the British with valuable combined arms and amphibious operational experience which would pay meaningful dividends later in the war.

In closing out this period, by the beginning of December 1941 the British could rightly feel a sense of relief and guarded optimism about the European conflict balanced against the realisation that untold hardships and challenges remained ahead. In highlighting the former, the British had successfully turned back two immense challenges to their national survival by avoiding a direct German invasion and blunting Germany's initial efforts to sever their all-important maritime lines of communication. Beyond this, the British had also enjoyed considerable success in the Middle East where they had stymied the designs of a numerically superior enemy and held their own in North Africa and the Mediterranean while attaining decisive victory in East Africa. Finally, they had also garnered a new and powerful ally in the form of the Soviet Union, which provided them with a realistic opportunity to not only survive, but attain outright victory against the European Axis. Still, by any measure, the attainment of this victory was uncertain and far off at best. Even as the British recounted their ongoing triumphs, Germany still wielded colossal military power and controlled a vast European empire ranging from Norway in the north to Greece in the south and France in the west to the doorsteps of Moscow in the east. Against this, the British were little more than outsiders looking in. One thing was certain, many years of trials and tribulation remained ahead before the stain of Naziism and Italian Fascism was eliminated from the European continent. Until then, Britain would remain committed to this contest.

CHAPTER 3

On the Brink in Asia

By any measure, British fortitude during the early years of World War II underwent a severe testing that made it hard to imagine the nation enduring further adversity. Yet, even as the British were fighting for their very survival in Europe, Africa and the surrounding waters, an ever-present and menacing threat lurked in the Pacific that portended to do just that. As discussed in Chapter 1, from almost its inception, the modern Japanese state had embarked upon a path of military and political expansion. This belligerence was driven by a Japanese desire to acquire an Asian empire that would provide Japan with the markets and resources it needed to attain economic self-sufficiency and relieve pressures on its excess population. In 1937, this quest for territorial growth had manifested itself into a Japanese invasion of China. Two years later, the Japanese were still bogged down in this protracted campaign as well as in an ongoing series of unproductive clashes with the Soviet Union along the border of Manchukuo and Mongolia. Yet, despite these disappointing results, the Japanese were not deterred in seeking additional opportunities for expansion as they covetously looked towards the resource-rich European colonies of Southeast Asia as a means to fulfill their imperial ambitions.

Sadly, this situation was only made worse by the onset of war in Europe. By the summer of 1940, the collapse of many European nations and Britain's preoccupation at home created a power vacuum in Asia. The Japanese wasted little time in taking advantage of this situation and assumed a more aggressive posture against their European colonial neighbours. On 18 July 1940 Japan pressured the British government into temporarily closing the Burma Road thus depriving China of its primary logistical gateway to the outside world. At roughly the same time, the Japanese also coerced Vichy French authorities into allowing them access to airfields and bases in northern French Indochina. On 27 September 1940 Japan signed the Tripartite Pact in Berlin with Germany and Italy. This agreement pledged its signatories to support each other in the event of an attack by a power not already engaged in the war. While not a direct alliance, this agreement clearly indicated that Japan was further migrating into the Axis camp. Finally, in July 1941 the Japanese demanded, and gained from the Vichy French, the right to exercise joint military control over French Indochina. This action brought the Japanese to within 700 miles of the important British naval base at Singapore and seriously threatened British security in the region.

Unfortunately, due to their commitments in Europe, the British were no longer capable of offering serious opposition to this growing threat. Instead, the United States was the only nation with a realistic capability to deter or confront Japan's growing aggression. Like Britain, the United States had territorial and economic interests in East Asia that gave it ample cause for intervention. Nevertheless, during much of this time the American government did little to counter Japan's growing belligerence other than lodge diplomatic protests. Finally, in July 1940 the United States implemented some meaningful sanctions against Japan by imposing an export embargo on scrap iron, steel and high-octane aviation fuel to that nation. This action failed to deter the Japanese, and when they assumed joint military control over Indochina, the Americans, with subsequent British and Dutch agreement, froze Japanese assets and imposed a near total trade embargo against Japan. The key provision of this embargo was a complete prohibition of fuel oil exports to Japan from the East Indies and the American continent. Although Japan maintained sizeable oil reserves, this embargo ultimately threatened to wreak havoc upon the Japanese economy and hinder its ability to wage war. Accordingly, the Japanese faced the unenviable prospect of either using their military forces or slowly losing them as a means to advance their national agenda. Given the debilitating nature of the embargo, which would only worsen with the passage of time, a moment of decision was clearly approaching.

If the Japanese chose the former option, they had a number of powerful weapons to wield in pursuit of their expansionist goals. This was particularly true regarding the Imperial Japanese Navy, which constituted the largest and most capable naval force present in the Pacific during this period. In December 1941 this force consisted of ten battleships, six fleet aircraft carriers, four light carriers, 18 heavy cruisers, 18 light cruisers, 113 destroyers, 63 submarines and some 1,750 combat and support aircraft.[1] While both Britain and the United States possessed larger navies as a whole, these nations were compelled to maintain sizeable portions of their strength outside of the Pacific, which allowed Japan to be the predominant naval power within the region. In fact, the Imperial Japanese Navy constituted a slightly larger force than that available to the entire American, British/Commonwealth and Dutch Pacific fleets combined. Nor was this the sole measure of Japanese naval power. The Japanese also enjoyed a level of materiel and operational quality that was at least comparable, and in some cases superior, to that of their American and European rivals. Similarly, Japanese personnel were generally well trained and fanatically loyal in the performance of their duties. Finally, the Japanese enjoyed a unity of command and purpose that was unmatched in the Allied camp. This latter point was highlighted by an American reluctance to conduct any joint planning with their British or Dutch counterparts regarding the defence of the Pacific.

Table 3.1. Available Japanese and Allied Naval Strength in the Pacific in December 1941.

	Japan	United States	British Empire	Dutch
Battleships/battlecruisers	10	9	2	–
Aircraft carriers	10	3	–	–
Heavy cruisers	18	13	1	–
Light cruisers	18	11	7	3
Destroyers	113	80	13	7
Submarines	63	56	–	13

Source: S. W. Roskill, *The War at Sea 1939–1945, Volume 1* (London: Her Majesty's Stationery Office, 1954), p. 560.

In terms of its naval strength, Japan's most potent weapon was its carrier-borne air arm. In the late autumn of 1941, the Japanese possessed the largest carrier fleet in the world with ten assorted aircraft carriers in commission. Added to this already considerable force, the Japanese had another seven aircraft carriers under construction including six that were due for completion in 1942. These were capable warships consisting of a variety of classes and designs including some that were conversions from other vessels. A major attribute of most Japanese carriers was their larger aircraft capacities than that of their British counterparts. This was demonstrated by the fact that all six Japanese active fleet carriers had capacities ranging from 63 to 72 aircraft compared to the British *Illustrious*-class, which could only operate between 36 and 55 aircraft depending upon the storage configuration used. Likewise, a typical Japanese light carrier was capable of carrying between 26 and 37 aircraft compared to 15 aircraft for the British *Hermes* and 21 aircraft for *Eagle*. Finally, Japanese aircraft carriers tended to have greater sailing speeds and range endurance

Table 3.2. Characteristics of Japanese Aircraft Carriers.

	Number of vessels	Tonnage	Normal aircraft capacity	Maximum speed
Akagi-class fleet carrier	1	36,500	72	31 knots
Kaga-class fleet carrier	1	38,200	66	28.3 knots
Sōryū-class fleet carrier	1	15,900	63	34.5 knots
Hiryū-class fleet carrier	1	17,300	64	34.3 knots
Shōkaku-class fleet carriers	2	25,675	72	34.2 knots
Hōshō-class light carrier	1	7,470	26	25 knots
Ryūjō-class light carrier	1	10,600	37	29 knots
Zuihō-class light carriers	1 + 1	11,260	30	28 knots
Taiyō-class escort carriers	1 + 2	17,830	27	21 knots
Ryūhō-class light carrier (building)	1	13,360	31	26.5 knots
Junyō-class fleet carriers (building)	2	24,140	53	25.5 knots
Taihō-class fleet carrier (building)	1	29,300	63	33 knots

than their British counterparts, which made them more suited for operating in the vast expanses of the Pacific Ocean.

In addition to the size and capabilities of this carrier fleet, the Japanese also possessed some of the finest naval aircraft and best trained air crews in the world. In December 1941 the Japanese naval air arm wielded a combat strength of some 660 fighters and 570 assorted bombers and torpedo-bombers.[2] The mainstay of this fighter force was the Mitsubishi A6M2 Zero, a highly manoeuvrable aircraft with a top speed of 332 miles per hour. Although not particularly fast or well armoured compared to contemporary shore-based fighters, the nimble A6M2 was a superb dog fighter in close quarter combat. As for the strike aircraft in the navy's arsenal, the Aichi D3A1 Val dive-bomber was superior in many respects to the German Stuka, which had already caused the Royal Navy considerable difficulties in the waters off Northwest Europe and the Mediterranean. With a top speed of 240 miles per hour and capacity to carry an 813-pound bomb load, the D3A1 Val was well suited for carrier operations and capable of delivering a deadly punch against Allied warships. The Nakajima B5N2 Kate torpedo-bomber was an all-metal monoplane with similar good performance and a load capacity for one 18-inch torpedo or one 1,764-pound armour-piercing bomb. A common attribute for all three of these aircraft was their excellent ranges, which could allow Japanese carriers to stand off at greater distances than their British counterparts when launching attacks. Finally, the navy possessed a number of shore-based designs for reconnaissance and strike purposes. Of these, the most notable were the Mitsubishi G4M1 Betty and G3M2 Nell twin-engine bombers, which could both carry an ordinance load of some 1,800 pounds in either a torpedo or conventional attack role.

The Japanese enjoyed a similar qualitative advantage regarding many portions of their surface fleet. Like the British, the vast majority of Japanese battleships came from the World War I era. However, unlike the British, the Japanese had invested far more time and resources into modernising their capital ships during the interwar years. Even more troubling, the Japanese also had three massive *Yamato*-class battleships under construction that were unparalleled in their size and striking power. The first of these behemoths, the namesake *Yamato*, was only weeks away from completion. The second, *Musashi*, still had a number of months to go, while *Shinano* would take considerably longer to complete. In fact, the Japanese would never complete *Shinano* as a battleship. Instead, they would convert it into an aircraft carrier during construction and commission it as such in 1944. Regarding other warship categories, Japanese heavy cruisers were generally larger, better protected and more heavily armed than their British counterparts. This advantage was highlighted by the Japanese *Takao*-class, which displaced 13,400 tons and was armed with ten 8-inch guns. Likewise, some classes of Japanese destroyers were larger and better armed than their British counterparts. Finally, Japanese cruisers and destroyers carried an exceptional anti-shipping weapon in the form of the Type 93 Long Lance torpedo.

Table 3.3. Characteristics of Selected Japanese Surface Warships.

	Number of vessels	Tonnage	Main armament	Maximum speed
Kongō-class battleships	4	27,613	8 × 14in guns	30 knots
Fusō-class battleships	2	34,700	12 × 14in guns	24.7 knots
Ise-class battleships	2	36,000	12 × 14in guns	25.3 knots
Nagato-class battleships	2	38,000	8 × 16in guns	25 knots
Yamato-class battleships (building)	3*	64,000	9 × 18.1in guns	27 knots
Myōkō-class heavy cruisers	4	13,000	10 × 8in guns	33.8 knots
Takao-class heavy cruisers	4	13,400	10 × 8in guns	34.4 knots
Mogami-class heavy cruisers	4	11,200	10 × 8in guns	35 knots
Kuma-class light cruisers	5	5,100	7 × 5.5in guns	36 knots
Agano-class light cruisers (building)	4	6,652	6 × 6in guns	35 knots
Minekaze-class destroyers	15	1,215	4 × 4.7in guns	36 knots
Fubuki-class destroyers	19	2,060	6 × 5in guns	34 knots
Shiratsuyu-class destroyers	10	1,900	5 × 5in guns	34 knots
Asashio-class destroyers	10	2,100	5 × 5in guns	35 knots

Note: Covers all classes of Japanese battleships but only covers selected cruiser and destroyer classes. The numbers of vessels reflect those on hand or under construction at the beginning of December 1941.

* Only two of the three *Yamato*-class were actually completed as battleships.

This oxygen-driven torpedo carried a heavier warhead and had four times the range of its British or American counterparts thus giving it the potential to be a particularly devastating weapon during naval surface engagements.

Augmenting these many materiel advantages was a similar high standard of training and tactical proficiency. Although generally lacking the recent combat experience of their British counterparts, the Japanese possessed a highly professional naval force in which standards of training were second to none. Already mentioned was the high level of proficiency present in Japan's naval aviation arm. The Japanese also excelled in night fighting skills rivaling that attained by the British in their many nocturnal encounters against the Germans and Italians. A second major attribute benefiting Japanese naval forces was high morale and confidence in their abilities. Although the Japanese lacked the extended, multi-century naval heritage enjoyed by the Royal Navy, they had yet to experience the sting of defeat, which helped foster these affirming sentiments. On a less positive note, while the Imperial Japanese Navy possessed a highly proficient cadre based upon years of training and professional development, the size of this force was limited. Once the Japanese started suffering substantial attrition, it remained to be seen how effectively they could replicate this same level of prowess in their replacement personnel.

Rounding out the Japanese fleet hierarchy were a number of lesser warship types. While the major combatants in the Japanese navy tended to be of excellent quality, the situation regarding these lesser vessels was more mixed. The Japanese had a number of submarine classes broken down into two major categories. The I-class designation was for large, long-range submarines typically displacing between 1,500 and 2,600 tons and armed with six to eight torpedo tubes and a 4.7 to 5.5-inch deck gun. These submarines possessed the range and speed necessary to operate in the vast expanses of the Pacific Ocean, but their large sizes tended to make them susceptible to detection, slow in diving and ungainly in their underwater performance. The second major category, the RO-class, consisted of smaller, short-range submarines earmarked for coastal operations. These types typically displaced between 600 and 1,000 tons and were armed with four to six torpedo tubes and a 3-inch deck gun. Finally, beyond these principal types, the Japanese also possessed a number of midget submarines of less than 50 tons, which could be transported on parent submarines for attacks against static targets.

On the other end of the maritime spectrum, the Japanese were grossly deficient in dedicated escort vessels generally depending upon fleet destroyers or a handful of older converted destroyers to fill this role. The exception to this was the recent construction of four *Shimushu*-class general-purpose escorts that displaced 860 tons and were armed with three 4.7-inch guns and a paltry 18 depth charges. The Japanese were also deficient in mine warfare vessels. This was particularly true regarding fleet minesweepers of which the Japanese only possessed 19 at the beginning of December 1941. These broke down into six different classes ranging in size from 580 to 720 tons and were armed with two to three 4.7-inch guns. The situation was much the same regarding minelayers as the Japanese possessed 17 such vessels of various classes ranging in size from 450 to 1,970 tons. Many of these vessels could serve in an escort capacity if the need arose, but they were hardly ideal for this purpose. From the Japanese perspective, this was of little consequence since their strategy was to wage a short, decisive war. It was only if the combat became protracted that their defensive deficiencies might become problematic.

Partnering with the navy was the Imperial Japanese Army. While any conflict in the region was sure to be maritime oriented, there would still be a significant role for ground forces to play. In this regard, the Japanese army consisted of 1.7 million men split between 51 divisions and several special purpose artillery, cavalry, anti-aircraft and armoured units.[3] Added to this was the Imperial Japanese Army Air Service, which was the army's air arm consisting of some 1,570 frontline aircraft including 550 fighters and 660 bombers.[4] The majority of these forces were needed to wage war in China or to garrison Manchukuo, Korea, Formosa and the home islands thus leaving only 11 divisions and two air groups (about 700 aircraft) immediately available for potential service against the European and American possessions in the

Southwest Pacific.[5] Yet, even with this limited force, the Japanese were still capable of matching, and in some cases outnumbering, the disjointed Allied formations directly present in the region. This factor was enhanced by the fact that the Japanese would likely hold the initiative and set the timing for any pending conflict.

The quality of the Japanese army was more varied. On the positive side, Japanese soldiers were generally well trained, highly disciplined and extremely tenacious in combat. Driven by their Bushido creed, the vast majority of these soldiers were prepared to fight to the death and willing to endure acute privations rarely acceptable to their European and American counterparts. This made them extremely formidable opponents. A less admirable aspect of this ethos was a tendency to show indifference or outright animosity towards established norms of warfare regarding the treatment of prisoners, wounded and civilians. In general, the Japanese officer corps was dedicated and competent in the execution of its duties with unwavering focus on mission accomplishment. At times, this staunchness and single-minded confidence bordered upon fanaticism. A large portion of the Japanese army had direct combat experience having seen service during the recent fighting in China and Manchukuo. In terms of combat proficiency, the Japanese were masters of small unit and infiltration tactics but were not as adept at larger combined arms operations.

In materiel and organisational terms, the outlook was equally mixed. Japanese equipment tended to be fairly rudimentary and, in some cases, clearly obsolete. A prime example of the latter was the quality of Japanese tanks, which were markedly inferior to contemporary European and American designs. To a lesser degree, Japanese artillery also lagged behind its western counterparts in terms of overall effectiveness. Meanwhile, the Japanese army was generally less mechanised than other premier armies of the era, and its logistical and support formations tended to be less abundantly staffed and equipped than similar western elements. These latter factors could serve as either a positive or a negative depending upon the situation. On one hand, the Japanese army was lighter and less dependent upon an overly cumbersome support infrastructure, which could be initially beneficial when operating in the harsh mountain and jungle terrain prevalent throughout much of Southeast Asia. On the other hand, this lack of a robust logistical and support organisation could become debilitating over a prolonged period of sustained combat operations.

This assorted quality situation was much the same in the Japanese Army Air Service. On the positive side, Japanese pilots and aircrews tended to be very well trained with many possessing practical combat experience. In 1941 first-line Japanese pilots had between 500 and 800 flying hours while 50 percent of army and 10 percent of navy pilots had combat experience in China or against the Soviet Union.[6] Against this strength, the performance characteristics of the available Japanese aircraft varied from reasonably good to obsolete. In terms of the latter, the main fighter of the Japanese Army Air Force was the Nakajima Ki-27 Nate, which had entered service in 1937 and seen extensive use in China but was now outmoded by more modern European and American designs. The Japanese possessed a newer fighter, the Nakajima Ki-43 Oscar, which had some similar performance characteristics to the navy's A6M2 Zero, but only existed in small numbers at the end of 1941. Meanwhile, the army's bomber force primarily consisted of the twin-engine Mitsubishi Ki-21 Sally and Nakajima Ki-49 Donryu Helen, both of which carried a 2,200-pound bombload, but otherwise had unremarkable performance. Finally, for reconnaissance purposes, the Japanese had the Mitsubishi Ki-46 Dinah, which was an exceptional aircraft capable of outrunning most contemporary fighters of the period.

In viewing the totality of Japan's military strength, it was clear that the Japanese possessed a powerful navy and a capable, if somewhat limited army. These forces were substantial in size and ability thus constituting a hazardous threat to the other regional powers. Enhancing this danger was the fact that the Japanese were immensely ambitious and possessed a degree of confidence bordering upon recklessness in the pursuit of their goals. On the greater strategic level, the Japanese did have some comparative weaknesses. In particular, the Japanese lacked the population, natural resources and industrial base to effectively compete with the Western Powers in an extended conflict. Of these, the Japanese might be able to obtain access to sufficient natural resources through the conquest of neighbouring territory, but they would then have to implement a vast, and potentially vulnerable, maritime transit system to effectively utilise these assets. On the other hand, these maritime lines of communication would be relatively close to the Japanese home islands compared to the long distances that American and British forces would have to operate from in order to impede them thus offering the Japanese a degree of geographical protection. One thing was certain, despite potential long-term vulnerabilities and the tendency of some military and political leaders, including Churchill, to underestimate the Japanese, most informed observers realised that Japan held the initial advantage in the event of a Pacific conflict.

From a British perspective, this sad reality had as much to do with their own weaknesses as it did with the prowess of Japanese strengths. Prewar British defence plans had called for the Royal Navy to dispatch a large battle fleet to the Singapore naval base in the event of growing tensions with Japan. Now, with the navy firmly committed to fighting the Germans and Italians, no fleet was readily available to send. Instead, all the British could amass was a token force consisting of the battleship *Prince of Wales*, the veteran battlecruiser *Repulse* and the new aircraft carrier *Indomitable*, which they ordered to Singapore in the autumn of 1941. No sooner did the Admiralty make this decision then problems arose. On 3 November *Indomitable* ran aground off Jamaica during a working-up exercise. This accident sufficiently damaged the carrier thus delaying its departure and preventing it from being immediately available to join the other two warships when they arrived in Singapore on 2 December. These two capital ships, plus a handful of British and Commonwealth cruisers and destroyers represented the totality of British naval strength within the region.

As previously alluded to, the biggest factor constraining the British was their need to retain the bulk of their forces in the Atlantic and Mediterranean theatres thus limiting what was available to send to the Far East. Not only did this disparity apply to the quantity of resources eventually deployed to this region, but it also applied to the quality. In many cases, the vessels and resources dispatched to the Pacific were older and less capable than those retained in the Atlantic and Mediterranean. The same was true regarding many of the crews and personnel involved as they lacked the training and experience of their European-based counterparts. Sadly, while these local British forces could hope to eventually receive additional reinforcements, starting with the arrival of the errant *Indomitable*, this situation of prevailing deficiency was unlikely to change anytime soon. As long as the conflict in Europe remained paramount in the overall British war effort, the Far East was certain to remain a secondary theatre.

Given this understanding, a general review of British naval strength is now in order. Starting first with the Fleet Air Arm, the British began the war with seven aircraft carriers, but by December 1941 three of these carriers had been lost in combat. Unfortunately, these casualties happened to consist of Britain's most capable pre-war carriers. The four remaining ships had insufficient aircraft capacities and were generally too slow to serve as effective fleet carriers. In fact, two of these, *Hermes* and *Argus*, were so limited in their capabilities that they were ill suited for anything other than trade protection and ferrying duties. The British compensated for these initial carrier losses with the construction of four new *Illustrious*-class aircraft carriers that were commissioned in 1940 and 1941. These *Illustrious*-class vessels possessed a robust design featuring an armoured flight deck that provided them with greater protection than their American or Japanese counterparts. However, this added protection came at a cost as these carriers only had an official hangar capacity of 36 aircraft, although this could be increased to 55 aircraft using a deck parking configuration.

Beyond these commissioned vessels, the British had further aircraft carrier designs under construction or in development. The first of these was the two-ship *Implacable*-class, which had a similar armoured flight deck as its *Illustrious* predecessor, but a greater storage capacity for up to 81 aircraft. A second was the aircraft repair ship *Unicorn*, which was designed to be a support vessel, but could function as a conventional carrier if needed with a capacity to operate 35 aircraft. Finally, the British had a number of escort carriers under development that were converted merchant ships or dedicated warships built along modified commercial lines. The British already had a rudimentary version on hand, the 5,540-ton

Table 3.4. Characteristics of British Aircraft Carriers.

	Number of vessels	Tonnage	Normal aircraft capacity	Maximum speed
Furious-class	1	22,450	36	30 knots
Eagle-class	1	22,600	21	24 knots
Hermes-class	1	10,850	15	25 knots
Argus-class	1	14,000	15	20 knots
Illustrious-class	4	23,000	55	30.5 knots
Implacable-class (building)	2	23,450	81	32 knots
Unicorn-class (building)	1	14,750	35	24 knots

Audacity, which would be sunk in December, while 11 more escort carriers were under conversion in the United Kingdom or on order from the United States under Lend-Lease.[7] Further escort carriers would be built as the war progressed. Generally displacing between 7,800 and 11,800 tons and capable of operating 15 to 28 aircraft, these escort carriers would become useful additions to the fleet hierarchy. Unfortunately, it would be several months before any of these new escort carriers became available while their larger brethren would take a year and a half to two years to complete. In the meantime, the British would have to make do with what they had.

The same was true regarding available aircraft for the Fleet Air Arm. Although the Royal Navy had pioneered the dawn of early naval aviation, the Fleet Air Arm had suffered significant neglect during the interwar years thus causing the British to lag behind the Japanese in terms of aircraft quality. In late 1941, the most prolific strike aircraft in the Fleet Air Arm's inventory was the Fairey Swordfish torpedo-bomber. A biplane designed in 1934 but looking more akin to a remnant from World War I, the Swordfish was laboriously slow with a top speed of only 139 miles per hour and a limited range of only 546 miles. Capable of carrying an 18-inch torpedo or 1,500-pound bombload, the Swordfish had enjoyed surprising success against the Germans and Italians, but it seemed unlikely to replicate these results against the more formidable Japanese. The British had a successor torpedo-bomber, the Fairey Albacore, in limited use, but this aircraft's performance was only moderately better than that of the Swordfish and thus did not constitute a major improvement. In terms of carrier-borne fighters, the British had three different types in service, the Fairey Fulmar, Hawker Sea Hurricane and American-built Grumman F4F Martlet. Of these, only the Martlet came remotely close to matching the performance of the Japanese A6M2 Zero while the other two types were markedly inferior. Given this, the British could reasonably hope to handle Japanese bombers, but would be hard pressed to cope with any fighter escorts.

During the war the British completed six armoured aircraft carriers that all saw service against the Japanese. Pictured here is *Victorious* in 1941. (Coote, R. G. G. (Lt), Royal Navy official photographer, public domain)

Turning now to the British battle line, the Royal Navy possessed 15 capital ships with two more under construction as of December 1941. Ten of these were veterans from World War I consisting of four *Queen Elizabeth-* and four *Royal Sovereign*-class battleships and two *Renown*-class battlecruisers. In their day, these warships had been among the most powerful capital ships afloat, but that had been more than two decades before. Now with the passage of time, these veterans were outclassed by more modern designs. This was particularly true since only *Queen Elizabeth, Warspite, Valiant* and *Renown* had undergone significant modernisation during the interwar years. The British augmented this force with the two *Nelson*-class battleships built in the 1920s. These ships were heavily armed with nine 16-inch guns and possessed good armour protection, but British designers had compromised speed and some ship handling characteristics to attain these attributes while still complying with the tonnage limitations set forth in the Washington Treaty. Closing out the battle line, the British had five *King George V*-class battleships in commission or under construction. These were stoutly designed ships with excellent armour protection and reasonably good speed. Armed with ten 14-inch guns capable of firing a 15,900-pound broadside some 38,560 yards, the *King George Vs* had a potent punch, but their quadruple gun turrets were initially prone to technical problems that could result in reduced rates of fire.

Beyond these capital ships, the British possessed several cruiser and destroyer classes. This included four different heavy cruiser designs that ranged in size from 8,300 to 10,000 tons and were armed with six to eight 8-inch guns thus making them less powerful than their Japanese counterparts. The British fared better in terms of light cruisers where they generally held a qualitative advantage over the Japanese. Amongst the navy's newest and most capable cruisers was the Town-class. Displacing between 9,100 and 10,000 tons (depending upon the grouping) and possessing a main armament of twelve 6-inch guns, the 'Towns' were arguably the best light cruiser class of the war. Based upon this design, the British then introduced the Colony-class. These cruisers maintained the same armament as the 'Towns' but had a reduced displacement of 8,800 tons. A final type that had already earned distinction in the Mediterranean was the *Leander*-class. Built in the early 1930s, the *Leanders* came in two groupings (the latter of which was also referred to as the *Amphion*-class) and displaced between 6,830 and 7,270 tons with a main armament of eight 6-inch guns. As for destroyers, the British had no fewer than 21 different

Table 3.5. Characteristics of Selected British Surface Warships.

	Number of vessels	Tonnage	Main armament	Maximum speed
Queen Elizabeth-class battleships	4	30,600–32,700	8 × 15in guns	24 knots
Royal Sovereign-class battleships	4	29,150	8 × 15in guns	21 knots
Renown-class battlecruisers	2	32,000	6 × 15in guns	29 knots
Nelson-class battleships	2	33,313	9 × 16in guns	23 knots
King George V-class battleships	3+2	36,700	10 × 14in guns	28.5 knots
County-class heavy cruisers	13	9,750–10,000	8 × 8in guns	31–32 knots
Leander-class light cruisers	7	6,830–7,270	8 × 6in guns	32.5 knots
Arethusa-class light cruisers	4	5,220–5,279	6 × 6in guns	32 knots
Town-class light cruisers	8	9,100–10,000	12 × 6in guns	32 knots
Colony-class light cruisers	4+6	8,800	12 × 6in guns	33 knots
S-class destroyers	10	905	1–3 × 4in guns	36 knots
Tribal-class destroyers	11+6	1,870	8 × 4.7in guns	36 knots
J-class destroyers	6	1,690	6 × 4.7in guns	36 knots
L-class destroyers	6+2	1,920	6 × 4.7in guns	36 knots

Note: Covers all classes of British battleships and battlecruisers but only covers selected cruiser and destroyer classes. The numbers of vessels reflect those on hand or under construction at the beginning of December 1941.

classes on hand or under development in late 1941 ranging in size from 905 tons to 1,920 tons. While generally capable warships, these destroyers tended to be smaller and less heavily armed than their Japanese counterparts. This latter point was highlighted by the fact that most British destroyers were armed with 4.7-inch guns compared to the 5-inch guns carried on many Japanese destroyers.

Finally, unlike the Japanese, a sizeable portion of British naval strength resided in the ranks of their lesser combat vessels. Of these, the most prevalent were the host of escort types consisting of escort destroyers, sloops, frigates and corvettes. Generally displacing between 900 and 1,500 tons and armed with a variety of anti-submarine weapons and small calibre guns up to 4-inch in size, the large volume of these vessels reflected the nature of the U-boat struggle underway in the Atlantic. The British also maintained a sizeable cadre of fleet minesweepers ranging in size from 600 to 900 tons. Finally, for offensive purposes, the British possessed several submarine classes. Of particular relevance for a potential Pacific conflict was the long-range T-class, which displaced some 1,300 tons and was armed with ten or eleven torpedo tubes depending upon the grouping. A second submarine type worth noting was the 1,810-ton *Grampus*-class, which was specifically designed for minelaying and could carry 50 mines as well as six 21-inch torpedo tubes and one 4-inch deck gun.

Through the composition of these various warships, the British possessed a capable and well-balanced fleet. In many respects, this fleet was more balanced than that possessed by the Japanese. Beyond this, the British also possessed a motivated and well-trained force, although there were some variations in this regard. This latter point was primarily due to the wartime expansion of the Royal Navy in which hundreds of thousands of civilians had swelled the ranks of the peacetime service as well as the need to quickly press forces into operational use to meet the various threats menacing Britain. In some cases, training proficiency suffered as a result of these factors, but in general the British maintained a skilled and effective fighting force. The same was true regarding Britain's logistical infrastructure, which allowed the British to maintain and operate naval forces and merchant shipping throughout the world including both the North and South Atlantic, Mediterranean, Indian Ocean and South Pacific. In this regard, Britain was truly a global naval power compared to the regional power projected by Japan. Still, within the confines of the Pacific region, Japan held the advantage.

The situation was much the same regarding the other British services. By the end of 1941 the British army possessed some two million men under arms with a nominal combat strength of one airborne, nine armoured and 27 infantry divisions and 11 independent tank brigades.[8] Added to this were hundreds of thousands of additional troops and several additional divisions coming from the Empire and Commonwealth. Yet, of this combined force, only a very small percentage was actually engaged in combat operations, almost exclusively in the Middle East. The vast bulk of the remaining personnel and units were stationed in Britain or the other home territories and countries where they were primarily engaged in organising, training and equipping themselves for eventual deployment. Much of this was due to the fact that even after two years of conflict, the British army was still very much in the process of mobilising its ranks while British industry strained to provide it with the implements of modern warfare. Likewise, with their constrained shipping situation, the British were limited in the number of divisions they could reasonably utilise overseas at this stage in the conflict. This reality meant that despite having been at war for over two years, the vast majority of British army personnel lacked combat experience with most having no experience at all. Against a potential Japanese foe tempered through extensive combat operations in China, the vast bulk of the British army along with its Imperial and Commonwealth contingents were untested.

This reality was particularly true regarding the forces defending Britain's interests in Asia and the Pacific region. With few British troops available to garrison and defend this territory, it substantially fell to the local Imperial and Commonwealth entities to fulfill this mission. Since the beginning of the war, authorities in India, Australia and New Zealand had followed the lead of Britain and instituted efforts to expand their armed forces. A prime example of this was in India, where the British launched a major initiative to expand and modernise the British Indian Army. This plan included a programme to create five new infantry divisions and an armoured division in 1940 followed by a further six divisions allocated in 1941.[9] However, this expansion went slowly as it took time to organise, train and equip the vast numbers of new recruits filling out these formations. In a typical Indian division, a majority of the officers and up to a third of the combat troops were British with the rest of the personnel coming from native Indian sources. Most of these latter personnel had limited education and came from a variety of ethnic groups, religions and cultures thus making smooth military integration more difficult. A second exacerbating factor was the low priority the British put in allocating resources to what was an inactive theatre. To this latter point, by October 1941 the divisions authorised in 1940 had only received 36 percent of their allotted field artillery, 19 percent of their Brenguns and 11 percent of their mortars from the United Kingdom.[10] Finally, much of this expansion was offset by the need to send forces to support the war effort in Europe thus making them unavailable to confront any possible Japanese aggression in Asia. By the end of 1941, these deployments included the 4th, 5th, 8th and 10th Divisions that had all been sent to the Middle East.

Mobilisation efforts in Australia and New Zealand encountered similar challenges. In 1939 the Australian government introduced conscription to expand the militia for home defence while creating a volunteer Second Australian Imperial Force (2nd AIF) to support the war effort in Europe. Initially, the 2nd AIF consisted of a single division, but as recruitment expanded (particularly after the fall of France), it eventually grew to five divisions, four of which were deployed by the end of 1941. Of these, the 6th, 7th and 9th Divisions were sent to the Middle East while the 8th Division deployed to Malaya. The creation of these 2nd AIF formations monopolised much of the training and materiel resources available thus leaving the home-based militia units in a less favourable state. A similar transformation and allocation occurred in New Zealand where the small country implemented conscription in 1940 and underwent a major expansion of its armed forces going from 2,570 total service personnel in September 1939 to 75,755 men and women under arms in August 1941 of which no fewer than 43,274 were serving overseas.[11] Much of these latter personnel were assigned to the 2nd New Zealand Division, which was employed in the Middle East. Given the small size of New Zealand's population, this contribution represented a major commitment to the British war effort and left little behind for service in the Pacific if needed.

In terms of the quality of British and Commonwealth soldiers and the overall performance of the British army thus far in the war, the results were mixed. Of the limited number of British and Commonwealth troops that had actually come to blows against the enemy, they had proven themselves more than capable of handling the Italians, but had generally struggled against the Germans. In fairness, during those times when British forces had faltered against the latter, they had often faced insurmountable odds that made defeat largely inevitable. Still, even in those defeats, the army had generally maintained good order and discipline thus attesting to the strength of its character. During those times when the odds were more even, such as during the siege of Tobruk or Operation *Crusader*, the army had generally performed better and even prevailed against its German adversaries. A key aspect of its performance was a tendency to depend upon firepower and materiel abundance to support its operations. This was particularly true regarding the use of artillery, which friends and foes alike recognised as a major British strength. Yet, despite this emphasis, the army was still amateurish on many aspects of combined arms operations, and it tended to perform better during static, set piece fighting than during battles of manoeuvre. How well this force might perform against a potential Japanese foe was very much an open question.

The situation regarding British equipment was much the same. In the two years since the start of the war, British industry had made great strides in remedying the equipment shortages plaguing the British army. Among the weapons produced, in 1940 and 1941 British industry completed 6,240 tanks and 21,400 assorted artillery pieces. By comparison, the Japanese only produced 910 tanks during the same two-year period while their artillery production in 1941 amounted to just 2,250 guns.[12] Beyond quantity, this British equipment tended to be of reasonable quality that was at least comparable if not superior to its Japanese counterparts. This was certainly true in the case of tanks, where British models such as the formidable Matilda, which had played a major role in routing the Italian Tenth Army during Operation *Compass*, and its successor, the Valentine, generally outclassed the prevailing Japanese designs. Still, this advantage in overall numbers and quality only applied if these weapons were available to use against the Japanese, which they were not. In December 1941, the British had virtually no tanks in Southeast Asia while the Australian 1st Armoured Division, which was in the process of forming up, possessed a mere 18. In a coming fight, it seemed likely that inferior Japanese tanks would prove superior to no tanks at all for the British.

Given these many factors and the overriding need to retain the bulk of their forces in Europe and the Middle East to confront the Germans and Italians, the British and local Commonwealth authorities could only muster about 100,000 men in a jumble of units to garrison the various imperial possessions most directly threatened by the Japanese. The majority of these men were stationed in Malaya with smaller garrisons located in Hong Kong, Borneo and Burma. Coming from a variety of sources including British, Indian, Australian and Canadian contingents as well as local native militias, many of these units were composed of hastily assembled and ill-prepared formations including some of dubious resolve and morale. Likewise, virtually none of these men had combat experience, and many of these formations lacked key equipment. Meanwhile, harsh terrain and limited communication assets would likely limit mobility and impede effective command and control. Finally, for isolated garrisons, such as that in Hong Kong, there could be little hope of relief or escape should the Japanese envelope their positions.

Adding to these difficulties, British ground forces could expect little immediate support from the Royal Air Force. In early December 1941 the RAF's total strength in Malaya consisted of 265 combat aircraft of which 181 were serviceable.[13] Beyond this, the British had a small contingent of aircraft in Burma, but Hong Kong and Borneo were almost entirely devoid of these assets. Given this situation, the Royal Air Force could expect to be outnumbered at the onset of any imminent conflict. Making matters worse, most of the aircraft that did exist within the region were second-line models. At the time, the Royal Air Force possessed a number of formidable aircraft types including many discussed in the previous chapter, but none of these were immediately present in Southeast Asia. Instead, the local RAF command had to settle for the American-built Brewster Buffalo Mk I to serve as its sole fighter. Slow and unwieldy, the Buffalo could hold its own against Japanese bombers and the obsolete Ki-27 Nate but was woefully outclassed by the Ki-43 Oscar and A6M2 Zero fighters. Meanwhile, the command's strike aircraft primarily consisted of the Lockheed A-28 Hudson and Bristol Blenheim Mk I and Mk IV light bombers, each of which had reasonable performance, but a limited bombload ranging from 750 to 1,320 pounds. Added to this was the woefully obsolete Vickers Vildebeest Mk IV torpedo-bomber, which was a biplane of similar capabilities to that of the Fleet Air Arm's Swordfish.

Nor was this the extent of the RAF's deficiencies in the Far East. Most of the local British pilots lacked combat experience and/or had limited flying hours on their designated aircraft types. In some cases, these pilots were fresh out of

Although the British possessed many capable aircraft types, these were generally unavailable in the Far East in 1941 thus forcing local commanders to depend upon lesser models such as the Brewster Buffalo pictured here. (U.S. Office for Emergency Management-Office of War Information Collection, public domain)

Flying Training School. Meanwhile, of the 26 RAF airfields located in Malaya, most lacked facilities and only 11 had all-weather concrete runways. The remaining airfields had grass runways making them susceptible to flooding during periods of heavy rainfall. Similarly, by early December Malaya only possessed 17 percent of its allocated anti-aircraft guns resulting in none of the airfields having their full allotment of anti-aircraft guns and some airfields having no anti-aircraft defences at all. Likewise, the British lacked adequate early warning and command and control assets thus further degrading their defensive capabilities. Finally, with only one of three Maintenance Units located in Malaya fully operational, the British were severely hampered in their ability to maintain the serviceability rates of the limited number of aircraft they had in the theatre.[14]

If war did come to the region, the men most directly responsible for leading the British effort against any Japanese incursions were Lieutenant-General Arthur Percival, Admiral Tom Phillips and Air Vice Marshal Conway Pulford. All three of these men had long and distinguished careers in their respective services, but each lacked recent combat or major operational command experience in the current conflict. In the case of Lieutenant-General Percival, he had joined the army in 1914 and served during World War I as well as in Archangel and Ireland in 1919 and 1920. During the first year and a half of the present war, Percival held various staff positions and briefly commanded the home-based 43rd and 44th Divisions before being appointed as General Officer Commanding Malaya in April 1941. Despite never having commanded anything larger than a division, Percival attained this position over the heads of many senior and more experienced officers. The situation was much the same with Admiral Phillips, who was a 38-year veteran of the Royal Navy but had spent the first two years of the war as Deputy and Vice Chief of the Naval Staff before being appointed Commander-in-Chief of the China Station in October 1941. Considered a 'desk admiral', Phillips attained this position over other officers with more operational experience. Finally, Air Vice Marshal Pulford had started his career in the Royal Navy in 1905 but transferred to the Royal Air Force in 1920. After serving in Headquarters Reserve Command for the first year and a half of the war, Pulford was appointed Air Officer Commanding RAF Far East in March 1941 and assumed this position despite suffering from poor health.

Notwithstanding the laudable determination displayed by each of these officers as well as the vast majority of the men they commanded, Britain's position in Southeast Asia was clearly precarious. Given the various deficiencies present in each of the British services, the best the British could realistically hope for was for American strength to serve as a deterrent to Japanese ambitions, and if that failed, that the United States would operate as an ally in the event of war. As previously discussed, in the late autumn of 1941 the United States Navy was roughly the same size as the Royal Navy, although like the British, the Americans were only able to position part of their fleet in the Pacific as roughly half of their naval strength resided in the Atlantic. Fortunately for the Americans, with their possession of the Panama Canal, they could move additional resources from the Atlantic to the Pacific with relative ease if the need arose. Meanwhile, the quality of the men, ships and planes making up the American fleet was generally high. This was particularly true in the area of carrier-borne aviation where the Americans held a marked superiority over the British Fleet Air Arm and were roughly equivalent to the capabilities possessed by the Japanese. The American Army Air Corps was also a powerful organisation containing a well-trained cadre and a number of capable aircraft types. Finally, and most important, the United States possessed vast human, natural and industrial resources that would allow it to substantially multiply its military power if called upon to do so.

Still, as capable as they were, the Americans were not fully ready for war, nor did their isolationist population embrace this prospect. As such, the American government sought other avenues to avoid direct confrontation. To this end, the United States engaged Japan in a series of peace negotiations throughout much of 1941. Unfortunately, these talks failed to produce meaningful results as both sides became increasingly intractable in their positions. This degree of intransigence was particularly surprising on the part of the Japanese, who were negotiating from the inferior position given the substantial economic leverage the United States wielded over them. Nevertheless, the Japanese remained immovable in their demands, which included the discontinuation of Western aid to China, an acceptance of Japan's position in Indochina, a moratorium on additional American and British forces stationed in the Far East and a full restoration of commerce with Japan. In return, the Japanese were willing to grant assurances not to used Indochina as a base for further military action against their American and European neighbours, guarantee the neutrality of the Philippines and agree to eventually leave Indochina once the conflict in China was over.

Yet, even as the Japanese engaged in these peace negotiations, their military leaders formulated plans to attack and seize the oil and resource rich Dutch East Indies, British Malaya and the American-supported Philippines. If successful, these actions would provide Japan with the territory and resources it had so long coveted, but this course also represented great danger to the island nation. Despite its immediate military advantages, Japanese planners knew that Japan, with its smaller industrial base, was ill suited to prevail in an extended conflict. Therefore, Japanese authorities planned to conduct a short, decisive war based upon an optimistic assumption that Britain was too preoccupied in Europe to offer much resistance while the United States, with all of its materiel power, was morally weak and would quickly agree to a negotiated settlement if dealt a series of stinging defeats. They also did this with the realisation that if they did not act soon, the various economic embargos enacted against Japan would progressively cripple the Japanese economy and eventually render their military forces impotent.

In early November the Japanese government finalised its plans for military action while concurrently sending two final diplomatic proposals to the United States in a last-ditch effort to avert war. In these, the Japanese offered to withdraw their forces from southern Indochina and proposed further Japanese withdrawals from northern Indochina and China proper (although not a complete withdrawal) once a peace treaty was concluded with the Chinese government. In return, the Japanese sought the cessation of Allied aid to China and a lifting of sanctions against Japan. After rejecting the first proposal on 14 November, the American Secretary of State, Cordell Hull, responded to the second overture with a blunt diplomatic note to the Japanese government twelve days later demanding the cessation of hostilities against China and the relinquishment of their quasi hold over French Indochina. Even before this note arrived, Japan had already begun dispatching naval forces to proceed to their war positions, although these forces were to await final approval from Tokyo before launching their coordinated attacks. Now in light of the American response and the Allied oil embargo, Japan faced two possible choices. It could acquiesce to the will of the United States and back down, or it could gamble and opt for war. Upon this decision hinged the fates of multiple millions throughout the Asia/Pacific region. The Japanese chose war.

On the eve of the Asia/Pacific war, the British had few resources immediately available to confront the Japanese. Pictured here is the battleship *Prince of Wales* arriving in Singapore in December 1941. (Abrahams, H. J. (Lt), Royal Navy official photographer, public domain)

CHAPTER 4

Japan Unleashed

Early on the morning of 7 December 1941 a Japanese task force, consisting of the aircraft carriers *Akagi*, *Kaga*, *Shōkaku*, *Zuikaku*, *Hiryū* and *Sōryū*, the battleships *Hiei* and *Kirishima*, three cruisers and nine destroyers, arrived some 275 miles north of the Hawaiian Islands. At 0600 hours the Japanese carriers turned into the wind and launched an air strike consisting of 183 bombers, torpedo-bombers and fighters. Their destination was the American naval base at Pearl Harbor, the home of the American Pacific Fleet, as well as various adjacent airfields on the island of Oahu. While en route, an American radar station located on the northern side of Oahu detected and reported the incoming formation of attacking aircraft, but a junior officer erroneously assumed it was a flight of B-17 bombers that were due in from the United States and took no action. At about the same time, the American destroyer *Ward* engaged and destroyed one of five Japanese midget submarines attempting to enter the harbour, but this action again failed to alert American authorities to the pending attack. Accordingly, when Japanese aircraft finally arrived over Pearl Harbor at approximately 0750 hours, they encountered no opposition and instead found the American fleet at anchor and in a state of complete unpreparedness.

At 0755 hours the Japanese began their coordinated attack. For the next two hours, these aircraft, plus a follow-up strike of a further 170 aircraft, bombed, torpedoed and strafed the hapless American ships and local military facilities. Particularly targeted was the line of battleships anchored off Ford Island. Early in the attack, one of these battleships, *Arizona*, exploded when an armour piercing bomb detonated its forward magazine. Results against the other battleships were not as spectacular, but each received varying degrees of damage from the attacking Japanese aircraft including *Oklahoma*, which capsized after receiving at least five torpedo hits, and three other battleships that sank on even keels in the shallow water. Meanwhile, on the adjacent airfields, the Japanese were able to catch the vast majority of American aircraft on the ground and inflict substantial damage against them. This process was assisted by the fact that many of the American aircraft were parked close together for security purposes thus making them easy targets for the Japanese raiders.

By 1000 hours the attack was over, and American authorities began assessing the immense damage inflicted against them. In terms of the fleet, eight battleships, three cruisers, three destroyers, a target ship, a minelayer, a seaplane tender and a repair ship were all sunk or damaged to varying degrees. The Americans also lost 188 aircraft destroyed with at least another 159 damaged. Finally, 2,403 American service men and civilians were killed with another 1,178 wounded. Japanese losses totalled 29 aircraft plus all five of the midget submarines dispatched to attack the American base.[1] These latter vessels had been transported to the harbour on parent submarines and were completely unsuccessful in their efforts. Fortunately for the Americans, much of this damage was repairable. In fact, of the vessels hit, only the battleships *Arizona* and *Oklahoma* and the former battleship turned target ship *Utah* were total losses. Still, it would take two years or more for some of these damaged warships to return to service. Thus, in one decisive blow, the Japanese had temporarily neutralised a substantial portion of the powerful American Pacific Fleet.

While this attack was Japan's most spectacular triumph for the day, it was by no means their only success. In the hours immediately preceding and following the strike against Pearl Harbor, the Japanese launched similar raids against British and American positions across Asia and the Pacific. Hong Kong, Malaya, Singapore,

The foundered wreck of the American battleship *Arizona* three days after the Pearl Harbor attack. (Department of the Navy, Fourteenth Naval District, Pearl Harbor Naval Shipyard, Fleet Salvage Unit, public domain)

the Philippines, Guam and Wake Island all endured Japanese bombing. Of these, the Japanese were particularly successful in attacking Clark and Iba airfields in the Philippines where they destroyed or damaged some 100 American aircraft, mostly on the ground, thus crippling American air power in the region. The situation was only marginally better in Malaya where Japanese raids destroyed or disabled 60 out of 110 British aircraft stationed on the peninsula's northern airfields. To the north, large Japanese ground forces crossed into the New Territories from China and began an invasion of the tiny enclave of Hong Kong. These forces met some resistance, but quickly forced the outnumbered British defenders into a fighting withdrawal. Finally, in China proper, Japanese army and naval units attacked and occupied the international settlement in Shanghai. At the onset of this operation, the Japanese demanded the surrender of the British river gunboat *Peterel* and its American counterpart *Wake*. While *Wake* complied, the defiant *Peterel* refused to surrender and was promptly sunk by overwhelming Japanese artillery and naval gunfire thus becoming the first British warship casualty of this new Asia/Pacific war. Beyond this inglorious incident, the Japanese also seized 17 Allied merchant ships totalling 34,330 tons in Shanghai.[2]

As bad as these events were, Britain's most serious calamity for the day occurred when Japanese invasion forces landed at Singora and Pattani on the Kra Isthmus in southern Thailand and at Kota Bharu in northeastern Malaya. Regarding the former, British defence planners had long anticipated a potential Japanese invasion of the Kra Isthmus and prepared a preemptive plan, codenamed Operation *Matador*, to occupy the area before the Japanese could arrive. Aware that Japanese forces were building up in Indochina, the British considered implementing *Matador* in early December, but vacillated at the last minute due to political considerations and limited resources. Even when British reconnaissance aircraft located elements of the approaching invasion convoys, the British opted to take no preemptive action to avoid giving the Japanese a pretext for war. Accordingly, when Japanese forces landed at Singora and Pattani, they encountered minimal resistance from Thai troops and easily captured their objectives. Immediately thereafter, the Thai government acceded to Japanese demands and granted Japan passage rights through the country. With this, Thailand became a quasi-Axis nation under Japanese domination, and on 25 January 1942, it declared war on both Great Britain and the United States. As it was, Thailand's contribution to the war was minimal, and the nation became little more than an occupied territory and Japanese puppet-state. Still, its abrupt capitulation in December 1941 did have an immediate adverse impact on the local military situation as Japanese troops were now ideally positioned to cross the border and advance down the western side of Malaya.

In Malaya itself, the Japanese encountered heavier resistance at Kota Bharu where the Indian 3/17 Dogra Regiment strongly contested their landings and inflicted heavy losses upon the assault forces. Commencing their invasion shortly after midnight on 8 December (about an hour before the Pearl Harbor attack given the differing time zones and the International Date Line), the first two waves of Japanese soldiers encountered withering fire from strongly entrenched Indian defenders that pinned them down on the beach. RAF and RAAF (Royal Australian Air Force) aircraft quickly joined the fight and carried out a number of low-level attacks against the invasion force. Particularly successful during these strikes were the Hudsons of No. 1 Squadron RAAF located at Kota Bharu airfield, which carried out 17 sorties that sank the 9,794-ton transport *Awajisan Maru*, damaged two other ships and destroyed a number of landing barges. Despite this opposition, the Japanese eventually breached the coastal defences and pushed inland. By mid-afternoon the British staff at Kota Bharu airfield received a false report of Japanese forces on their perimeter. This erroneous report prompted them to conduct a confused withdrawal that soon compromised the entire British position and allowed the Japanese to complete their capture of Kota Bharu and its important airfield. In turn, this sad result ceded a firm foothold on the Malaysian peninsula to the Japanese and made the RAF's local situation, which had always been tenuous, even more disadvantaged. Still, the price in attaining this victory was high as the assaulting Japanese forces suffered some 800 casualties during the day-long battle.

In response to these events, the British took what measures they could to strike back at the Japanese. Of particular consequence, at 1735 hours on 8 December Admiral Phillips departed Singapore with the battleship *Prince of Wales*, battlecruiser *Repulse* and four destroyers. This small battle fleet, designated Force Z, sailed northeast to the Anambas Islands and then turned north with the intention of attacking the Japanese landing force at Singora. Early the next morning Phillips received word from Singapore that the Japanese had captured or neutralised the airfields in northern Malaya thus rendering air support impossible. Still later that day the British spotted various Japanese reconnaissance aircraft shadowing their ships. With the element of surprise lost and with no prospect of air support, Admiral Phillips abandoned his sortie and turned Force Z back towards Singapore. Shortly after midnight on the 10th Phillips again altered course westward to investigate a report, which later proved to be false, of Japanese landings at Kuantan in east-central Malaya. In making this manoeuvre, he opted to maintain radio silence and did not inform Singapore of his new destination or request air support out of Kuantan. Unbeknown to him, the Japanese submarine *I-58* observed this movement and sent a position report back to Saigon. Thus, despite strict security precautions, the Japanese had good knowledge regarding Force Z's whereabouts, whereas the British staff in Singapore did not.

With the coming of dawn, the Japanese put plans in motion to destroy Force Z. At 0600 hours the Japanese 22nd Air Flotilla dispatched three reconnaissance aircraft and nine bombers out of Saigon to seek out and shadow the retiring British warships. They followed this up shortly thereafter with a large strike force consisting of

34 high-level bombers and 51 torpedo-bombers made up of Mitsubishi G3M2 Nells and G4M1 Bettys. To put the size of this force in perspective, this was more than four times the number of aircraft the British had used to cripple the Italian fleet at Taranto or to help sink the German battleship *Bismarck*. Making matters worse, the majority of these aircraft carried the Type-91 torpedo, which was a powerful weapon with a 452-pound warhead. By comparison, the FAA's primary torpedo only possessed a 300-pound warhead. Sadly, even as this aerial armada proceeded towards him, Admiral Phillips remained tragically unaware of the danger he was in, and he made no efforts to coordinate with the RAF to obtain shore-based fighters, which were available and within range, to cover his ships.

Despite this perilous situation, for a moment it looked like Force Z might actually avoid disaster as the Japanese strike force initially missed its quarry. Unfortunately, the Japanese aircraft found the British ships on their return flight to Saigon and commenced an attack at 1113 hours. Despite a spirited anti-aircraft barrage and effective manoeuvring to comb the tracks of the oncoming torpedoes, the sheer weight of the aerial onslaught soon overwhelmed the British defences. Within minutes, both capital ships were hit by four to six torpedoes and one bomb each. This had a devastating effect on the British warships. At 1233 hours *Repulse* rolled over and sank taking 513 men with it. *Prince of Wales* held on a little longer, but at 1320 hours it capsized and joined its companion. Admiral Phillips, the ship's captain and 325 men perished along with the ship. The attending destroyers quickly rescued the remaining 2,081 officers and men from the dispatched vessels, but this did little to mitigate the scope of the disaster.[3]

In a little more than two hours and at a cost of only three aircraft to themselves, the Japanese had inflicted one of the worst defeats ever to befall the Royal Navy. In a practical sense, the British could ill-afford these losses in light of their stretched resources and ever-expanding global commitments. Equally dire, the destruction of Force Z came as a major blow to British morale and standing in the region. Finally and most important, Southeast Asia now lay wide open to Japanese assault. Churchill summarised the situation when he later described his reaction to the loss of these two warships:

> In all the war I never received a more direct shock. The reader of these pages will realise how many efforts, hopes, and plans foundered with these two ships. As I turned over and twisted in bed the full horror of the news sank in upon me. There were no British or American capital ships in the Indian Ocean or the Pacific except the American survivors of Pearl Harbour (*Sic*), who were hastening back to California. Over all this vast expanse of waters Japan was supreme, and we everywhere weak and naked.[4]

Yet, the addition of the United States as a new and powerful ally more than compensated for these immediate and pending disasters. On 8 December 1941 the American president asked Congress for a declaration of war against Japan. Congress responded with an overwhelming affirmation and approved the measure 470 to one.

The British battlecruiser *Repulse* leaving Singapore on 8 December 1941. It would be sunk two days later along with *Prince of Wales*. (Adams, W. L. G. (Captain), Commanding Officer, HMS *Corinthian*, public domain)

Three days later Germany and Italy came to the support of their Tripartite ally and declared war on the United States.[5] The American government promptly reciprocated and expanded the war into a truly global conflict with the British Empire, the Soviet Union, and the United States in one camp and Germany, Italy and Japan in the other. From a British point of view, this was a monumental improvement over the situation of just six months prior when they had stood alone against the combined power of Germany and Italy. Again, Churchill wrote in regards to America's entry into the war:

> Hitler's fate was sealed. Mussolini's fate was sealed. As for the Japanese, they would be ground to powder. All the rest was merely the proper application of overwhelming force. The British Empire, the Soviet Union, and now the United States, bound together with every scrap of their life and strength, were, according to my lights, twice or even thrice the force of their antagonists. No doubt it would take a long time. I expected terrible forfeits in the East; but all this would be merely a passing phase. United we could subdue everybody else in the world. Many disasters, immeasurable cost and tribulation lay ahead, but there was no more doubt about the end.[6]

For the Allied forces trying to stem the overwhelming Japanese onslaught in Asia and the Pacific, the truth of these sentiments came as a difficult proposition.

In Hong Kong, a garrison made up of British, Indian, Canadian and local forces put up a determined, but hopeless, defence against an enemy that was more than twice its size and had complete control of the air. The battle began on the morning of 8 December when three regiments of the Japanese 38th Division crossed the Sham Chun River and advanced into Hong Kong's New Territories from the north. Here, they met British and Indian forces, which conducted a fighting withdrawal to a series of strong defensive positions known as the Gin Drinkers' Line. Meanwhile, that morning Japanese bombers attacked Kai Tak airport and effectively destroyed the meagre RAF force stationed there as well as several civilian aircraft. On the 9th the first Japanese forces reached the 10-mile-long Gin Drinkers' Line, which was only defended by three British battalions, and began a series of probing attacks. That night the Japanese seized the Shing Mun Redoubt, a key position on the line. Then on the morning of the 11th the Japanese carried out attacks against positions in the Golden Hill area. With these events, Major-General Christopher Maltby, the garrison commander, realised that the Gin Drinkers' Line was now dangerously compromised and ordered a full withdrawal to Hong Kong Island, which the British carried out over the next two days.

Supporting this ground struggle was a small naval contingent stationed at Hong Kong consisting of the veteran destroyers *Scout*, *Thanet* and *Thracian* along with a handful of auxiliaries and motor torpedo boats. Almost immediately this small force was reduced when authorities ordered *Scout* and *Thanet* to break out and proceed to Singapore, which they successfully did despite a hazardous journey through Japanese controlled waters. While this was underway, the vessels that remained behind engaged in a number of minelaying, ferrying and ground support operations as well as various offensive sweeps in which they claimed the destruction of several Japanese coasters and launches. Despite this yeoman service, the constant grind of air attacks, ground fire and dwindling support resources steadily depleted this force. This was highlighted by the loss of *Thracian*, which was scuttled following bomb and grounding damage on the 16th.

Meanwhile, the battle for Hong Kong continued. By 13 December the British completed their withdrawal from the New Territories and Kowloon, and the garrison settled in to defend Hong Kong Island. Over the next six days the Japanese relentlessly shelled and bombed the garrison as the British rejected two calls to surrender. During this time, the British also repulsed a Japanese probing attack against the Lye Mun Peninsula. Finally, on the night of 18/19 December the Japanese successfully landed a large force consisting of six battalions on the northern portion of the island. From there, the Japanese advanced inland, and over the next week split the British defenders seizing many key features including the island's main water reservoirs. Throughout this period, the British continued to put up fierce resistance, including the launching of many local counterattacks. This was supported by the handful of surviving motor torpedo boats that carried out attacks that sank or damaged a number of Japanese troop-laden launches bringing reinforcements to the island. Yet, despite these valiant efforts, the British were unable to stem the unrelenting Japanese advance.

By 25 December the situation was clearly hopeless. With no prospect of reinforcement or escape and realising that further resistance would only lead to needless bloodshed, at 1530 hours Governor Mark Young and General Maltby surrendered Hong Kong to the Japanese. With this, the widespread fighting ended, although certain isolated British formations continued to resist for the next few days. In their failed attempt to hold the colony, the British suffered 11,848 military casualties, most of whom were taken prisoner. Japanese losses are more difficult to ascertain. The official Japanese casualty figure for the battle was 675 killed and 2,079 wounded, but this may have been an understatement of their true losses.[7] Many participants and scholars believe that Japanese casualties were much higher, perhaps as high as 6,000 or more. In addition to this personnel toll, the British also lost the destroyer *Thracian*, one minelayer, four gunboats, eight motor torpedo boats and four auxiliaries sunk or scuttled, and the Japanese seized 26 Allied merchant ships totalling 52,604 tons.[8]

The situation was equally bleak for the British in Malaya. Upon the Japanese landings at Singora and Pattani, a small force of Indian troops advanced into Thailand in an attempt to reach a key feature known as the Ledge, a six-mile stretch of road cut into a steep hillside. By blowing up the hillside, the British hoped to block the road thus effectively obstructing a Japanese advance from Pattani. Delayed by resistance from Thai police who felled trees across their route, the Indian troops encountered strong Japanese forces, supported by tanks, already in possession of the Ledge by the time they arrived. Unable to dislodge the Japanese, the Indians eventually withdrew after two days of heavy fighting. The Japanese quickly followed this withdrawal and captured Betong on the Thai side of the border on 13 December. A similar British attempt to delay Japanese forces advancing from Singora was equally unsuccessful, and the Japanese entered northwest Malaya where they drove the 11th Indian Division from its defensive positions at Jitra on the night of 12/13 December. During the process of this battle, 11th Indian Division suffered heavy losses thus making it incapable of further largescale resistance without benefit of reorganisation and reinforcements.

Together, this battle, along with a rapid advance of Japanese forces out of Kota Bharu, compromised the entire British defensive position in northern Malaya. In mid-December follow-up Japanese convoys arrived in Thailand and Kota Bharu with reinforcements and supplies for the invading Japanese army. Given the loss of Force Z and neutralisation of their northern airfields, the British were powerless to impede these deployments. Immediately upon consolidating his positions on the Kra Isthmus and northern Malaya, Lieutenant-General Tomoyuki Yamashita sent his 60,000-man Twenty-Fifth Army into Malaya proper. General Percival and

88,000 British and Commonwealth soldiers opposed this advance. Despite being outnumbered, the Japanese enjoyed several important advantages in their offensive. First, due to the circumstances outlined in the previous chapter, Percival's army was largely composed of hastily assembled and ill-prepared formations. By comparison, Yamashita's army was made up of first-rate units that were generally better organised and trained than their British counterparts. The Japanese also possessed some 200 tanks and 600 aircraft compared to no tanks and fewer than 100 operational aircraft for the British. This materiel disparity quickly demoralized British resolve and proved to be a decisive factor during many engagements. This was particularly true regarding many of the Indian troops, who had never seen tanks before and were often unnerved by their appearances on the battlefield. The Japanese also benefitted from the use of bicycles, which they regularly employed to make swift advances across the country.

One by one, key positions in northern and central Malaya fell as the Japanese continued their relentless push southward. In this, the Japanese firmly controlled the tempo of the battle and always enjoyed the initiative, whereas the British constantly found themselves responding to Japanese moves. This put the British in a very confused situation where they were always under pressure with little or no opportunity to rest and regroup. At times, British forces were able to make stands that frustrated Japanese ambitions, but these respites were always temporary and invariably the British were compelled to retreat. At the end of December, the British held up the Japanese advance at Kampar for four days inflicting heavy losses upon them, but the Japanese responded with a seaborne landing near Telok Anson that outflanked the British position and forced them to retreat. A few days later on 7 January, a Japanese force spearheaded by tanks scored a stunning victory on the Slim River that once again sent the British reeling back and forced them to cede Kuala Lumpur to the Japanese. The fall of this city, which occurred on the 11th, brought the Japanese army to within 200 miles of the key British base at Singapore.

While this fighting was underway, the Royal Navy supported the local defensive efforts to the best of its limited ability. Immediately following the loss of *Prince of Wales* and *Repulse*, Vice-Admiral Geoffrey Layton took command of the handful of cruisers and destroyers that now made-up the British Eastern Fleet. The first priority for this force, and indeed that of the other Allied navies, was to bring reinforcements into the area. From 1 January to 8 February British and Dutch warships successfully escorted seven convoys consisting of 44 transports and troopships into Singapore. For the loss of only one ship, these convoys delivered some 45,000 men and large quantities of equipment to the besieged colony.[9] Amongst these reinforcements was the British 18th Division, which had been diverted to Singapore while en route to the Middle East. During the same period other British and Allied warships successfully escorted similar convoys to the Dutch East Indies, New Guinea and Australia. Considering the dangers arrayed against them, these convoys suffered miraculously few losses. Added to this, the Allies were able to score a few successes against the Japanese navy. On 17 January the British destroyer *Jupiter* sank the Japanese submarine *I-60* off the Sunda Strait. Three days later the Australian minesweepers *Deloraine*, *Lithgow* and *Katoomba* teamed up with the American destroyer *Edsall* to sink the Japanese submarine *I-124* off Darwin.

Augmenting these defensive efforts were a handful of Allied submarines that attempted to wage offensive operations against the Japanese. The British did not possess any submarines in the Far East at the outbreak of hostilities, but they did have operational control over a handful of Dutch submarines. During the first two months of the Pacific war these Dutch submarines operated out of Singapore and sank five Japanese merchant ships totalling 27,528 tons and the destroyer *Sagiri*.[10] They may have sunk or participated in the destruction of two additional ships worth 4,460 tons and damaged at least another five (possibly seven) merchant ships totalling 41,702 tons (53,816 tons).[11] While these successes were not insignificant, they failed to seriously impede the local Japanese operations and cost the Dutch four boats in return. The British partially made up these losses with the arrival of the British submarines *Trusty* and *Truant* from the Mediterranean at the end of January. Unfortunately, due to a combination of technical problems and bad luck, these British boats were unable to have an immediate impact upon the battle and then only sank two Japanese merchant ships totalling 11,719 tons through April 1942.[12]

Despite these efforts and the large influx of reinforcements, the situation for the British continued to deteriorate in Malaya as the Japanese Twenty-Fifth Army made steady progress down the peninsula. By the middle of January Japanese forces reached the southern Malayan state of Johore where they finally encountered effective opposition that checked their advance. This was particularly true in the Segamat and Muar sectors where Australian and Indian forces repulsed several local Japanese attacks and inflicted heavy losses upon the assaulting formations. However, this success was fleeting as the Japanese applied consistent pressure along the front while conducting seaborne landings in the vicinity of Batu Pahat to outflank the British position. These operations once again forced the British to give ground, and over the period of 18–23 January they conducted a fighting withdrawal from the Segamat and Muar fronts suffering heavy losses in the process.

While this calamity unfolded on the ground, the situation in the air was equally bleak. Under constant pressure from their numerically superior enemy, the Royal Air Force and its Allied contributors struggled to gain a footing in the uneven contest. On numerous occasions British aircraft carried out strikes against Japanese positions, but these garnered meagre results for the expenditure of heavy losses. By comparison, Malaya's outnumbered force of Buffalo fighters repeatedly rose to challenge the incessant tide of air raids plaguing the colony, but while they were able to inflict some losses upon the attacking Japanese, they were unable to stem the tempo of their assaults. Through this period the British received some aircraft

Constantly operating at a materiel and qualitative disadvantage, the British were unable to stem the Japanese advance in Malaya. Pictured here is an Australian anti-tank gun crew in action near Bakri. (Unknown author, public domain)

reinforcements, including the arrival of 51 Hurricane fighters in mid-January, but these barely kept pace with losses, and the British were never able to seriously erode Japan's numerical advantage. To this point, on 18 January the British could still only muster a serviceable strength of 74 bomber/reconnaissance aircraft and 28 fighters on Malaya against an estimated Japanese strength of 250 bombers and 150 fighters in the area.[13] Making matters worse, as the amount of British-controlled territory on the peninsula shrank, the RAF's ability to function and support itself equally diminished as it was forced to operate on fewer airfields with less warning time to defend itself. The time was quickly approaching when the RAF's position in Malaya would become untenable.

Sadly, the Japanese offered no respite to the beleaguered British defenders. On 26 January the Japanese dispatched a landing force to occupy the port of Endau on the east coast of Malaya. A cruiser and six destroyers directly supported this force while the light carrier *Ryūjō* and other warships provided distant cover. By comparison, the British could only muster some 36 aircraft and two old destroyers to counter the landing. In a series of costly air attacks that effectively destroyed Britain's remaining offensive air power in Malaya, the British claimed hits on two transports and a cruiser, but this had little impact on the landing operation. Meanwhile, the old British destroyer *Thanet* and the equally old Australian destroyer *Vampire* sortied out of Singapore to attack the invasion force. Early on the morning of the 27th these destroyers encountered the Japanese covering force, and in a short, desperate battle, lost *Thanet* to a cruiser and three destroyers while *Vampire* was just able to make good its escape. Four days later the British withdrew their land forces from Malaya and retreated to Singapore Island thus entering the final stage of the tragic campaign.

By 1 February the end was clearly approaching. The Japanese had complete control of the air, and Singapore endured increasingly heavy bombing. Given these attacks, the use of the naval base became increasingly untenable, and the British began demolitions of the local stores and facilities. On the night of 8/9 February the Japanese crossed the Johore Strait and landed on Singapore Island. In a situation reminiscent of the battle of Hong Kong Island a month and a half earlier, the Japanese pushed inland and advanced towards Singapore City. On the 13th the British began a final limited evacuation with those ships still available to do so. The large ships had already departed, but 80 overcrowded minor vessels ventured out of Singapore harbour to make good their escape. Of these, no fewer than 69 were captured or destroyed by patrolling Japanese naval and air units or were lost due to unknown causes.[14] One of these lost vessels, *ML310*, carried Air Vice Marshal Pulford and Rear-Admiral Ernest Spooner, the highest-ranking air force and naval officers remaining in Singapore. Hit by Japanese aircraft, the motor launch was forced aground on the island of Chibia where both senior officers died from malaria and exhaustion.

Against this carnage, the British were able to score a minor, but moral, victory with one of their evacuating craft, the auxiliary patrol vessel *Li Wo*. On 14 February this auxiliary ship, a 707-ton converted passenger river boat armed with a single 4-inch gun and two machineguns, encountered a Japanese convoy en route to invade Sumatra north of the Banka Strait. Although facing insurmountable odds and only possessing 13 rounds plus three practice rounds for its main gun, the lone British auxiliary attacked the Japanese convoy and succeeded in sinking one of the transports through gunfire and ramming. However, this latter action left *Li Wo* dead in the water, and it was subsequently sunk by the convoy's cruiser and destroyer escort. Of *Li Wo*'s crew of 84 men, a mere seven survived as prisoners of war. Included in the ship's fatalities was its commanding officer, Lieutenant Thomas Wilkinson, who was later awarded a posthumous Victoria Cross for the action.

Meanwhile, on the morning of 15 February General Percival met with his senior staff to review the situation. With their water supply under threat, their provisions quickly running out and the civilian population pressed into an ever-shrinking perimeter, the attendees decided that surrender was the only viable option remaining to the garrison. Unbeknown to them, the Japanese were also running low on supplies, but this was a moot point to their deliberations. That afternoon a delegation led by Percival met with General Yamashita at the local Ford Motor Company factory and formally surrendered Singapore. With this, the British concluded the worst defeat ever to befall their military forces in the history of the nation. Beyond the loss of British Malaya and its substantial resources, the British suffered 138,708 casualties including over 130,000 men taken prisoner. The British also sustained substantial materiel losses. Official Japanese casualties for the campaign numbered just 9,824 in return.[15]

Unfortunately, this debacle was not unique for the Allies. All across Southeast Asia and the Pacific, the Allies suffered a series of defeats at the hands of the Japanese. In December a 43,000-man Japanese army invaded the Philippines where they encountered 130,000 poorly trained and equipped American and Filipino defenders under the command of American General Douglas MacArthur. By early January these defenders found themselves trapped on the Bataan Peninsula. Although they held out longer than their British counterparts at Singapore, the outcome was just the same. On 22 February President Franklin Roosevelt ordered General MacArthur to relinquish his command and escape to Australia. A month and a half later on 9 April the American and Filipino defenders at Bataan surrendered. The island fortress of Corregidor held out a little longer, but it too fell on 6 May. With this, the Japanese completed their conquest of the Philippines, and America, like Britain at Singapore, suffered the worst military defeat in its history. During the same period the Japanese also captured the American island possessions of Guam and Wake and drove into the Bismarck Archipelago, the Solomon Islands, New Guinea and Burma.

Meanwhile, to the south, the Japanese executed a brilliant campaign to seize their primary war objective, the oil fields of the Dutch East Indies. To combat this incursion, the Allies formed the new ABDA (American-British-Dutch-Australian) Command under the leadership of British General Archibald Wavell in January 1942. During its short existence. ABDA fought a series of inconsistent defensive actions against the Japanese invaders. British and Commonwealth contributions to this fight were generally limited and ineffective, but they did attain moderate success on rare occasions. One example of this occurred on 14 February when a force of Hudson, Blenheim and Hurricane aircraft attacked a Japanese invasion convoy in the Banka Strait and sank the 989-ton transport *Inabasan Maru*. The next day British aircraft carried out a series of attacks against Japanese maritime traffic moving up the Moesi River in southern Sumatra and claimed the destruction of at least five troop-laden barges and damage to the transport *Otawa Maru*. Yet, despite this and other infrequent successes, the Allies were unable to stem the tide of Japanese conquest, and the Japanese were able to capture Borneo, Sumatra, Celebes, Ceram, Bali and Timor in little more than two and a half months. By the end of February, Java was the only significant territory in Southeast Asia still under Allied control.

As ABDA Command hastily gathered its limited resources to defend Java, the Japanese prepared to launch their final assault in the conquest of the Dutch East Indies. As part of these preparations, the Japanese moved to isolate Java from Australia. On 18 February a Japanese naval force consisting of two battleships, four fleet carriers, three cruisers and nine destroyers proceeded into the Timor Sea. Early the next morning this force, under the command of Vice-Admiral Chūichi Nagumo, launched 188 aircraft to attack the port of Darwin on Australia's northern coast. Like Pearl Harbor a few months earlier, the Japanese achieved complete surprise and inflicted heavy losses upon the unsuspecting Allied ships and installations located in and around the northern Australian port. For the loss of only four aircraft, the Japanese sank five merchant ships totalling 37,530 tons, the American destroyer *Peary* and two minor naval vessels. They also damaged seven merchant ships, the Australian sloop *Swan*, the depot ship *Platypus* and three boom defence vessels to varying degrees. Finally, they destroyed or damaged a number of Allied aircraft, port facilities and warehouses and killed 243 servicemen and civilians.[16] With this, the Japanese temporarily neutralised Darwin and eliminated the prospect of Allied support from Australia to Java.

It did not take long for the Japanese to exploit this isolation. On 26 February Allied aircraft observed two large Japanese convoys approaching Java. To counter this threat, the Allies immediately dispatched Dutch Rear-Admiral Karel Doorman with an Allied naval squadron to seek out and engage the invaders. This squadron consisted of the British heavy cruiser *Exeter*, the American heavy cruiser *Houston*, the Dutch light cruisers *De Ruyter* (flagship) and *Java*, the Australian light cruiser *Perth* and nine destroyers (three of which were British). Over the next several hours these warships scoured the northeastern approaches to Java in a vain attempt to locate the elusive enemy. Instead, all they encountered were Japanese aircraft that delivered heavy, but ineffective, bombing against the Allied ships. By the afternoon, Doorman decided to call off his sortie and return to port to refuel his destroyers. Just as his squadron was about to do so, he received word that a large Japanese invasion force was less than 90 miles away, and he dutifully altered course to investigate this new sighting.

At 1605 hours on the 27th, Doorman's squadron finally encountered the Japanese. However, instead of finding an invasion convoy, they found the Japanese covering force consisting of two heavy cruisers, two light cruisers and 14 destroyers. On the face of it, the Allied and Japanese forces seemed evenly matched, but as was often the case during the early months of the Pacific war, these appearances were deceiving. The Allies were handicapped by the disparity of their force, a lack of common signal codes, the fact that they had never trained or exercised together and a lack of air support. Despite these disadvantages, the Allied squadron proceeded forward and engaged the Japanese. The fighting began at 1616 hours when both sides formed traditional lines of battle and engaged each other with long-range gunfire. This gunnery duel failed to cause significant damage until approximately 50 minutes into the action when an 8-inch shell hit the British cruiser *Exeter* and reduced its speed to 11 knots.

This began a series of events that spelled disaster for the Allied squadron. Unable to keep up with the other Allied ships, *Exeter* pulled out of the line and withdrew.

This manoeuvre caused confusion in the succeeding Allied ships, and the Allied line quickly fell into disarray. In the melee that followed, a Japanese torpedo hit and sank the Dutch destroyer *Kortenaer* while heavy gunfire dispatched the British destroyer *Electra*. It took Admiral Doorman several minutes to regain control over his now depleted squadron. With darkness beginning to fall, Doorman again attempted to manoeuvre his ships around the Japanese screen. In the process of doing so, Doorman's ships erroneously passed through a Dutch inshore minefield, and the British destroyer *Jupiter* struck a mine and sank. Now seriously weakened but undeterred by this loss, Doorman turned his squadron north in another attempt to reach the invasion convoy. Unfortunately, Japanese floatplanes observed and reported this manoeuvre, and Doorman's ships again encountered the covering screen. At approximately 2320 hours Japanese cruisers launched a mass torpedo attack against Doorman's ships. These torpedoes hit and sank the Dutch cruisers *De Ruyter* and *Java* killing Admiral Doorman in the process. With this final disaster, the remaining Allied ships withdrew, and the Japanese Sixteenth Army successfully executed its landings at Bantam Bay in Java.

On the 28th the Allies accepted defeat and ordered their remaining ships out of the Java Sea. In the morning the Australian and American cruisers *Perth* and *Houston* departed Batavia to make good their escape through the Sunda Straits to Tjilatjap. While en route that evening, these ships happened upon and attacked the Japanese invasion force at Bantam Bay. Despite being heavily outnumbered, the Allied cruisers sank the transports *Horai Maru* and *Sakura Maru* (9,192 and 7,167 tons respectively) and damaged three Japanese destroyers and a minesweeper. They were then overwhelmed by the Japanese covering force and sunk. In a similar engagement the next morning, the damaged British cruiser *Exeter*, the British destroyer *Encounter* and the American destroyer *Pope* encountered four Japanese heavy cruisers and four destroyers off Bawean Island. In a desperate two-hour battle against hopeless odds, the Japanese sank *Exeter* and *Encounter*. *Pope* survived the battle only to be crippled a few hours later by Japanese aircraft from the carrier *Ryūjō* and then finished off by Japanese cruisers. In related fighting during this and the next couple of days, the Japanese sank or forced the scuttling of a number of other Allied ships including one British, three Dutch and three American destroyers, an American aircraft depot ship, an Australian sloop and an American escort. By 4 March the Japanese had completely destroyed or driven out all Allied naval forces in the area, and Java capitulated four days later.

With this fall, the remaining British and Commonwealth forces in the theatre concentrated around Australia and in the Indian Ocean. With Japan's expansion to the south complete, the Allies realised that these areas were increasingly vulnerable to Japanese attack. To the east, the Japanese continued their conquest of the Bismarck Archipelago, the Solomon Islands and the northern portion of Papua New Guinea. This put them in an ideal position to directly threaten Australia and New Zealand. In response to this threat, the Allies sent hastily assembled Australian and American reinforcements to bolster their defences in northern Australia, southern Papua New Guinea, the Fiji Islands, the New Hebrides Islands and New Caledonia. The United States Navy primarily carried out these defensive moves with augmentation from the handful of Australian and New Zealand cruisers and destroyers remaining in the region. Meanwhile, British warships escorted large troop convoys bringing Australian forces back to Australia from the Middle East. Fortunately, there was no Japanese interference, and the Allies accomplished these troop movements without incident.

Meanwhile, to the west the Allies faced a growing crisis in British-controlled Burma. Before the war British defence planners had minimized the Japanese threat to Burma due to its harsh terrain and geographical location. In terms of the former, most of Burma was covered in dense jungle, mountainous topography and crisscrossing waterways that would seem to pose a natural impediment to any invading army. In terms of the latter, the presence of neutral Thailand theoretically provided a defensive buffer on Burma's eastern border while the naval base at Singapore protected Burma's seaborne flank. Unfortunately, these assumptions were quickly proven wrong when the Japanese launched an invasion into Burma from a complicit Thailand in January 1942. The initial antagonists in this assault were two Japanese divisions (the 33rd and 55th) followed by two more divisions (the 18th and 56th) as the campaign developed. The Japanese also employed considerable air assets in conducting this operation.

For their part, The British contested the invasion with two divisions of their own, the 1st Burma and 17th Indian, but these forces were heavily outclassed by their Japanese opponents. In particular, the Japanese were far more adept at jungle fighting than were their British counterparts. As such, the British were largely restricted to operating along the handful of roads that existed within Burma, whereas the Japanese regularly travelled through the jungle with little difficulty including terrain that the British considered impassable. This allowed them to repeatedly outflank or bypass British positions thus forcing the impacted British formations to give ground or face likely isolation and piecemeal destruction. Other British problems included the fact that both of their divisions were relatively new, having been formed within the previous year, and thus lacked adequate training and preparation for the task at hand. Likewise, at the onset of the invasion these divisions were widely dispersed thus making it difficult for the British to properly mass their forces to meet the various Japanese assaults. Finally, the Allies only possessed a few dozen modern combat aircraft within the country compared to hundreds available to the Japanese thus again condemning the British to operate in an environment of likely Japanese air superiority.

Given these realities, the British quickly found themselves repeating a disastrous script that had already been played in Hong Kong, Malaya and a dozen other places throughout Asia and the Pacific. After conducting successful preliminary operations that seized key British airfields in southeast Burma, the Japanese launched their main assault from Raheng towards the capital city of Rangoon on 20 January. Bypassing or sweeping aside sporadic British resistance, the Japanese made good progress and captured the important coastal city of Moulmein on 31 January. In doing so, they also captured large amounts of supplies and equipment abandoned by the British. The Japanese then turned northward to continue their advance towards the Sittang River. Using manoeuvre and speed, the Japanese repeatedly kept their more cumbersome British counterparts off balance and in a general state of retreat. The British briefly blunted this advance for a couple of days in the middle of February along the Bilin River, but Japanese infiltration tactics eventually compromised their defences and compelled the 17th Division to once again retreat. In the process of doing so, the 17th Division increasingly fell into a state of disorder.

The situation reached a crisis point on 23 February when an unexpected appearance of Japanese forces on the Sittang River spooked local British authorities into prematurely destroying the railway bridge spanning the expanse thus trapping most of the 17th Indian Division on the river's eastern bank. Utilising other means, about half of these trapped men eventually made good their escape, but in doing so, they abandoned most of their equipment and lost their ability to function as a coherent fighting unit. Unfortunately, this costly sacrifice had little impact upon the Japanese, who crossed the river in force after a week-long delay and continued their advance towards Rangoon. Against this, despite the arrival of reinforcements, which included the British 7th Armoured and 63rd Indian Brigades, General Harold Alexander, the recently appointed commander of British forces in Burma, realised that he could not hold the city, and on 7 March the British began a full evacuation.

In doing so, the British benefitted from the only bright spot that had occurred in their defensive effort. During the previous two and a half months, the Japanese air force had launched a series of air raids against Rangoon utilising some 400 bombers and fighters. Opposing these raids was an initial force of 21 American P-40 and 16 British Buffalo fighters followed by a reinforcement of 30 more British Hurricanes and a squadron of Blenheim light bombers under the command of Air Vice Marshal Donald Stevenson. The American portion of this force consisted of a squadron from the American Volunteer Group (the Flying Tigers) that had previously been stationed at Kunming for the defence of the Burma Road. With the invasion of Burma, the squadron was ordered south to help defend Rangoon. Despite being heavily outnumbered, these American and British fighters were able to effectively challenge the Japanese raids and claimed the destruction of at least 123 Japanese aircraft in aerial combat while the Allied bombers destroyed a further 58 aircraft on the ground during counterattacks against local Japanese airfields.[17] Given these heavy losses, the Japanese air force suspended operations over Rangoon at the end of February, and this pause allowed the British to carry out their evacuation free from aerial interference or undo loss. As part of this, not a single Allied ship was sunk during the evacuation, and the British were able to conduct a thorough demolition of the port and other critical assets before their departure.

Still, the loss of Rangoon represented a major setback that threatened to endanger Britain's position throughout the entire region. With southern Burma in Japanese hands and the British struggling to form a viable defence in central and northern Burma, the British now also had to plan for the direct defence of India itself. This latter mission represented a daunting task as British forces in India were primarily oriented towards maintaining internal security and providing resources for the global war effort and were thus ill prepared to confront an external threat. In terms of ground units, the main formations available to defend India and Ceylon consisted of one British and six Indian divisions. Unfortunately, none of these divisions were fully combat ready as some were just in the process of forming, and all were deficient in staffing and equipment. Similarly, three of the divisions only possessed two brigades instead of the normal three. Finally, other than the British 70th Division, which had recently served in North Africa and participated in the fighting around Tobruk, none of these divisions had any meaningful combat experience and all required additional training.

The situation in terms of air strength was equally bleak. In March the British possessed a mere 15 air squadrons available for the immediate defence of India and Ceylon against a requirement of 64 squadrons deemed necessary to fulfill this task. Of these 15 squadrons, one existed on paper only as it possessed no serviceable aircraft while five more were equipped with obsolete types that would be of little use against the Japanese. This left the British with an effective strength of just nine squadrons or roughly one-seventh of their stated requirement. Of these, five were fighter squadrons with four possessing Hurricanes while the fifth possessed Mohawk aircraft that were of limited capability. Rounding out this force were one Blenheim light bomber, one Hudson general reconnaissance and two Catalina naval reconnaissance squadrons. Regrettably, this dearth of suitable aircraft was made worse by a lack of airfields and facilities and a grossly inadequate early warning and command and control system that promised to impede effective air operations throughout the region. Given these limited resources, the British had no realistic ability to effectively defend the entire country and instead concentrated the bulk of their forces to defend Ceylon.

In response to this dire situation, the British service chiefs in London directed the dispatch of substantial reinforcements to India, including the British 2nd and 5th Divisions as well as additional air units, but it would take time before these reinforcements arrived. An essential factor in executing this critical replenishment mission as well as ongoing logistical operations centred upon the British retaining effective control over the Indian Ocean. This vital body of water was not only crucial to the maintenance of Britain's entire position in India, but it also served as a key transportation artery supporting British forces in the Middle East and Allied materiel sustenance to the Soviet Union. Unfortunately, this vital sea lane was under growing threat from the Imperial Japanese Navy, which could now operate out of Singapore or other bases in Southeast Asia to menace British shipping around India and beyond.

To defend against this threat, the Admiralty hastily assembled a new and more powerful Eastern Fleet stationed out of Ceylon. By the end of March this fleet consisted of the battleships *Warspite, Resolution, Revenge, Royal Sovereign* and *Ramillies*, the aircraft carriers *Formidable, Indomitable* and *Hermes*, seven cruisers, 16 destroyers and seven submarines. Unfortunately, while this new fleet was sizeable in numbers, it suffered from numerous qualitative deficiencies that threatened to put it at a grave disadvantage if confronted by a comparable Japanese force. First, many of its ships were old and in need of modernisation or maintenance. All of the battleships were veterans from World War I, and of these, only *Warspite* had been modernised. The remaining *Royal Sovereign*-class battleships were notoriously slow, had poor endurance and lacked adequate anti-aircraft defences. As for the carriers, *Formidable* and *Indomitable* were both modern, capable warships, but *Hermes* was too slow and small to be useful for anything other than convoy protection. Equally important, the three carriers only embarked a total of 57 strike aircraft and 33 fighters between them, all of which were inferior in performance to their Japanese counterparts. Finally, due to the haste in which the British had assembled this fleet, some of the ships were not completely worked-up and many of the crews lacked sufficient training and experience in working with each other.

Fortunately, the fleet had at least one thing going for it in the form of its seasoned and capable commander, Vice-Admiral James Somerville. Somerville was born at Weybridge, England on 17 July 1882. A 45-year naval veteran having first entered the Royal Navy in 1897, Somerville had held a variety of command and staff positions including service in both the Mediterranean and Grand Fleets during World War I where he earned a DSO and mentions in dispatches. In early 1939 Somerville briefly retired from the navy having contracted suspected tuberculosis, but he was recalled back onto active duty a few months later when war appeared on the horizon. Starting the war on special service to the Admiralty where he performed important work on naval radar development, Somerville later transferred to Dover Command where he helped organise the Dunkirk evacuation under the overall command of Admiral Bertram Ramsay. In June 1940, Somerville assumed command of the newly formed Force H in Gibraltar, which initially consisted of the battlecruiser *Hood*, the battleships *Resolution* and *Valiant*, the aircraft carrier *Ark Royal*, two light cruisers and 11 destroyers to secure the western Mediterranean following the collapse of France. Somerville commanded Force H for the next year and a half where he oversaw numerous convoys and air ferrying missions in support of Malta. While these various replenishment operations were vital to Malta's survival and Britain's naval position in the Mediterranean, they offered Somerville little opportunity to offensively engage the enemy.

Of course, there were some exceptions to this. Within days of taking command of Force H, Somerville carried out Operation *Catapult* to neutralise the French fleet at Mers-el-Kébir. Arriving off the French port with Force H on the morning of 3 July 1940, Somerville offered the French four options regarding the disposition of their fleet. First, they could join the British and continue the fight against the Germans and Italians. Second, they could sail with reduced crews to any British port and be interned with the crews being repatriated. Third, they could sail to a French West Indies port and demilitarise their ships or entrust them to the United States. Again, the crews would be repatriated. Finally, they could scuttle their ships in place within six hours.[18] Unfortunately, the French commander refused to acquiesce to Somerville's petitions, and after extending the deadline to no avail, Somerville reluctantly ordered his ships to open fire. In the resulting bombardment, the British sank one French battleship and disabled three other warships. Somerville found the entire undertaking extremely distasteful, and his performance at Mers-el-Kébir merits some criticism since he hesitated too long and then failed to press home his attack thus allowing the battlecruiser *Strasbourg* to escape. Still, given the fact that he was engaging a former ally, one can reasonably understand Somerville's reluctance in the matter.

In other actions against Italian or German forces, Somerville was far more resolute. The best example of the former occurred some seven months later when on 9 February 1941 Somerville brought his Force H warships to the very threshold of Italy itself and carried out a bombardment of the key commercial/military port of Genoa. In this, Somerville was able to fire 273 15-inch shells, 782 6-inch shells and 400 4.5-inch shells causing considerable damage to the hapless port before withdrawing his vessels unmolested from the area.[19] A few months later, Somerville's Force H sortied into the Atlantic where it took part in the effort to destroy the German battleship *Bismarck*. Although a late participant in this operation, Force H played a critical role in bringing about the demise of this powerful adversary, as a last-minute strike by *Ark Royal*'s Swordfish aircraft scored two torpedo hits on *Bismarck* that crippled its steering gear and rendered it incapable of manoeuvring. At the time, *Bismarck* was heading for St. Nazaire on the French Atlantic coast and had almost reached the safety of German air cover, but this damage ensured that the great battleship would never arrive. Instead, elements of the British Home Fleet, which included the battleships *Rodney* and *King George V*, were able to catch up to *Bismarck* and destroy it in a classic surface engagement.

Clearly a veteran combat commander with extensive sea service, Somerville arrived at Ceylon on 26 March to assume command of the Eastern Fleet. Hoisting his flag on the battleship *Warspite*, Somerville took stock of his situation. More than anything else, Somerville needed time to mould his new fleet into an effective fighting force, but this was a luxury the Japanese were not about to grant. On 2 April 1942 a large Japanese carrier strike force, consisting of the aircraft carriers

Akagi, Shōkaku, Zuikaku, Hiryū and *Sōryū*, the battleships *Kongō, Haruna, Hiei* and *Kirishima*, three cruisers and eight destroyers, passed south of Sumatra and sortied into the Indian Ocean. Admiral Nagumo, the architect of the Pearl Harbor and Darwin attacks, commanded this force and possessed some 300 carrier aircraft. The objective of this sortie was to strike at the British naval and military bases at Ceylon and destroy or neutralise the new British Eastern Fleet. At the same time a second Japanese force, consisting of the light carrier *Ryūjō*, six cruisers and four destroyers under Vice-Admiral Jisaburō Ozawa, proceeded from Mergui in southern Burma to strike against Allied shipping in the Bay of Bengal.

On the afternoon of the 4th a British Catalina reconnaissance aircraft spotted Nagumo's force some 360 miles southeast of Ceylon. Fortunately, the British had expected this incursion, and the majority of the Eastern Fleet was safely out of harm's way at Addu Atoll, some 600 miles southwest of Ceylon. From there, Somerville, who believed that his primary mission was to preserve his fleet, deployed his ships to keep them out of the reach of Nagumo's aircraft. Meanwhile, Admiral Layton, the new Commander-in-Chief of Ceylon, ordered all seaworthy ships out of Colombo and Trincomalee harbours and prepared his defences to meet the expected Japanese attack. In this, he did not have long to wait. On the morning of 5 April the Japanese launched 91 bombers and 36 fighters against Colombo. The British opposed this onslaught with 42 Hurricane and Fulmar fighters. In the battle that followed, the Japanese destroyed 19 of these fighters, sank the armed merchant cruiser *Hector* and the destroyer *Tenedos* and damaged the depot ship *Lucia* and a merchant ship. This cost them seven aircraft in return.

Despite the apparent disparity in these results, the damage inflicted upon Colombo was relatively light compared to other recent Japanese successes, and the Japanese were generally disappointed with the attack. This disappointment quickly moderated a few hours later when a Japanese reconnaissance aircraft happened upon the British heavy cruisers *Cornwall* and *Dorsetshire* some 300 nautical miles southwest of Ceylon. The Japanese immediately dispatched 53 dive-bombers to attack these ships, and both were quickly overwhelmed and sunk. Following this attack, Nagumo's carrier force retired to the south and then spent the next three days manoeuvring around Ceylon in preparation for their next attack. While this was underway, Admiral Ozawa's cruiser force swept into the Bay of Bengal and destroyed 23 Allied merchant ships worth 112,312 tons while Japanese submarines operating off of India's west coast added another five merchant ships totalling 32,404 tons.[20]

On 9 April Admiral Nagumo renewed his offensive against Ceylon and launched 91 bombers and 38 fighters against Trincomalee. Again, the British were alerted to this threat, and the Japanese found their attack force opposed by 23 Hurricanes and Fulmars. Despite their numerical advantage, the Japanese only succeeded in destroying a merchant ship and nine British fighters and damaging the monitor *Erebus*. Their own losses amounted to six aircraft shot down. However, as luck would have it, a Japanese floatplane from the battleship *Haruna* sighted the British aircraft carrier *Hermes* and a few accompanying ships some 65 miles south of Trincomalee. In a repeat of events just a few days before, Admiral Nagumo sent 80 dive-bombers to attack this force. In a matter of minutes, the Japanese found the hapless British carrier, which was not carrying any aircraft at the time, and sank it after scoring a reported 40 direct hits. They also sank the Australian destroyer *Vampire*, the British corvette *Hollyhock* and two tankers. When this attack was complete, Nagumo turned his ships back towards home thus concluding the Ceylon operation.

As Admiral Nagumo's force withdrew, the British took stock of their situation and counted their losses. In this, they were able to take some solace in the fact that the bulk of the Eastern Fleet survived the raid intact, but their losses had been grievous nevertheless. Making matters worse, the raid coincided with a continuing deterioration of the situation in Burma. After the fall of Rangoon, the British coordinated with the Chinese to take over the defence of northern Burma while their own forces attempted to establish a new defensive line in the central part of the country. At the end of March through the first three weeks in April the Japanese launched a new offensive that routed these Chinese forces in the north and progressively forced the British to give ground. Realising that the situation was now hopeless, on 26 April the British abandoned all hopes of holding Burma and began a general retreat across the Irrawaddy River towards the Indian border. Despite interference from the Japanese, the British successfully extricated the bulk of their forces into India by the middle of May thus completing the longest retreat in the history of the British army (as measured from Southeast Burma where the campaign had first begun). This failed campaign cost the British 13,463 casualties compared to just 2,431 for the Japanese.[21]

When added to other recent reversals, the loss of Burma culminated an unprecedented period in British military history. In just five months, the British had lost their Southeast Asian empire and suffered the worst series of defeats ever to befall the British army and navy. In terms of the former, British ground losses during this tragic period (including those from Commonwealth and Imperial sources) totalled 166,867 casualties of which nearly 94 percent were taken prisoner.[22] Meanwhile, the British and Commonwealth navies lost a battleship, a battlecruiser, a light carrier, four cruisers, eight destroyers, two sloops, a corvette, an armed merchant cruiser, several minor warships and auxiliaries and dozens of merchant ships. Against this, the British had only inflicted negligible losses upon the Japanese. In particular, Japanese ground casualties during the related campaigns were only about an eighth of those sustained by the British while their naval losses consisted of just two submarines and a handful of merchant ships sunk solely or partially by British or Commonwealth means.

With this record of defeat, the British had little reason for future optimism. The Japanese were in full command of the initiative with strong and powerful

Highlighting Japan's stunning series of early victories was the surrender of British forces in Singapore. Pictured here is General Percival (far right) and his party on their way to surrender. (Unknown author, public domain)

forces that were seemingly capable of striking whenever and wherever they chose. Against this, the British were weak and vulnerable everywhere with little ability to do anything other than respond to these Japanese moves. More than anything else, the British needed time to regroup and properly prepare their defences for the next Japanese onslaught. Already, additional reinforcements, including the battleship *Valiant* and the aircraft carrier *Illustrious*, were en route or earmarked for service in the Indian Ocean, but it would take time for these forces to arrive. Once there, it would take even more time for these forces to be made fully combat ready and integrated into effective command structures that were capable of meeting the Japanese on something approaching equal terms. Unfortunately, the British had little reason to believe the Japanese would grant such a respite. Instead, all they could do was wait and make ready as best they could for the next Japanese push that seemed sure to come.

CHAPTER 5

Turning the Tide

By any measure, Japan's surprise attack against the American Pacific Fleet at Pearl Harbor constituted a substantial military victory, but as the Japanese themselves would acknowledge, it was also explicitly incomplete in its strategic impact. In late 1941 the United States Navy possessed seven aircraft carriers consisting of *Lexington*, *Saratoga*, *Enterprise*, *Ranger*, *Yorktown*, *Wasp* and *Hornet*. Of these, the first three were stationed in the Pacific while the remainder were based in the Atlantic. Through a stroke of fortunate timing, none of the Pacific-based carriers were in Pearl Harbor at the time of the attack, which meant that while the Japanese were able to inflict heavy damage upon the American battle line, they left the primary targets for the operation, the aircraft carriers, untouched. In early January 1942, the Japanese submarine *I-6* torpedoed *Saratoga* and damaged it sufficiently to put it out of action for five months. Fortunately, this temporary absence was more than offset by the corresponding arrivals of *Yorktown* and *Hornet*, which were transferred into the Pacific from the Atlantic. A few months later *Wasp* also arrived in the theatre thus leaving *Ranger* as the only American aircraft carrier remaining in the Atlantic. Although still outnumbered by their Japanese counterparts by a factor of roughly two to one, the presence of these carriers meant that the American Pacific Fleet remained a force to be reckoned with.

The veracity of this threat rapidly materialised as the Americans quickly put their aircraft carriers into operational use. In February and March, American naval forces conducted a series of hit and run raids and sweeps against the Marshall and Gilbert Islands, Rabaul, and Lae-Salamaua in Papua New Guinea using *Enterprise*, *Lexington* and *Yorktown*. In some cases, they supplemented these actions with shore bombardments carried out by the attending cruisers and destroyers. During these operations, the Americans destroyed an armed merchant cruiser and four merchant ships worth a combined 31,106 tons as well as a minor auxiliary. They further damaged at least 15 other vessels including the light cruisers *Katori* and *Yūbari* and two destroyers and destroyed some 30 Japanese aircraft for little loss to themselves. While these results were not substantial, they proved that the American carriers

Table 5.1. Characteristics of Selected Japanese, American and British Carrier-borne Aircraft in 1942.

	Role	Top Speed (mph)	Range (miles)	Armament
Japanese				
Mitsubishi A6M2 Zero	Fighter	332	1,930	2 × 7.7mm MGs and 2 × 20mm Cannons
Aichi D3A1 Val	Strike	240	915	3 × 7.7mm MGs, 813lbs of bombs
Nakajima B5N2 Kate	Strike	235	1,237	1 × 7.7mm MG, 1 × 18in torpedo or 1,764lb bomb
American				
Grumman Wildcat*	Fighter	331	845	4 or 6 × .50 MGs, 200lbs of bombs
Douglas Devastator	Strike	206	716	2 × .30 MGs, 1 × 22in torpedo or 1,000lbs of bombs
Douglas Dauntless	Strike	250	1,345	2 × .50 and 2 × .30 MGs, 1,200lbs of bombs
British				
Fairey Fulmar	Fighter	280	800	8 × .303 MGs
Hawker Sea Hurricane	Fighter	300	450	8 × .303 MGs
Fairey Swordfish	Strike	139	546	2 × .303 MGs, 1 × 18in torpedo or 1,500lbs of bombs
Fairey Albacore	Strike	161	930	2 × .303 MGs, 1 × 18in torpedo or 2,000lbs of bombs

* The Grumman Wildcat also saw service in the FAA where it was initially referred to as the Martlet.

were formidable weapons capable of operating with considerable impunity in the vast expanses of the Pacific Ocean despite Japan's overall dominance in the region.

In mid-April the Americans drove this point home in a spectacular fashion. Early on the morning of the 18th a special American strike force, consisting of the aircraft carriers *Hornet* and *Enterprise*, four cruisers and eight destroyers, approached within 700 miles of Japan. Shortly after 0800 hours, *Hornet* turned into the wind and launched the first of 16 specially modified United States Army Air Force (USAAF) B-25 Mitchell medium bombers. Over the next hour the remaining twin-engine B-25s lifted off the aircraft carrier and proceeded towards Japan. By 1215 hours this force, commanded by Lieutenant-Colonel James Doolittle, arrived unmolested over the main Japanese home island of Honshu and commenced bombing attacks against various targets in Tokyo, Kobe, Yokohama, Nagoya and Yokosuka. After dropping their bombs, these aircraft continued on towards China to seek refuge from the Nationalist Chinese. Due to poor weather conditions and fuel exhaustion, all 15 aircraft that made it into Chinese airspace either crash-landed or were abandoned in flight by their crews. In the process, three American crewmen died, and eight others were taken prisoner. The sixteenth American bomber diverted to Vladivostok in southeastern Russia, where it was interned by Soviet authorities.[1]

Despite the loss of all 16 American aircraft and the fact that the operation only inflicted minor damage upon the Japanese, the Doolittle Raid had a psychological effect far exceeding its materiel achievements. After four and a half months of uninterrupted defeats and disasters, the raid represented the first noteworthy piece of good news out of the Pacific and provided a much-needed boost to Allied morale and confidence. This was particularly true for the Americans, who reveled in the fact that their aircraft had mounted a seemingly impossible operation and struck directly into the heart of the Japanese Empire. For the Japanese, the raid had an equally profound, although opposite, effect upon the national sentiment. The Japanese civilian population was shocked and horrified to learn that the Americans had attacked their sacred homeland and threatened the emperor's life. This latter outrage was emphasised by the fact that one of the American bombers actually flew in the vicinity of the Imperial Palace during the course of the raid. In an act of reprisal, all eight captured American crewmen were tried and convicted as war criminals, and three were executed while a fourth died in captivity. Meanwhile, Japan's military leadership and Imperial General Staff considered the raid to be a colossal embarrassment and affront to their prestige. This quickly prompted them to embrace a more aggressive and risky offensive strategy to counter the perceived American threat. Therefore, although a minor event in terms of damage inflicted, the Doolittle Raid represented the first appreciable crack in Japan's aura of military supremacy.

Yet, despite this change in perception, the overall trend within the theatre remained one of overwhelming Japanese success. In a period of less than five months, the Japanese had defeated the combined military forces of the United States, the United Kingdom, the British Commonwealth and the Dutch colonial authorities. In doing so, they had seized an empire containing 90 million people, 88 percent of the world's rubber, 54 percent of its tin, 30 percent of its rice, 20 percent of its tungsten and substantial oil reserves.[2] These victories cost the Japanese the relatively meagre price of less than 50,000 casualties, several hundred aircraft and a couple dozen ships lost, none of which were larger than a destroyer. By comparison, combined Allied casualties during the same period topped roughly 350,000 men along with substantial air and naval assets including the irretrievable loss of three battleships, one battlecruiser, one light aircraft carrier, seven cruisers and 20 destroyers.[3] This result gave the Allies little cause for future optimism and was particularly hard on the British who had just lost much of their Asian Empire and undergone the worst series of defeats ever to befall their military services.

Making matters worse, this pattern of defeat and struggle was not limited to the Pacific or Southeast Asia. Instead, the first half of 1942 ushered in a period of almost uninterrupted defeats in which the British seemed to be on the defensive everywhere. In the Middle East, the British began the year on a high note as their forces consolidated control over Italian Cyrenaica following the Eighth Army's victory during Operation *Crusader*. Unfortunately, this victory was short lived as an unexpected Axis counteroffensive in the latter half of January caught the British off guard and forced them to relinquish half the territory they had gained during the *Crusader* offensive. After a few months of uneasy stalemate, the German/Italian Panzerarmee Afrika renewed its offensive in May and inflicted a devastating defeat upon the British Eighth Army at Gazala that was only surpassed in its magnitude by the defeat the British had suffered in Malaya.[4] With this, the British were sent reeling back into Egypt, and by late June it looked like Britain's position in the eastern Mediterranean might collapse. Meanwhile, in the central Mediterranean, an intensified Axis bombing campaign threatened to render Malta impotent while the Royal Navy struggled to provide sustenance to the beleaguered colony. On a number of occasions during the first half of 1942, the British attempted to run convoys through to Malta, but only a handful of merchant ships actually arrived, and this came at a heavy cost to the forces involved.

The situation was much the same 2,500 miles to the north where the British endeavoured to run a series of convoys through to their Soviet allies in Murmansk. These convoys represented extremely difficult and dangerous undertakings given the conditions arrayed against them both natural and manmade. In terms of the former, the convoys had to endure some of the world's harshest climatic conditions ranging from oppressive cold to intense gales and blizzards. Likewise, given the routes the British were compelled to take, these convoys passed through a relatively narrow corridor on a 2,000-mile journey through German-dominated waters that exposed them to a myriad of threats ranging from U-boats, surface warships and air attacks. To counter these substantial and comprehensive dangers, the British were forced to commit extensive resources to the defence of each convoy, which often included battleships and aircraft carriers. As such, the dispatch of each Arctic convoy was the equivalent of a minor fleet operation, and in many cases the British suffered heavy losses in their executions.

Nor was this struggle a uniquely British challenge as all of the major Allied powers suffered similar hardships within their own theatres of operation. Despite having the opportunity to observe and learn from the Royal Navy during the first two years of the Atlantic struggle, the United States was shockingly unprepared to deal with the foreseeable U-boat threat that arrived off its eastern seaboard in January 1942. Capitalising upon this flagrant weakness, the Germans immediately directed the bulk of their U-boat forces into this region, where they operated in an environment of near impunity against a plethora of shipping targets transiting through the area. As such, Allied merchant shipping losses in the North Atlantic, which had been declining during the last six months of 1941, shot up to a staggering 526 ships sunk for a total of 2,831,689 tons during the first half of 1942. Corresponding Kriegsmarine losses during this timeframe amounted to just 21 U-boats sunk thus prompting the Germans to refer to this period as the 'second happy time'.[5] In materiel terms, these shipping losses constituted a far greater calamity than that suffered by the Allied maritime forces in the Pacific and Indian Oceans during the same period, and this debacle arguably constituted America's greatest maritime failure of the war.

Meanwhile, on the Eastern Front the Soviets were still reeling from the unimaginable losses they had suffered in stemming the initial German invasion into their country. In 1941 alone, the Soviets suffered a staggering 4,473,820 personnel casualties, and this massive attrition continued into the new year.[6] This carnage was highlighted in May when the Germans encircled and destroyed three Soviet armies in the area around Kharkov. In just a few weeks of fighting in this single battle, the Soviets suffered more casualties than the British and Commonwealth forces had suffered during six months of fighting against the Japanese in the Asia/Pacific theatre. Now with the oncoming spring, the Germans had plans for a major new offensive into the Caucasus where they hoped to cause more destruction to the Soviet forces and deprive them of their vast oil reserves. It remained to be seen how long the Soviets could persevere under these unprecedented conditions or if they might crack under the immense pressure applied by the Germans. Such an event would be disastrous for the British as it would release substantial German forces to operate against the West, and it was for this reason they believed it so necessary to send materiel support to their Soviet allies despite the cost.

Given this difficult global situation, the British were still fighting for their very survival in the Atlantic and Middle East. As such, they were obliged to concentrate most of their resources in these other theatres, and there was little left over to utilise against the Japanese. This presented the British service chiefs with the daunting task of trying to secure their remaining Asian possessions with what continually seemed to be inadequate and ill-prepared forces. Given these realities, British defence planners contemplated a nightmare scenario in which the Japanese coordinated their efforts with the German/Italian forces in North Africa and the Caucasus to launch concurrent offensives from both east and west to seize Egypt, the Arabian Peninsula, Iran and India. If successful, this would put the entire length of North Africa and southern Asia under Axis control and deprive the Allies of substantial resources as well as an important communication link to the Soviet Union. It would also sever direct British access to Australia and New Zealand. In retrospect, it seems highly unlikely that the Axis could have mustered the immense logistical resources to carry out such an undertaking, but given Japan's recent string of astonishing victories as well as the deteriorating situation in the Mediterranean and North Africa, one can certainly understand the origins of this fear.

To further complicate this situation, the British also faced a huge potential threat to their critical lines of communication from the Vichy French-controlled Island of Madagascar. Located some 250 miles east of Mozambique, Madagascar was perfectly positioned to menace Allied maritime traffic in the western portion of the Indian Ocean. Beyond this, the large harbour at Diego Suarez on Madagascar's northern tip was ideally suited to serve as a base for naval and air operations against

Allied shipping traversing the area thus imperiling Allied links to the Middle East, Persian Gulf and India. As such, the Allies determined it a high priority to deny the Axis potential use of the island. In this regard, they had little confidence in the local Vichy authorities given recent events in Indochina and Syria where Vichy officials had caved to Japanese and German pressure thus granting them territorial access or logistical support for their ambitions. In regards to Madagascar, Allied planners feared that a Vichy response to any Axis incursion might range from token resistance to outright collaboration. Even if the French chose to offer more strident opposition, they would be hard pressed to do so given their small garrison and limited defensive capabilities.

British authorities had long contemplated the potential threat that Madagascar posed to their critical lines of communication. With the collapse of France in 1940, German forces had occupied the northern half of the country including Paris and the French Atlantic coast while a semi-independent French government was established in the spa town of Vichy to administer the southern half of the country and France's colonial possessions. This Vichy regime had limited autonomy and was not in a position to overtly contest Germany's strategic ambitions. Given this unequal power arrangement and the threat of Japanese military force, French authorities in Madagascar clearly appeared susceptible to Axis coercion. Even before Japan's entry into the war, the British Chiefs of Staff had openly contemplated intelligence reports indicating that the French might cede control of Madagascar over to the Japanese or at least grant them basing rights on the island. On 16 December 1941 General Charles de Gaulle, the leader of the small Free French movement, urged Churchill to launch an expedition to occupy Madagascar. Although acutely aware of the potential peril confronting his position in the Indian Ocean, Churchill initially resisted this proposal citing a lack of resources as the reason. However, with the advent of recent events and the receipt of signal intelligence indicating German attempts to lobby Japan to occupy the island, the Allies decided they could no longer accept the status quo. Therefore, on 12 March 1942 the British War Cabinet, with American concurrence, ordered the seizure of Diego Suarez and the nearby naval base at Antsirane on Madagascar's northern coast.

With this decision made, the British began the process of marshalling the ships and forces necessary to implement their invasion plans. This was no easy task given the many commitments confronting the British at the time as well as their recent heavy losses sustained in both the Mediterranean and Far East. Still, by requisitioning ships from a variety of sources including the Home Fleet, Force H and the Eastern Fleet, the British gathered a sizeable naval force under the command of Rear-Admiral E. N. Syfret and consisting of the battleship *Ramillies*, the aircraft carriers *Illustrious* and *Indomitable*, two cruisers, 11 destroyers, six corvettes, six minesweepers and 18 assorted transports and support vessels.[7] Likewise, they further assembled an invasion force, commanded by Major-General R. G. Sturges, Royal Marines, consisting of the British 13th, 17th and 29th Infantry Brigades and No. 5 Royal Marine Commando. Finally, in terms of aerial assets, the two carriers possessed 20 Martlet, 13 Fulmer and nine Sea Hurricane fighters and 20 Swordfish and 24 Albacore strike aircraft while the South African Air Force provided a number of shore-based patrol and reconnaissance aircraft to support the operation. Opposing this vast undertaking was a markedly inferior French force consisting of some 8,000 men, although only a portion of these were in the Diego Suarez area, along with a couple dozen aircraft and a handful of minor warships.

By the end of April everything was ready, and the various naval elements departed South Africa and Ceylon to rendezvous to the east and west of Diego Suarez on 3 May. Concurrently, Admiral Somerville and elements of the Eastern Fleet, including the battleships *Warspite* and *Resolution* and the aircraft carrier *Formidable*, positioned themselves further to the east to screen against any potential Japanese interference. Two days later the British commenced their invasion, which they designated Operation *Ironclad*. Traversing a series of reefs, channels and minefields that the French considered impassable, British assault forces made their initial landings on three beaches in Ambararata and Courrier Bays to the west of Diego Suarez at 0439 hours on 5 May. In doing so, they were aided by the fleet's minesweepers, which opened a route through the dangerous approach removing 17 mines in the process. This audacious action caught the French completely by surprise, and the British landings went in without incident or serious opposition. By daybreak, the British had firm control over all the beaches having seized a battery of 6.1-inch coastal defence guns and some 300 prisoners. Thereafter, they began the process of landing follow-up forces while consolidating and expanding the lodgment area. In this, they were overwhelmingly successful, and by the end of the next day they had at least 13,650 personnel as well as 339 assorted vehicles and guns and 590 tons of stores ashore.[8] The only mishap marring this process was the loss of the corvette *Auricula*, which struck a mine on the 5th and sank the following day while under tow.

Meanwhile, the coming of dawn also brought an expansion to the operation as *Indomitable* and *Illustrious* launched a series of air strikes to neutralise the local French air and naval forces. In this, *Indomitable* primarily concerned itself with an attack against Antsirane airfield, where its Albacores scored hits on hangars and destroyed or damaged ten French aircraft on the ground. While this was underway, *Illustrious* launched a strike of 18 Swordfish to attack shipping in Diego Suarez harbour. Armed with a combination of torpedoes, bombs and depth charges, these Swordfish sank the armed merchant cruiser *Bougainville* and the submarine *Bévéziers*, but failed to inflict meaningful damage against their primary target, the colonial sloop *D'Entrecasteaux*. Still, this reprieve was short lived as a follow-up strike in the afternoon scored a bomb hit that heavily damaged the elusive sloop and forced it to ground in shallow water. A final strike by Swordfish and Martlets later in the day inflicted further damage against the immobilised *D'Entrecasteaux* thus rendering it a total loss.

As Operation *Ironclad* proceeded into the succeeding days, the fighting continued on both land and sea. In terms of the former, British forces pushed inland towards the main French bases at Diego Suarez and Antsirane, but encountered growing resistance from French garrison troops that slowed their progress. Fortunately, the Royal Navy provided valuable support that helped overcome or circumvent these obstacles. Much of this centred upon the Fleet Air Arm, which attacked various ground targets, conducted a diversionary parachute drop and sheltered the British from any remaining French aerial interference. Meanwhile, British warships carried out a number of fire support missions expending a total of 515 shells ranging from 3-inch to 15-inch in size against various French positions.[9] Finally and perhaps most important, on the night of 6/7 May the destroyer *Anthony* braved dangerous conditions to land 50 Royal Marines behind the French defenders at Antsirane. These marines seized the French artillery command post and other key locations thus seriously compromising French resolve. At about the same time, troops from the 17th Brigade broke through the French defences and entered Diego Suarez shortly thereafter. Sporadic fighting continued the next day, but the main ground resistance was now broken as the bulk of French forces withdrew to the south. Meanwhile, in related naval combat, a patrolling Swordfish from the aircraft carrier *Illustrious* sank the French submarine *Le Héros* on 7 May while the destroyer *Active* sank the submarine *Monge* as the latter was attempting to attack *Indomitable* on the morning of the 8th.

This final action proved to be the closing shot in Operation *Ironclad* as the two sides entered into negotiations resulting in a formal French surrender effective at 1625 hours on 8 May. With this cessation of hostilities, the British assumed control over Diego Suarez thus fulfilling the primary objective for the undertaking and removing a potential threat to their regional lines of communication. The importance of this was demonstrated by the 3,250,700 tons of military cargo shipped into the region from the United Kingdom and North America in 1942 alone.[10] This inflow of resources supported combat operations in both the Middle East and Southeast Asia and provided direct sustenance to the beleaguered Soviet Union. The cost in attaining this success was relatively light consisting of the corvette *Auricula*, 105 men killed, 283 wounded and four missing. Against this, the Vichy French lost three submarines, a sloop and an armed merchant cruiser sunk along with 171 men killed, 343 wounded and several hundred men taken prisoner.[11] Finally, the British seized the 4,669-ton Vichy-controlled merchant ship *General Duquesne* and forced the scuttling of three Axis merchant ships (the 2,315-ton Italian *Duca Degli Abruzzi*, the 2,699-ton Italian *Somalia* and the 6,181-ton German *Wartenfels*) that had taken refuge in Diego Suarez.[12]

Beyond its strategic implications, *Ironclad* provided the British with other important benefits. The first of these was psychological. After months of defeats and disasters, the British found it extremely heartening to finally enjoy a victory. True, this victory was scored against the Vichy French and not the Japanese, Germans or Italians, but it was victory nevertheless. Likewise, *Ironclad* provided the British with valuable training and experience in the conduct of joint amphibious operations that would later prove beneficial in Africa, Europe and Asia. Finally, *Ironclad* demonstrated that FAA aircraft operating from carriers could prevail over land-based air power when the conditions were right. During the battle *Indomitable* and *Illustrious* flew a total of 309 sorties during which they successfully gained and maintained air superiority, neutralised French naval power, spotted for shore bombardments and provided close air support for the ground forces. These operations cost the British four aircraft that were lost through combat while British fighters shot down at least six French aircraft and claimed 11 more as probably destroyed.[13]

Notwithstanding these successes, the British soon found themselves embroiled in additional fighting in and around Madagascar. The first such incident occurred on the night of 30/31 May when two Japanese Type-A midget submarines attempted to penetrate into Diego Suarez harbour and attack British shipping located there. The Type-A was a self-contained two-man submarine that displaced 46 tons and was armed with two 18-inch torpedoes. Incapable of extended travel, the Type-As were transported to Madagascar by the fleet submarines *I-16* and *I-20*. At least one of these midget submarines penetrated into the harbour and carried out a highly effective torpedo attack that damaged the battleship *Ramillies* and the nearby 6,993-ton tanker *British Loyalty*. British escort vessels immediately counterattacked, and the offending Type-A was subsequently beached at Nosy Antalikely with its crewmembers taking refuge in the nearby jungle. Three days later, these crewmen were killed in a fight with Royal Marines. Meanwhile, the second Type-A was lost due to an unknown cause with the body of one of its crewmen washing up on shore. Fortunately, this proved to be Japan's only intervention into the battle, but it gave a foretaste of what might have happened had the Japanese acted more aggressively in supporting the French.

For their part, in the succeeding months the British conducted follow-up operations to solidify their control over Madagascar. In July the British captured the small, nearby island of Mayotte. Then, on 10 September they launched Operation *Stream* and landed the 29th British Infantry Brigade at Majunga on the west side of Madagascar. This was followed by a similar landing at Tamatave on the east side of the island eight days later. A number of British ships, including the battleship *Warspite* and the aircraft carrier *Illustrious*, supported these operations, but they encountered little French opposition. Still, this show of force proved beneficial as British warships conducted a brief bombardment at Tamatave that immediately induced the local French garrison to surrender. In other related actions, on 24 and 29 September the Australian destroyer *Nizam*, with support from South African aircraft, captured the French transports *Marechal Gallieni* and *Amiral Pierre* in the Mozambique Channel and off Lourenco Marques respectively.[14] Meanwhile, British ground forces enjoyed a similar lack of serious opposition and completed their conquest of Madagascar on 6 November 1942. The eight-week campaign cost the British 142 casualties. French losses were much higher including some 1,300 prisoners taken during the period of 13–29 October alone.[15]

While these operations were underway, Admiral Somerville and the Eastern Fleet prepared to defend the Indian Ocean from further Japanese incursions. In doing so, the British were well aware of their many weaknesses in this area. Fortunately, the Japanese were too preoccupied in the Pacific to mount a serious challenge to this tenuous position. Instead, the Japanese limited their activities in the Indian Ocean to a minor submarine offensive and a halfhearted surface raider campaign. In terms of the former, the Japanese employed a handful of submarines from their 8th Flotilla against Allied shipping in the Indian Ocean and Red Sea approaches. The British were hard pressed to counter this limited offensive due to their lack of resources and the immense areas involved, and the Japanese succeeded in sinking a total of 31 Allied merchant ships worth 144,224 tons from May through October 1942.[16] In turn, the Japanese lost a single submarine, *I-30*, which was sunk by a British mine off Singapore on 13 October. While these losses were not insignificant, they were not particularly serious either. In the grand scheme of things, the toll in the Indian Ocean was a pittance compared to the carnage underway in the Atlantic, and these losses would soon abate as the Japanese substantially subsided their submarine offensive in November.

During the same month the British scored a small, but decisive, victory against Japan's surface raider force. In the autumn of 1942 the Japanese, hoping to imitate previous German surface raider successes, dispatched the armed merchant cruisers *Hōkoku Maru* and *Aikoku Maru* (10,439 and 10,438 tons respectively) into the Indian Ocean to prey upon Allied shipping. Early on the morning of 11 November these merchant cruisers encountered the Royal Indian Navy minesweeper *Bengal* and the Dutch tanker *Ondina* some 550 miles south-south-west of the Cocos Islands. The Japanese enjoyed an overwhelming firepower advantage and should have easily destroyed their Allied adversaries. Together, the Japanese merchant cruisers possessed sixteen 5.5-inch guns and eight 21-inch torpedo tubes against a single 3-inch gun for the *Bengal* and a single British-manned 4-inch gun for the *Ondina*. Despite this disparity, the Allied vessels courageously and effectively defended themselves and scored a number of well-placed hits on *Hōkoku Maru*. These hits caused numerous fires that quickly engulfed the armed merchant cruiser resulting in its destruction.

As for the Allies, *Ondina* was badly damaged during the battle, but ultimately reached port. This victory against seemingly insurmountable odds signalled the end of Japan's fledgling surface raider campaign. With the loss of *Hōkoku Maru*, the Japanese suspended further such operations, and the Indian Ocean became free from this threat.

Nor were all of the British efforts during this period strictly defensive. During the last eight months of 1942, the British took what limited opportunities they had to strike back at the Japanese. Given the Eastern Fleet's inability to directly challenge the Japanese navy at this time, these offensive efforts primarily centred upon the handful of British and Dutch submarines present in the region. On 4 June the British submarine *Trusty* sank the 7,031-ton Japanese merchant ship *Toyohashi Maru* in the Malacca Straits. One month later the British *Truant* sank the 3,019-ton *Tamon Maru* in the same area. Then on 2 August the Dutch submarine *O-23* sank the 6,440-ton *Zenyo Maru* and may have sunk a second vessel, the 5,873-ton *Ohio Maru*, off Penang. Finally, in October and November *O-23* and *Trusty* damaged two Japanese merchant ships worth a combined 10,238 tons.[17] Added to this, on 12 September British aircraft sank the 1,350-ton merchant ship *Niyo Maru* in the Bay of Bengal off Burma's west coast.[18] Yet, despite the best efforts of the crews involved, these actions amounted to little more than pinpricks as the Indian Ocean increasingly became a secondary theatre devoid of significant naval and maritime action by either side.

This secondary status and same level of inactivity was also generally true regarding the local ground war. As discussed earlier in the chapter, at the conclusion of the Burma invasion, the British feared that the Japanese might continue their offensive into India. This was a prospect they were ill prepared to counter, and they needed time to prepare their defences. Fortunately for the British, with Japan's attention firmly affixed on events in the Pacific, the Japanese were content to remain in place and consolidate their recent gains in Burma. As such, other than the execution of occasional bombing raids, the Japanese took no further offensive action within the region, and the British were spared the realisation of an immediate invasion into India. By year's end, the nightmare spectre of a combined, converging Axis offensive through southern Asia was largely nullified, and the British were able to rebuild their depleted forces free from Japanese interference.

In fact, it was the British, and not the Japanese, who initiated the only ground actions that occurred during this period. The first was a limited offensive by a heavily reinforced 14th Indian Division designed to capture territory in the Arakan region of Burma's western coast. The purpose of this was to gain bases and staging areas that could be used for follow-up operations into the country at large. Launched in December 1942, this offensive gained some initial success, but quickly bogged down due to logistical restraints and strong Japanese resistance. As the fighting continued, the Japanese brought in reinforcements and launched a series of counterattacks that put increasing pressure on the exposed British positions. After a five-month struggle the British finally pulled back relinquishing all of their earlier gains for a cost of 5,057 casualties compared to 1,775 casualties for the Japanese.[19] Although clearly a failure, the battle still represented an improvement over earlier British performance within the theatre and provided them with valuable lessons for future operations.

These latter points were even more prevalent in the second British action; a large-scale commando raid that was the brainchild of British Colonel Orde Wingate. A 19-year veteran of the army at the end of 1942, Wingate had started his career as an artillery officer, but had gained considerable experience in the area of irregular warfare during his subsequent service. The first major example of this occurred prior to the war when Wingate was assigned as a staff officer in the British Mandate of Palestine where he created the Special Night Squads (SNS) to counter Arab attacks against British and Jewish interests in the region. Under his command, the SNS carried out multiple ambushes and raids against Arab insurgents that helped quell their activities and earned Wingate a Distinguished Service Order (DSO). The second major example of this occurred in 1940 when Wingate created and commanded an irregular unit called Gideon Force to operate against the Italians in East Africa. Beginning operations in February 1941, Gideon Force, which consisted of some 70 British officers and NCOs and 1,600 Sudanese and Ethiopian troops, conducted a successful campaign in western Abyssinia where they collected some 15,600 Italian prisoners for minimal loss to themselves thus contributing to the British conquest of Italian East Africa as outlined in Chapter 2.

In March 1942 Wingate arrived in the Far East where he was tasked to create guerilla units to wage irregular warfare against the Japanese. Upon Britain's expulsion from Burma, Wingate advocated for the creation of long-range penetration units to carry out extended operations behind Japanese lines. Considered arrogant and a bit eccentric by many of his peers, Wingate was not particularly popular within the senior ranks of the army, but he had key supporters in high places. Amongst these was General Wavell, who now led India Command and was a longtime patron of Wingate's from his earlier service in Palestine and East Africa. Accordingly, Wavell assigned Wingate the 77th Indian Brigade as a means to put his ideas to test. After undergoing an extensive training programme under Wingate's tutelage, the 77th Brigade, which now operated under the moniker as the Chindits, prepared to execute its own brand of unconventional warfare.

The initial result of this was Operation *Longcloth*, a deep penetration raid carried out by the 3,000-man strong brigade. Operating over a three-month period beginning in February 1943, the Chindits used aerial re-supply to allow seven marching columns to penetrate deep inside Japanese-controlled territory and attack various infrastructure targets. Although the damage these columns inflicted was not substantial and the operation cost them 818 casualties, the raid provided the British with valuable experience and proved they could successfully operate in the jungle for extended periods of time without the use of roads or significant ground infrastructure.[20] Even more important, the undertaking provided the British with an important morale boost as they slowly reversed the aura of invincibility the Japanese had gained in the opening months of the war. When combined with the Arakan offensive, these operations served as stepping stones leading to the day when the British army would confront the Japanese in far greater numbers and capacity. Until then, the British bided their time as the front remained relatively quiet.

By comparison, the conflict in the Pacific was anything but serene as American and Commonwealth forces battled against the vast bulk of Japan's military power. For Australia and New Zealand, this battle was literally one of national survival. With Britain's retreat from the Pacific and the loss of northern New Guinea and the Solomon Islands, both Australia and New Zealand faced the imminent prospect of isolation and potential invasion. This was particularly true for Australia, which was most immediately threatened by the ever-encroaching Japanese. Prior to the war, Australian authorities had garnered some sense of security from their country's substantial distance from Japan and the promised deterrent of the Royal Navy operating out of Singapore, but those bulwarks were now gone. Increasingly, the Australians looked to the United States to fill the void left by the departure of British forces from the region, and in February 1942 the British and American governments agreed that the United States would assume strategic responsibility for the defence of the Commonwealth nation.

Accordingly, in March American General Douglas MacArthur arrived in Australia to assume command of the South West Pacific Area (SWPA). Serving under MacArthur was Australian General Thomas Blamey, who commanded the local ground forces. Available to MacArthur and Blamey for the defence of Australia were ten Australian divisions in various states of organisation and readiness as well as two American divisions, the 41st and 32nd, which would arrive in April and May respectively. These Australian formations included elements of the 6th and 7th divisions, which were in the process of returning from the Middle East as well as the 1st Armoured Division, which was forming up and almost completely devoid of tanks. The remaining Australian divisions were militia units that were only partially trained and equipped. For their part, the arriving American units would also prove to be understrength and only partially trained. Filling out MacArthur's command were a few hundred aircraft and a few dozen warships immediately available in the area to confront the Japanese.

Hoping to avoid a direct assault against Australia and New Zealand, the Allies sent reinforcements into southern Papua New Guinea, the Fiji Islands, New Caledonia and the New Hebrides. Likewise, they also provided logistical support to a small Australian commando force still operating on the Japanese-occupied island of Timor. A number of Australian and New Zealand warships participated in these operations and helped establish a new Allied defensive perimeter based upon these island outposts. This effort did not come without risks as the Japanese dispatched submarines to operate in these areas. This threat was amply demonstrated on the night of 31 May–1 June when three Japanese Type-A midget submarines attempted to penetrate into Sydney harbour and repeat the success their counterparts had achieved at Diego Suarez. Fortunately, alert Australian defences detected and countered the intruders, and the Japanese lost all three submarines for the meagre return of the 447-ton Australian auxiliary ship *Kuttabul*, which was destroyed by two torpedoes originally intended for the American cruiser *Chicago*.

Despite reinforcements, the new Allied defensive perimeter was tenuously held. A key position in this perimeter was the Australian base at Port Moresby on the southern coast of Papua New Guinea. This base represented a last line of defence before Australia itself, and its retention was vitally important to the beleaguered commonwealth. This fact was not lost upon the Japanese, who also recognised Port Moresby's vast strategic value. As such, in late April the Japanese dispatched an invasion force from the Caroline Islands to seize Port Moresby. This force was supported and covered by strong Japanese naval units including the large fleet aircraft carriers *Zuikaku* and *Shōkaku* and the light carrier *Shōhō*. Fortunately, Allied Intelligence quickly learned of these moves, and the Americans consolidated two naval task forces in the Coral Sea to intervene. These forces, under the overall command of American Rear-Admiral Frank Fletcher, consisted of the aircraft carriers *Lexington* and *Yorktown*, five cruisers and nine destroyers. They also included an Allied cruiser squadron commanded by British Rear-Admiral John Crace and consisting of the Australian cruisers *Australia* and *Hobart*, the American cruiser *Chicago* and two (later increased to three) American destroyers. Admiral Fletcher detached this squadron to patrol the Jomard Passage to prevent any Japanese ships from getting through to Port Moresby while he manoeuvred his carriers to intercept the main Japanese force. For the first time in the war, the Allies prepared to meet the Japanese on roughly even terms. With the defence of Australia hanging in the balance, Fletcher moved to confront the oncoming enemy.

This engagement, known as the battle of the Coral Sea, was fought on 7–8 May 1942 and represented a unique turning point in the annals of naval warfare. For the first time, a major naval battle was fought on the open seas without either fleet ever coming into direct contact with the other. Instead, the combatants fought each other through a series of carrier air strikes directed against their opponent's forces. During these attacks the Americans sank the light carrier *Shōhō* and heavily damaged *Shōkaku* while the Japanese sank the large fleet carrier *Lexington*, a destroyer and an oiler and damaged the carrier *Yorktown*. Corresponding aircraft losses amounted to 68 destroyed and 16 damaged for the Americans compared to at least 80 lost to the Japanese.[21] In materiel terms, the battle was a tactical victory for the Japanese as the Americans clearly suffered the heavier warship losses, but it also represented an important strategic victory for the Allies. Alarmed by the determined American opposition, the Japanese abandoned their plans to capture Port Moresby and withdrew their invasion force. Thus, for the first time in the war, the Allies checked an expansionist move by the Japanese. This was almost exclusively an American success, as Admiral Crace's cruiser squadron played no direct part in the battle. Nevertheless, his ships did successfully repel two air attacks during which they destroyed at least four Japanese aircraft.[22]

Undeterred by this setback, the Japanese prepared for a new and bolder operation to solidify their naval supremacy in the Pacific. Provoked by the embarrassing Doolittle Raid, the Naval General Staff approved a plan to seize Midway Island and force the American Pacific Fleet into one final, decisive battle. To carry this out, the Japanese assembled an impressive force consisting of nearly 200 warships and support vessels split into four major fleets and assault groups. The main spearhead of this force was the 1st Carrier Fleet commanded by Vice-Admiral Chūichi Nagumo. This fleet consisted of the large aircraft carriers *Akagi*, *Kaga*, *Hiryū* and *Sōryū*, the battleships *Haruna* and *Kirishima*, three cruisers and 12 destroyers. This was followed by the main Battle Fleet under the command of Admiral Isoroku Yamamoto, who was also the overall commander for the operation. Yamamoto's fleet consisted of the battleships *Yamato*, *Mutsu*, *Nagato*, *Ise*, *Hyūga*, *Fusō* and *Yamashiro*, the light carrier *Hōshō*, three cruisers and 13 destroyers. The Japanese further assigned the battleships *Kongō* and *Hiei*, the light carriers *Zuihō*, *Ryūjō* and *Junyō*, 15 cruisers and 34 destroyers in direct support of their Midway Assault Group and a diversionary Aleutian Assault Group. They rounded out this force with 15 submarines positioned between Midway and Hawaii.

Supremely confident and full of high morale, the Japanese dispatched this seemingly overwhelming force against Midway at the end of May. In the eyes of its leaders and membership, the Imperial Japanese Navy was now poised to fulfill its final destiny against the American Pacific Fleet. The Japanese had good reason for their confidence. They were entering the battle with the largest and most powerful naval force assembled since the British Grand Fleet had engaged the German High Seas Fleet at Jutland some 26 years earlier. By comparison, the Americans could only match a fraction of this power. Still reeling from the heavy damage inflicted at Pearl Harbor, the United States could only muster three aircraft carriers and a couple dozen cruisers and destroyers to confront the massive Japanese force. True, the American carriers had proven their effectiveness during the battle of the Coral Sea, but this had been against an enemy of roughly equal strength. Now they faced an enemy that was overwhelmingly their superior, and there seemed little reason to believe they could prevail against such heavy odds. Even if they managed to trade carrier losses with the Japanese as they had done so in the Coral Sea, this would only ensure a Japanese victory.

Fortunately, the Americans enjoyed one important advantage that would turn the battle decisively in their favour. Unbeknown to the Japanese, the Americans had broken their naval codes and were forewarned of their intentions. As such, the Americans were able to deploy two task forces, consisting of the aircraft carriers *Enterprise*, *Hornet* and *Yorktown*, eight cruisers and 15 destroyers, to the northeast of Midway. Of these carriers, the presence of *Yorktown* was particularly remarkable as American yard workers in Pearl Harbor had performed substantial emergency repairs in just a 48-hour period to make it ready for the battle. When Admiral Nagumo's 1st Carrier Fleet commenced operations against Midway on 4 June, it did so completely unaware of this American naval presence on its flank. Taking advantage of this ignorance, the Americans launched a large carrier air strike that surprised the Japanese and destroyed three of their carriers in quick succession. The fourth carrier, *Hiryū*, immediately counterattacked and launched two strikes that crippled *Yorktown*, but this success was short-lived. A follow-up strike from *Enterprise* soon found and destroyed the troublesome *Hiryū* thus depriving the Japanese of their vaunted air power. As night fell, Admiral Yamamoto reviewed the situation and decided it was too risky to continue the battle. Fearing America's newly won air superiority, he

In June 1942 the United States Navy scored a spectacular victory at Midway that abruptly turned the tide of the Asia/Pacific war. Pictured here is the mangled wreck of the Japanese heavy cruiser *Mikuma* prior to it sinking. (National Museum of the U.S. Navy, public domain)

cancelled the operation and ordered his forces to withdraw. Over the next couple of days American carrier aircraft harried the retreating Japanese and sank the heavy cruiser *Mikuma*. Meanwhile, on the 6th the Japanese submarine *I-168* succeeded in sinking the crippled *Yorktown* and an attending destroyer.

The battle of Midway was a resounding victory for the United States and signalled the primary turning point of the Pacific war. In many respects, this battle was the single most important naval engagement of the entire global conflict and represented the greatest victory in American naval history. In one fell swoop, the United States Navy delivered a staggering blow against the Japanese from which they would never fully recover. With the loss of four fleet carriers along with 253 aircraft and large numbers of highly trained aircrew, maintenance and deck crew personnel, America had irreparably damaged the Imperial Japanese Navy's most effective weapon, its naval air arm.[23] This loss forced the Japanese to abandon the strategic initiative and assume a more defensive posture. As such, the battle effectively signalled the end of largescale Japanese expansion and served as the transition point from which the Allies could successfully move onto the offensive. It also ended once and for all the myth of Japanese invincibility and proved to be a major boost to Allied morale and confidence. Finally, the battle solidified the role of the combat aircraft as the primary weapon in modern naval warfare and designated the aircraft carrier as the principal capital ship within the fleet organisation.

The United States wasted little time in capitalising upon this victory and seizing the initiative. Based upon intelligence reports indicating the construction of a Japanese airfield on the island of Guadalcanal in the eastern Solomon's chain, the Americans promptly resolved to remove this potential threat to their lines of communication with Australia and New Zealand. Accordingly, on 7 August the bulk of the American Pacific Fleet, supported by elements of the Royal Australian Navy, landed the American 1st Marine Division on Guadalcanal and the small neighbouring island complex of Tulagi-Tanambogo-Gavutu. The British Eastern Fleet indirectly supported this operation by conducting a concurrent sweep into the Bay of Bengal as a diversionary effort. While this sweep successfully attracted the attention of various Japanese reconnaissance aircraft, one of which was shot down by FAA fighters, it caused little other discernible reaction. Still, the American invasion of Guadalcanal caught the Japanese completely by surprise, and the landings went in virtually unopposed. The newly landed American marines then advanced against light opposition and within 36 hours captured their main objective, the nearly completed airfield located on the northern end of the island. Thereafter, the Americans renamed their new prize Henderson Field and feverishly began efforts to finish it for use against the Japanese.

Unfortunately, this ease of operation soon ended as the Japanese quickly recovered from their initial surprise and dispatched new forces into the battle area. On 7 August the Japanese 8th Fleet, consisting of five heavy cruisers, two light cruisers and a destroyer, departed Rabaul and proceeded south to engage the American transport fleet off Guadalcanal. Although detected by an American submarine and Australian reconnaissance aircraft, an intelligence breakdown allowed this impending threat to go unreported to the Allied leadership on the scene. On the night of 8/9 August this Japanese force successfully avoided American destroyer screens and surprised an Allied cruiser squadron, commanded by British Rear-Admiral Victor Crutchley, patrolling the waters north of Guadalcanal near Savo Island. Unleashing a deluge of gunfire and torpedoes against the unsuspecting Allied warships, the Japanese quickly destroyed the Australian heavy cruiser *Canberra* and the American heavy cruisers *Astoria*, *Quincy* and *Vincennes* and severely damaged the American cruiser *Chicago* and two American destroyers. The Japanese then withdrew after suffering insignificant damage to themselves. As bad as this debacle was, it could have been far worse. In concentrating their efforts against the Allied warships, the Japanese failed to engage the nearby American transport fleet thus missing their primary target for the operation. Still, the salvation of the transports was of little solace to the local Allied leaders as the Japanese had clearly won a striking victory and demonstrated their resolve to fight for Guadalcanal.

This engagement, known as the battle of Savo Island, was the first shot in what proved to be a long and difficult campaign. Over the next six months the Americans fought tenaciously to retain their tentative hold on Guadalcanal while the Japanese fought equally hard to evict them. During the course of this struggle, the Americans and Japanese fought six major naval battles and numerous minor engagements as both sides attempted to reinforce and support their ground combatants on the island. Carrier forces fought two of these battles in a similar manner to those fought at Coral Sea and Midway. The first was an American victory; the second, a tactical victory for the Japanese. The remaining battles consisted of a series of nocturnal surface engagements fought between various forces ranging in composition from battleships to destroyers. These battles pitted superior American radar technology against superb Japanese night fighting capabilities, and both sides suffered heavy losses. The same was true on Guadalcanal itself, where American marines and later army personnel fought a series of desperate clashes against fanatical Japanese troops bent on recapturing Henderson Field and driving the Americans off the island.

The outcome of this struggle remained in serious question for some time, but America's stubborn retention of Henderson Field eventually tilted the battle permanently in their favour. In February 1943 the Japanese finally ceded defeat and withdrew their remaining forces from the island. In doing so, they ended a campaign that had cost them the battleships *Hiei* and *Kirishima*, the light carrier *Ryūjō*, four cruisers, 11 destroyers, one patrol boat (ex-destroyer), six submarines, 13 transports, 682 aircraft and some 30,343 combatants. American materiel losses were equally high with the destruction of the aircraft carriers *Wasp* and *Hornet*, eight cruisers (including the Australian *Canberra*), 15 destroyers, three fast transports (converted destroyers), one transport and 615 aircraft. Fortunately, American personnel fatalities, at 7,100 including 92 Australians and New Zealanders, were only a fraction of those suffered by the Japanese.[24] Likewise, due to America's vastly superior industrial base, the Americans were far better positioned to replace their materiel losses than were the Japanese. Thus, not only had the Americans achieved their strategic objective for the campaign by eliminating a potential Japanese threat to their lines of communication, but they also facilitated a costly battle of attrition that the Japanese could ill afford to wage.

Nor was this Japan's only misfortune during this period. In Papua New Guinea the Japanese encountered increasingly stiff resistance as they tried to expand their presence on the island. On 21 July Japanese forces landed at Buna and Gona on Papua New Guinea's northeast coast. From there, the Japanese pushed inland to capture Kokoda and its strategically important airfield on 29 July. They then continued southward on an overland trek along the jungle-clad Kokoda Track with the aim of capturing Port Moresby, but their offensive made slow progress against the inhospitable terrain and the stubborn Australian resistance. In particular, two battalions of the Australian 30th Brigade (a militia unit) were able to hold up the Japanese advance in the area between Kokoda and Isurava for a month. While this was underway, the Australians moved reinforcements into the Kokoda area through Port Moresby, which eventually included two brigades (the 21st and 25th) of the veteran 7th Australian Division. On 29 August the navy enjoyed a small victory when the Australian destroyer *Arunta* sank the Japanese submarine *RO33* ten miles southeast of the endangered port. Meanwhile, bolstered by their growing strength, the Australians finally halted the Japanese advance at Ioribaiwa and the Imita Ridge in mid-September. Although less than 20 miles from Port Moresby, the Japanese were now at the end of their logistical endurance. Even more important, with the fighting underway in Guadalcanal, the Japanese decided they could not support both operations and on 24 September began withdrawing forces from their forward positions on the Kokoda front.

In concurrent fighting, on 25 August the Japanese launched a small seaborne assault against the newly established Australian airfield at Milne Bay on the far eastern tip of Papua New Guinea. This assault met strong opposition from two Australian infantry brigades, two Australian artillery units, an American engineer unit and two RAAF Kittyhawk fighter squadrons. For ten days the Australians successfully repulsed every Japanese attempt to capture the airfield. During the battle, they received excellent support from the two Kittyhawk squadrons and other RAAF units that operated against both ground and maritime targets. In one action of particular consequence, RAAF Kittyhawks destroyed seven barges off Goodenough Island that stranded 350 Japanese marines of the 5th Sasebo and prevented them from participating in the battle. These strikes, along with stubborn ground resistance, quickly degraded Japanese resolve to continue the battle, and on 4 September the

Japanese cancelled the operation and began evacuating their forces. In doing so, they left behind 751 dead and missing and brought back 335 wounded.[25] Australian losses amounted to 123 dead and 198 wounded.[26] Although a minor battle compared to the larger contests underway at Guadalcanal and the Kokoda area, Milne Bay represented the first Allied land victory scored against the Japanese during the war.

Meanwhile, seventeen hundred miles to the west the Australians enjoyed success of a different sort with a small commando force on the occupied island of Timor located some 400 miles northwest of Darwin. Primarily built around the 2/2 and 2/4 Independent Companies, this force also included various native and Dutch contingents and eventually attained a peak strength of about 1,000 men. For a period of almost a year, these irregular forces carried out a series of hit and run raids and guerilla operations against the Japanese using the island's mountainous and jungle-covered terrain to conceal their movements. In turn, the RAAF and Royal Australian Navy conducted numerous replenishment sorties to provide logistical support to the isolated commandoes. During one of these operations on 23 September 1942, the Australian destroyer *Voyager* ran aground off Betano Bay and had to be scuttled following bomb damage by Japanese aircraft. A few months later a similar fate fell upon the Australian minesweeper *Armidale* when Japanese aircraft sank it in the same area on 1 December. Yet, despite these losses, the Allies considered the overall campaign a success as the commandoes tied down significant Japanese forces on the island including the 12,000-man 48th Division. By the end of the year Australian authorities decided to wind down the mission, and in January and February 1943, the Australians safely evacuated their remaining forces from Timor thus successfully concluding the operation.

Returning now to Papua New Guinea, on 28 September the 7th Australian Division went onto the offensive to pursue the retreating Japanese on the Kokoda front. Advancing with two brigades, the 16th and 25th, the Australians retraced the route used by the Japanese during their earlier offensive. This was no easy task as the Japanese conducted a measured, fighting retreat while the Australians had to deal with extremely harsh terrain and their own logistical constraints. Over the next six weeks the Australians maintained steady pressure and slowly pushed the Japanese back across the Owen Stanley Mountain Range. On 2 November Australian forces captured Kokoda village and eleven days later reached the Kumusi River after routing a Japanese rearguard in the vicinity of Oivi-Gorari. Up to this point, the Japanese had largely conducted an orderly retreat, but this substantially broke down during this latter action as the Japanese suffered an estimated 600 fatalities including their commander, Major-General Tomitarō Horii, who drowned while attempting to cross the river.[27] Other Japanese losses during this engagement included the abandonment of large amounts of materiel including 15 artillery pieces.

The victory at Oivi-Gorari signalled an end to the Kokoda campaign, but the fighting in eastern Papua New Guinea was far from over. On 15 and 16 November, the Australian 25th and 16th Brigades crossed the Kumusi River at Wairopi and began an advance towards the Japanese beachhead positions in the Buna-Gona area. In this, they were joined by the American 32nd Division, which had flown into a newly established airfield on the northeast side of Papua and was advancing on Buna from the southeast along the coast. Upon reaching their objectives, the Allies encountered strong resistance from a force of roughly 11,000 Japanese defenders. This quickly turned into a protracted battle of annihilation as the Allies had to overcome a succession of strongly-held Japanese positions. Even with the influx of substantial Allied reinforcements, which included the arrival of four additional Australian brigades (the 18th, 21st, 30th and 14th) and a squadron of Australian M3 Stuart light tanks, it took over two months of heavy fighting for the Allies to fully secure the area. In the process, they destroyed most of the Japanese defenders, although a few thousand eventually escaped to the west. By the end of January 1943, the Allies controlled all of eastern Papua New Guinea having inflicted an estimated 12,000 fatalities upon the Japanese during the previous six months of fighting with another 350 taken prisoner. Their own losses in attaining this victory amounted to 5,698 Australian and 2,848 American casualties of which 2,165 and 930 were killed respectively.[28]

After Midway, the Allies secured the strategic initiative by scoring follow-up victories at Guadalcanal and Papua New Guinea. Pictured here are Australian forces assaulting a Japanese position at Buna. (Australian War Memorial, copyright expired, public domain, image 014001)

With this triumph and their roughly concurrent victory on Guadalcanal, the Allies took a brief pause to consolidate their positions and take stock of the situation. In doing so, they had great cause for satisfaction. In the spring of 1942, Japan had been at the zenith of its power having amassed a great empire in a short period of time and inflicted an unprecedented series of defeats upon the British Empire and the United States. To many observers, this string of Japanese victories seemed likely to continue. Nevertheless, in a few short months the Allies had completely reversed this trend. The abruptness of this turnaround was nothing short of miraculous. Prior to the war Admiral Yamamoto had guaranteed Japanese victories for the first six months to a year of the conflict with no certainty of success after that. As it was, this prediction proved overly optimistic since Japan's string of victories ran out after only four and a half months. This reversal began modestly with the Doolittle Raid, Britain's preemptive seizure of Madagascar and America's strategic victory in the Coral Sea, but it was the battle of Midway that finally turned the fortunes of war decisively against Japan. After Midway, the Japanese suffered two long and debilitating defeats in the Solomons and Papua New Guinea. These defeats solidified Japan's reversal and put them firmly on the defensive. Although much heavy fighting remained ahead, the course of the Pacific war had unalterably shifted in favour of the Allies, and Japan's future prospects were increasingly bleak.

CHAPTER 6

Commonwealth Contributions in the South Pacific

By the spring of 1943 Japan found itself ensnared in a trap of largely its own design. In 1941 Japan had entered the war with the objective of attaining quick, decisive victory that would force the Allies to accept a negotiated settlement favourable to Japan's imperial ambitions. After a series of unexpected defeats in 1942, the possibility of this outcome was definitively shattered, and the Japanese found themselves embroiled in a prolonged total war that they were hopelessly ill-equipped to wage. This was a conflict in which the Japanese had no prospect of matching the immense power that the United States and British Commonwealth could ultimately employ against them. As such, the impetus behind Japan's overall war effort changed from attaining victory to fending off defeat. In this, the Japanese were now in the unenviable position of having to secure their newly attained empire and the essential natural resources it provided against an enemy that would only get stronger with time. At stake was not only the retention of this empire, but also the survival of the Japanese regime.

Nor could the Japanese expect any decisive relief from their Axis cohorts, who had suffered their own series of reversals during this period. On the Eastern Front against the Soviet Union, the major Axis offensive in the Caucasus was reversed by Russian counterattacks that trapped the German Sixth Army in the city of Stalingrad. When this embattled army finally surrendered at the end of January 1943, some 91,000 German soldiers went into captivity while another 160,000 were left dead in the ruins of the devastated city. Unfortunately for the Germans, this prominent disaster only represented a small portion of their overall losses on the Eastern Front, which in 1942 totalled 1,080,950 casualties.[1] Concurrent Soviet losses were substantially higher, but the Russians were far better positioned to absorb these losses than were the Germans. Meanwhile, in North Africa the British Eighth Army halted and then repulsed the German-Italian Panzerarmee at El Alamein in Egypt while an Anglo-American army landed in French North Africa to confront an improvised Axis force in Tunisia. The resolution of these operations would take a little longer than at Stalingrad, but the final result was equally pronounced—the destruction of all Axis forces in North Africa by May 1943 including the seizure of more than 300,000 prisoners.[2] In turn, these actions culminated a campaign in Africa that had lasted almost three years and cost the Axis some 950,000 casualties, 2.4 million tons of shipping, 8,000 aircraft, 2,500 tanks, 6,200 guns and 70,000 trucks.[3]

The situation was much the same in the naval conflict. In the last half of 1942 and first four months of 1943 the struggle in the Atlantic intensified in both scope and ferocity. This was increasingly a battle of brute force against brute force as the expanding German U-boat arm was able to dispatch 50 to 70 U-boats into the Atlantic each month to prey upon transiting Allied convoys. During this period the Allies lost 674 merchant ships worth 3,812,676 tons in the North Atlantic.[4] Despite these heavy losses, the entry of the United States into the war brought an additional 10 million tons of merchant shipping into the Allied shipping pool while American and British shipyards produced a further 5.4 and 1.3 million tons respectively in 1942 alone.[5] As such, Germany's quest to cause appreciable harm to the Allied merchant fleet quickly became unattainable. Meanwhile, in the ten-month period culminating in April 1943 the Germans lost a total of 121 U-boats of which the vast majority were sunk by British forces. In May the situation came to a head when the Germans lost a record 40 U-boats during the month against only 34 Allied merchant ships worth 163,507 tons sunk in the North Atlantic.[6] Even with their expanded U-boat force, the Germans could not afford this exchange rate, and at the end of May they temporarily suspended the majority of their U-boat operations in the North Atlantic. The Germans would never again regain the initiative, and their U-boat activities thereafter would only garner minimal successes against heavy losses to themselves.

Moving now to the skies over Europe, throughout 1942 the British strategic bombing offensive grew in size and intensity as German cities came under increasing attack. Many of these raids were carried out by between 100 and 300 bombers, and in May 1942 the Royal Air Force conducted its first 1,000-bomber raid. In 1943 the United States Army Air Force joined this offensive thus subjecting Germany to round the clock bombing. Meanwhile, in 1942 British interdiction efforts resulted in the loss of over 350 German and German-affiliated commercial and military vessels in the waters off Northwest Europe with this rate of destruction continuing into the new year.[7] Together, these various activities took a modest, but growing toll on German economic output and increasingly forced the Germans to divert valuable resources to defensive applications to counter these attacks. In just one example of the former, in 1942 Ruhr crude steel production was down 16.06 percent compared to 1939 levels, and this output would decline a further 12.41 percent by 1944.[8] Meanwhile, in terms of the latter, in November 1943 the Germans had a staggering 1,002,695 service personnel manning some 39,200 assorted anti-aircraft guns positioned in Germany and Northwest Europe to counter the Allied air offensive.[9]

Against this ongoing erosion of German resources, Allied strength during this period progressively increased. With each passing month, growing numbers of men and materiel arrived in Britain and the Middle East from the United States and to a lesser extent Canada where they joined the ranks of British forces that had reached the zenith of Britain's mobilisation effort. This build-up would eventually bring the Western Allies back onto the European mainland starting first with operations in the Mediterranean to drive Italy out of the war followed by landings in both northern and southern France to liberate that country and provide a base of operations for subsequent advances into Germany itself. Eventually, the Western Allies would commit over 100 divisions to these various undertakings supported by tens of thousands of tanks and artillery pieces and vast armadas of ships and aircraft. Facing the prospect of a multi-front war, there was little the Germans could do to impede this build-up or regain the initiative other than make preparations to blunt these blows once they occurred.

Given these many events, it was clear that the tide of war had decisively turned against the Axis everywhere bringing truth to Churchill's confident prediction regarding the grand breakdown of the competing powers once the United States entered the conflict (see Chapter 4). Nevertheless, much heavy fighting remained ahead. This harsh reality was certainly true in the Pacific where the Japanese had established a formidable defence in depth using the vast expanses of the ocean and a variety of outlying, fortified island chains to protect their home islands and the inner core of their fledgling empire from Allied intrusion. To counter this, the Allies embarked upon a strategy to progressively break down these outer barriers along two major avenues of advance. The first of these was already underway in the Southwest Pacific where General MacArthur proposed to proceed through key portions of the Solomon Islands, Papua New Guinea and the Bismarck Archipelago. The second avenue of advance would occur in the central Pacific under the command of American Admiral Chester Nimitz targeting the Gilbert, Marshall and Mariana Islands. Given the need to build up resources, it would be a number of months before the Allies commenced this second advance.

As had been the case during the first year of the Pacific conflict, the United States served as the primary participant in these various advances, but the Commonwealth nations also made ongoing contributions to the efforts. During the latter part of 1942 and well into 1943, various Australian and New Zealand warships and auxiliaries participated in and covered numerous supply and reinforcement missions throughout the South Pacific. While this was generally mundane and unglamorous duty, it nevertheless represented a vital contribution to the Allied war effort in the area. Meanwhile, the RAAF, under the operational command of Air Vice Marshal William Bostock, played an equally important interdiction role against Japanese lines of communication. Operating from various bases in Australia and Papua New Guinea, the RAAF carried out numerous strikes against Japanese maritime traffic, port facilities, airfields and logistical centres throughout the region. In terms of the former, typical targets included barges, coasters and other minor vessels, but occasionally, RAAF aircraft were able to score against more substantial prey. An example of this occurred on 22 July 1942 when a RAAF Hudson joined American aircraft in destroying the 9,788-ton Japanese merchant ship *Ayatosan Maru* off Buna, Papua New Guinea.[10] Later, on 11 September a force of RAAF Hudsons and American B-17 bombers attacked and sank the Japanese destroyer *Yayoi* off Vakuta Island.[11] On 24 November RAAF Beaufighters and Beauforts participated in an American strike that sank the destroyer *Hayashio* in Huon Gulf.[12] Finally, on 7 January 1943 a RAAF Catalina sank the 5,447-ton Japanese merchant ship *Nichiryu Maru* off New Britain.[13]

While limited in scale, these successes served as a precursor to a far more substantial victory in the Bismarck Sea a few months later. On 28 February 1943 the Japanese, alarmed by their recent reversals in Papua New Guinea, dispatched a large troop convoy from Rabaul to Lae. This convoy carried some 6,900 men from the 51st Division on eight transports and eight supporting destroyers. Augmenting this force were about 100 shore-based fighters that were assigned to provide aerial protection to the convoy from airfields along its route. On 1 March an Allied reconnaissance aircraft discovered the convoy northeast of the Dampier Strait, and Allied aircraft commenced efforts to attack it the next day. Part of this included a raid by RAAF A-20 Boston bombers from No. 22 Squadron that targeted the Japanese airfield at Lae to suppress aerial opposition while American B-17s launched a series of strikes against the convoy itself. During these latter attacks, the American bombers sank one of the Japanese transports and damaged two others.

That night RAAF Catalina aircraft maintained contact with the convoy, and the next day, 3 March, the Allies launched an all-out aerial assault against the Japanese force. Once again, the battle began with the dispatch of 22 RAAF Boston bombers to attack Lae and suppress Japanese fighter opposition. Similar attacks continued throughout the day. Meanwhile, a force of some 90 Allied aircraft departed the Port Moresby area to attack the convoy itself. Thirteen RAAF Beaufighters from No. 30 Squadron led this latter assault and strafed the Japanese ships to suppress return anti-aircraft fire. One of the merchant ships, probably the 6,869-ton *Teiyo Maru*, exploded in flames under the Beaufighters' heavy cannon and machine-gun fire while other ships were rendered impotent.[14] Immediately behind this came an assorted force of American B-17, B-25 and A-20 bombers that attacked the convoy and scored numerous bomb hits on various vessels. The onslaught continued that afternoon and into the next day as successive waves of Allied aircraft attacked the hapless Japanese ships. This included five RAAF Bostons from No. 22 Squadron that attacked and scored at least two bomb hits and many near misses on the Japanese destroyer *Tokitsukaze*, which later sank.[15]

By the evening of the 4th the battle was all but over. In three days of air strikes, the Allies had destroyed all eight transports totalling 37,335 tons and four of the attending destroyers.[16] Of the nearly 9,000 Japanese army and naval personnel on board these vessels, 2,890 were killed and only scattered groups of survivors ever reached Papua New Guinea.[17] Like at the Coral Sea and Midway, the battle of the Bismarck Sea proved to be another monumental event in the annals of aviation and maritime history. For the first time, air power had completely destroyed a major reinforcement effort at sea. Prior to this, many Allied and Axis convoys had suffered heavy losses due to air attacks, and some had even turned back in the face of heavy aerial opposition, but none had suffered anything approaching the utter devastation inflicted upon the Japanese during this engagement. With the destruction of these 12 ships, the USAAF and RAAF had all but annihilated the Japanese convoy and severely weakened Japan's strategic position within the region. Allied losses in attaining this great success were minimal at just six aircraft destroyed and four more heavily damaged.

While this battle represented a spectacular victory, the RAAF soon introduced a new, less dramatic weapon that would become far more indicative of its anti-shipping efforts. In April the Allies determined that the Japanese were about to establish a new fleet anchorage at Kavieng on the northern coast of New Ireland. The RAAF quickly moved to counter this threat and commenced an aerial mining campaign to render the potential anchorage unusable. Beginning on 22 April 1943 and continuing for seven months, RAAF PBY-5 Catalina aircraft carried out a series of missions during which they laid a total of 104 mines in and around the approaches to Kavieng. American submarines further augmented this effort by laying 24 moored mines in the same area. Together, these mines sank five ships worth 8,233 tons and damaged seven more worth an estimated 20,701 tons.[18] Of these, at least three of the sunk vessels, the merchant ships *Seikai Maru* and *Ryuosan Maru* (2,663 and 2,455 tons respectively) and the 1,400-ton armed survey ship *Tsukushi*, were lost to Australian-laid mines.[19] These losses eventually persuaded the Japanese to abandon their plans for Kavieng and helped prompt the Australians to expand their aerial minelaying campaign. Through the remainder of the year the RAAF laid hundreds of additional mines in 14 different locations around Papua New Guinea, Celebes and the surrounding areas. These mines sank a number of Japanese vessels including the 2,913-ton merchant ship *Mie Maru* and the minesweeper *W16* and forced the Japanese to restrict their maritime traffic throughout the region.[20]

Beyond these offensive applications, the RAAF also made strides in protecting their own lines of communication. An example of this was the defence of Darwin, which was an important logistical centre located in northern Australia. Initially bombed by Japanese carrier aircraft in February 1942, Darwin and the surrounding area now sustained regular raids from Japanese land-based bombers operating out of Timor and

Table 6.1. Characteristics of Select RAAF, RNZAF and RAF Aircraft in the Pacific/Asian War.

	Roles	Top speed (mph)	Range (miles)	Maximum ordnance load (lbs)
Hawker Hurricane II	Fighter, fighter-bomber	339	460	500
Curtiss P-40 Kittyhawk	Fighter, fighter-bomber	354	850	700
Supermarine Spitfire V	Fighter, fighter-bomber	374	470	500
Supermarine Spitfire VIII	Fighter, fighter-bomber	404	660	500
Lockheed Hudson	Reconnaissance, Strike	246	1,500	750
Douglas Boston	Light bomber	304	1,020	2,000
Bristol Beaufighter	Night fighter, strike	330	1,470	2,127
Consolidated PBY Catalina	Patrol, minelaying, strike	175	2,350	4,000
Consolidated B-24 Liberator	Heavy bomber, minelaying	303	2,850	8,000

some of the surrounding islands. To counter this, in January 1943 the Australians deployed three squadrons of Spitfires (two RAAF and one RAF) to bolster Darwin's defence. Over the next several months these fighters fought a series of engagements with intruding Japanese aircraft. Of particular consequence was a large battle fought on 20 June when Darwin's Spitfires claimed nine Japanese bombers and five fighters shot down for the loss of two of their own number. By summer's end the Japanese ceased their daylight incursions, and the threat to Darwin subsided. In all, Darwin's Australian and British defenders claimed 63 Japanese aircraft destroyed and 13 more probably destroyed during this period against the loss of 17 Spitfires destroyed in combat and 27 more written off due to operational causes.[21]

While this was underway, the Allies resumed their offensive in the Solomon Islands. Beginning with unopposed landings on the Russell Islands on 21 February, American naval and ground forces conducted a series of amphibious operations that slowly worked their way up the Solomon's chain culminating in landings on Bougainville in November. These undertakings were overwhelmingly American affairs, but there were some Commonwealth contributions. This included forward-deployed Australian and New Zealand Coastwatchers, which provided intelligence regarding Japanese movements. More directly, New Zealand naval and air units participated in peripheral fighting in and around the area. On 29 January the New Zealand minesweepers *Kiwi* and *Moa* sank the Japanese submarine *I-1* off Kamimbo Bay on the northwest coast of Guadalcanal. Seven months later the New Zealand minesweeper *Tui*, with assistance from American aircraft, scored a similar success in sinking the Japanese submarine *I-17* off Espiritu Santo on 19 August. Meanwhile, from April 1943 through February 1944, five Royal New Zealand Air Force (RNZAF) squadrons armed with American-built P-40 Kittyhawk fighters operated from Guadalcanal and other nearby locations on a rotating basis claiming the destruction of 99 Japanese aircraft and a number of barges and other minor craft within the area. On 8 May No. 15 squadron scored a particularly notable success when it participated in a combined strike along with American aircraft against three Japanese destroyers stranded in a minefield off Rendova Island. During this operation the New Zealand fighters strafed the stricken Japanese vessels to suppress their anti-aircraft fire while the American dive-bombers attacked them with 1,000-pound bombs. Together, this assault resulted in the destruction of two of the destroyers, *Oyashio* and *Kagero*.[22]

Nor were minesweepers and aircraft the only New Zealand assets to inflict damage against the Japanese during this period. In July the New Zealand light cruiser *Leander* was assigned to Task Force 36.1 consisting of the American cruisers *Honolulu* and *St. Louis* and ten American destroyers. On the night of 12/13 July 1943 this force intercepted a Japanese squadron consisting of the light cruiser *Jintsū* (flagship) and nine destroyers off Kolombangara on a reinforcement mission to Vila. The Japanese were first off the mark and began launching torpedoes at the Allied warships at 0108 hours. The American destroyers immediately followed suit, and at 0112 hours the Allied cruisers commenced firing. The Allied cruisers concentrated their fire on the Japanese flagship, and within a few minutes the hapless *Jintsū* was literally shot to pieces by the incoming barrage of 6-inch shells. *Jintsū* later broke in half and sank at 0145 hours along with most of its crew. *Leander*'s contribution to this action included the firing of several gun salvos plus the launching of four torpedoes. Unfortunately, this success came at a heavy price. At 0122 hours a torpedo struck *Leander* causing serious damage that prompted the New Zealand cruiser to withdraw from the battle area. A short time later the Japanese launched a follow-up torpedo attack that damaged both American cruisers and sank the American destroyer *Gwin*. Thereafter, both sides disengaged, and what later became known as the battle of Kolombangara abruptly ended.

In reviewing *Leander*'s role during this engagement, the New Zealand warship helped sink the Japanese cruiser *Jintsū* but sustained heavy damage in return that would take over a year to repair. This damage, plus a long refit afterwards, effectively ended *Leander*'s wartime career. Likewise, 26 members of the ship's crew, which consisted of a mixture of both British and New Zealand personnel, were killed while several others sustained injuries. Among the latter was the ship's executive officer, Commander Stephen Roskill RN, who was wounded in the leg. Despite his injury, Commander Roskill remained on duty for several hours directing the damage control efforts and played an important role in saving the ship. He would later receive a DSC for his performance during the action. After the war, Roskill became a renowned naval historian and author. His greatest work was the four-volume official British history of the maritime conflict during World War II entitled *The War at Sea 1939–1945*, which is often cited in this book.

Beyond the contributions made by the Royal New Zealand Navy, a major British warship also played a small part in the Solomon Islands campaign. In October 1942 the American Chiefs of Staff requested the use of a British aircraft carrier to help rectify recent American carrier losses in the Pacific. During the previous six months the United States had lost four aircraft carriers, *Lexington*, *Yorktown*, *Wasp* and *Hornet*, while a fifth, *Enterprise*, was temporarily out of service due to battle damage. New aircraft carriers were under construction, but until these started to arrive, this left the American Pacific Fleet with just a single carrier, *Saratoga*, immediately available for use. American authorities ascertained that without additional carrier support, they might have to cancel or delay some of their offensive plans scheduled in the Pacific for 1943. Although the Royal Navy was already heavily committed in the Mediterranean, Atlantic and Indian Oceans, which included a pending invasion of French North Africa scheduled for November, Churchill and the Admiralty altruistically agreed to support this American request.

In December the aircraft carrier *Victorious* detached from the Home Fleet and proceeded to the Pacific. After an intermediate stop at Norfolk for equipment upgrades and to receive new American-built aircraft, *Victorious* arrived at Pearl Harbor in March 1943 where it continued its familiarisation with American operating procedures. In May *Victorious* joined the American aircraft carrier *Saratoga* to form Task Group 36.3. One month later on 27 June this task group served as the covering force for the American invasion of New Georgia, which was part of Operation *Cartwheel*. For this undertaking, the Allies cross-decked their squadrons so that most of the fighters (British and American) operated from *Victorious* while the strike aircraft operated from *Saratoga*. For 28 days *Victorious* stayed on station and flew 614 sorties in support of the American invasion.[23] Disappointingly given the substantial preparations involved, Japanese opposition was limited, and Task Group 36.3's aircraft saw little action other than the destruction of a single Japanese flying boat. This less than dramatic debut proved to be *Victorious'* only contribution to the campaign. The introduction of new *Essex*- and *Independence*-class aircraft carriers to the American Pacific Fleet at the end of July (which was ahead of schedule) rendered *Victorious'* continued service unnecessary, and the British carrier departed the Pacific shortly thereafter to safely return home in September.

Although *Victorious'* participation in the Solomon Islands campaign was limited, it heralded to a day when the Royal Navy would once again return to the Pacific conflict in a consequential way. In the meantime, the Commonwealth nations continued to shoulder the burden as the near-exclusive 'British' contributors to the theatre-wide war effort. In this, they encountered plenty of action to keep them occupied. During the latter half of 1943 and continuing on for the remainder of the war, the conflict in the Pacific grew in size and intensity as the various Allied offensives and campaigns gained momentum and progressively encroached upon Japan's territorial, security and economic interests. From the Aleutian Islands in the north to the jungles of Papua New Guinea in the south, the Allies increasingly seized the initiative and steadily pushed the Japanese back towards their home

Although the Solomons campaign was predominantly an American affair, a number of British/ Commonwealth air and naval units also participated. Pictured here are American pilots from squadron VF-6 aboard the British aircraft carrier *Victorious*. (U.S. Navy, public domain)

islands while concurrently subjecting them to ever-increasing blockade and bombing interdiction. Undoubtedly, this onslaught remained predominately an American affair, but various Commonwealth formations provided significant support to these efforts thus contributing to the ongoing success.

Of these various impacts, none was more important than the provision of ground forces to the Allied cause. In this, Australia was by far the biggest contributor providing a significant, and often prevailing, portion of the ground forces involved in the re-conquest of Papua New Guinea and the final securing of the Bismarck Archipelago and Bougainville. Included in these endeavours were a total of six Australian divisions (the 3rd, 5th, 6th, 7th, 9th and 11th) along with several lesser units that saw action in these areas. Invariably, this fighting took place against a tenacious enemy under conditions of extreme hardship as the units involved had to contend with treacherous terrain, disease-ridden surroundings and primitive or non-existent infrastructure. Similarly, as the fighting progressed, these operations were increasingly overshadowed by concurrent American efforts that reduced the Australian areas to strategic backwaters in the grand scheme of the Pacific conflict. Still, despite these many adversities, the engaged Australian units diligently persevered in their assigned missions.

Shepherding these efforts was General Thomas Blamey, a tried and accomplished leader who was the Commander-in-Chief of the Australian Military Forces and the commander of Allied Land Forces SWPA. Born in 1884 in New South Wales, Blamey entered the Australian army in 1906 as a lieutenant and later attended the British Staff College in Quetta, India in 1912. During World War I Blamey saw service in Gallipoli and on the Western Front eventually attaining the rank of brigadier general. He left the permanent military forces during the interwar years but continued to serve in the militia. At the onset of World War II, Blamey was promoted to lieutenant-general and appointed commander of the 6th Australian Division followed by that of the 2nd AIF, which deployed to the Middle East and saw action in North Africa, Greece and Syria. With the onset of the Pacific conflict, Blamey (now a full general) was recalled home and assigned the roles described above. In this capacity, he effectively cooperated with General MacArthur, the Supreme Allied Commander SWPA despite the latter's propensity to be overbearing, but his relationships with other Australian military and political leaders could be strained. As a commander, Blamey was a competent administrator and tactician who regularly incorporated new technical innovations and concepts into his operational planning and took many prudent steps to mitigate disease and other hardships experienced by his troops. Finally, despite his vast responsibilities, Blamey would directly intervene in battlefield matters when necessary and could bring prudent leadership to difficult situations.

With the conclusion of their successful defence and expulsion of Japanese forces from eastern Papua, the Australians embarked upon an extended campaign to capture northern New Guinea and neutralise all Japanese forces located there. The first major step in this process was the successful defence of Wau in late January and early February 1943. Alarmed by the growing threat that Australian forces presented to their control of Lae and other positions south of the Huon Peninsula and hoping to open a new drive towards Port Moresby, the Japanese opted to launch an assault against the Australian outpost of Wau located some 30 miles southwest of Salamaua. On 6 January the Japanese dispatched a convoy from Rabaul to Lae containing the 102nd Infantry Regiment and other units to facilitate this move. Forewarned of this deployment through signal intercepts, Allied aircraft attacked the convoy resulting in the destruction of the 5,447-ton transport *Nichiryu Maru* by a RAAF Catalina aircraft as mentioned earlier in the chapter, but the rest of the convoy made it through to disembark some 4,000 men at Lae on the 7th. From there, about 2,500 of these men moved down the coast in barges to Salamaua and then proceeded inland to carry out their assault against Wau.

While this was underway, the Allies prepared to meet the attack. Upon learning of the Japanese convoy movement, General Blamey correctly surmised that Wau was the ultimate target and ordered the Australian 17th Brigade to reinforce the outpost's small garrison. Utilising Dakota transport aircraft from the American

374th and 317th Troop Carrier Groups, the Allies flew in three battalions of the 17th Brigade along with various supporting arms including two 25-pounder artillery pieces thus bringing the Australian force in Wau to 201 officers and 2,965 other ranks by 1 February.[24] Even as these troops were arriving at the end of January, the fighting around Wau began with preliminary engagements on the 28th and 29th followed by a major Japanese assault on the 30th. Initially, the Australians were forced to give some ground, but their positions substantially firmed up with the arrival of the 25-pounder guns and the timely support of RAAF aircraft. Fighting continued for the next several days, but the intensity of the Japanese assaults declined in the face of the ever-increasing Australian firepower, and the Australians increasingly assumed the initiative. In the final phase of the battle Australian forces began systematically reducing the Japanese positions around Wau, and on 8 and 9 February the Japanese executed a full retreat from the area. In doing so, they left behind at least 753 dead as counted by the Australians with further undocumented losses probably bringing this fatality total up to around 1,200. Australian casualties in return, which included those suffered by the garrison before the battle, numbered 30 officers and 319 other ranks.[25]

With Wau now secured, the Australians used it as a base for the next step in their offensive, the capture of Salamaua and Lae. Beginning in April, this would be a substantially larger and more protracted campaign eventually involving four Australian and one American divisions as well as several lesser units. Initially, this fighting centred upon the Australian 3rd Division, which operated from Wau and engaged in a series of battles at Mubo, the Bobdubi Ridge and other areas to slowly erode the Japanese defences around Salamaua. In this, they were aided by the American 162nd Regimental Combat Team, which landed unopposed at Nassua Bay south of Salamaua at the end of June and began an advance up the coast. Despite these efforts, progress was slow against the determined Japanese resistance, and in August the Australian 5th Division relieved the 3rd in the area battle. Still, even as the Japanese continued to hold out, their forces sustained continuing losses, and in early September the Australians made key penetrations in the final Japanese defensive line before Salamaua.

Concurrent with these latter actions, the Allies made moves in the north that rendered the entire Japanese position in the region untenable. On 4 September the American VII Amphibious Force landed the Australian 9th Division near Malahang east of Lae. This action constituted the first major amphibious landing carried out by Australian forces since their ill-fated expedition to Gallipoli some 28 years earlier. The next day an American parachute regiment carried out an unopposed airborne assault at Nadzab some 30 miles to the west. Securing the local airfield, the Allies then flew in the Australian 7th Division thus forming a pincer to envelope Lae. Having sent many of their reserves south to defend Salamaua, the Japanese lacked sufficient forces to counter these assaults and realised that their position in the region was now hopelessly compromised. Accordingly, on 8 September the Japanese began a phased withdrawal from the area abandoning both Salamaua and Lae in the succeeding days. Although hampered by difficult terrain and rearguard actions, the Australians secured Salamaua and Lae on 11 and 16 September respectively. Thereafter, the Allies turned Lae into a major base for future operations, but Salamaua was found to be too badly damaged to be of much use. Meanwhile, the bulk of the Japanese forces escaped northward, but they left behind substantial losses including at least 2,722 dead from the fighting around Salamaua through August. Australian authorities later estimated that total Japanese casualties for the campaign amounted to over 10,000. Corresponding Australian losses amounted to 546 dead and 1,277 wounded while the American 162nd Regimental Combat Team suffered a further 81 killed and 396 wounded.[26]

Having captured Lae ahead of their original timetable, the Allies next moved to clear the Huon Peninsula. A key to this was the capture of Finschhafen, a town located some 50 miles east of Lae on the tip of the peninsula. On 22 September the 20th Brigade of the Australian 9th Division made an amphibious landing at the mouth of the Song River six miles north of Finschhafen. Unlike the unopposed

In 1943 Australian forces (with some American participation) conducted a series of operations to secure Lae and the Huon Peninsula in Papua New Guinea. Pictured here is the Japanese merchant ship *Myoko Maru* beached near Lae. (Australian Department of Information, public domain)

landing carried out a few weeks earlier at Malahang, this landing encountered stiff opposition on the beach, but the Australians still managed to take their initial objectives and land some 5,300 troops, 180 vehicles, 32 guns and 850 tons of stores by day's end. The cost in attaining this success was 20 killed, nine missing and 65 wounded.[27] From there, the Australians set out for Finschhafen, which they captured on 2 October. Meanwhile, a separate Australian battalion cleared the coastal area south of Finschhafen having advanced overland from Lae. On 4 October the Allies began operating aircraft from the Finschhafen airfield thus fulfilling the primary objective for the operation.

However, this success soon garnered a strong Japanese response. Intent on recapturing Finschhafen, the core of the Japanese 20th Division moved into the area from Madang to launch a counter-attack. Concentrating their forces in the area around Sattelberg, the Japanese eventually gathered some 6,200 men to carry out this attack. Fortunately, Allied intelligence learned of these moves, and the Australians brought in the 24th Brigade to reinforce the 20th. On 16 October the attack commenced, and over the next four days the Japanese made some inroads against the Australian positions including the splitting of the 24th and 20th Brigades at Siki Cove, but the abundance of Australian firepower repeatedly stymied their attempts to attain decisive results. Then with the arrival of the Australian 26th Brigade and a squadron of Matilda tanks on the night of 19/20 October, the balance of power substantially shifted in favour of the Australians. On the 21st the Japanese withdrew from Siki Cove, and four days later they called off their offensive withdrawing their forces back to Sattelberg. During the battle, the Japanese suffered at least 679 dead as counted by the Australians with their total casualties estimated at 1,500. Australian casualties in return numbered 228 including 49 killed.[28]

After this, the Allies continued their efforts to clear the Huon Peninsula. There were several components to this. In the middle of November, the Australian 26th Brigade fought a difficult battle to capture Sattelberg, which was a highly defensible position and not finally secured until the 25th following a five-day Allied bombardment. Thereafter, the 26th and 24th Brigades began a northward advance and secured an area between Wareo and Gusika in early December. The recently arrived Australian 4th Brigade then began an advance up the coast reaching Fortification Point on 20 December. From there, the 20th Brigade took over the advance with the 26th Brigade covering its inland flank. At this point in the campaign, Japanese resolve substantially collapsed, and the Australians were able to make speedy and extended advances against minimal opposition. Assisting them in this process was a landing on Long Island by American and Australian forces followed by a second American landing at Saidor farther to the west. These actions convinced the Japanese to abandon the Huon Peninsula, and Australian forces captured Sio on 15 January 1944. Although mopping up operations would continue for another two months, the major fighting on the peninsula was now over. Japanese losses for the battle included

3,099 counted dead, 38 captured and an estimated 4,000 to 5,000 further killed or wounded. Casualties for the Australian 9th Division amounted to 283 killed, one missing and 744 wounded during the period of 2 October 1943 through 15 January 1944.[29]

Closing out this phase of the New Guinea campaign was a series of battles to clear the inland territory south of the Huon Peninsula and the coastal strip from Sio to Mandang. Following the capture of Lae in September, the Australian 7th Division embarked upon a largely unopposed overland advance through the Markham and Ramu valleys to Dumpu some 100 miles away. Using aerial resupply as their primary means of logistical support, the Australians then shifted their advance northward towards the sea where they finally encountered strong resistance from Japanese forces on the mountains of the Finisterre Range. From October through January the division fought a series of battles to clear the range. Of particular consequence was a month-long struggle to secure the Shaggy Ridge and the nearby Kankiryo Saddle. At the end of January, the Australians finally took possession of these features thus forcing the Japanese to withdraw. Thereafter, 7th Division paused to consolidate its positions and bring up supplies, although it continued to send patrols forward to probe towards Bogadjim and the coast.

Meanwhile, operations continued in the north and east. On 21 January the 5th Australian Division relieved the 9th Division on the Huon Peninsula and immediately dispatched its 8th Brigade to clear the area between Sio and Saidor. In the process of carrying this out, 8th Brigade killed 734 Japanese, found 1,793 more dead and took 48 prisoners through the end of February. Its own losses during this period amounted to three killed and five wounded.[30] While this was underway, elements of the American 32nd Division began an advance from Saidor towards Mandang supported by the landing of two battalions at Yalau Plantation on 5 March. Over the next few weeks, these American forces made tentative advances while units of the Australian 7th Division continued to fan out from the Finisterre area. Finally, on 8 April the Australian 11th Division relieved the 7th Division and launched a concerted push using the 15th Brigade towards Bogadjim. Proceeding along various avenues of advance, the Australians encountered some resistance but made steady progress entering Bogadjim on the 13th. Then with the arrival of a battalion from the 8th Brigade, which was shipped in from Saidor, the Australians pushed northward with a combined force from both brigades and captured Mandang on the 24th. With this, the Allies secured their hold on the Huon Peninsula and culminated an impressive series of victories that cost the Japanese an estimated 35,000 men since the end of January 1943. Corresponding Australian casualties since the beginning of the offensive against Salamaua and Lae amounted to 1,231 dead and 2,867 wounded.[31]

Nor were the Australians the only Commonwealth contributors to the theatre ground fighting. In late 1943 and early 1944 elements of the New Zealand 3rd Division carried out a series of amphibious landings and mopping up operations in conjunction with American forces to seize or secure some of the minor islands in the Solomon's chain. On 18 September some 3,700 men of the New Zealand 14th Brigade landed to secure the northern part of Vella Lavella Island, which the Americans needed for the establishment of a radar station and naval base. Over a three-week period, the New Zealanders carried out this task declaring the area clear on 9 October. In the process, they accounted for between 200 and 300 Japanese dead for a loss to themselves of 31 killed and 32 wounded. The 3rd Division followed this up with landings by its 8th Brigade to seize the Treasury Islands located some 30 miles south of Bougainville. Augmented by American supporting units, the New Zealanders completed their capture of the islands on 12 November having accounted for 223 confirmed Japanese dead and eight prisoners for a cost of 40 New Zealand and 12 American dead and 145 New Zealand and 29 American wounded. Then, on 15 February the 14th Brigade landed on the Green Islands, a small coral atoll located between Rabaul and Buka. Supported again by the Americans, the brigade secured the atoll on 27 February along with 120 Japanese dead for the cost of ten New Zealand and three American dead and 21 New Zealand and three American wounded.[32] Finally, in a wholly unrelated operation, on 15 August 1943 a reinforced Canadian infantry brigade participated in an American invasion of Kiska Island in the Aleutians. However, this operation proved to be somewhat inconsequential as the Japanese had already abandoned the island by the time the Allies landed.

Augmenting these ground operations were a number of Commonwealth ships that served alongside the United States Navy during this period. While most of these were minor combatants or support vessels, this included a handful of major surface warships. Amongst these, during the latter half of 1943 and first half of 1944, Britain's Rear-Admiral Victor Crutchley commanded an Allied cruiser squadron that was part of the U.S. Seventh Fleet. This squadron, designated Task Force 74, consisted of both American and Australian warships including at times the Australian cruisers *Australia*, *Shropshire* and *Hobart* and the Australian destroyers *Arunta* and *Warramunga*. Throughout this period Task Force 74 conducted various escort and bombardment duties in support of General MacArthur's Southwest Pacific campaign. Then in June 1944 this squadron intercepted a Japanese force attempting to bring reinforcements to Biak Island. In a running engagement, Crutchley's ships forced the Japanese to withdraw after abandoning several troop-laden barges to fend for themselves.

Meanwhile, the RAAF and RNZAF also played an important role in the growing Allied air offensive engaging a wide array of targets throughout the region. Of these, none were more important than the Japanese air and naval bases located on Rabaul. From October 1943 through February 1944 the Allies embarked upon an extended bombing campaign to neutralise Rabaul. While predominately an American effort, a number of RAAF and RNZAF squadrons participated in these operations. Included in this were three squadrons of Australian Beaufort light bombers that carried out a series of night attacks against Rabaul while the Americans bombed during the day thus exposing the Japanese to a form of round the clock bombing. Allied estimates of Japanese losses during this bombing campaign and related air fighting numbered almost 900 aircraft.[33] Japanese records put their losses at only about a quarter of this number, but were nevertheless compelled to abandoned Rabaul as a main operating base at the end of February. Although Rabaul would remain in Japanese hands, it was now thoroughly neutralised as a base for air and naval operations. Meanwhile, in an example of the RAAF's support for the fighting in New Guinea, in February 1944 No. 10 Group, which operated from Nadzab and consisted of seven squadrons of Vengeance, Kittyhawk and Wirraway aircraft, flew a total of 1,467 sorties in 62 missions during which it dropped some 210 tons of bombs.[34] Many of these sorties directly supported Allied ground forces while others included attacks against regional airfields and infrastructure targets.

The RAAF also continued to play an important role in the Allied maritime interdiction effort. Of the various weapons employed in this endeavour, none was more important than the aerial mine. Throughout 1944 RAAF PBY-5 Catalina aircraft laid over 1,000 mines against 34 different targets in the Dutch East Indies, the Bismarck Archipelago and around Borneo. Key amongst these was Balikpapan harbour, which was a major access point to substantial oil refining and storage facilities critical to the Japanese war effort. From 22 February through 19 October 1944 RAAF aircraft laid 118 mines in and around this harbour that sank five ships worth 18,063 tons and damaged another six worth an estimated 14,415 tons. A second major target was Kau Bay, which was the recipient of 62 RAAF-laid mines from 14 January through 20 July 1944 that sank another five Japanese ships worth 13,500 tons and damaged seven more worth 12,393 tons.[35] As important as this direct materiel destruction was in these and the other impacted locations, the mere presence or threat of RAAF mines often caused port closures and transportation delays that substantially amplified the disruptive impact this aerial mining campaign had to the regional Japanese logistical network and proved it to be a highly cost effective interdiction method.

The RAAF supplemented its mining activities with conventional air strikes. During this period RAAF and RAAF-affiliated Dutch aircraft flew thousands of anti-shipping sorties against the local Japanese maritime traffic. Amongst their more substantial successes, on 15 and 16 December 1943 five Mitchell bombers and 16 Beaufighters carried out a series of strikes against a Japanese convoy off Timor that sank the merchant ships *Wakatsu Maru* and *Genmei Maru* (5,123 and 3,180 tons respectively) and destroyed a third vessel worth an estimated 500 tons.[36] Then on 27 March 1944 RAAF Catalina aircraft sank the 575-ton cargo ship *Shinsei Maru* in a conventional bombing attack northeast of Timor. Three months later on 19 July RAAF Mitchell bombers sank the auxiliary minesweeper *WA4* at Dili harbour and two minor cargo vessels in the adjacent waters. Finally, on 6 August and 20 December Dutch aircraft sank the 824-ton *Uwajima Maru 15* and the 898-ton *Shoeki Maru* off Ceram and Celebes respectively.[37]

While these periodic successes against larger Japanese ships garnered notice, the steady attrition inflicted against local coastal traffic arguably had a greater impact upon Japan's regional supply situation. This was true because maritime transport was often the only viable means the Japanese had to transfer men and materiel to and between their numerous garrisons manning the islands and long stretches of undeveloped coastline prevalent in the theatre. Since ocean going vessels were in limited supply and often unsuitable for use in these restricted waters, the Japanese utilised large quantities of coasters, barges and other minor craft, many of which were produced locally, to fulfill these needs. In all, the Japanese eventually acquired upwards of 6,000 of these useful vessels. In turn, losses were heavy. In May 1943 the Japanese admitted to the loss of 600 barges, and this wastage continued through the remainder of the war.[38] Examples of the interdiction contributions

Using both aerial mines and direct attacks, the RAAF carried out an aggressive campaign against Japanese shipping in the Southwest Pacific. Pictured here is a burning Japanese oil barge following a RAAF Beaufighter strike. (JohnnyOneSpeed, CC0, public domain)

made by the RAAF in this regard included the Beaufighters of No. 9 Group, which conducted 130 sorties that claimed 33 barges destroyed and 51 more damaged in September 1943. One year later this attrition continued as the Bostons and Beaufighters of No. 77 Attack Wing sank 24 vessels in October 1944 while No. 81 Wing claimed 26 barges destroyed and 72 damaged from October through December. Finally, in February 1945 No.79 Wing destroyed or damaged 38 assorted vessels of which half were claimed by No. 13 Squadron RAAF operating off the coast of Sumbawa.[39]

While these Commonwealth contributions of men and materiel were undoubtedly beneficial, the driving engine behind the growing Allied ascendancy in the Pacific was the unprecedented buildup of American military power. This was nowhere more evident than in the naval war where America's industrial might and vast human resources produced and manned immense numbers of new ships and aircraft. The scope of this unparalleled buildup was demonstrated by the fact that on 30 June 1944 the United States Navy possessed 46,032 vessels of all types and 3,623,205 service personnel (including coast guardsmen and marines).[40] Obviously, the vast bulk of this materiel force consisted of minor craft and support vessels, but the United States Navy also possessed well over a thousand principal warships in its fleet organisation ranging from battleships and aircraft carriers to submarines and fleet minesweepers. This vast materiel abundance was clearly demonstrated during a single operation against the Marianas in June 1944 when the Americans utilised a force that included 14 battleships, 15 aircraft carriers, ten escort carriers, 24 cruisers and some 140 assorted destroyers and escort vessels. As a point of comparison, only two years before the United States Navy had employed a mere three aircraft carriers, eight cruisers and 15 destroyers during the crucial battle of Midway. The Japanese, with their inferior industrial base and limited resources, were simply incapable of competing against this vast materiel onslaught.

To this point, during the second half of the war the United States Navy steadfastly squeezed the lifeblood out of the Japanese Empire. Across the Pacific, America's

Table 6.2. Comparative Strength of Primary American and Japanese Naval Forces in the Pacific as of 31 August 1944.

	Battleships	Aircraft carriers	Escort carriers	Cruisers	Destroyers	Submarines
United States Navy	17	21	47	38	249	155
Imperial Japanese Navy	9	9	3	25	73	48

Source: S. Woodburn Kirby, *The War against Japan, Volume III: The Decisive Battles* (London: Her Majesty's Stationery Office, 1961), p. 518.

Note: In addition to these totals, both navies possessed large numbers of lesser warships including escort destroyers, frigates and minesweepers. Likewise, the American figures only represent a portion of their total strength since warships employed in the Atlantic and Mediterranean are not included.

ever-expanding carrier task forces attacked Japanese strong points at will. Starting in September 1943 and continuing on through the next several months, these forces conducted a series of strikes against Japanese garrisons on the Gilbert and Marshall Islands, Wake, Rabaul, Kavieng, Kwajalein, Truk, Palau and the Mariana and Bonin Islands targeting both Japanese air and naval units. During these attacks the Americans destroyed more than 1,000 Japanese aircraft while destroying or heavily damaging dozens of military and commercial vessels. In terms of the latter, this included the destruction of two light cruisers, six destroyers, one patrol boat (ex-destroyer), one minesweeper and 374,205 tons of merchant shipping from September 1943 through June 1944.[41] Together, these strikes increasingly rendered Japan's forward outposts impotent and forced the Japanese navy to substantially withdraw its forces into the interior portions of the empire.

An even greater factor in this progressive Japanese decline was the impact that American submarines had in ravaging Japan's maritime lines of communication. This development was particularly devastating, since Japan, like Britain, was an island nation dependent upon maritime commerce for its very survival. However, unlike the British, the Japanese were far less adept at defending their lines of communication. First, Japan started the war with a merchant fleet that was only a third of the size of Britain's. Similarly, as previously discussed in Chapter 3, the Japanese navy entered the war severely delinquent in defensive assets. As hostilities progressed, the Japanese remained stubbornly negligent in addressing these materiel deficiencies. Beyond this, they initially failed to implement rudimentary defensive measures including the introduction of a comprehensive convoy system. The Americans were quick to take advantage of these deficiencies, and by the end of 1943 Japanese merchant shipping losses numbered almost three million tons of which nearly two thirds were sunk by American submarines. Making matters worse, this rate of attrition was accelerating as nearly 30 percent of these total losses occurred in the last four months of this period.[42]

Given this ongoing carnage, the Japanese were finally forced to address their defensive deficiencies. Starting modestly in 1942 and substantially expanding thereafter, the Japanese embarked upon a major shipbuilding programme to produce escort vessels. Referred to as Kaibōkans (sea defence or coastal defence ships), these ocean-going warships were more akin to frigates or escort destroyers in the Allied navies. Displacing between 740 and 940 tons and armed with two to three 4.7-inch guns and up to 120 depth charges, the Japanese eventually produced 164 of these versatile vessels in five different variants. Beyond this, the Japanese also converted existing warship designs to perform escort functions. This was particularly true regarding their remaining fleet minesweepers, which had their minesweeping gear removed to accommodate depth charges. To protect coastal traffic, the Japanese further produced a number of submarine chasers ranging in size from 100 to 420 tons while converting numerous civilian craft, such as trawlers and fishing boats, to serve as naval auxiliaries. Finally, the Japanese earmarked five small aircraft carriers to perform escort duties while beginning construction to convert a number of merchant ships into auxiliary escort carriers.

In other actions, in November 1943 the Japanese established a new entity called General Escort Command to coordinate and protect their shipping movements. At about the same time the Japanese instituted a basic convoy system, which expanded over the next several months to eventually cover their primary transit routes. By mid-1944 General Escort Command possessed over 100 ocean-going escort vessels, and most Japanese merchant ships now travelled in protected convoys.[43] Unfortunately for the Japanese, these actions did little to reverse the growing attrition plaguing their merchant fleet. Despite its increased numbers, General Escort Command was largely a hollow force lacking the technical, tactical and operational proficiency of its Allied counterparts. Nor was this force large enough to effectively counter the threat arrayed against it. To this point, Japan's 100 assorted escort vessels compared quite feebly to the 426 assorted destroyers, frigates, sloops and corvettes used by the British just to secure their home waters in January 1945.[44] Given these factors, the Japanese only succeeded in sinking about 50 American and Allied submarines during the course of the war.[45] This was an extremely poor result compared to the 692 German U-boats attributed as sunk in direct action by the Western Allies during the European conflict.[46] It was also an inadequate result as demonstrated by the fact that Japanese merchant shipping losses continued to mount totalling 1,777,248 tons during the first six months of 1944.[47] Putting this attrition into perspective, this tally almost equated to the totality of losses suffered by the Japanese merchant fleet in all of 1943. A number of Allied weapons including aircraft and mines contributed to this carnage, but none was more prevalent than America's ever-increasing submarine force.

While this decline was underway, the main elements of the Imperial Japanese Navy made little effort to challenge the American offensive. Debilitated by heavy losses sustained during the battle of Midway and the Solomon Islands campaign, the Japanese fleet focused most of its energies on reconstituting its strength. This situation changed in June 1944 when the Americans launched their aforementioned invasion of the Mariana Islands. Realising that the loss of these islands would put Japan within range of American long-range bombers, the Japanese fleet was compelled to act. Employing five battleships, nine aircraft carriers, 13 cruisers and 28 destroyers, the Japanese struck at an American force, the U.S. Fifth Fleet, that was more than twice its size. The result was the last purely dedicated carrier battle of the war and another substantial victory for the United States. In all, the Japanese lost three aircraft carriers sunk and four others damaged and some 450 aircraft along with their invaluable aircrews. This engagement, referred to as the battle of the Philippine Sea, broke the back of Japan's once vaunted carrier air arm, which would never again rise as an effective fighting force. American losses were negligible in return.

In other respects, this victory represented a transition point in the Pacific war. Up to this time, America, with its Commonwealth allies, had been progressively chipping away at Japan's outer defensive zone. Now with the capture of the Marianas, the focus of the Allied efforts transitioned to waging war against Japan's vital inner empire as well as its home islands. Over the next two months, the Americans completed their capture of Saipan, Guam and Tinian, which put them in a position to launch a strategic bombing campaign against Japan. Meanwhile, from late August through early October America's fast carrier task forces rampaged through Japan's inner empire launching a series of raids against various targets in the Bonin Islands, Philippines, Formosa and Okinawa that destroyed some 1,600 Japanese aircraft and over 160 assorted vessels for the loss of fewer than 200 American aircraft.[48] By this time the United States fully controlled the initiative, and there was little the Japanese could do except react to each American incursion. Japan was losing the war, and unless circumstances changed radically, this outcome was assured. The only real question confronting the Allies was how long it would take and how much it would cost.

To this latter point, despite their increasing misfortunes, the Japanese remained formidable opponents. By the summer of 1944 the Imperial Japanese Army had more than doubled in size compared to its strength at the beginning of the war. Eventually, it would number over five million men. A similar expansion had occurred in terms of frontline aircraft for the various Japanese air services. Likewise, despite the neutralisation of its vaunted carrier force, the Imperial Japanese Navy remained numerically strong possessing large numbers of surface warships and submarines. Together, each of these services continued to offer fanatical resistance against the Allies. Meanwhile, in terms of territory, the Japanese still occupied a vast empire stretching across much of East Asia and the Southwest Pacific including considerable terrain taken from the British. Clearly much heavy fighting remained ahead despite the fundamental hopelessness of Japan's long-term situation.

For the British, who were still predominately focused on the conflict in Europe, the retrieval of their lost territory represented a long and arduous task against an enemy that was determined and well-entrenched. This pending process was made more difficult by the harsh terrain and enormous logistical challenges involved. In terms of the latter, this included a requirement to wage largescale operations many thousands of miles from home on what was literally the other side of the world. Such operations would require a massive, sustained seaborne effort to assemble and support the forces involved, which would necessarily include substantial naval, air and ground components. This represented a daunting task almost as challenging as the fierce opposition the British could expect to encounter from the Japanese. Yet, despite these many difficulties, the British were determined to reenter the Pacific war and play their part in helping defeat Japan. For them, this process would begin in the Indian Ocean and Burma.

CHAPTER 7

Return to the Indian Ocean

By the summer of 1943, British naval strength in the Indian Ocean was at a precarious level. During the previous year, Admiral Somerville's Eastern Fleet had suffered a continuing haemorrhage of assets as the Admiralty diverted numerous ships to more critical theatres. The first major combatant to depart the area was the aircraft carrier *Indomitable*, which left for the Mediterranean in July 1942. This was followed during the next couple of months by the aircraft carrier *Formidable* and the battleship *Ramillies*. Then during the first five months of 1943, the fleet lost the aircraft carrier *Illustrious* and the battleships *Valiant* and *Warspite*. When adding in other vessels, by July 1943 the Admiralty had transferred no fewer than 48 ships from the Eastern Fleet to the Mediterranean to participate in the pending invasion of Sicily.[1] This left Somerville with only two *Royal Sovereign*-class battleships and no aircraft carriers to secure the vast Indian Ocean. The Eastern Fleet also suffered from a chronic shortage of destroyers and escort vessels, which hampered both fleet and convoy operations. This destroyer deficit deteriorated to a point where Somerville was often unable to dispatch his dwindling number of capital ships to sea due to a lack of sufficient anti-submarine protection.

Unfortunately, this was only the beginning of the Eastern Fleet's difficulties. Beyond its dangerous lack of numbers, the fleet also suffered from numerous qualitative issues that posed a serious impediment to its projected effectiveness against the Japanese. First, many of the warships remaining in the fleet were old and obsolete with some in a poor state of repair or at least not in ideal fighting condition. In some cases, a contributing factor to Somerville's retention of these vessels was the disheartening fact that no other commands wanted them. Likewise, due to the inactivity of the Eastern Fleet, it was difficult to maintain any semblance of operational prowess as ships and crews often languished in ports for extended periods of time. This unfortunate condition sapped the fleet's fighting spirit and technical competence. Even when they did go to sea, British ships had little practical opportunity to strike at the enemy thus further eroding morale and any sense of purpose within the command. Finally, from a structural point of view, the fleet's lack of aircraft carriers meant that it would be at a distinct disadvantage in directly confronting the Imperial Japanese Navy, which still possessed a substantial carrier air arm at this stage in the war.

Nor were these maritime deficiencies entirely limited to the navy. The British also suffered from a lack of modern shore-based patrol and maritime strike aircraft within the theatre. In terms of the former, the Indian Ocean represented an extremely large body of water requiring substantial numbers of patrol aircraft to fully cover the vast shipping routes stretching throughout the region as well as to maintain vigilance against any Japanese incursions into the area. In July 1943, India Command possessed a mere six Catalina flying boat squadrons to perform this vital function. Additional patrol aircraft were stationed in East Africa and Aden, but this combined force could only provide intermittent coverage to ships transiting the area. Meanwhile, the maritime strike component within India Command consisted of just two Beaufort torpedo-bomber squadrons. This shortage of shore-based aircraft was made worse by a rigid command structure and intense interservice rivalry that kept these aircraft firmly under RAF control to the detriment of the navy. Sadly, this lack of effective collaboration was not an isolated problem, but rather a systemic feature plaguing the local British war effort. Across the board, the various British service commands failed to adequately integrate and cooperate with each other. This proved to be a persistent obstacle in their efforts to plan and conduct joint operations, and often the different services seemed more intent on contesting each other than fighting the Japanese.

Under these conditions, the British Eastern Fleet lacked sufficient resources to properly defend itself or its lines of communication from even minor Japanese incursions. Fortunately for the British, the Japanese were too preoccupied in the Pacific to exploit this weakness. Given the colossal events described in the previous chapters, the Japanese were compelled to keep the vast bulk of their military forces in the Pacific. Accordingly, the Japanese, like the British, relegated the Indian Ocean region to that of secondary theatre status and only dedicated sufficient resources to consolidate and secure their territorial gains from the previous year. The only offensive actions they did undertake came in the form of periodic submarine sorties against British shipping routes and regular bombing raids against targets in eastern India that generally garnered meagre results. Even against these minor assaults, the British were hard pressed to mount an appreciable defence, and this lack of Japanese success was more indicative of Japanese shortcomings than the effectiveness of the limited British countermeasures opposing them. During this period, British escort vessels failed to sink a single Japanese submarine, and the RAF's responses to the air raids were often ineffective due to inadequate early warning and command and control systems. On 27 March 1943 the British did score a rare defensive victory when Hurricane fighters from Nos. 79 and 135 Squadrons intercepted and destroyed nine unescorted Japanese bombers attempting to attack Cox's Bazaar, but this was not a typical result. In most cases, the Japanese raiders got through unscathed or at minimal loss to the aircraft involved.

Meanwhile, British offensive activities within the region were practically non-existent. Somerville's only effective offensive force during this time consisted of three Dutch submarines that were under his operational control and an occasional British boat operating out of Ceylon or East Africa. Hampered by a grossly insufficient support base and a lack of suitable targets in their patrol areas, these Allied submarines achieved even less than their Japanese counterparts. In particular, during the first eight months of 1943, Somerville's Dutch submarines sank just three Japanese merchant ships and one minor vessel worth a combined 13,595 tons.[2] Added to this was a single 3,000-ton merchant ship reportedly sunk by the British submarine *Trusty* on 11 February 1943 in the Java Sea. Unfortunately, post war analysis could not confirm this latter success, and *Trusty*'s claim went unsubstantiated. However, in light of British eyewitness accounts that reported seeing the vessel sink within eight minutes of being struck by a single torpedo and the chaotic and incomplete state of Japanese records at the end of the war, it is entirely possible that *Trusty* did sink a vessel of some sort on this date.[3] On a more positive note, no British or Dutch submarines were lost during this period thus providing a degree of solace to counter the meagre results attained during these patrols.

Augmenting this limited seaborne offensive were the efforts of the Royal Air Force. In this regard, results were mixed. On one hand, local British aircraft failed to sink any sizeable Japanese warships or merchant ships (of 500 tons or greater) in 1943. In fairness, much of this was due to a lack of suitable targets, but the British also suffered from limited numbers of strike aircraft that had the range and payload to effectively operate against the targets that did exist within the region. On a more positive note, the RAF conducted a series of strikes against the multitude of sampans, coasters, barges and fishing vessels that operated along Burma's vast coastal and river waterways. Summarising this effort, from 1 December 1942 through 31 December 1943, No. 224 Group (RAF) claimed 88 sea-going and 636 river craft destroyed while a further 441 and 3,137 such vessels were claimed as damaged.[4] These were almost exclusively native-built vessels of very minor tonnage, but some were presumably used to support Japanese military and logistical operations.

The only other significant British/Commonwealth success that occurred during this period was a daring commando raid carried out in September 1943. The instrument of this operation was a captured, 78-foot Japanese fishing vessel and a few brave men in canoes. This vessel, the Japanese *Kofuku Maru*, had been seized by the British at Singapore at the beginning of the conflict and used by them to transfer evacuees from the colony. Now rechristened *Krait* by its new owners, the unassuming fishing vessel assumed a new role. On 2 September *Krait* departed Exmouth Gulf on the western coast of Australia. On board was a special commando force consisting of three British and 11 Australian naval and military personnel.[5]

For the next 15 days the unarmed *Krait*, which was disguised to look like a native craft, travelled some 2,000 miles deep into Japanese-controlled territory. On the night of 17/18 September *Krait* arrived at Pandjang Island located some 30 miles south of Singapore and disembarked three two-man commando teams along with three canoes and associated equipment. *Krait* then withdrew to shelter off Borneo while the commandoes proceeded on alone.

Over the next several nights these teams paddled up the Bulan Strait and eventually established themselves on Subar Island located just eight miles south of Singapore. On the night of 26/27 September, the commandos paddled into Singapore harbour and attached limpet mines to a number of merchant ships. They then made good their escape, rendezvoused with *Krait* on 1–3 October and retraced their 2,000-mile voyage back to Australia. This return journey was generally uneventful, but there was one tense moment when a Japanese auxiliary minesweeper approached *Krait* in the Lombok Strait. Fortunately, the Japanese auxiliary made no attempt to investigate the disguised vessel, and *Krait* proceeded on arriving in Exmouth Gulf on 19 October. Meanwhile, the limpet mines left behind sank the Japanese merchant ships *Kizan Maru* and *Hakusan Maru* worth 5,077 and 2,197 tons respectively.[6] This raid, which was designated Operation *Jaywick*, further damaged at least four (and possibly five) other Japanese vessels worth an additional 18,000 tons.

While this operation was underway, major events were occurring in Europe that would profoundly impact Britain's war against Japan. Paramount amongst these were events in the Mediterranean. In July British and American forces launched a seaborne invasion of Sicily, which fell after a month of fighting. With the war now on Italy's doorstep, Mussolini's own Fascist Grand Council voted to depose him, and he was placed under arrest by the Italian king, Victor Emmanuel III. The new government that replaced Mussolini quickly sought out an armistice with the Western Allies to end the war. This armistice was signed on 3 September 1943 and went into effect five days later. A key provision of this armistice was the surrender of the Italian fleet, which generally occurred over the next two weeks. By 21 September the Allies had possession of the battleships *Vittorio Veneto*, *Italia* (ex-*Littorio*), *Giulio Cesare*, *Andrea Doria* and *Caio Duilio*, eight cruisers, 33 destroyers/torpedo boats, 20 assorted escorts, 34 fleet submarines and 33 miscellaneous vessels.[7] With this capitulation, a major chapter in Britain's maritime war came to an end. After nearly 39 months of conflict, the Regia Marina, which had been the world's fifth largest navy at the beginning of the war, ceased to exist as a hostile combatant. When viewed in a global context, of the three major naval powers that had confronted Britain and the Allies since December 1941, only two now remained.

Meanwhile, in the Atlantic and waters off Northwest Europe the Allies enjoyed a series of complementary successes against the German Kriegsmarine. As discussed in the previous chapter, May 1943 represented the final turning point in the U-boat war. From this point on, the Allies retained their ascendancy over the Germans, and for the remainder of the year, another 142 U-boats were sunk. In terms of major surface warships, in September the British launched an attack with X-craft midget submarines against the battleship *Tirpitz* located at Kaafjord in Norway. This operation crippled the German battleship, and it would never again attain operational status, but was instead further damaged by FAA aircraft and then eventually destroyed by RAF Lancaster bombers in 1944. Meanwhile, in December 1943 a British naval force, centred upon the battleship *Duke of York*, encountered and destroyed the German battlecruiser *Scharnhorst* off Norway's North Cape. With *Scharnhorst* sunk and *Tirpitz* disabled, the German surface threat from Norway effectively ceased to exist. Also in December, two British cruisers fought an action against a combined German force of 11 destroyers/torpedo boats in the Bay of Biscay during which they destroyed one destroyer and two torpedo boats for no loss to themselves. This action reflected the growing ascendency the British had attained over the relative handful of German surface warships still operating along the French Atlantic coast and heralded to a time when the Allies would soon conduct major landing operations in France itself.

Together, these various events had two major impacts on Britain's maritime position in the Far East. First, with the naval threats substantially reduced in Europe and the Mediterranean, the British were finally free to send significant naval reinforcements to Somerville's over-stretched command. This pending expansion covered all categories of warships ranging from battleships and aircraft carriers down to destroyers and submarines and would predominantly be made up of modern or modernised vessels. Second, with the collapse of Italy, the Allies effectively gained control over the full length of the Mediterranean thus transforming this central body of water into a major transportation artery between the Atlantic and Indian Oceans. This ended the need to route shipping around the Cape of Good Hope, which eliminated some 5,000 miles off each convoy passage to and from India. This new routing scheme saved an estimated 2,000,000 tons of cargo space or the equivalent of about 225 merchant ships thus substantially simplifying British efforts to reinforce and sustain their forces in the Far East.[8]

Spurred on by these factors, from September through December 1943, an average of 800 Allied ships traversed the Mediterranean in convoys each month, and in 1944 this number increased to 1,100–1,200.[9] Many of these various convoys culminated in Italy and the surrounding area to support local operations, but some passed all the way through to the Far East. In naval terms, the deployment of new reinforcements began modestly with the arrival of the submarine depot ship *Adamant* and the first boats of the 4th Submarine Flotilla to Ceylon in October 1943. By the end of the year the British had seven submarines operating with this flotilla. Meanwhile, during the same month the escort carrier *Battler* joined the fleet, thus ending a nine-month absence of British carrier air power in the Indian Ocean. As for the fleet carriers and battleships, it would still take a few months before these ships arrived, but the commitment was now there. Soon, the Admiralty would begin sending some of its newest and most powerful warships into the Indian Ocean to join the Eastern Fleet.

In this, the navy followed its army and air force counterparts, which also benefitted from the opening of the Mediterranean and were already farther along in the regeneration process. Despite their low priority for global resources, these services had painstakingly used the 18-month period following their expulsion from Burma to reconstitute and expand their strength in eastern India. In terms of the former, the army assembled several divisions from British, Indian and African origins that were earmarked for service against the Japanese. As a whole, each of these divisions were better trained and equipped than the unfortunate formations that had first opposed the Japanese in 1941 and 1942. Likewise, the British bolstered these forces with the deployment of substantial command and control, logistical, engineering, artillery and armoured elements thus creating more balanced combined arms teams than had existed during those earlier contests. Of equal importance, the British used this period to substantially expand and improve the region's logistical infrastructure to ensure the availability of adequate support once major combat operations recommenced.

Meanwhile, a similar expansion occurred in regards to air power as both Britain and the United States sent several squadrons of modern combat aircraft to the region. For the British, this process was highlighted by the arrival of Spitfire fighters in October 1943. Other key aircraft that joined the British ranks during this time included Liberator bombers, Beaufighter fighter-bombers and Vengeance dive-bombers. An example of the impact these new aircraft types had occurred in January 1943 when a flight of Beaufighter night fighters arrived in the Calcutta area and immediately shot down four Japanese bombers thus significantly curtailing further nocturnal raids against the city. Meanwhile, with the arrival of the Spitfires, Japan's high-flying Ki-46 Dinah reconnaissance aircraft, which were largely impervious to Hurricane interception, suddenly found themselves vulnerable to these new adversaries. This was amply demonstrated in November 1943 when Indian-based Spitfires promptly shot down three Dinahs in just a nine-day period. Over the next 15 months these Spitfires accounted for a further 17 Dinahs destroyed thus severely degrading the latter's ability to collect photographic intelligence.

Corresponding with these personnel and materiel enhancements, the Allies decided to improve interservice and international cooperation by establishing a new command authority for the area. During the Trident Conference held in Washington in May 1943, Britain and the United States agreed to better coordinate their various military activities in Southeast Asia. This understanding was formalised three months later during the first Quebec Conference when Allied leaders agreed to the creation of South East Asia Command (SEAC) to oversee all Allied air, land and sea activities in Burma, Malaya, Sumatra and the surrounding waters with further authority extending into Thailand and French Indochina for certain clandestine and offensive operations. Churchill and the Combined Chiefs of Staff considered several officers, including Admiral Somerville, to assume the role of Supreme Allied Commander South East Asia, but eventually decided upon Admiral Lord Louis Mountbatten to fill this position.

The selection of Mountbatten as Supreme Allied Commander was a seemingly unorthodox choice given his relative youth and lack of substantial command experience. Born in Windsor, England, on 25 June 1900, Mountbatten was the second son of a prominent Battenberg family that had connections to the British royal family. After attending the Royal Navy College, Osborne, Mountbatten entered the Royal Navy in 1916 and saw wartime service on the battlecruiser *Lion* and battleship *Queen Elizabeth*. During the interwar years, Mountbatten remained in the Royal Navy and eventually advanced to the rank of captain. With the onset of World War II, Mountbatten was appointed commander of the 5th Destroyer Flotilla and saw action off Norway, in the English Channel and in the Mediterranean. After the loss of his flagship, the destroyer *Kelly*, to German dive-bombers off Crete in May 1941, Mountbatten briefly commanded the aircraft carrier *Illustrious* and then became Chief Advisor (and later Chief) of Combined Operations Headquarters in October. Attaining the rank of acting vice-admiral, Mountbatten served in this capacity for almost two years where he oversaw the planning and execution of a number of combined arms raids against occupied Europe as well as substantial planning for future amphibious operations.

Promoted to the rank of acting admiral, the 43-year-old Mountbatten arrived in India on 7 October to assume command of SEAC, which was formally activated one month later. While lacking experience as a battlefield or fleet commander, Mountbatten brought a number of useful attributes to his new position. The most obvious of these was his recent experience running a joint headquarters and overseeing combined arms operations. This gave him substantial exposure to high-level planning and the immense interservice coordination necessary to successfully execute these undertakings. This would serve him well as Mountbatten's primary role as SEAC commander was to provide overall direction and effectively orchestrate the numerous and varied elements of his command to allow his more experienced combat commanders to successfully engage the enemy. This would often require Mountbatten to exercise a delicate balance between firm leadership and loose diplomacy as he dealt with the various services and nationalities within his command. To be sure, there were some difficulties in doing this, particularly early on, but these were resolved over time. Eventually, Mountbatten developed effective command relationships that generally allowed his combat commanders substantial freedom of action in managing their battles and confronting the Japanese. Finally, Mountbatten was a man of boundless energy who exuded confidence and a drive to be victorious, which would eventually permeate throughout his entire command thus boosting confidence and morale within the ranks.

With its activation on 15 November 1943, SEAC constituted an immense organisation that would eventually encompass well over a million men of which the vast majority were British or British affiliated, but also included smaller contingents coming from China and the United States. In recognition of this latter point, SEAC's deputy commander was American Lieutenant-General Joseph Stilwell. This was just one of three positions that Stilwell fulfilled within the theatre as he was also the commander of all American forces in China, Burma and India and the Chief of Staff to Generalissimo Chiang Kai-shek, the Nationalist Chinese leader. Likewise, Stilwell commanded Chinese forces in northern Burma. These various roles, plus Stilwell's generally abrasive personality, would result in some unusual (and often strained) command relationships developing in regards to his presence. In terms of combat formations, the main headquarters responsible for ground operations within SEAC was the 11th Army Group under the command of General George Giffard. In turn, the main subordinate command within the 11th Army Group was the British Fourteenth Army, which eventually contained a total of eight Indian, two British and three colonial (African) divisions. SEAC's primary air component was Eastern Air Command under Air Chief Marshal Richard Peirse, which in December 1943 possessed some 800 aircraft assigned to 10 bomber, 33 tactical strike/fighter, six transport and five photo-reconnaissance squadrons broken down between British and American contingents at roughly a 65 to 35 percent ratio.[10] Finally, the naval portion of SEAC was overwhelmingly British with the Eastern Fleet under Admiral Somerville providing its combat assets.

Despite its many promises and eventual success, the initial rollout of SEAC generated some tension between certain command elements and senior leaders within the organisation. This was no truer than in the case of the Eastern Fleet and Admiral Somerville. At first, Somerville was enthusiastic about Mountbatten's appointment, but this enthusiasm quickly turned to antagonism as a rift developed between the two leaders. Part of this was due to the fact that Somerville's area of responsibility encompassed the entire Indian Ocean and not just the SEAC area of operation. As such, he had a different perspective regarding the scope and execution of his mission. Likewise, disputes over contrasting command styles and the fact that Somerville was senior to Mountbatten in both age and rank became issues of contention between the two men and their corresponding staffs. It took a number of months for Mountbatten and Somerville to reconcile their differences, but eventually they came to an accommodation with each other, and SEAC ultimately improved interservice planning and cooperation despite its tumultuous start.

In the meantime, Somerville wasted little time putting his newly acquired combat strength to good use. Immediately upon their arrival, the boats of the 4th Submarine Flotilla began offensive operations against the Japanese with a patrol area encompassing the Bay of Bengal, the Strait of Malacca and the seas adjacent to Northwest Sumatra. This area was largely devoid of major Japanese shipping, and the British primarily contented themselves with attacks on junks, coasters and other minor vessels. Of course, there were some notable exceptions to this when the British were able to score against more sizeable targets. On 10 November 1943 the flotilla scored its first major success when the submarine *Tally Ho* sank the 1,914-ton Japanese merchant ship *Kisogawa Maru* in the Strait of Malacca. Three days later the submarine *Taurus* sank the Japanese submarine *I-34* off Penang. Then on 11 and 15 January *Tally Ho* sank the Japanese light cruiser *Kuma* and the 2,962-ton merchant ship *Ryuko Maru* off Penang and Port Blair respectively.

This former event represented Britain's first success against a major Japanese warship as *Kuma* displaced 5,100 tons and had a main armament of six 5.5-inch guns and eight torpedo tubes. Two days earlier, on 9 January, *Tally Ho*, which was commanded by Lieutenant-Commander L. W. A. Bennington, had sighted *Kuma* off Penang, but was unable to get within range to engage the cruiser. Surmising *Kuma*'s route into and out of Penang, Bennington remained in the area, and on the morning of the 11th sighted a Mitsubishi F1M2 floatplane flying along a route that he expected the cruiser to follow. Shortly thereafter at about 0900 hours, *Kuma* and the accompanying destroyer *Uranami* came into view, and Bennington was able to put his submarine into position to launch an attack. Engaging *Kuma* at a range of 1,900 yards some ten miles northwest of Penang, *Tally Ho* fired a spread of seven torpedoes at the light cruiser. Lookouts on *Kuma* spotted the incoming torpedo tracks, and the cruiser attempted to turn to avoid the salvo, but two torpedoes struck *Kuma* on its starboard aft causing it to quickly sink by the stern. In the process of doing so, a number of *Kuma*'s depth charges exploded thus causing further distress to crewmen in the water. In all, 138 crewmen perished with the ship. Despite a counter-attack from *Uranami*, *Tally Ho* was able to make good its escape, and Lieutenant-Commander Bennington was later awarded a Bar to his DSO for this action.

Fifteen days later on 26 January, this success was almost repeated when the British submarine *Templar* seriously damaged the Japanese light cruiser *Kitakami* in the same area. Like *Tally Ho*, *Templar* was able to score two torpedo hits on *Kitakami*, but in this case, the Japanese cruiser did not sink. Instead, *Kitakami* was towed to Angsa Bay to undergo emergency repairs followed by further repairs in Singapore that would keep the ship out of service until 21 June. Meanwhile, the British continued their offensive into February as the submarine *Stonehenge* sank the 889-ton Japanese merchant ship *Choko Maru* on the 12th while *Tally Ho* added to its already impressive score by sinking the German U-boat *UIT23* (formally the Italian submarine *Reginaldo Giuliani*) and the 510-ton merchant ship *Daigen Maru* on the 14th and 21st respectively. Still, not all of these encounters were entirely one sided as the indomitable *Tally Ho* sustained heavy damage during an encounter with two Japanese warships on the night of 23/24 February. During this engagement a Japanese torpedo boat passed so close to *Tally Ho*'s side that its rotating screws ripped large gashes along the full length of the submarine's port ballast tanks. Yet, despite this damage, *Tally Ho* survived the encounter and eventually made port to enact repairs.

While the threat posed by the Imperial Japanese Navy was an obvious and pressing concern, the destruction of *UIT23* emphasised the fact that Japan was not the only Axis antagonist in the Indian Ocean. Throughout much of 1943 a handful of German and Italian submarines also operated within the theatre. Some were there to carry out offensive patrols while others were used as blockade runners to transport vital materials and resources to and from the Far East. Initially these submarines originated out of the French Biscay port of Bordeaux, but during the latter half of the year some also began operating out of the Japanese base of Penang on Malaya's western coast. This latter development represented one of the few examples of direct cooperation that occurred between the Kriegsmarine and the Imperial Japanese Navy during the war. When Italy departed the conflict in September, the Japanese seized three Italian submarines located in the Far East and subsequently turned them over to the Germans. It was in this manner that *UIT23* came under German control.

For its part, the Kriegsmarine found combat in the Indian Ocean to be both a difficult and profitable undertaking. Hampered by the great distances involved and the limited support structure available despite the emergence of Penang as a local base, the Germans were rarely able to operate more than six U-boats within the theatre at any given time. Nevertheless, these participating U-boats often attained meaningful results despite their limited numbers. In fact, it was the Germans, and not the Japanese, who sank the lion's share of the 82 Allied merchant ships worth 486,324 tons that were lost due to enemy action in the Indian Ocean in 1943.[11] This was an anomaly since German U-boat fortunes were declining in all other theatres during this stage in the war, but in the Indian Ocean the U-boats benefitted from the vast expanses of the region and the limited defences arrayed against them. Accordingly, they were able to hunt Allied shipping, often independently sailed, with little risk of detection or interference to themselves. This latter point was emphasised by the fact that only two U-boats, *U197* and *U533*, were lost in the Indian Ocean during the whole of the year. Of these, both succumbed to RAF aircraft on routine anti-submarine patrols off Madagascar and the Gulf of Oman respectively.

Fortunately for the Allies, the advent of the new year brought some relief to British lines of communication as Somerville's forces increasingly gained the upper hand against their undersea adversaries. A key factor in this ascendancy was the destruction of two German merchant tankers operating in the Indian Ocean. Guided by Ultra intelligence, the British destroyer *Relentless* intercepted and forced the scuttling of the first, the 7,747-ton *Charlotte Schliemann*, some 500 miles south of Diego Garcia on 12 February. Three weeks later Ultra intelligence prompted the dispatch of a British hunter-killer group, built around the escort carrier *Battler*, to search for the 9,925-ton merchant tanker *Brake*. On 12 March a Swordfish from *Battler* located *Brake* some 200 miles southeast of Mauritius and guided the destroyer *Roebuck* to intercept and sink the German tanker. With the destruction of these vessels, the British eliminated German mid-ocean refuelling and re-supply capabilities thus significantly reducing the amount of time the U-boats could remain in their patrol areas.

Adding to this misfortune, the build-up of British and affiliated Allied forces within the theatre soon resulted in the sinking of a number of German and Japanese submarines. Already mentioned was *Tally Ho*'s victory against *UIT23* on 14 February. Also in February, British destroyers and escort vessels sank the Japanese submarines *RO110* and *I-27* in two separate actions on the 11th and 12th respectively. One month later on 11 March, South African aircraft sank *UIT22* (the former Italian *Alpino Bagnolini*) off the Cape of Good Hope. British aircraft scored a similar success on 1–3 May when they carried out a series of attacks that crippled and forced the scuttling of *U852* off Cape Guardafui, East Africa. On 17 July the British submarine *Telemachus* sank the Japanese submarine *I-166* in the Strait of Malacca. Later, on 12 August a British hunter-killer group dispatched *U198* northwest of Seychelles in the western Indian Ocean. Likewise, on 23 September and 6 October the British submarine *Trenchant* and the Dutch submarine *Zwaardvisch* sank *U859* and *U168* in the Strait of Malacca and in the Java Sea respectively. Finally, in November *U537* and *U196* were lost to American and unknown causes in the Java Sea.

The British destroyer *Petard* had the distinction of sinking a submarine from each of the three Axis navies during the war including the Japanese *I-27*, which was sunk on 12 February 1944. (Royal Navy official photographer, public domain)

This steady attrition of submarines and support vessels, coupled with improved British defences and deteriorating operational conditions, soon had a profound impact upon regional Allied shipping losses. During the first three months of 1944 German and Japanese submarines sank 29 Allied merchant ships worth a total of 188,040 tons in the Indian Ocean.[12] Fortunately, this toll quickly subsided as the Allies increasingly gained ascendancy in the area. Whereas regional Allied losses from all causes in March amounted to 12 ships worth 75,498 tons, there were no losses in April and May and only three ships worth 19,319 tons were lost in June. The Allies suffered a temporary reversal in July and August when 14 vessels worth 87,908 tons were sunk, but this trend was short-lived, and losses fell precipitously thereafter. For the remainder of the war, the Allies only lost another four merchant ships worth 26,871 tons in the Indian Ocean, and this vital maritime region became a virtual safe zone for Allied shipping.[13]

A key factor in this defensive victory, as well as the offensive operations that were about to begin, was the steady stream of new ships and other reinforcements that arrived to bolster the Eastern Fleet. On 28 January 1944, Vice-Admiral Arthur Power arrived in Ceylon with the battlecruiser *Renown*, the battleships *Valiant* and *Queen Elizabeth*, the aircraft carrier *Illustrious*, the aircraft maintenance carrier *Unicorn* and six destroyers. In March the depot ship *Maidstone* arrived at Trincomalee, and the British activated a second Ceylon-based submarine flotilla, the 8th. This activation enabled the British to increase their number of offensive submarine patrols within the theatre, and sinkings rose accordingly. Later that same

Table 7.1. Combat Losses of Allied Merchant Ships and Axis Submarines in the Indian Ocean and Adjacent Areas, 1943–1945.

	Allied merchant ships sunk through enemy action	Allied merchant tonnage sunk through enemy action	Axis submarines lost
Jan–Mar 1943	13	78,090	–
Apr–Jun 1943	24	138,994	–
Jul–Sep 1943	30	183,086	1
Oct–Dec 1943	15	86,154	2
Jan–Mar 1944	30*	195,880	4
Apr–Jun 1944	3	19,319	1
Jul–Sep 1944	15	93,578	3
Oct–Dec 1944	2	14,025	3
Jan–Mar 1945	1	7,176	–
Apr–Jun 1945	–	–	2**
Jul–Aug 1945	–	–	–

* Axis submarines sank twenty-nine of these vessels while Japanese cruisers accounted for the thirtieth.

** These losses consist of *U183* sunk by the American submarine *Besugo* in the Java Sea and the Japanese-controlled submarine *K-XVIII* sunk by the British submarine *Taciturn* near Surabaya. This latter victim was a captured Dutch submarine that was not in an operational state at the time of its demise.

month the American aircraft carrier *Saratoga* and three destroyers rendezvoused with British warships southwest of Cocos Island to begin a short period of service with the Eastern Fleet. Finally, in April the British welcomed the arrival of the Free-French battleship *Richelieu* and the escort carriers *Shah* and *Begum* thus further enhancing their growing strength in the region.

In addition to these new warships, the British also benefitted from the arrival of new carrier-borne aircraft. Gone were the days when the lumbering Swordfish and Albacore torpedo-bombers served as the FAA's sole strike aircraft, although the former still fulfilled an anti-submarine patrol function on certain escort carriers. Instead, the FAA could now call upon a whole series of new and improved aircraft types that were immediately available or would arrive in the theatre shortly. In terms of British designs, this included the Fairey Barracuda strike aircraft, which could effectively serve in either a torpedo or dive-bombing role. The British also produced the Supermarine Seafire and Fairey Firefly, which despite having marginal deck-landing performance in the case of the former, proved to be formidable seaborne fighter-bombers by the end of the war. Meanwhile, in terms of American-built designs, the British had the Chance Vought Corsair and Grumman Hellcat, which were both well-armed, powerful and rugged carrier-borne fighters. Another American design that would eventually attain widespread use within the fleet was the Grumman Avenger strike aircraft. Although designed as a torpedo-bomber, the British did not use the Avenger in this capacity, but rather used it as a glide bomber armed with four 500-pound bombs.

These improved aircraft types were just the beginning of the FAA's renaissance within the theatre. In addition to better aircraft designs, the FAA also benefitted from having greater numbers of aircraft available to use on its carriers. Equally important, the British now had adequate numbers of trained aircrews available to fully utilise these aircraft. Coming from a series of training establishments throughout the Empire and Commonwealth under the British Commonwealth Air Training Plan (BCATP), the FAA now benefitted from a steady stream of trained aircrews to fill its ranks.

Table 7.2. Characteristics of Selected Fleet Air Arm Aircraft.

	Top speed (mph)	Range (miles)	Armament
Torpedo/strike aircraft			
Fairey Barracuda II	228	686	2 × .303 MGs, 1,620lbs of assorted ordnance
Grumman Avenger	271	1,215	3 × .30/.50 MGs, 2,000lbs of assorted ordnance
Fighter/fighter-bombers			
Supermarine Seafire LIII	358	725	4 × .303 MGs, 2 × 20mm CAN, 500lbs of bombs
Fairey Firefly	316	1,300	4 × 20mm CAN, 8 × rockets or 2,000lbs of bombs
Chance Vought Corsair	425	1,015	6 × .50 MGs, 2,000lbs of bombs
Grumman Hellcat	376	1,090	6 × .50 MGs, 2,000lbs of bombs

Most of these pilots and aircrews had limited or no combat experience, but they were technically competent and capable of matching or surpassing the performance of their Japanese rivals at this stage in the war. Given this abundance of men and machines, the British were no longer compelled to operate their carriers with partial air groups as had often been the case during the opening years of the war. Instead, they were finally in a position to maximise the hangar and deck parking capacities of their carriers. Although it still lagged behind the sheer power and competence of the American carrier force, the FAA was now poised to become a major weapon in the Royal Navy's war against Japan.

The first example of this resurgent strength occurred in April 1944. With the arrival of the aforementioned reinforcements, Admiral Somerville immediately moved to put his new resources to good use against the Japanese. On 16 April he departed Trincomalee with the battleships *Queen Elizabeth*, *Valiant* and *Richelieu*, the battlecruiser *Renown*, the aircraft carriers *Illustrious* and *Saratoga*, six cruisers and 15 destroyers. This marked the beginning of Operation *Cockpit*, the fleet's first major offensive action in nearly two years. Early on the 19th this force arrived off northern Sumatra and launched a large air strike against the oil and military installations at Sabang. This strike consisted of 17 Barracuda bombers and 13 Corsair fighters from *Illustrious* and 29 Avenger and Dauntless bombers and 24 Hellcat fighters from *Saratoga*. The attack caught the Japanese completely by surprise, and the Allied aircraft were able to inflict heavy losses upon their unsuspecting foes. Altogether, they destroyed 24 Japanese aircraft on the ground, sank the merchant ships *Kunitsu Maru* and *Haruno Maru* (2,724 and 776 tons respectively), destroyed three oil storage tanks and heavily damaged other oil and port facilities. This cost the striking force just one American Hellcat in return; the pilot of which was rescued by the British submarine *Tactician*. As the fleet withdrew, an American Combat Air Patrol intercepted and shot down three Japanese torpedo bombers without loss to itself thus providing a fitting end to a successful inaugural operation.

No sooner did the fleet return to Ceylon then Somerville began planning follow-up strikes. *Saratoga* was already earmarked to return to the United States, and Somerville was determined to utilise the carrier one last time before its departure. In May the fleet once again departed Trincomalee to conduct Operation *Transom*, a strike against Japanese bases at Surabaya in Java. For this undertaking, the British replace their Barracuda aircraft with American-built Avengers to extend their operational range. On the 17th the fleet arrived off Surabaya and launched 85 aircraft. For the loss of one of their number, these aircraft destroyed the 987-ton merchant ship *Shinrei Maru*, two small auxiliary warships and 12 Japanese aircraft. They also heavily damaged the Japanese patrol vessel *P36/Fuji*, which was a former Japanese destroyer that had been converted to perform an escort role. Displacing 935 tons and armed with two 4.7-inch guns, *P36/Fuji* was damaged so severely that it would never be put back

By 1944 a rejuvenated Fleet Air Arm was ready to reenter the Asia/Pacific war with new and improved aircraft types. Pictured here is an American-built Grumman Avenger strike aircraft. (U.S. Navy, public domain)

into service and essentially became a total loss. Finally, the striking aircraft wrecked the oil refinery at Wonokromo and damaged other shore installations throughout the area. Other than the one aircraft shot down during the strike and two others lost through accidents, there were no Allied losses, and the fleet was able to withdraw without encountering any meaningful Japanese interference.

This operation marked the end of *Saratoga's* service with the Eastern Fleet, but despite this loss, the British continued to maintain their newly rejuvenated offensive pressure against the Japanese. During the period of 10–13 June, the fleet carried out a diversionary sweep in the Bay of Bengal to draw Japanese attention away from the forthcoming American invasion of the Mariana Islands in the Pacific. Then on the 21st the fleet conducted Operation *Pedal*, a strike against Port Blair in the Andaman Islands. Centred upon the aircraft carrier *Illustrious* with the battlecruiser *Renown* and battleship *Richelieu* in support, the British launched 15 Barracudas and 16 Corsairs to attack military targets within the area. Unfortunately, poor weather conditions hampered the raid, and results were generally disappointing. Nevertheless, the British did destroy at least two, and perhaps as many as a dozen, Japanese aircraft on the ground and sank at least one, and possibly more, Japanese coastal vessels.[14] British losses for the operation amounted to two aircraft.

In early July the aircraft carriers *Victorious* and *Indomitable* joined the Eastern Fleet thus significantly increasing its striking power. Unfortunately, these arrivals were partially offset by the need to withdraw *Illustrious* for a short refit. Before this occurred, however, *Illustrious* participated in one final sortie, designated Operation *Crimson*, against Sabang. On 22 July Somerville departed Trincomalee with the battleships *Queen Elizabeth*, *Valiant* and *Richelieu*, the battlecruiser *Renown*, the carriers *Illustrious* and *Victorious*, seven cruisers and 10 destroyers. On the morning of the 25th the carriers launched air strikes against airfields and oil storage facilities on Sabang. These attacks caused considerable damage including the destruction of at least two Japanese aircraft on the ground. Immediately following this, Somerville moved the fleet close inshore and conducted a heavy bombardment of the port area. As the heavy guns of the battleships and battlecruiser shelled the harbour from a distance, Captain R. G. Onslow led a squadron of cruisers and destroyers across the harbour entrance launching torpedoes at the docks and shooting up everything in sight. This bombardment inflicted severe damage upon the various harbour installations, barracks and oil storage facilities and sank two small vessels worth an estimated 1,500 tons.[15] Meanwhile, British fighters rounded out the engagement by shooting down four Japanese aircraft over the fleet.

This proved to be Somerville's final operation as Commander-in-Chief of the Eastern Fleet. Concerns over his health and his relationship with Mountbatten prompted the Admiralty to remove him from command. The rationale for this action was at least partially flawed since Somerville and Mountbatten had largely reconciled their differences by this time. Likewise, from a strictly personal perspective, it seemed modestly unfair removing Somerville from his position just at the very moment his Eastern Fleet was finally attaining success against the Japanese following the two disappointing years he had steadfastly shepherded it through. Still, the Admiralty was determined to remove Somerville, and they directed him to proceed to Washington to head the British naval delegation located there. While many in the Eastern Fleet lamented the loss of their long-serving and capable commander, this turned out to be a wise appointment. In his new capacity, Somerville proved to be extremely effective in dealing with the less than cordial American Chief of Naval Operations, Admiral Ernest King.

Meanwhile, back in Southeast Asia, Admiral Bruce Fraser assumed command of the Eastern Fleet on 23 August. Although new to the region, Fraser was no stranger to the rigours of naval warfare and senior command. A 40-year veteran of the Royal Navy with combat experience in two world wars, Fraser had excelled as a gunnery officer, commanded the cruiser *Effingham* and the aircraft carrier *Glorious* and proven himself a capable leader and administrator in both seaborne and shore assignments. In his most recent posting, Fraser had served as the Commander-in-Chief of the Home Fleet where he oversaw numerous combat actions against the Germans. In particular, he was aboard the battleship *Duke of York* and commanded the engagement that resulted in the destruction of the German battlecruiser *Scharnhorst* during the battle of North Cape in December 1943. Beyond this, Fraser oversaw the triumphant execution of several Arctic convoys to and from the Soviet Union and successfully conducted several carrier air strikes against German shipping off Norway that destroyed 13 assorted vessels worth 57,912 tons and damaged the battleship *Tirpitz* and 14 other vessels of 41,477 tons from October 1943 through June 1944.[16] Given these various experiences plus his earlier background, Fraser had a good understanding of both fleet and carrier operations, which would bode well in his new assignment. Finally, he had an agreeable personality and could be quite diplomatic and persuasive in advocating his positions to both peers and subordinates alike. This would serve him well both in the Eastern Fleet and then later when dealing with Allied counterparts in the Pacific.

The departure of Admiral Somerville and arrival of Admiral Fraser were not the only changes to impact the fleet during this time. Shortly after the completion of Operation *Crimson*, the fleet lost two veteran warships when the aircraft carrier *Illustrious* and the battleship *Valiant* withdrew to South Africa and Britain respectively. The former departed for a short refit; the latter to repair damage sustained in the collapse of a floating dock. Despite these losses, the general trend within the Eastern Fleet continued to be one of expansion and improvement. On 8 August the battleship *Howe* arrived in Trincomalee thus becoming the first modern British battleship to join the effort against Japan since the arrival of the ill-fated *Prince of Wales* some two and a half years earlier. This was followed in the next few months by a steady flow of reinforcements that joined the fleet covering all categories of warships and support vessels including the battleship *King George V* and the aircraft carrier *Indefatigable*. Enhancements in training and morale matched these materiel improvements. With each successful operation mounted against the Japanese, the British gained valuable combat experience that enhanced morale and confidence within the ever-expanding fleet. These factors, both materiel and personnel-related, would prove to be invaluable assets during later operations in both the Indian and Pacific Oceans.

To this end, the fleet continued its offensive posture against the Japanese. The first such event under Fraser's new leadership occurred on 24 August when the aircraft carriers *Indomitable* and *Victorious*, along with the battleship *Howe* and two cruisers in support, launched 61 Barracudas and Corsairs against Japanese installations on Sumatra. Their primary target for this undertaking, which was designated Operation *Banquet*, was the cement works at Indaroeng. This was the largest facility of its kind in Southeast Asia and a primary supplier for all Japanese military construction in the theatre. For the loss of one Corsair, the British accurately bombed the cement works and reduced its output for several months. During this operation British aircraft also attacked Emmahaven harbour where they damaged the merchant ships *Senko Maru* and *Chisho Maru*. Three weeks later the same ships conducted Operation *Light*, a strike against the railway yard at Sigli. This operation was marred by technical issues and inadequate intelligence that generally impeded results, but it came at no significant cost to the British and thus contributed to their ongoing learning curve.

Things went better a month later when the Eastern Fleet conducted Operation *Millet*, a series of raids and bombardments against the Nicobar Islands. The purpose of this was two-fold. First, the British hoped to draw attention away from the pending American landings at Leyte in the Philippines. The second was to continue the fleet's offensive presence within the region. On 15 October a force under the direct command of Vice-Admiral Power and consisting of the battlecruiser *Renown*, aircraft carriers *Indomitable* and *Victorious*, four cruisers and 11 destroyers departed Trincomalee. Two days later this force arrived off the Nicobar Islands where the British carriers conducted strikes on the 17th and 19th while the accompanying warships carried out bombardments on the 17th and 18th. A high point in these assaults occurred on the first day when 10 Barracudas and eight Hellcats from *Indomitable* attacked Nancowry harbour and sank the 830-ton merchant ship *Ishikari Maru* and a number of minor craft located there. The Japanese initially offered no meaningful

The Royal Navy's resurgence in the Indian Ocean was highlighted by the use of aircraft carriers. Amongst these was *Illustrious*, which participated in Operations *Cockpit*, *Transom*, *Pedal* and *Crimson* from April through July 1944. (U.S. Navy, Commander Joseph C. Clifton, public domain)

opposition to this assault, but on 19 October 12 Japanese torpedo-bombers attempted to attack the British fleet. This resulted in a substantial air battle in which British fighters shot down seven of the attacking Japanese aircraft for the loss of three of their own number. No British ships were hit, and the fleet was able to withdraw having suffered no damage to itself.

While these fleet operations were underway, the British submarine force in the area continued to grow in size and capability. In August the depot ship *Wolfe* arrived at Trincomalee thus allowing the British to activate the 2nd Submarine Flotilla. This action brought the fleet's overall submarine strength to three flotillas and 26 boats. Given this influx of combat assets and support capabilities, the British were now positioned to substantially expand their submarine operations throughout the region. Accordingly, on 4 September the British, with American agreement, moved one of these flotillas, the 8th, to Fremantle in Australia and extended its patrol area to include the South China and Java Seas. For the remainder of the year these 8th Flotilla boats, along with their compatriots from the 2nd and 4th Flotillas operating out of Ceylon, scored a continuing number of victories against Japanese maritime assets throughout the theatre. As discussed earlier, most of these successes occurred against minor vessels and local coastal craft operating under Japanese control, but this tally also included periodic triumphs against more sizeable ships.

Summarising these results, from 1 October 1943 through 31 December 1944 British and British-controlled Dutch submarines sank the light cruiser *Kuma*, the minelayer *Itsukushima*, three German and two Japanese submarines, two auxiliary warships, 23 sizeable merchant ships totalling 42,741 tons and approximately 268 minor vessels worth an estimated 31,000 tons through conventional attacks. Also sunk by British submarines during this period were the converted escort destroyers *W5* and *W7*. The Japanese originally designed these vessels to serve as minesweepers, but as discussed in the last chapter, they subsequently converted them to serve as escort destroyers to counter the growing Allied submarine threat. In this configuration, these vessels displaced 620–630 tons and were armed with one or two 4.7-inch guns, multiple smaller calibre guns and 36 depth charges. Although these ships retained their original designations as minesweepers, they were in fact escort destroyers in both composition and function, and I have therefore counted them as such here. All other converted escort destroyers listed in the remainder of the book underwent similar conversions.

Nor were these the extent of British submarine successes during this period. In addition to conventional attacks, mines laid by British submarines sank another two auxiliary warships and a 3,029-ton merchant ship during 1944. Likewise, the submarine *Trenchant* carried out a Chariot human torpedo attack against Phuket harbour on 28 October. The Chariot was a man-operated torpedo, crewed by two men in shallow water diving suits, that had a detachable warhead for placement and delayed detonation against a ship's hull. The British had first introduced Chariots in the Mediterranean where they used them to destroy the Italian cruisers *Ulpio Traiano* and *Bolzano* in separate operations. In the case of Phuket harbour, the results were not so grandiose, but the British still managed to sink the 984-ton merchant ship *Sumatra Maru* during the attack. Finally, British and British-controlled Dutch submarines damaged a number of ships including the light cruiser *Kitakami*, the minelayers *Hatsutaka* and *Wakataka* and the torpedo boat *Kari* in 1944.[17] British casualties during this same period amounted to just two submarines, *Stonehenge* and *Stratagem*, that were lost to unknown causes and a Japanese escort vessel respectively.

Beyond these naval exploits, Eastern Air Command also played an increasing role in the anti-shipping campaign during this time. This was primarily achieved through the use of aerial mines. As far back as 22 February 1943, American aircraft stationed in India had begun laying mines against local Japanese-controlled harbours. On 7 January 1944 RAF Liberators joined this effort. Over the next several months these Liberators assumed the predominant role in the campaign by conducting over 200 sorties and laying well over 1,000 mines against various targets along the coasts of Burma, Thailand and the Malaya Peninsula. While these mines only sank a handful of vessels, they caused great delays to regional maritime traffic and thus had a disruptive effect far exceeding their materiel results. The Allies also bombed area ports and harbours to cause further disruptions and impede Japanese lines of communication. Finally, on a local basis, RAF fighter-bombers from No. 224 Group carried out numerous anti-shipping strikes claiming 1,246 minor vessels destroyed and 6,552 damaged along Burma's coastal and internal waterways in 1944.[18]

Together, this aerial onslaught, coupled with submarine operations, forced the Japanese to move many of their supply activities inland where they were hampered by inhospitable terrain and a limited transportation infrastructure. Similarly, these ground infrastructure assets were equally vulnerable to Allied air attacks, which occurred on a regular basis. As part of this, in the first five months of 1944 the Strategic Air Force dropped 6,741 tons of bombs (split almost equally between its RAF and USAAF contingents) against local targets of which 54.7 percent were dropped on military installations and dumps, 22.6 percent on railroad communications, 10.2 percent on airfields and landing grounds and 5.5 percent on bridges.[19] Taken as a whole, this combined interdiction campaign seriously reduced Japan's ability to adequately support its armies in Burma. By comparison, the British were able to use the Indian Ocean as a major transportation artery to build-up and support their forces in India with little opposition encountered from Japanese or German interference. Once arrived, the British were able to move these resources to the needed areas much more efficiently than their Japanese counterparts and with little interference from the Japanese air force. While the territory comprising the SEAC area of operations represented a distant battlefield for both the British and the Japanese, the British were clearly doing a better job winning the local logistical contest.

At the core of this triumph was the successful application of British maritime power both globally and within the region. During the first half of 1943 the British had been hard pressed to adequately defend their tentative hold on the Indian Ocean or exert pressure against the Japanese. The only thing that saved them from major adversity during this period was Japan's preoccupation with events in the Pacific. During the latter half of 1943 the British finally made strides in improving the situation, and this progress accelerated through the first three quarters of 1944. By October of that year, the British were in a position to fully exploit the Indian Ocean for their own purposes while preventing the Japanese from doing the same. With the arrival of additional resources, the British could expect this ascendancy to continue, and soon they would begin sending substantial naval forces eastward to join the handful of British submarines already operating in Australia to wage war in the Pacific. In the meantime, they had to continue their critical maritime support to help facilitate British ground victories in the epic battle for control over India and Burma, which was already underway.

CHAPTER 8

The Battle for India and the Opening of the Burma Offensive

At the onset of 1944, the war in Southeast Asia entered a period of momentous decision as events were already underway to bring the competing British and Japanese armies positioned along the India-Burma border into decisive conflict with each other. This promised to be a contest of brute force against brute force as the contenders in this pending clash were substantially larger than any of the forces thus far engaged in the regional conflict. Perhaps even more daunting, the two sides intended to take the offensive over the same territory with much the same timing thus foreshadowing the likelihood of head-on collisions between the oncoming armies. For the British, the ultimate goal in their efforts was the reconquest of Burma and the destruction of all Japanese forces located there. For the Japanese, the goal was primarily defensive, but believing that offense was the best form of defence, they proposed to seize key staging locations within India to impede expected British attacks into Burma. The results of these competing campaigns over the next eight months would likely shape the outcome of the entire regional war.

The main British contender in this pending series of battles was the Fourteenth Army under the command of Lieutenant-General William Slim. At the start of 1944, Fourteenth Army consisted of two active corps containing six divisions and other lesser units with further units held in reserve. The first of these subordinate formations was IV Corps located around the Imphal plain with its main logistical base located in Dimapur some 130 road miles to the northwest. Under the command of Lieutenant-General Geoffry Scoones, IV Corps consisted of the 17th, 20th and 23rd Indian Divisions, the 50th Indian Parachute Brigade and the 254th Indian Tank Brigade. The second major formation was XV Corps under the command of Lieutenant-General Philip Christison. With a primary combat strength consisting of the 5th and 7th Indian Divisions and the 81st West African Division, XV Corps was earmarked to operate on the Arakan front with its main logistical base located at Chittagong.

Beyond these two corps, which were directly under Slim's command, the British had several other units within SEAC that were available for use against the Japanese. Paramount amongst these was the Northern Combat Area Command, which technically fell under Slim's authority, but effectively operated as an independent element commanded by American Lieutenant-General Joseph Stilwell. Based out of the small town of Ledo in northern Assam, the Northern Combat Area Command had a main combat strength of six British special forces brigades, an American infantry regiment and three Chinese divisions (the 22nd, 30th and 38th). Another important command available to operate against the Japanese was XXXIII Corps under the command of Lieutenant-General Montagu Stopford. At the beginning of 1944, XXXIII Corps was located in southern India where it was undergoing training and other preparations to carry out amphibious operations against the Japanese. Units assigned to this corps or held in reserve within India included the British 2nd Division and the Indian 19th, 25th and 36th Divisions. Of these forces, 36th Division contained two British brigades and would later be redesignated a British division during the course of operations. At the time, XXXIII Corps fell under the authority of the 11th Army Group, which also commanded Fourteenth Army.

Under the overall command of SEAC's Admiral Louis Mountbatten, the British were intent on beginning their reconquest of Burma. Previously, limited resources had forced the cancellation of numerous undertakings including several proposed amphibious operations. Now with the advent of the new year, limited landing craft allocations once again precluded any amphibious operations for the next several months. Accordingly, the British realised that any immediate advances would have to occur overland, and they proposed a series of phased offensives along a broad front. In the centre, IV Corps would conduct a limited advance to contain Japanese forces west of the Chindwin River. To the north, Allied forces would advance eastward from Ledo to seize Myitkyina and other key locations to compromise the Japanese hold on northern Burma. To the south, XV Corps would conduct a limited offensive into the Arakan with the immediate objective of capturing Maungdaw and Buthidaung. Once these tasks were complete, the British would conduct follow-up operations as dictated by the situation.

To carry out these various tasks, the British possessed an army that was far more powerful than anything previously employed against the Japanese within the theatre. Not only was this army numerically strong, but it also enjoyed a number of qualitative improvements that promised to garner great dividends on the battlefield. Long gone were the days when the British were compelled to use ad hoc or half-trained formations to confront the Japanese. Instead, Fourteenth Army and the other major British commands predominantly possessed units that were properly organised, amply equipped, well trained and soundly led. In fairness, most of these troops lacked practical combat experience, but they had a clear understanding of who their enemy was and what actions were necessary to defeat him. In this regard, they had no illusions about the martial prowess of their opponents or the difficult tasks that lay ahead, but they approached these challenges with a burgeoning confidence in their own abilities and a stoic acceptance of the necessity of their mission.

In materiel terms, Fourteenth Army was well provisioned with a wide range of supporting arms including a substantial allocation of artillery units. Within the British army, the Royal Artillery was widely considered to be one of its most effective components having earned an excellent reputation from friends and foes alike in the European conflict. The mainstay of this force was the indomitable 25-pounder field gun, which was extensively used by British and Commonwealth forces throughout the war including with the Fourteenth Army. This quick firing gun could fire a 25-pound shell some 13,000 yards and was extremely reliable, easy to maintain and highly mobile. These latter qualities made the 25-pounder a particularly valuable asset for the Fourteenth Army given the remote and inhospitable terrain it was consigned to operate in. Another key artillery piece used by the Fourteenth Army was the 5.5-inch medium gun. Considerably larger than the 25-pounder, the 5.5-inch gun could fire a 100-pound shell some 16,000 yards or an 82-pound shell 18,100 yards thus giving it substantially greater destructive power. The British rounded out these core weapons with various other guns including the 3.7-inch pack howitzer, which was ideally suited for mountain fighting, and the 7.2-inch howitzer for heavy bombardment duties.

The Army also possessed a number of armoured units that could be used as mobile artillery or to engage bunkers and other hardened positions in support of the infantry. A mainstay of this force was the M3 medium tank, which came in two variants, dubbed Lee or Grant, depending upon the design and construction of the turret. Originally used by the British Eighth Army in North Africa during the spring of 1942, the M3 was no longer considered viable for European operations, but some 900 had been sent to India for use against the Japanese. Possessing reasonably thick armour that made it impervious to most Japanese weapons and a 75mm hull-mounted gun along with a 37mm turret-mounted gun, the M3 had the

Table 8.1. Characteristics of selected British/Commonwealth and Japanese artillery pieces.

	Shell weight (lbs)	Range (yards)	Rate of fire (rpm)	Gun weight (lbs)
British/Commonwealth				
QF 3.7-inch pack howitzer	20	5,900	8	1,610
QF 25-pounder field gun	25	13,400	3–5	3,600
BL 5.5-inch medium gun	82/100	18,100/16,200	2	13,647
BL 7.2-inch howitzer	202	16,900	3	22,900
Japanese				
Type 92 70mm battalion gun	8	3,060	10	476
Type 38 75mm field gun	13	12,700	8–10	2,088
Type 91 105mm field howitzer	34	11,779	6–8	3,300
Type 96 150mm howitzer	69	13,014	3–4	9,103

potential to be quite formidable under the right conditions. The other main tank available to the Fourteenth Army was the M4 Sherman. A successor to the M3, the M4 possessed an improved design that featured increased armour protection and a turret-mounted 75mm gun that gave it enhanced survivability and a better 360° engagement capability. The M4 had already proven itself to be a highly reliable and capable tank in Africa and Europe, and its introduction in Southeast Asia would likely emulate that performance to the detriment of the Japanese.

Beyond this internal firepower, Fourteenth Army could also call upon Eastern Air Command to provide close air support and interdiction operations against the Japanese. The primary formation tasked to do this was the Third Tactical Air Force, which was established in December 1943 under the command of Air Marshal John Baldwin. The primary strike aircraft used within the command for close air support was the Hawker Hurricane Mk II, which equipped 13 squadrons at the beginning of 1944. Now long obsolete in its day fighter role, the Hurricane Mk II proved to be an effective fighter-bomber capable of carrying two 250- or 500-pound bombs. Another key strike aircraft was the Vultee Vengeance, a dedicated dive-bomber that equipped five squadrons and was capable of carrying a 2,000-pound bombload. Finally, the versatile Bristol Beaufighter fulfilled a number of roles including long-range interdiction and could carry various combinations of guns, rockets and bombs in this capacity. Still, while these various aircraft constituted potent weapons, they were only as effective as their ability to locate and hit elusive ground targets. Timely and effective cooperation between air and ground units was often challenging under even ideal conditions, and this difficulty was only exacerbated by the jungles and harsh terrain in which Fourteenth Army would soon operate in. Still, the British had already made great strides in perfecting this valuable mission through the acquisition of effective radio equipment, adoption of standardised procedures and the placement of dedicated air liaison teams within the forward deployed units to call in and direct these strikes.

Of course, notwithstanding the impressive firepower available to the British, an ultimate factor gaging Fourteenth Army's success would be its ability to maintain adequate logistical support. Given the harsh terrain and limited infrastructure present in eastern India and Burma, the British realised that aerial resupply would have to be a key component in their logistical effort. To help facilitate this, Eastern Air Command possessed six transport squadrons in December 1943, and this number would increase to an eventual strength of 17 squadrons by campaign's end of which nine were British and eight were American. In most cases, transport aircraft would fly supplies and materiel into forward bases for storage and subsequent distribution, but they could also directly air drop provisions to deployed units in the field as needed. Yet, even with this massive aerial contribution, a substantial portion of the army's logistical needs would have to be maintained using ground infrastructure. Accordingly, Fourteenth Army also possessed a large number of

Of the various RAF aircraft that participated in the Asia/Pacific war, none saw more service than the Hawker Hurricane Mk II, which was used as both a fighter and a fighter-bomber. (Royal Air Force official photographer, public domain)

engineer and transportation units to help facilitate this task. Among the missions the engineers would perform included building and improving roads and bridges, constructing bases, depots and airfields and opening ports as they became available. The transportation units would then facilitate the actual movement of supplies to the sprawling army.

A final factor worth considering regarding the status of the local British forces was the effectiveness of their leadership. In this regard, the British were generally well served as SEAC possessed a number of quality officers in its senior command positions. Of these, none was more critical to the upcoming struggle than the commander of the Fourteenth Army, Lieutenant-General William Slim. Born in Bishopston, England on 6 August 1891, Slim began his army career in 1914 when he was commissioned as a temporary second lieutenant in the Royal Warwickshire Regiment. During World War I Slim saw action in both Gallipoli and Mesopotamia where he was twice wounded and earned the Military Cross. At the end of the war, Slim was an acting major in the 6th Gurkha Rifles, and he spent the interwar years in the British Indian Army where he held a variety of command and staff positions eventually attaining the rank of colonel. At the onset of World War II, Slim was given command of the 10th Indian Infantry Brigade and later saw action in

East Africa where he was wounded a third time. In May 1941, Slim attained the rank of acting major-general and assumed command of the 10th Indian Division leading it during the short Iraq, Syria-Lebanon and Iran campaigns. In 1942 Slim briefly commanded Burma Corps during its retreat from Burma and then was given command of XV Corps.

In October 1943 Slim, now an acting lieutenant-general, assumed command of Fourteenth Army. In doing so, he brought a number of talents and attributes to his new command. Among these traits were strong and steady leadership, competent tactical prowess and excellent organisational skills. As an experienced leader who had personally tasted the sharp end of combat on numerous occasions, Slim was determined to defeat the Japanese and had a realistic understanding of what was necessary to do this. An unflappable fighter who had often shown great personal bravery in the past, Slim was not easily rattled and had strong instincts to come to grips with the enemy, but he was not foolhardy in his approach or decision-making process. While not a particularly flamboyant or verbose leader, Slim demonstrated a clear devotion to the welfare of his soldiers and instilled a growing sense of morale and confidence within his command. At his core, he understood the need to reinvigourate British fortunes within the theatre and give his newly created Fourteenth Army the means and confidence it needed to carry out the tasks at hand.

This would be no easy undertaking as Slim faced a determined and formidable foe in the form of the Japanese army. The main formation confronting SEAC was the Japanese Burma Area Army under the command of Lieutenant-General Masakazu Kawabe. At the beginning of 1944, this command was divided into several subordinate formations including two (and later three) field armies, each of which was roughly the size of a British corps. The first of these was the Fifteenth Army under the command of Lieutenant-General Renya Mutaguchi, which contained three divisions (the 15th, 31st and 33rd) and was responsible for the defence of central Burma. The second was the Twenty-Eighth Army under the command of Lieutenant-General Shōzō Sakurai that defended the Arakan region with two divisions, the 54th and 55th. Also located in the Arakan was the recently arrived 2nd Division. Finally, the Japanese possessed two divisions (the 18th and 56th) located in northern Burma, where they were soon joined by a third division (the 53rd) to form the Thirty-Third Army. When combined together and including the 5th Air Division, the Japanese army possessed a total strength of 316,700 men in Burma as of March 1944.[1]

Quality attributes associated with these Japanese forces included uncommon tenaciousness and a willingness to endure great hardships beyond the threshold of most other combatants. In combat, the Japanese gave very little quarter, and they expected none in return. Japanese soldiers were generally very obedient in the execution of their duties and exercised an exceptional readiness to sacrifice themselves in pursuit of their missions. Given the Bushido honour code practiced by the Japanese army, most Japanese soldiers would continue fighting even under the most hopeless circumstances, and the only way to overcome them was to kill them. Beyond their absolute doggedness, the Japanese were skilled fighters particularly versed in small unit infantry tactics. Likewise, the Japanese had proven themselves far more adept at operating in the jungle and living off the land than their British counterparts. On the other hand, the Japanese were often overconfident, inflexible in the face of changing circumstances, and dismissive of the legitimate needs of their forces. Accordingly, the Japanese were occasionally prone to rely upon sheer force of will to overcome adversities instead of sound military planning and execution.

In terms of equipment, the Japanese lacked the same materiel abundance available to the British, but this lighter force structure had some advantages. To be clear, the Japanese were not entirely devoid of supporting arms as the Burma Area Army did possess a number of artillery and armoured units, but these units were not as numerous as their British counterparts or as lavishly equipped. Likewise, the equipment available to the Japanese was generally of lesser quality than that used by the British. An example of this was the Type 95 Ha-Go light tank, which was substantially lighter and less heavily armed than the British M3 and M4 tanks. While this arrangement provided the Japanese with less firepower, it also unencumbered them so they could better move and operate within the harsh jungle and mountainous terrain prevalent in the theatre. Less tied to roads given their lighter force structure, the Japanese were often able to advance through territory considered impassable by the British. Time and again in the past, the Japanese had used infiltration tactics to successfully bypass and compromise exposed British positions, and this remained a key tenet of their tactics. In a battle of manoeuvre in the jungle, the Japanese possessed a flexibility previously unmatched by the British, but if the British could

Table 8.2. Characteristics of selected British/Commonwealth and Japanese tanks.

	Weight (tons)	Max armour	Max speed (mph)	Armament
British/Commonwealth				
Matilda II infantry tank	25	78mm	15	1 × 2pdr gun, 1 × 7.92mm MGs
Valentine infantry tank	16	65mm	15	1 × 2pdr gun, 1 × 7.92mm MGs
M3 Stuart light tank	14	51mm	36	1 × 37mm gun, 3 × 7.62mm MGs
M3 Lee/Grant medium tank	27	51mm	26	1 × 75mm, 1 × 37mm, 3 × MGs
M4 Sherman medium tank	30	76mm	30	1 × 75mm gun, 2 × 7.62mm MGs
Japanese				
Type 94 tankette	3.4	12mm	25	1 × 6.5mm MG
Type 95 Ha-Go light tank	7.4	12mm	28	1 × 37mm gun, 2 × 6.5mm MGs
Type 89 I-Go medium tank	13	17mm	16	1 × 57mm gun, 2 × 6.5mm MGs
Type 97 Chi-Ha medium tank	15	25mm	24	1 × 57mm gun, 2 × 7.7mm MGs

hold their ground and force a protracted fight, their superior firepower was likely to pay dividends. Likewise, even though the Japanese tended to travel lighter and were more adept at living off the land, they still had to exercise some degree of conventional logistical support that would become increasingly vulnerable in a prolonged struggle given their less abundant engineering and transportation assets.

Beyond these internal units, the Japanese had access to another organisation, the Indian National Army (INA), to help achieve their objectives. The Indian National Army was initially formed in April 1942 with the consent and support of the Japanese government using dissident Indian prisoners of war to fill out its ranks. This first version of the INA was short lived as leadership disagreements resulted in its dissolution in December 1942, but the Japanese revived it again under the leadership of Subhas Chandra Bose some six months later. Pursuing a goal to end British rule in India, the INA eventually reached a peak strength of between 40,000 and 50,000 men of which roughly half were ex-prisoners of war while the other half were Indian expatriates living in Southeast Asia. Serving at the pleasure of the Japanese and heavily dependent upon them for support, the INA clearly represented an adjunct to the local Japanese power. Still, it remained to be seen how effective this force would perform as relations between the Japanese and Indians were often strained and most INA formations were poorly equipped and/or insufficiently trained.

As mentioned in the beginning of the chapter, the main Japanese orientation within the theatre was defensive, but they sought to use offensive action as the best way to secure this outcome. Impressed by the recent Chindit operation and convinced that further attacks were inevitable, General Mutaguchi of the Fifteenth Army devised a plan to launch a pre-emptive offensive against British IV Corps. The objective of this action was to seize Imphal and Kohima. The former served as the administrative centre for IV Corps and contained several important airfields and supply depots. The latter, Kohima, was of no particular importance itself, but its capture would allow the Japanese to sever the road link between Imphal and the even larger British administrative base at Dimapur. If successful, the seizure of these key assets would seriously impede SEAC's ability to launch any offensive actions into central Burma for the foreseeable future. Likewise, if the Japanese could seriously maul or even destroy IV Corps in the process, this would make the situation even worse for the British. Beyond this immediate benefit, the Japanese also hoped to gain a foothold in Indian territory that would allow them to establish a 'Free India' provisional government to undermine British rule on the subcontinent.

Gaining approval from the Imperial General Headquarters in Tokyo, General Kawabe of the Burma Area Army devised a phased, two-pronged offensive to execute this plan. First, on or about 4 February, the Japanese Twenty-Eighth Army would launch a limited offensive against British XV Corps in the Arakan. The purpose of this undertaking, which was designated HA-GO (Operation Z), was to fix XV Corps in place and draw British reserves into the region. Then later in the month Fifteenth Army would launch the main Japanese attack, designated U-GO (Operation C), against IV Corps. Major units assigned to U-GO included all three divisions of the Fifteenth Army as well as a division from the Indian National Army. Two of these Japanese divisions, the 15th and 33rd, would envelope Imphal from the north and south while the third division, the 31st, seized Kohima and cut the Dimapur–Imphal road. The INA division, which was split into sections, would primarily serve as support. If all went according to plan, General Mutaguchi hoped to capture Imphal within three weeks.

Of course, before this occurred, Twenty-Eighth Army first had to launch its HA-GO offensive. At the time, XV Corps was already engaged in its own offensive to capture Maungdaw and Buthidaung in the northern Arakan. The main portion of this offensive consisted of the 5th Indian Division advancing down the coastal plain of the Mayu Peninsula while the 7th Indian Division advanced through the Kalapanzin Valley. On 9 January 5th Division captured Maungdaw and then pressed on towards Razabil. While this was underway, 7th Division advanced down the Mayu Range and established a large administrative base at Sinzweya. From there, the British hoped to continue their offensive by capturing the road running between Maungdaw and Buthidaung. However, before this advance occurred, the Japanese 55th Division launched HA-GO against the exposed 7th Division. If all went well, the local Japanese commander hoped to destroy XV Corps and even garnered ambitions to advance across the border to capture the British staging base at Chittagong.

Commencing on 5 February, the Japanese used infiltration tactics to bypass the forward-deployed British units and cut their lines of communication. Dispatching one battalion to cross the Mayu Range and block the coastal road supplying 5th Division, the bulk of the Japanese force descended upon the Ngakyedauk Pass to isolate and destroy 7th Division, which was commanded by Major-General Frank Messervy. Once accomplished, the Japanese would then attack westward to destroy the sequestered 5th Division in a piecemeal fashion. Fortunately for the British, General Slim had other ideas. Disregarding his severed lines of communication, Slim ordered his besieged units to stand and fight where they were. Surmising that the Japanese were not strong enough or adequately supported to prevail in a protracted battle against two divisions, he coordinated with Troop Carrier Command to supply his isolated formations by air while he assembled additional reinforcements to send into the area. In doing so, Slim wagered that the weight of superior British resources would eventually overwhelm the Japanese incursion, but this all depended upon how effectively his exposed forces could hold their positions against the initial Japanese assaults.

The primary result of these competing ambitions was a growing battle that developed around the 7th Division's administrative base located at Sinzweya near the eastern end of the Ngakyedauk Pass. Roughly 1,200 yards in diameter, the British initially defended this area, known as the admin box, with an infantry battalion from the 9th Indian Brigade, a mountain artillery regiment, two squadrons of M3 Lee tanks and various headquarters and administrative units under the command of Brigadier Geoffrey Evans. Later as the battle developed, further reinforcements arrived to support the defenders including a second infantry battalion from the 89th Indian Brigade. During a period of more than two weeks, this ad hoc garrison successfully repulsed a series of Japanese attacks around the perimeter of the box. This was no easy task as the fighting was often desperate and sometimes hand to hand. In one notorious event that occurred on 7 February, Japanese soldiers briefly captured the base's main dressing station where they killed 35 medical personnel and patients. A week later, the Japanese carried out a particularly heavy attack that gained them a key hill on the western side of the perimeter, but the British regained this feature the next day through a combined infantry/armour counter-attack.

With each passing day, the situation for the Japanese became increasingly dire. There were a number of factors that helped facilitate this deteriorating situation. Foremost amongst these was the British ability to keep the garrison adequately provisioned using aerial resupply. Through the duration of the battle, Troop Carrier Command flew 714 sorties that delivered 2,300 tons of supplies to bypassed British units including the defenders of the admin box.[2] Although Japanese fighter aircraft did attempt to impede these operations, they were generally thwarted by British Spitfire fighters operating out of Chittagong, which gained air superiority over the contested area. In terms of their ground forces, the Japanese had no way to replicate the materiel support the British were receiving, and their engaged units quickly depleted the limited resources they had started the battle with. A subsequent Japanese effort to use a mule train to bring supplies forward came to naught when the British captured it en route. Thus, instead of isolating the British, it was their own forces which became increasingly isolated and devoid of support. An example of the latter was the fact that the Japanese had no effective counter to the British Lee tanks located in the admin box. Time and again, these tanks were used to help repulse Japanese attacks or reverse any progress they might make.

By the beginning of the battle's third week, heavy losses and acute supply shortages rendered the Japanese incapable of continuing a structured assault. Making matters worse, British reinforcements were now entering the area in increasing numbers. On 24 February some Japanese units began to disengage without authorisation, and the operation was officially halted two days later. In the process of withdrawing back to their lines, the Japanese suffered further heavy losses thus bringing their total casualties for the battle to 5,335 including 3,106 fatalities. Corresponding British losses amounted to 3,506 casualties.[3] This action, which became known as the battle of Ngakyedauk Pass, or more commonly referred to as the battle of the Admin Box, constituted the first significant British ground victory in Southeast Asia. Not only did the British retain the battlefield, but XV Corps was able to resume its own offensive resulting in the captures of Buthidaung and Razabil on 9 and 12 March respectively.

Soldiers of the 7th Indian Division during the battle of Ngakyedauk Pass, the first major British ground victory in Southeast Asia. (No. 9 Film & Photographic Unit, public domain)

Perhaps more important, the battle shattered the aura of Japanese invincibility that had haunted the British up to this point in the war. In this regard, the battle was a true turning point within the theatre.

As momentous as this event was, the battle of Ngakyedauk Pass was quickly eclipsed by the launching of the U-GO offensive. Originally, the Japanese had intended to launch U-GO in February to better synchronise it with the diversionary HA-GO action in the Arakan, but delays in bringing up some of the formations assigned to the offensive caused it to be postponed until early March. Nevertheless, when the Japanese Fifteenth Army finally launched its offensive against British IV Corps, it did so with a powerful force consisting of some 85,000 Japanese and 7,000 INA soldiers. To put this in context, this constituted a substantially larger force than what the Japanese had initially used to invade Malaya in December 1941. Accompanying this force was the Japanese 14th Tank Regiment, which possessed 66 assorted tanks, and the 3rd Heavy Artillery Regiment. Likewise, the Japanese also brought large herds of pack animals and cattle to serve as beasts of burden and to feed their troops. At a time when Japanese fortunes were waning almost everywhere, U-GO constituted a rare Japanese attempt to regain the strategic initiative and decisively rebuff Allied designs within the theatre. Thus, for the armies involved, this represented the most important battle to be waged since the struggle for Malaya two years before. Depending upon its outcome, the course of the entire Southeast Asia campaign hung in the balance.

The Fifteenth Army executed the U-GO offensive using a phased advance over a broad front that eventually extended some 170 miles. The 33rd Division in the south was the first to go beginning its advance on 8 March. Divided into three primary columns, the division had an aggressive goal of destroying the 17th and 20th Indian Divisions located in the vicinities of Tiddim and Tamu respectively and then advancing on Imphal from the south and east. One week later, on 15 March, the Japanese 15th and 31st Divisions joined the fray as the former sought to advance through Ukhrul to cut the Dimapur–Imphal road and then attack Imphal from the north while the latter proceeded towards Kohima. The British had long anticipated this attack and were determined not to let their forward-deployed units become engaged in a piecemeal fashion. Instead, Slim and Scoones ordered the 17th and 20th Divisions to conduct a fighting withdrawal back towards the Imphal plain. There, the British could fight in a relatively compact area close to their logistical centres against an enemy that was operating at the end of a long and tenuous supply line.

Unlike previous retreats carried out by British forces during earlier operations, this redeployment was no undisciplined rout or harried retirement. Instead, the British carried out an effective fighting withdrawal according to their own designs and timetable. Nevertheless, there was one dangerous moment in the middle of the month when the 17th Division had to fight its way through a Japanese roadblock near Tongzang. Thereafter, the 17th Division encountered further Japanese impediments, but overcame them all and made good its redeployment to Imphal with assistance from the 23rd Division. In the central area, the 20th Division defeated multiple Japanese attempts to advance up the Tamu–Palel road and only relinquished territory when it chose to do so. Included in this fighting was a rare clash between opposing armour when British M3 medium tanks repulsed an attempted Japanese mechanised advance destroying six Japanese tanks in the process. The situation was much the same in the north where the 50th Indian Parachute Brigade made two determined stands at Ukhrul and Sangshak against elements of both the 15th and 31st Divisions that delayed Japanese advances for two and six days respectively thus gaining the British valuable time to shore-up their defences around Imphal and bring in reinforcements.

By 4 April the British had completed their repositioning, and the units of IV Corps were now firmly ensconced along a defensive arc stretching some 90 miles around the Imphal plain. By this time, the Japanese had cut the Dimapur–Imphal road thus isolating IV Corps from external ground support, so the British once again turned to air transport to bolster and maintain the garrison. In this, they gained critical support from Admiral Mountbatten, the SEAC Supreme Commander, who on his own authority, diverted 20 transport aircraft engaged in Chinese airlift operations to support the fighting around Imphal. Among other things, this diversion of air assets allowed the British to fly in the 5th Indian Division from XV Corps to bolster the Imphal defence. At the onset of the battle, the British possessed enough supplies in the Imphal area to sustain combat operations for about a month, and during the next several weeks Allied transport aircraft delivered some 12,550 reinforcements and 18,800 tons of supplies to Imphal while concurrently evacuating some 43,000 administrative personnel and 13,000 casualties.[4]

This inflow of men and resources had a major impact upon the fighting around Imphal. The original Japanese plan carried out by Fifteenth Army had called for it to destroy the divisions of the British IV Corps in quick succession and then capture Imphal within 15 days, but it had failed in attaining either of these objectives. With this lack of success, the Japanese 33rd and 15th Divisions now found themselves bogged down in a protracted battle against a well-provisioned and supported enemy that was twice their size. Adding to this Japanese misfortune was their own precarious supply situation, which would only worsen with the passage of time. Yet, despite this clearly adverse tactical situation, the Japanese continued their offensive and attempted to batter their way through the strong British defences. Over the next month both Japanese divisions launched a series of disparate attacks along the length of the Imphal perimeter, but they were rebuffed in each case by the stout British defenders who gave up little ground and inflicted a growing tally of casualties upon the attacking Japanese forces.

While the fighting around Imphal unfolded in a manner generally favouring the British, the situation in the north was far more desperate as the Japanese 31st Division encroached upon Kohima. The British had anticipated the potential for this attack, but were surprised by the timing and scale of the assault. In particular, they thought it unlikely that the Japanese would target both Imphal and Kohima at the same time and surmised that any assault launched against the latter would be no stronger than regimental strength. Accordingly, when the British learned that an entire Japanese division was approaching Kohima, they were caught off balance with limited resources immediately available to meet the threat. In response, Slim directed General Stopford and XXXIII Corps to assume responsibility for the defence of Kohima and Dimapur. Likewise, he directed reinforcements into the area, including the 2nd British and 7th Indian Divisions, but only a small contingent of troops actually made it to Kohima before the Japanese enveloped the outpost. At the time of this occurrence, the British had a garrison of about 2,500 men in Kohima of which 1,500 were dedicated combat troops with the rest being administrative personnel. Under the command of Colonel Hugh Richards, the main combat elements of this force were a battalion from the Assam Regiment and the 4th Battalion of the Queen's Own Royal West Kent Regiment. This latter battalion came from the 161st Indian Brigade, which was also in the area, but blocked from directly augmenting the Kohima garrison by Japanese forces that had cut the Kohima–Dimapur road west of the town.

The battle of Kohima began on 4 April when Japanese troops made initial contact with the Kohima garrison, and within two days the town was effectively encircled. Colonel Richards organised his defence on the Kohima Ridge, a hilly spur about a mile long overlooking a hairpin turn on the Dimapur–Imphal road. At the onset of the siege, Richards benefitted from the fact that his garrison was generally well-provisioned with food and ammunition and could depend upon Eastern Air Command to airdrop further supplies as necessary. Likewise, he could call upon fire support from RAF aircraft and the 3.7-inch pack howitzers of the 24th Mountain Regiment (of the 161st Brigade), which was located some two miles away near the village of Jotsoma. Still, his garrison was outnumbered by a factor of at least five to one, and this weight of numbers was quick to have an impact. After seizing some of the garrison's southernmost positions in the first few days of the battle, the main focus of the fighting shifted north to a feature called Garrison Hill and a nearby administrative area. This latter area contained the local deputy commissioner's bungalow as well as other government buildings and structures on a series of terraces. Early in this struggle the Japanese captured some of the lower terraces while the British clung to the high ground. A focal point of this fighting became the commissioner's tennis court, where the opposing sides were only separated by the width of the court, a distance of about 20 yards.

As the battle moved into its second week, the British continued to hold out against repeated Japanese attacks. A major factor in this was the exceptional shooting of the 24th Mountain Regiment, which often laid artillery fire a mere 15 yards in front of the forward British positions. Equally important was the yeoman's service performed by Eastern Air Command, which flew some 2,200 Hurricane fighter-bomber sorties against the Japanese 31st Division during a 16-day period while Vengeance dive-bombers carried out similar attacks against both forward and rear echelon Japanese positions.[5] On the night of 17/18 April the Japanese finally captured the bungalow area and a feature called Kuki Picquet. This latter development effectively cut the garrison in two with the areas still under British control measuring just 350 yards square. Fortunately, relief was finally at hand when on the same day (the 18th) the 161st Brigade, reinforced by elements of the 2nd Division, finally broke through the Japanese defences west of Kohima and lifted the siege. Thereafter, the British 6th Brigade relieved the garrison, and Colonel Richards formally relinquished command of the area on the morning of the 20th. By this time, the battlefield was a scene of utter devastation, and many of the relieving British troops were shocked by the emaciated appearance of the surviving garrison members. Still, the battle was won. Even though the Japanese would continue their attacks against Garrison Hill for the next several days, it was now clear that Kohima was saved. The price in attaining this feat included over 800 casualties for Richards's brave little command of which over 300 were killed. Of these, 199 casualties came from the Royal West Kents including 61 fatalities out of 444 men employed.[6]

The 31st Division's failure to subdue the Kohima garrison was matched by similar results on the Imphal front where repeated Japanese attacks made no appreciable gains against IV Corps' formidable defenders, and by the beginning of May it was unmistakably evident that Fifteenth Army had failed in attaining its offensive objectives. Still, the Japanese remained unwilling to cede this point, and the fighting continued on at an unrelenting pace as both sides launched a series of attacks to dislodge the other. In this, the Japanese made no appreciable headway while the British only attained marginally better results. Still, with each passing day, the momentum of the battle slowly shifted in favour of the British. Much of this resulted from the substantial combat power they were able to bring into the fight, which included the eventual commitment of 150,000 men spread across two corps with six divisions, four independent brigades and various other units. Equally important, the British were able to keep these forces adequately supplied through their aerial resupply efforts and bolstered them with substantial air, armour and artillery support. By comparison, the Japanese received little more than what they had started the offensive with in terms of reinforcements, and the harsh terrain and unrelenting Allied air attacks reduced their logistical support to a trickle.

Increasingly, this disparity of forces made an impact on the battlefield. This was particularly true in the north where the British began making meaningful gains against the dogged Japanese resistance. At Kohima, the British 2nd Division waged a series of hard-fought battles over a three-and-a-half-week period to clear the Japanese from the Kohima Ridge. Thereafter, 2nd Division and the newly arrived 7th Indian Division, which had come in from the Arakan, began a push down the Dimapur–Imphal road towards Imphal. In this, they were aided by a decision of the 31st Division commander, Lieutenant-General Kotoku Sato, to withdraw from the Kohima area on 31 May and begin a retreat. This action was not authorised by Fifteenth Army, but Sato made it on his own authority citing a critical logistical situation that had brought his men to the brink of starvation. While this was underway, the 5th Indian Division in Imphal slowly advanced northward against the Japanese 15th Division, which was also facing a critical logistical situation. Finally, on 22 June the 2nd and 5th Divisions attained a link-up at Milestone 109 some ten miles north of Imphal thus lifting the three-month siege of IV Corps.

Up to this point, the Japanese 33rd Division had continued to launch costly attacks against the southern portion of the Imphal perimeter, but even with the arrival of some rare reinforcements, including the II/154 Regiment and 151st Regiment from the 54th and 53rd Divisions respectively, it was unable to make any meaningful headway against the strong British defences. The fighting around Bishenpur was particularly fierce with many of the participating Japanese battalions reduced to just a handful of men. British casualties were also high, but given their numerical advantage, they were in a substantially better position to replace their losses. Fifteenth Army was being bled dry, and no amount of fighting spirit or sheer force of will could overcome the stark realities of military feasibility. Now with the siege broken in the north and General Mutaguchi effectively losing control over his 31st and 15th divisions, the situation was clearly hopeless. Still, it took an intransigent Mutaguchi another two weeks before ordering a total withdrawal from Imphal beginning on 4 July. For a large portion of his emaciated army, it was already too late. Many thousands of Japanese soldiers had already died during the fighting, and many thousands more would die during the retreat due to starvation, disease, battle wounds and sheer exhaustion.

When the final cost for the U-GO offensive was tallied, the enormity of this disaster became clear. Altogether, the Japanese suffered a staggering 53,505 casualties out of a total force of 84,280 men committed. Of these casualties, 30,502 were killed or missing in action. Meanwhile, of the 30,775 men that remained available for duty with their units, the majority suffered from varying combinations of minor wounds, diseases and malnutrition.[7] In terms of equipment, the Japanese lost or abandoned every heavy weapon they had started the offensive with. They also lost 17,000 mules and pack ponies. Finally, the 1st Division of the Indian National Army suffered some 4,400 casualties out of 7,000 men employed.[8] A large number of these were taken prisoner or simply deserted. Against this, the British suffered 16,667 casualties, which was a heavy toll, but nothing compared to the calamity that had befallen the Japanese.[9] If there had been any doubt regarding the changing momentum occurring within the theatre following the battle of Ngakyedauk Pass, the twin battles of Imphal and Kohima decisively settled this matter. Not only had India been saved, but Fourteenth Army had inflicted a devastating defeat upon the Japanese Burma Area Army from which it would never fully recover. In the grander scheme of things, the battle constituted the worst defeat ever to befall the Imperial Japanese Army up to this point in its history.

Making matters worse from a Japanese perspective, this defeat was not an isolated event. Even as the Fourteenth Army was successfully defending Imphal and Kohima from the Japanese U-GO offensive, the Allies carried out a series of offensive actions of their own into northern Burma to seize territory and disrupt Japanese lines of communication. The units involved in this undertaking included five British Chindit Special Forces brigades, a 2,832-strong American composite infantry unit, large contingents of Chinese troops and later the British 36th Division. For the Chindit forces involved, this incursion, designated Operation *Thursday*, represented an undertaking six times larger than the first Chindit raid carried out the year before. Expanding off the lessons learned during that earlier raid as well as more recent operations, the British planned to use transport aircraft to deploy and supply the majority of their units so they could operate deep within Japanese-controlled territory. The objectives of this were three-fold. First, the British hoped to cause a diversion and disrupt the lines of communication of the Japanese 18th Division thus assisting a proposed Chinese and American offensive towards Myitkyina. The second was

At Imphal and Kohima, the British Fourteenth Army inflicted a decisive defeat against the Japanese from which they would never recover. Pictured here are British Gurkha troops advancing with Lee tanks to clear the Imphal–Kohima road. (British Information Service, public domain)

to encourage a similar Chinese offensive from Yunnan into northern Burma. The final was to cause as much disruption as possible to impede Japanese operations in northern Burma and eventually compromise their position there while potentially drawing away resources from the ongoing U-GO offensive.

To carry this out, the Chindits, under the command of recently promoted Major-General Orde Wingate, planned to establish a number of jungle bases in the area southwest of Myitkyina near the railway line running between that city and Mandalay. Initially, one Chindit brigade, the 16th, would advance overland from Ledo towards Indaw and establish a base nearby, referred to as Aberdeen, from which they could fly in additional resources. While this was underway, elements of the 77th and 111th Brigades would fly in and land on three designated landing zones, codenamed Broadway, Piccadilly and Chowringhee, using Hadrian gliders for their initial assaults. Once secured, the British would establish rough landing strips in these zones to fly in additional forces using Dakota transport aircraft. From there, they would branch out and establish further bases in the area from which to menace Japanese lines of communication. Meanwhile, as conditions allowed, the British would fly in the last two brigades, the 14th and the 3rd West African, to participate in the undertaking.

On 5 February 16th Brigade began its trek into northern Burma. Travelling through extremely difficult terrain, the brigade was able to advance towards its objective garnering little attention from the Japanese. One month later, on 5 March, the British commenced the airborne portion of their offensive with the dispatch of elements of the 77th Brigade. Just prior to this departure, aerial reconnaissance indicated that large logs had been placed across the length of the Piccadilly landing zone thus rendering it unusable. This sparked fears that the Japanese might have gained advanced knowledge of the British plans, but it was later learned that the logs were placed there by local inhabitants harvesting the wood. Regardless of this last-minute surprise, the British continued the operation diverting the forces earmarked for Piccadilly to Broadway. As it was, the landing ground at Broadway proved to be very rough, and a number of gliders crashed in the initial assault, but engineers quickly fashioned a crude landing strip capable of receiving follow-up Dakota aircraft. That night, 62 Dakotas arrived at Broadway while a second glider assault occurred at Chowringhee, and in a week's period Allied transport aircraft conducted some 600 sorties to deploy the 77th and 111th Brigades into the area. This resulted in the delivery of 9,052 men, 175 ponies, 1,183 mules and 509,082 pounds of supplies. No Dakota aircraft were lost in attaining this great success, but the British did sustain 121 casualties during the initial glider operations.[10] These forces were bolstered by the 16th Brigade, which arrived in the area and established its Aberdeen base north of Indaw during the latter part of the month. From there, the British flew in their last two brigades, the 14th and 3rd West African, thus completing this deployment by the middle of April.

With the arrival of these various forces, the Chindits began their efforts to disrupt the Japanese rear area. Much of this staged out of another base, designated White City, that the British established astride the main railway line north of Indaw. From there, the British effectively blocked the main transportation artery supporting Japanese operations in northern Burma. Meanwhile, various Chindit elements carried out a series of raids across the region that destroyed a number of Japanese dumps and installations. Not surprisingly, this British presence in their rear area evoked an immediate and harsh response from the Japanese 18th Division, which launched a series of attacks against both White City and Broadway. This resulted in much heavy fighting in which the British successfully repulsed each attack, often with the assistance of artillery flown into the area. On a less positive note, on 24 March General Wingate died in an air crash thus robbing the Chindits of their flamboyant leader, and the next day a British attempt to capture Indaw failed. Yet, notwithstanding these mishaps, the Chindits were generally successful in fulfilling their overriding obstruction and diversionary roles throughout the next month, although the strain on the forces involved increasingly took its toll.

At the end of April, the Chindits, now under the command of Brigadier Walter Lentaigne, assumed a new mission as they were ordered by General Stilwell to directly assist in his efforts to capture Mogaung and Myitkyina. Accordingly, the Chindits, now minus 16th Brigade which had already been withdrawn, abandoned their positions around Indaw and established a new blocking position, called Blackpool, some 30 miles south of Mogaung on the main railway and road line. Once again, this garnered a violent Japanese response including attacks carried out by the Japanese 53rd Division, which had recently arrived in the area from southern Burma (minus its one regiment detached to reinforce the 33rd Division at Imphal). The British repulsed a major attack on Blackpool on 17 May, but a subsequent attack one week later compromised key positions within the perimeter thus prompting the British to abandoned the base. By this time, the Chindit brigades were in rough shape having endured several weeks of hard fighting in the harsh jungle environment made worse by the monsoon rains that were now in full swing. Still, the Chindits carried out one last mission when 77th Brigade executed a brilliant attack capturing Mogaung on 27 June.

This action essentially signalled the end of the Chindit operation. By this time, 77th and 111th Brigades were largely spent forces, and they were both withdrawn from the area in July. The 14th and 3rd West African Brigades remained in the area a little longer, but these too were withdrawn from Burma in August. Once back in India, the Chindits were disbanded, although some of their components were reformed into the new 44th Airborne Division and the headquarters element for the XXXIV Corps. During the Chindit portions of the fighting, the British inflicted 5,311 casualties upon the Japanese including 4,716 fatalities for the loss of 3,786 combat casualties to themselves.[11] Of course, their main contribution was the impact they had in helping to perpetuate Stilwell's offensive in the north. To this end, on 3 August Chinese forces finally captured Myitkyina thus claiming the ultimate prize for the entire offensive. Even before this occurred, Allied forces captured the nearby airfield, and the British 36th Division flew in to support operations. Thereafter, the division began an advance down the railway corridor from Mogaung towards Indaw.

On a strategic level, this success in northern Burma had implications beyond the immediate region. One of the consequences of the fall of Burma in 1942 had been the severing of the Burma Road, which had been the only direct land route connecting China to the outside world. Prior to this, the Allies had used the Burma Road to transport supplies into China, but when this was cut, they resorted to aerial resupply from airbases in India to fulfill this function. This required the flying of transport aircraft over the treacherous Himalaya Mountain chain, which proved to be a dangerous undertaking due to the harsh terrain, unpredictable weather and occasional Japanese opposition. With the capture of Myitkyina, the Allies eliminated Japan's primary fighter base menacing these movements, and this allowed them to alter their transit route to a more direct, and less dangerous, course thus helping to reduce losses and increase deliveries. Even more important, the seizure of this territory allowed the Allies to build a new road that connected into the northern portion of the old Burma Road thus reestablishing their direct connection with China. This road was completed at the end of 1944 with usage beginning in January. Together, these supply operations helped sustain Chinese participation in the war while allowing the United States to establish and maintain an air command, the Fourteenth Air Force, within China itself to wage an aerial campaign against Japanese assets throughout the region.

This success in northern Burma augmented the Fourteenth Army's crushing victory at Imphal and Kohima and its recent success in the Arakan thus irrevocably passing the initiative into British hands. For the remainder of the year the British moved quickly to exploit their newly gained advantage. On Fourteenth Army's front, the British followed up the defeated and retreating Japanese Fifteenth Army and eventually crossed the Chindwin River to firmly establish itself on Burma's west central frontier. During the process of this advance, the British continued to inflict heavy losses upon their beleaguered Japanese opponents. A partial accounting of this included 8,859 Japanese fatalities (as confirmed by body counts) and 234 prisoners taken by Fourteenth Army from 1 July through 1 November. Fourteenth Army losses during the same period consisted of 583 dead, 2,001 wounded and 110 missing.[12] Much of this British success was highlighted by the 11th East African Division, which spearheaded the British offensive and accounted for 7,868 Japanese fatalities, 387 prisoners and the seizure of over 40 guns through the middle of December.[13] Meanwhile, in the north, Allied forces continued to expand their hold over northern Burma. This included the activities of the newly arrived British 36th Division, which claimed over 600 Japanese killed and 20 taken prisoner by infantry as well as another 630 Japanese found dead as a result of artillery, air attacks, wounds and disease during the first three months of its advance down the railway corridor.[14] Altogether, Japanese losses in this northern sector (including those inflicted by American and Chinese forces) from 1 July through 1 November included 3,724 fatalities and 246 prisoners. Related British losses consisted of 513 dead, 1,389 wounded and 47 missing.[15]

A major factor in bringing about these ground victories was a similar success the Allies enjoyed in the air. In the autumn of 1943, the Allies had a total of 48 British and 17 American squadrons within the theatre of which the majority were in Eastern Air Command. By May 1944 this strength had increased to 64 British and 28 American squadrons respectively.[16] During the intervening period, this expanding force, which was led by Air Chief Marshal Richard Peirse, played an indispensable role in bringing about the great victories just mentioned. Of particular consequence, without the essential transit and logistical support provided by the Allied transport aircraft, none of these victories would have been remotely possible or at best would have been exceedingly more difficult to attain. The scale of this undertaking was demonstrated by the fact that from January through July these transport aircraft

In late 1944 the British went onto the offensive and began operations to re-conquer central and southern Burma. Pictured here are men of the British 36th Division advancing near Pinwe. (Stubbs, A. (Sgt), No. 9 Army & Photographic Unit, public domain)

flew some 15,000 sorties within the theatre.[17] Beyond this, British strike aircraft flew thousands of additional sorties attacking Japanese ground forces in direct contact with the army as well as their local supply dumps and camps. Meanwhile, other Allied aircraft ranged deep into Burma attacking infrastructure and support targets. Given these actions, Eastern Air Command proved to be an indispensable partner in helping the army overcome its Japanese opponents.

By comparison, despite the presence of some 740 aircraft within the region at the end of 1943 including 200 fighters, 110 bombers and 60 reconnaissance aircraft that were located in Burma, the Japanese air force was unable to give comparable support to its ground forces or seriously disrupt the efforts of the British.[18] This latter point was demonstrated by the fact that Japanese fighters only succeeded in shooting down a total of four Allied transport aircraft during the first seven months of 1944. Instead, during this period Japanese efforts were largely limited to conducting periodic raids against Calcutta and other set targets as well as regular fighter sweeps over the battle areas. The British contested these incursions with their newly arrived Spitfire squadrons, and from the middle of December 1943 through the end of July 1944 these British fighters claimed 90 Japanese aircraft destroyed and 46 probably destroyed in aerial combat.[19] At the same time Allied fighter-bombers destroyed at least three times this number of aircraft on the ground during strikes against Japanese airfields. As part of this, from March through May alone, Eastern Air Command fighter-bombers claimed at least 309 Japanese aircraft destroyed during these raids.[20]

Given these losses and the limited number of replacement aircraft that arrived in the area, Japanese regional air strength was cut in half by June including only about 125 aircraft remaining in Burma.[21] Against this, British losses from all causes (aerial combat, ground fire, accidents and mechanical failure) during the first seven months of 1944 included 34 fighters, 135 fighter-bombers and 15 dive-bombers.[22] However, unlike the Japanese, the British were able to make good their losses and actually expand their strength through the continuous flow of new aircraft arriving in the theatre. The same held true for the American portion of Eastern Air Command. As such, by the end of this period, the Allies had attained a degree of air superiority within the theatre that was now irreversible. Although the local Japanese air force would continue to offer sporadic resistance, the Allies had clearly gained a decisive advantage that would greatly assist their future efforts within the region.

This growing ascendancy was equally true regarding all of the British services in the SEAC area of operations. In less than a year the British had gone from frustrating stalemate to success on a variety of levels within the theatre. At sea, the British had secured their own maritime lines of communication while progressively degrading Japan's ability to do the same. In doing so, they maintained and expanded the vital flow of war materiel into the region while establishing an increasing ability to exploit sea power to their own advantage. On land, the British had decisively defeated two major Japanese offensives, inflicted heavy losses upon their antagonists, recaptured much of northern Burma and positioned themselves to liberate the remainder of the country. In the air, the British had effectively exercised a degree of air-ground coordination far exceeding anything previously experienced in Southeast Asia while rendering their Japanese counterparts impotent. Going forward, the British had every reason to believe that they would continue to maintain the substantial progress already made in their SEAC area of responsibility including the re-conquest of Burma and a subsequent recapture of Malaya and Singapore.

Given these events, it was clear that Britain was reengaging in the war against Japan, and this commitment was only likely to increase in the upcoming year. This expansion was aided by events in Europe where the war was rapidly advancing towards a victorious conclusion. In June 1944 the Allies launched a successful invasion of Normandy in northern France thus reestablishing their presence in Northwest Europe. By the beginning of autumn, the Allies had no fewer than seven powerful field armies (including one British and one Canadian)[23] encroaching upon Germany's western border after having liberated most of France and Belgium. In the process, the Allies inflicted heavy losses upon the Germans, which included the taking of 567,374 German prisoners during a period of about three and a half months of which 156,951 were taken by the British and Canadian forces as of 26 September.[24] During this heady time there was wild speculation within the Allied camp that the war might be over by Christmas. As it turned out, it would take an additional four and a half months beyond this Christmas deadline to bring about this outcome, but the final matter was never in doubt. Given this situation, many British officials, including Churchill, were now eager to reenter the Pacific war. It would take some time to bring this about, but the commitment was undeniable. Even as they continued their efforts in Burma and the Indian Ocean, the British were once again poised to reenter the Pacific conflict in a meaningful way.

On the day when this occurred, the British could expect to confront a Japanese adversary every bit as tenacious as the one they had unsuccessfully battled in 1941 and 1942. If nothing else, it seemed certain that the Japanese would continue to offer fanatical resistance to every Allied advance. Still, regardless of their actions, the Japanese could not hope to prevail against the military juggernaut arrayed against them. This was predominantly an American juggernaut, but British and Commonwealth elements were also present. Fighting hand in hand, these British and Commonwealth partners had participated in the successes already attained in the Southwest Pacific and Southeast Asia. Now with the Japanese Empire caught in a death grip of powerful converging forces, these same Allied partners would soon join the Americans in bringing the war directly to Japan's doorstep. For three years the Japanese had wreaked havoc upon their Asian neighbours. The time was quickly approaching when Japan would reap the bitter harvest of its criminal aggression.

CHAPTER 9

Tightening the Noose

On 20 October 1944, after days of preliminary operations, powerful forces of the American Sixth Army landed on the island of Leyte in the central Philippines. Brought in on some 300 assorted transports and landing ships of the American Seventh Fleet, these landings were initially made by four divisions against minimal Japanese opposition. This was the opening of America's re-conquest of the Philippines, which represented the first effort to seize one of the key possessions in Japan's inner empire. Prior to this, the Allies had reclaimed substantial territory from the Japanese, but this had all been on the periphery. With the seizure of the Philippines, Japan would not only be deprived of this prime territorial possession, but American forces would be ideally positioned to sever Japanese lines of communication between their home islands and the vast resources of Malaya and the Dutch East Indies. Appropriation of these resources had been the reason for Japan's entry into the war, and now they were on the verge of losing access to these critical assets. Likewise, the capture of the Philippines would provide the Allies with further staging bases for their advance towards Japan.

Given the stakes involved, the Imperial Japanese Navy felt compelled to launch an all-out effort to reverse this prospect. Executing a multipronged plan utilising most of the remaining heavy warships available to them, the Japanese sent three distinct forces towards the Americans from different directions. The first consisted of their remaining aircraft carriers approaching from the north, which were now largely devoid of aircraft due to recent heavy losses. No longer useful as effective weapons, the Japanese planned to use these carriers as decoys to draw the American covering force, the U.S. Third Fleet, away from the invasion area. Once accomplished, the Japanese planned to strike the exposed American invasion fleet with two converging battle groups approaching from the west consisting of a combined seven battleships, 16 cruisers and 26 destroyers. Using these surface warships, along with ground-based aircraft, the Japanese hoped to cause enough damage against the exposed American transports and support vessels to halt or seriously impede their landing efforts on Leyte.

The result of these manoeuvres was a series of engagements that collectively became known as the battle of Leyte Gulf. This combined battle constituted the largest fleet action of the war and a decisive defeat for the Japanese that signalled a death knell to the Imperial Japanese Navy. In the grand scheme of things, the battle unfolded according to Japanese designs, but it utterly failed in its local execution to fulfil their objectives. Although successful in their efforts to draw the Third Fleet away to the north, the Americans still retained enough strength around Leyte to effectively deal with the converging battle groups and prevent them from engaging the transport fleet. The result of this was a slaughter of Japanese forces. For the loss of one aircraft carrier, two escort carriers, three destroyers and one submarine; the Americans sank four Japanese aircraft carriers, three battleships, 10 cruisers and 11 destroyers. Not only did the Japanese entirely fail in their attempt to impede the American invasion, but these heavy losses effectively destroyed the Japanese navy as a cohesive fighting force, and its remaining ships could now only be used on a limited and local basis.

Although overwhelmingly an American endeavour, there were some British and Commonwealth contributions to the Philippines' invasion and subsequent battle of Leyte Gulf. In terms of indirect support, the Eastern Fleet's conduct of Operation *Millet* against the Nicobar Islands on 17–19 October (see Chapter 7) was timed to draw Japanese attention away from the pending landings at Leyte. More directly, amongst the vast armada of American vessels operating off the Philippines during this period were a number of ships flying the white ensign (flag) of the British and Commonwealth navies. Many of these were support vessels, but this included the Australian cruisers *Australia* and *Shropshire* and the destroyers *Arunta* and *Warramunga*, which were part of the bombardment force. Also present was the British fast minelayer *Ariadne*, which was used as an assault troop carrier for the landings. In the case of the latter, *Ariadne* was the first British surface warship to serve in the Pacific since *Victorious*' short stint in the Solomons the year before. In fact, *Ariadne* had arrived in the Pacific in February to help compensate for a lack of dedicated minelaying capacity in the United States Navy and had already conducted two minelaying operations off Wewak, New Guinea prior to this assignment.

With the commencement of the Leyte landings, these Commonwealth warships quickly found themselves embroiled in action against the Japanese. On the 21st a Japanese suicide bomber hit *Australia* killing 30 of its crew and forcing the damaged cruiser to withdraw from the combat area. A few nights later *Shropshire* and *Arunta* exacted revenge for this mishap when they joined an American battle group in repulsing one of the Japanese pincers attempting to break through to the American landing area. This action, which was fought in the Surigao Strait on the night of 24/25 October, was part of the larger battle of Leyte Gulf and proved to be history's final naval engagement involving competing battleships. During this fight, *Shropshire* and *Arunta* concentrated their fire on the Japanese flagship *Yamashiro*. In this, *Shropshire* was particularly successful scoring at least ten straddles

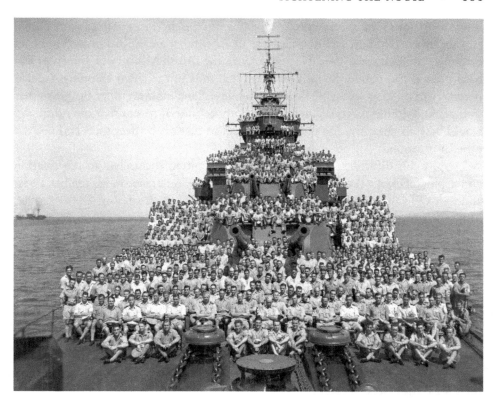

The Australian heavy cruiser *Shropshire* and crew some four months after participating in the battle of Surigao Strait where its 8-inch guns helped sink the Japanese battleship *Yamashiro*. (Royal Australian Navy, public domain)

and a number of presumed hits out of the 214 8-inch shells it fired at the stricken battleship.[1] *Shropshire's* fire control personnel later claimed sixteen direct hits during the engagement. This was just a small part of the deluge of shells that brought about *Yamashiro's* demise, but *Shropshire's* and *Arunta's* participation in helping sink the Japanese battleship, which capsized at 0419 hours, gave the British a degree of revenge for the loss of *Prince of Wales* and *Repulse* three years earlier.

Of course, this was only a portion of the desired retribution the British planned to exact against the Japanese. Even as the fighting was underway at Leyte Gulf, the British were making their own preparations to return to the Pacific. As far back as the Sextant Conference in Cairo on 26–27 November 1943, the Allies had agreed in principle to the creation of a British Pacific Fleet. Considering the condition of the Eastern Fleet at the time, this prospect seemed little more than wishful thinking. Nevertheless, the British Chiefs of Staff and the Admiralty began preliminary planning and coordination to bring this fleet into being. Their biggest challenge was the creation of an adequate fleet train and logistical support system.

These provisions were necessary to compensate for the sheer size of the Pacific Ocean and the absence of port facilities near the likely combat areas. This proved to be an extremely difficult task. After five years of war, the British Ministry of Transport was hard pressed to provide the million and a half tons of merchant shipping deemed necessary to build an adequate fleet train while still maintaining all of Britain's other military and domestic requirements. It quickly became apparent that the Admiralty would have to tailor the size of its Pacific fleet to that of the fleet train and not the other way around.

Despite this difficulty, the British firmly committed themselves to the creation and deployment of a Pacific fleet during the Quebec Conference in September 1944, and they officially activated this fleet at Ceylon two months later on 22 November. This newly established force predominantly consisted of the most modern ships out of the Eastern Fleet plus new arrivals from Europe. This included the battleships *Howe* and *King George V* and the aircraft carriers *Illustrious, Indomitable, Victorious* and *Indefatigable*. This latter carrier joined the fleet on 10 December 1944 and embarked two new aircraft types not previously utilised against the Japanese, the Seafire short-range fighter and the Firefly long-range fighter-bomber. Admiral Bruce Fraser commanded this new fleet with Second-in-Command going to Vice-Admiral Bernard Rawlings. They assigned the main combat portion of the fleet, the 1st Aircraft Carrier Squadron, to Rear-Admiral Philip Vian. Finally, Vice-Admiral Arthur Power assumed command over the remains of the Eastern Fleet, which was now redesignated the East Indies Fleet.

No sooner had Admiral Fraser assumed command of the British Pacific Fleet then he left Ceylon to meet with his American counterpart, Admiral Chester Nimitz, in Pearl Harbor. The purpose of this meeting was to pave the way for Britain's return to the Pacific. In this matter, Fraser was able to quickly gain acceptance and support from Nimitz. Before their meeting ended, the two admirals signed a document known as the Pearl Harbor Agreement. This agreement stipulated four major tenets to help facilitate the Royal Navy's return to the Pacific. First, the British Pacific Fleet would operate under Nimitz or MacArthur. Second, the fleet would adopt American signal procedures. Third, the fleet would have access to Manus in the Admiralty Islands as an intermediate base. Finally, the British task force commander would hold the same status as an American task force commander. With this agreement in hand, Fraser departed Pearl Harbor and returned to Australia arriving on 24 December to establish his headquarters and prepare the way for the arrival of his new fleet.

In his absence, the fleet conducted its first offensive operation. On 17 December Admiral Vian led Force 67, consisting of the aircraft carriers *Illustrious* and *Indomitable*, three cruisers and seven destroyers, out of Trincomalee to conduct Operation *Robson* against the oil refinery at Pangkalan Brandan. This force arrived off Sumatra on the 20th and launched a strike of 27 Avenger bombers with fighter escort. Poor weather conditions forced the British to divert to a secondary target, the harbour and railway yards at Belawan Deli, but this area was also shrouded in low clouds and rain squalls, and their bombing results suffered accordingly. Fighter strikes against surrounding airfields were more successful as the British claimed the destruction of a number of Japanese aircraft on the ground. Likewise, two British Hellcat fighters from *Indomitable* intercepted and shot down a Mitsubishi KI-21 Sally bomber. The British accomplished these feats for no combat losses to themselves, although an Avenger from *Indomitable* was lost due to operational causes. Yet, despite these latter successes, the British were generally disappointed with the results of their strike, and they viewed the operation as a fairly inauspicious debut for their new fleet.

Fortunately, the British had little time to dwell on this disappointment as they were quickly assigned a more substantial task to carry out consisting of a series of heavy air strikes against the strategically important oil refineries at Palembang in southern Sumatra. These facilities were vitally important to the Japanese war effort as they were the largest oil refineries in Southeast Asia with a capacity to satisfy half of Japan's total oil usage and 75 percent of its aviation fuel requirements.[2] Despite their strategic significance, the Palembang refineries had thus far largely escaped the ravages of war. An American attempt to attack them with heavy bombers had failed to cause any significant damage, and now Admiral Nimitz requested that the newly established British Pacific Fleet launch a more targeted assault. Even as they were preparing to leave the Indian Ocean for the Pacific, this was an opportunity the British dared not refuse, and they eagerly accepted the mission.

Prior to the conduct of these strikes, the British launched what was essentially a dress rehearsal with another raid against Pangkalan Brandan in northeast Sumatra. On 31 December 1944 Admiral Vian led elements of the British Pacific Fleet, including the aircraft carriers *Victorious, Indefatigable* and *Indomitable*, out of Trincomalee to conduct Operation *Lentil*. Four days later the fleet arrived off Sumatra and launched its attack. The carriers first launched a strike of 16 Corsair and Hellcat fighters to conduct 'Ramrod' offensive sweeps against four airfields in the target area. These Ramrods destroyed seven Japanese aircraft on the ground and two more in aerial combat while a further five Japanese aircraft were assessed as damaged. Ninety minutes later the British launched a second strike consisting of 32 Avengers and 12 Fireflies escorted by 32 Corsairs and Hellcats against the oil refinery at Pangkalan Brandan and shipping in the nearby harbour at Pangkalan Soe Soe. This attack was very successful as the British heavily damaged the oil refinery thus causing a significant reduction in output for several months. They also damaged a small tanker in the harbour and destroyed five Japanese aircraft in aerial combat. The British suffered no combat losses during this operation, but two aircraft were lost due to engine failure.

With a successful rehearsal now complete, the fleet turned its attention to the Palembang refineries. The British knew that these refineries represented one of the toughest targets yet assigned to the Fleet Air Arm. Just getting there was going to be a challenge as the attacking aircraft would have to traverse the 7,000-foot Barisan Mountain Range and then fly 150 miles over hostile territory. Once there, the British faced a formidable defence, which included six Japanese fighter squadrons from the 9th Air Division stationed on airfields around the refineries. The Japanese also had one of the heaviest concentrations of anti-aircraft guns in all of Southeast Asia and a balloon barrage located in and around the target areas.[3] To meet these challenges, the British assembled a powerful strike force consisting of the battleship *King George V*, the aircraft carriers *Indomitable, Illustrious, Victorious* and *Indefatigable*, three cruisers and nine destroyers. The key striking power behind this force was the fleet's combined air strength of 83 Avengers, 76 Corsairs, 40 Seafires, 29 Hellcats and 12 Fireflies plus two Walrus floatplanes for the recovery of downed aircrews. Given this force, the British planned to hit Palembang with more aircraft than had been utilised during any other combined Fleet Air Arm strike of the war.[4]

On 16 January 1945 Admiral Vian led the British Pacific Fleet, now designated Force 63, out of Ceylon for the last time. On the morning of 24 January the fleet arrived at its first fly-off position and launched Operation *Meridian One* against the Palembang refinery at Pladjoe. This strike consisted of 43 Avengers and 12 Fireflies escorted by 32 Corsairs and 16 Hellcats. A secondary strike of five Avengers and four Hellcats attacked Mana airfield on the southwest coast while 24 Corsairs conducted two Ramrod sweeps against airfields in the target area. Despite heavy Japanese opposition, these attacks were very successful. At Pladjoe, the British striking force fought its way through heavy Japanese defences and extensively damaged the oil refinery. In related fighting, the British destroyed 34 Japanese aircraft on the ground and at least 11 more in aerial combat and damaged a vessel that was adjacent to the refinery. The fleet suffered no reprisals as a result of these attacks and was able to withdraw unmolested to the southwest for refuelling.

On the 29th the British returned to Sumatra and launched *Meridian Two* against Palembang's second major oil refinery located at Soengei Gerong. This operation was essentially a repeat performance of the strike conducted five days earlier, and it attained similar positive results. Utilising a strike force of 123 aircraft, the British completely crippled the oil refinery, destroyed 38 Japanese aircraft on the ground and another 30 in aerial combat. The Japanese reacted to this onslaught by launching seven Mitsubishi KI-21 Sally bombers from the Shichisci Mitate Unit of the Army's Special Attack Group in a counter-attack against the fleet. Despite a determined effort, this attack ended in utter failure. Patrolling British fighters and naval anti-aircraft fire shot down all seven Japanese bombers and a KI-46 Dinah reconnaissance aircraft before they could inflict any damage upon the fleet. This action signalled the end of the *Meridian* operations, and the fleet departed Sumatra to proceed to Australia and the Pacific war.

The *Meridian* operations were the Fleet Air Arm's largest combined air strikes of the war and represented the Royal Navy's single greatest contribution to the Allied war effort against Japan. As a result of these strikes, monthly crude oil output at Pladjoe dropped from 1,039,000 barrels to 265,000 and 173,000 barrels in February and March respectively. Soengei Gerong suffered a similar impact on production with overall output dropping from 666,000 barrels to 160,000 barrels in February.[5] Neither oil refinery ever achieved pre-strike production levels for the remainder of the war, and this shortfall reduced aviation fuel output from Sumatra to only 35 percent of its previous level.[6] In turn, this loss of aviation fuel crippled or hampered Japanese air operations across a series of fronts. These attacks also cost the Japanese at least 121 aircraft destroyed with damage inflicted to vessels and other local assets. British losses were much smaller in comparison amounting to 16 aircraft destroyed in combat and 25 more from operational causes. This represented a great victory and a more fitting start for the fledgling British Pacific Fleet.

This triumph was also indicative of the continuing string of disasters befalling Japan. By the beginning of 1945 Japanese fortunes were declining everywhere, and Japan was clearly losing the war. This was particularly true in the maritime realm where the Japanese were quickly losing their ability to use sea power as a means to advance their national objectives. As already discussed, with its defeat at Leyte Gulf, the Imperial Japanese Navy could no longer conduct largescale fleet operations or even operate beyond localised areas. Although the Japanese still possessed numerous warships, these tended to be of smaller designs and were almost entirely relegated to defensive applications. Even more devastating for the Japanese was the ongoing disintegration of their merchant fleet. In the latter half of 1944 Japanese shipping losses continued to accelerate culminating in an annual toll of 3,892,019 tons sunk by years end.[7] As covered in Chapter 6, the Americans were responsible for most of these losses, but British and Commonwealth forces made some contributions to this attrition. In terms of means, almost two-thirds of these merchant ships were sunk by submarines while aircraft, mines and surface warships accounted for most of the rest.

The result of this carnage was a severe withering of the Japanese merchant fleet. At the beginning of the Pacific war Japan possessed 5,996,607 tons of merchant shipping. In the succeeding three years the Japanese lost 6,836,094 tons of this shipping against a gain of 3,551,334 tons through acquisitions and new construction. The net result of this was a merchant fleet reduced to 2,711,847 tons by the end of 1944 thus representing a 54.8 percent reduction compared to its prewar level.[8] This, in turn, contributed to a significant decline in Japanese imports, which dropped from a prewar annual level of 67 million tons to a mere 16 million tons in 1944. Even more devastating, oil imports dropped from 1.75 million barrels per month in August 1943 to just 360,000 barrels in July 1944.[9] With this, the entire Japanese war effort suffered from a growing lack of resources that plagued both its industry and military alike. Just one example of the former was an 85.68 and 95.04 percent decline in Japanese steel and aluminum production respectively from 1943 to 1945 due largely to shortages of ore, coke and bauxite.[10] Meanwhile, Japanese oil stockpiles dropped from some 43 million barrels at the beginning of the war to just 3.71 million barrels available on 1 April 1945.[11]

The situation was much the same in the air where the Japanese struggled to counter the growing aerial onslaught confronting them. Much of this was simply a matter of materiel strength as the Japanese increasingly found themselves outnumbered by their Allied opponents. From 1942 through 1944 the United States and Britain produced 230,052 and 76,396 military aircraft respectively compared to only 53,734 aircraft produced by Japan.[12] While the majority of these Allied aircraft were dedicated to the European war, enough were left over to significantly outnumber the Japanese. As such, in January 1945 the Americans possess 17,976 frontline aircraft in the Pacific compared to just 4,600 for Japan.[13] When British and Commonwealth contributions were added in, this disparity became even greater. The Japanese also suffered from growing disadvantages in terms of aircraft and pilot quality. At the beginning of the war the Japanese had possessed some very capable aircraft types, but in the succeeding years, subsequent Japanese designs had failed to keep pace with ongoing Allied innovations. As a result, by 1945 most Japanese aircraft were inferior to their Allied counterparts. This situation was even more pronounced when it came to pilot proficiency. Whereas in 1941 the Japanese had possessed some of the best trained pilots and aircrews in the world, by 1945 this proficiency had substantially dropped to a point where many Japanese pilots were only partially trained. Much of this was due to chronic shortages of aviation fuel, which limited training time as well as operational flying. Of course, this matter was only made worse by the recent British strikes against Palembang and other oil refineries in Southeast Asia.

The result of these growing disparities was Allied attainment of air superiority over all the major regions of the conflict. This was even true in China where the United States, through support from India, established a sizeable air force in the interior of the nation. Of even greater consequence, the Americans were able to begin a strategic bombing campaign against the Japanese home islands. This onslaught initially emerged out of China in June 1944, but this quickly proved to be an unsatisfactory base of operations due to logistical constraints and the great distances involved. In late November the Americans began launching raids out of the Marianas, and this proved to be a much better option. Within three months the Americans were subjecting Japanese cities to largescale firebombing raids, and soon every major city in Japan, along with its embedded war industry, was susceptible to these attacks. While this was underway, the Americans launched a concurrent effort to lay aerial mines in Japanese ports and coastal waterways. Christened Operation *Starvation*, the purpose of this was to further isolate Japan from its overseas trade. Finally, in February and March American carrier forces launched their own series of air strikes against military targets in Japan. The Japanese attempted to counter these various actions and were able to inflict some losses against the Americans, but generally their efforts were inadequate in curbing the aerial tempest engulfing them.

Nor was the Imperial Japanese Army able to provide any meaningful relief. By 1945 the Japanese had over five million men under arms of which roughly half were stationed in Japan with the rest spread across Asia. Still, despite its vast size, the army lacked the means to proactively counter the various threats engulfing Japan. In terms of its deployed formations, many were stationed in isolated locations cut off and bypassed by the advance of the war. In others, large contingents of Japanese troops garrisoned vast imperial possessions that were increasingly incapable of providing material benefit to the home islands given Japan's waning maritime situation. In nearly all cases, these disparate formations were incapable of operating in a coordinated manner supporting a common goal. Instead, about the only thing the Japanese army was still capable of doing was defending in place wherever it was located, be that on the home islands or thousands of miles away on an isolated outpost. As such, the Japanese army was almost completely reactive to the events unfolding around it without an ability to take the initiative or seriously change the course of the war.

A case in point, by the beginning of 1945 the Japanese still had upwards of 200,000 men stationed in the Solomon Islands, Bismarck Archipelago and New Guinea. This was territory that had largely been bypassed in the Allied advance across the Southwest Pacific. As such, the sizeable Japanese forces marooned there were incapable of providing meaningful benefit to the Japanese war effort other than tying down Allied forces in containment and mopping up operations. To this end, in late 1944 the Australian army assumed full responsibility for this area thus freeing up American units to participate in the liberation of the Philippines. Since much of this was Australian territory, the Australians eagerly accepted this task and employed four infantry divisions and two armoured brigades to carry it out. Over the next several months these Australian forces would apply growing pressure to progressively tighten their grip around the isolated Japanese formations and liberate additional Allied territory. Against this, the Japanese were powerless to decisively alter their situation as disease and starvation proved to be as much of an adversary as were their Australian antagonists.

For Japanese forces stationed in other parts of the empire or on the home islands, the immediate situation was not as dire, but their long-term prospects were equally bleak. Japan was in the unenviable position of being under multidimensional assault by a more powerful adversary with no meaningful ability to decisively strike back or do anything other than respond to each blow as it occurred. Yet, as bad as this was, the Japanese still clung to a hope that they could stave off total defeat. With an eventual invasion of Japan now an assumed outcome, the Japanese hoped to inflict such cost upon the Allies that these losses, or the threat of catastrophic losses, would convince the Allies to accept a negotiated settlement short of Japan's unconditional surrender. To carry this out, the Japanese were willing to endure immense hardships and employ extreme measures as they sought to grind down Allied resolve through fierce and relentless resistance wherever challenged. Thus, like a wounded animal, the Japanese were still extremely dangerous despite, or because of, their increasingly desperate situation.

It was against this backdrop that the Royal Navy joined the Pacific war and added its weight to the contest. On 10 February the major ships of the British Pacific Fleet arrived in Sydney where they joined dozens of military and merchant ships already there. The majority of these latter ships were part of Rear-Admiral Douglas Fisher's newly formed fleet train. For the next two and a half weeks, the fleet remained in Sydney to replenish and prepare itself for action. Then on 28 February it departed for the intermediate staging base of Manus in the Admiralty Islands. Despite these activities, there was a great deal of uncertainty about the fleet's upcoming role. The U.S. Chief of Naval Operations, Admiral Ernest King, wanted to use the fleet to support General MacArthur's Southwest Pacific campaign. The British and Admiral Nimitz opposed him on this matter. They instead wanted to utilise the fleet in the upcoming invasion of Okinawa. After much internal debate and a great deal of lobbying by the British government, Admiral King finally relented and agreed to release the fleet to Nimitz. He did so, however, with the proviso that he could transfer the fleet to MacArthur's command after giving a seven-day notice.

On 15 March the British Pacific Fleet reported itself ready for action to Admiral Nimitz, who in turn assigned it to Admiral Raymond Spruance's Fifth Fleet for Operation *Iceberg*, the invasion of Okinawa. For this invasion, the Fifth Fleet had assembled over 1,300 warships and auxiliaries and 1,700 aircraft. Spruance divided these ships and aircraft into an assault force, Task Force 51, a covering force, Task Force 58, and a logistical supply group. Joining this colossal force was the British Pacific Fleet, now designated Task Force 57. Vice-Admiral Rawlings commanded this British task force with Rear-Admiral Vian in command of the carrier squadron. It consisted of the battleships *King George V* and *Howe*, the aircraft carriers *Indomitable*, *Victorious*, *Indefatigable* and *Illustrious*, five cruisers, 11 destroyers and about 220 combat aircraft. The British Fleet Train, now designated Task Force 112, provided logistical support to this force and eventually reached a peak strength of 125 ships worth 712,000 tons and some 26,200 men.[14]

On 19 March Admiral Rawlings took the fleet to Ulithi to replenish and receive final orders for Operation *Iceberg*. Task Force 57 acquired the mission to secure the Fifth Fleet's southern flank by neutralising Japanese airfields in the Sakishima Gunto Island Group. There were six principal airfields located on the islands of Ishigaki and Miyako in the Sakishima Gunto. These airfields were ideally situated to serve as staging areas for air attacks and air reinforcements sent from Formosa to Okinawa. The British planned to hit these airfields on a rotating basis with two days of strikes followed by two replenishment days. During the replenishment periods the American escort carriers of Task Group 52.1.3 were designated to come on station and continue the strikes. In this manner, the Allies hoped to maintain continuous pressure against the airfields thus mitigating their usefulness to the enemy.

The importance of this mission and the dangers facing the British fleet were facilitated by a new and deadly threat recently introduced by the Japanese. Realising they could no longer prevail against America's immense materiel superiority using conventional methods, the Japanese had adopted Kamikaze tactics to counter this imbalance. The Kamikazes were volunteer Japanese suicide pilots who purposely attempted to crash their bomb-laden aircraft into Allied ships thus turning themselves into human missiles. Throughout the war Japanese pilots had occasionally performed similar acts on an impromptu basis, but now this was an organised effort with dedicated units earmarked for this purpose. The use of Kamikazes suited the Japanese in two ways. First, given the technology that existed at the time, the Kamikazes represented the ultimate guided weapon to multiply the effectiveness of their limited resources. Second, it allowed the Japanese to compensate for the increasingly poor state of their pilot proficiency since it took far less training and skill to crash an airplane into a warship than it did to hit the same warship with a bomb or torpedo.

The Allies were well aware of this threat since the first dedicated Kamikaze attacks had occurred during the battle of Leyte Gulf. In fact, it was during one of these attacks that the aforementioned cruiser *Australia* was hit. Unfortunately, this was only the beginning of *Australia*'s ordeal. In January *Australia* participated in follow-up operations in the Lingayen Gulf where it was hit by no fewer than five Kamikazes. Despite being heavily damaged with 44 dead and 72 wounded, the Australian cruiser survived the onslaught and even managed to remain on station until ordered to retire.[15] The same was not true for a number of American warships. From October 1944 through February 1945 Kamikaze strikes sank 23 American vessels including three escort carriers, three destroyers and a minesweeper. These same attacks damaged dozens of additional ships including battleships and aircraft carriers. One of these damaged warships was the battleship *New Mexico*, which sustained a Kamikaze hit to its navigation bridge during operations off Luzon on 6 January. British Lieutenant-General Herbert Lumsden, the British liaison to General MacArthur's headquarters, was among the 30 dead resulting from this incident. Also present on the bridge at the time of the strike was Admiral Fraser, who was there as an observer. Fortunately, Fraser was standing on the opposite side of the bridge when the aircraft impacted and thus escaped the calamity uninjured. Nevertheless, the incident gave the British fleet commander a personal appreciation of the immense danger posed by the Kamikaze threat.

As bad as it was, the Allies knew this was only a precursor to what they would likely encounter off Okinawa, and they girded themselves for a gruelling campaign. On 23 March Task Force 57 departed Ulithi for the Sakishima Gunto. Three days later the fleet arrived 100 miles south of Miyako and commenced Operation *Iceberg*.

During the next two days the British launched a series of air strikes against airfields and other targets of opportunity in the area. The British found relatively few Japanese aircraft on these airfields and instead concentrated on cratering the runways to deny their use to the Japanese. This proved to be an elusive task since the runways were made out of crushed coral and were thus easily repairable due to the abundance of this material on each island. The British encountered little air opposition to their attacks but had to contend with heavy and accurate anti-aircraft fire. By the close of operations on the 27th, the British had conducted 273 offensive and 275 defensive sorties which cost them six combat losses and a further 11 aircraft lost through ditching and deck landing accidents. In return, they claimed the destruction of 28 Japanese aircraft.[16] At least some of these claimed aircraft were probably decoys. Likewise, they hit various ground targets including barracks, hangars and fuel depots and sank or damaged a number of coasters and other minor vessels.

After three replenishment days, the fleet returned to Sakishima Gunto and conducted a second series of strikes beginning on the 31st. This set the pattern for the remainder of the campaign. Over the next two months, Task Force 57 conducted a rigid routine of air strikes followed by replenishment periods. This routine quickly taxed the endurance and morale of the aircrews, who saw little appreciable results for their efforts. With each series of strikes the British bombed the airfields and cratered the runways only to have the Japanese repair them again at night. This pattern repeated itself day after day with little relief. The British also attacked other targets of opportunity with particular emphasis paid to harbour installations and small maritime craft. In terms of the latter, the British attacked hundreds of minor coastal vessels during the course of Operation *Iceberg*. The majority of these vessels were of small sizes ranging from a few dozen to a few hundred tons.

On 1 April Task Force 57 underwent its first Kamikaze attack. British fighters shot down four would-be attackers before they could inflict any damage, but a fifth Kamikaze got through to hit the aircraft carrier *Indefatigable*. Thankfully, *Indefatigable*'s armoured flight deck protected the ship from serious damage, and the carrier was able to resume air operations within an hour of being struck. In the days and weeks that followed, the British fleet endured additional Kamikaze attacks and sustained hits to all of its aircraft carriers. Fortunately, as in the case of *Indefatigable*, none of these carriers suffered serious damage due to their armoured flight decks, and all were able to remain on station. In fact, the only British ship to sustain serious damage during Operation *Iceberg* was the destroyer *Ulster*, which had to be towed out of the area after being heavily damaged by a near miss from a conventional bombing attack.

Unfortunately, the same cannot be said for the Americans. While Task force 57 neutralised Sakishima Gunto, the American Fifth Fleet conducted landings on Okinawa followed by an extended period of support operations to sustain the invasion. Not surprisingly, the Japanese threw the vast bulk of their resistance against

A Fairey Firefly taking off from the aircraft carrier *Indefatigable* during the strike against Pangkalan Brandan in January 1945. A few months later the same carrier participated in extended operations off Okinawa where it, along with its partner aircraft carriers, all withstood Kamikaze hits. (Trusler, C. (Lt), Royal Navy official photographer, public domain)

this prolonged assault, and the American fleet endured far heavier Kamikaze and conventional air attacks than did their British counterparts. During this onslaught the Japanese scored hits on dozens of American ships, many of which were sunk or severely damaged. To help alleviate some of this pressure, Admiral Spruance requested that Task Force 57 launch a series of strikes against Formosa, which was the source of some of these attacks. The British eagerly accepted this request and hit Formosa on 12 and 13 April. These British attacks destroyed at least eight Japanese aircraft on the ground and caused heavy damage to area airfields, maritime targets, industrial plants and transportation infrastructure. Meanwhile, British fighters destroyed a further 16 Japanese aircraft in aerial combat including an acclaimed encounter when two Fireflies from *Indefatigable* intercepted and shot down four out of five Japanese Sonia bombers that were en route to Okinawa for no loss to themselves.

Immediately following these strikes, Admiral Spruance approached Task Force 57 with another urgent request. In the British fleet's absence, the situation at Sakishima Gunto had deteriorated as the American escort carriers of Task Group 52.1.3 struggled to adequately neutralise the airfields there. During this period the

American fleet had continued to suffer heavy losses to Kamikaze attacks including two aircraft carriers put out of action, three battleships damaged, seven destroyers sunk and another 13 destroyers damaged. To help counter these losses, Spruance requested that Task Force 57 postpone a scheduled departure to San Pedro Bay in Leyte and instead conduct one more series of strikes against Sakishima Gunto. The British again dutifully accepted this request and launched their strikes on the 16th, 17th and 20th. They did so with a new aircraft carrier among their number. On 14 April *Formidable* joined the fleet replacing *Illustrious*, which began a long journey back to the United Kingdom for a much-needed refit. Meanwhile, at the conclusion of operations on the 20th, Task Force 57 departed for San Pedro Bay in the Philippines to undergo a week of rest, replenishment and repairs.

On 4 May the fleet renewed offensive operations against Sakishima Gunto. In addition to their normal programme of air strikes, the British commemorated their return to action by conducting a fleet bombardment against the island of Miyako. During this bombardment the battleships *King George V* and *Howe*, five cruisers and six destroyers fired some 200 tons of heavy-calibre shells against Japanese positions on the island. In the absence of these heavy ships, the Japanese launched a series of air attacks against the exposed British aircraft carriers. British fighters and anti-aircraft fire destroyed 12 of these attackers, but two Kamikazes got through to score hits on the aircraft carriers *Formidable* and *Indomitable*. Five days later the fleet underwent another Kamikaze attack that scored hits on *Formidable* and *Victorious*. These attacks destroyed large numbers of aircraft on the flight decks but failed to significantly damage any of the British carriers. Finally, on the 18th *Formidable* experienced an accidental hangar fire that further exacerbated British losses by destroying 30 aircraft.

Despite these adversities, Task Force 57 successfully remained on station and continued its interdiction efforts against Sakishima Gunto. In all, the British carried out strikes on 11 separate days in May. These strikes helped neutralise Japanese resistance in the area, and aerial opposition soon waned. In fact, during the fleet's last eight strike days following the 9 May Kamikaze attack, the British encountered minimal opposition and only managed to locate and destroy a handful of Japanese aircraft in the air or on the ground. Nevertheless, the British continued their cratering efforts against the regional Japanese airfields while concurrently carrying out attacks against local Japanese shipping and other targets of opportunity. On 25 May Admiral Spruance released Task Force 57 from operational status, and the fleet departed for Sydney. Meanwhile, heavy ground fighting continued on Okinawa, and it wasn't until 22 June that American authorities finally declared the island secure.

Operation *Iceberg* firmly established the British Pacific Fleet as a viable force alongside its American allies. During this operation Task Force 57 spent 62 days at sea and carried out 23 strike days and one naval bombardment against Japanese targets. Altogether, the British conducted 5,335 sorties of which roughly 40 percent were offensive. During the latter, the British expended 927 tons of bombs, half a million rounds of ammunition and 950 rockets. In doing so, they claimed 42 Japanese aircraft destroyed in the air (excluding eight aircraft destroyed in Kamikaze strikes) with over 100 destroyed or damaged on the ground. They also sank a definite six minor vessels with a further 180 vessels either probably sunk or damaged worth an estimated 30,000 tons. This cost the British some 160 aircraft in return of which 26 were shot down in combat and at least 32 were destroyed in Kamikaze attacks. Operational causes and accidents accounted for the remaining aircraft losses. Finally, the fleet's personnel casualties amounted to 85 killed and 83 wounded.[17]

By comparison, during Operation *Iceberg* the mighty U.S. Fifth Fleet destroyed 16 Japanese warships, including the 64,000-ton super-battleship *Yamato*, a cruiser and five destroyers, along with untold numbers of Japanese aircraft. Japanese ground losses were even worse as the Japanese army suffered an estimated 100,000 casualties in its failed attempt to hold Okinawa. Of these, the vast majority were killed, but this included 7,400 men taken prisoner.[18] Putting this immense slaughter into perspective, this was roughly twice the number of casualties sustained by the Japanese during their epic defeats at Imphal and Kohima, which up to that point had constituted the worst defeats in the history of the Imperial Japanese Army. While clearly a substantial victory, this triumph came at a heavy price for the Americans as the Fifth Fleet lost 36 assorted vessels sunk and another 368 damaged, mostly due to Kamikaze and conventional air attacks. American aircraft losses amounted to 763 while the navy lost some 4,900 men killed and missing and 4,824 wounded out of a total American butcher's bill of 49,144 battle casualties for the campaign.[19]

Put in this perspective, Britain's contribution to Operation *Iceberg* seemed small, but these materiel results only partially measured the fleet's success. Despite the unglamorous nature of its mission, Task Force 57's relentless campaign to neutralise the airfields of the Sakishima Gunto helped minimize these islands as potential staging areas for large-scale air strikes against the invasion area. In this manner, the British fulfilled their primary function and contributed to the operation's overall success. Likewise, the fleet gained valuable experience and earned the respect of their American allies. The Americans were particularly impressed by the durability of the British aircraft carriers as they withstood multiple Kamikaze hits with no appreciable damage. By comparison, during the same period Kamikaze and conventional bomb hits forced the withdrawal of no fewer than seven American aircraft carriers from the operational area to undergo repairs. This American admiration was amply demonstrated during the fleet's replenishment period in San Pedro Bay when Admiral King tried to implement his seven-day notice to divert the British fleet away to support the upcoming invasion of Borneo. Admirals Nimitz and Spruance so vehemently opposed him on this matter, that King was forced to reverse himself and relented to leave the British fleet under Nimitz's control. Now with Operation *Iceberg* complete, Admiral Spruance reported the British Pacific Fleet ready to form part of the American fast carrier force thus securing a British role in the upcoming assault against Japan.

While these events were unfolding in the Pacific, the war in Burma and the Indian Ocean continued unabated. In terms of the former, by the end of 1944 the British were poised to begin their re-conquest of central and southern Burma. The main force assigned to carry this out was General William Slim's Fourteenth Army consisting of some 260,000 men in six divisions, two independent brigades and two tank brigades targeting Japanese forces in central Burma. This force was split into two corps, IV and XXXIII, with the former commanded by Lieutenant-General Frank Messervy, who had replaced General Scoones in December 1944, while the latter was commanded by Lieutenant-General Montagu Stopford. The British had a further five divisions performing or earmarked for concurrent operations in the north and south. Supporting this proposed assault were 49 tactical squadrons with a frontline strength of 464 British and 186 American fighters and 74 British and 103 American bombers, along with six photo-reconnaissance, four troop carrier and 16 transport squadrons.[20] Opposing the British in Burma were three Japanese armies containing a combined ten divisions (plus one division from the Indian National Army), two independent brigades and a tank regiment. While this was clearly a formidable force, it was tempered by the fact that many of these Japanese units were significantly understrength. Meanwhile, the situation in the air was even more uneven as the Japanese only possessed 195 frontline aircraft in the region.[21]

In November 1944 Fourteenth Army established two bridgeheads across the Chindwin River at Sittaung and Kalewa on the western edge of central Burma. On 29 November and 4 December British IV and XXXIII Corps launched advances using the 19th and 20th Indian Divisions out of these bridgeheads towards Pinlebu and Mandalay respectively. In the north the 19th Division captured Pinlebu on 14 December followed the next day by a link-up with the British 36th Division, which was advancing southward from Mogaung. This action secured the army's left flank and established a continuous front with the Northern Combat Area Command. In the south, XXXIII Corps made equally good progress and was able to draw up to the Irrawaddy River. Slim had anticipated that the Japanese would attempt to hold the Shwebo Plain located between the Chindwin and Irrawaddy Rivers and had hoped to cut off and destroy the Japanese there. However, when it became apparent that the bulk of the Japanese forces had already withdrawn across the Irrawaddy, he devised a new plan to entrap these forces around Mandalay. Accordingly, Slim transferred the 19th Division to XXXIII Corps and ordered it to operate against Mandalay, which is located on the eastern side of the Irrawaddy River near a point where the river makes a major bend to the west before continuing its southward flow. Meanwhile, the rest of IV Corps covertly shifted to the south along the Gangaw Valley to operate against Meiktila, located some 80 miles south of Mandalay along the primary transportation line running to the north. In doing so, the British set up a dummy corps headquarters near Sittaung and conducted other deception operations to shield IV Corps' movement from Japanese observation.

In January and February 1945 XXXIII Corps launched a series of assaults across the Irrawaddy River with the 19th, 20th and British 2nd Divisions that established bridgeheads north and west of Mandalay. The Japanese, believing that these crossings represented Slim's main effort, mounted a series of unsuccessful and costly counterattacks against these bridgeheads. While the Japanese expended their forces in this manner, Slim launched his main assault using IV Corps at Nyaungu to the west of Meiktila on 14 February. This attack, carried out by the 7th Indian Division, initially encountered heavy resistance from INA units, but succeeded in establishing a bridgehead across the Irrawaddy River. Thereafter, mechanised units of the 17th Indian Division and the 255th Indian Tank Brigade passed through the bridgehead and began an advance towards Meiktila. Unlike most terrain in Burma, which was dominated by jungles and mountains, this area was relatively flat and open thus making it ideal for mechanised movements. This action caught the Japanese completely by surprise, and they were hard pressed to counter the advance. On 28 February 17th Division enveloped Meiktila and began a comprehensive assault against the town, which was defended by a hastily-assembled Japanese garrison consisting of about 4,000 men including administrative and support personnel. Assisted by substantial armour, air and artillery support, 17th Division quickly destroyed this garrison and took possession of Meiktila on 5 March.

With this development, the Japanese found themselves in an extremely exposed position as the seizure of Meiktila severed their supply line to Mandalay. To remedy this situation, the Japanese 18th and 49th Divisions launched a series of disjointed counterattacks to retake Meiktila, but these achieved nothing except heavy losses for the attacking divisions, which collectively suffered some 8,273 casualties and lost 67 artillery pieces during the battle.[22] While this was underway, the various divisions of XXXIII Corps broke out of their bridgeheads and advanced upon Mandalay. Entering the city on 8 March, it took two weeks of fighting for the British to fully secure the prestigious prize. This process was made more difficult by the thick walls of the massive fortress Fort Dufferin, which proved largely impervious to British air and artillery bombardment. Despite this difficulty, the British secured Mandalay on 20 March, and at the end of the month the Japanese Fifteenth and Thirty-Third Armies broke off the battle and began a desperate retreat to the south. In doing so, they ceded central Burma to the Fourteenth Army and abandoned large stocks of supplies and most of their equipment.

Following a short period of regrouping, the British gave pursuit and continued their offensive towards the capital city of Rangoon. This consisted of a dual advance down the Sittang and Irrawaddy River valleys by IV and XXXIII Corps respectively. Of these two routes, the former was shorter and thus became the

In the opening months of 1945, the British Fourteenth Army conducted a series of brilliant operations to seize Meiktila and Mandalay in central Burma. Pictured here are men of the South Wales Borderers advancing towards Mandalay. (Stubbs, A. (Sgt), No. 9 Army & Photographic Unit, public domain)

primary British effort. By this time, the Japanese lacked the means to form a continuous defence, but the British still encountered ongoing opposition from isolated Japanese formations along their line of advance. For the Fourteenth Army, this was a race against time as it strained to reach Rangoon before the monsoons broke and rendered its logistical situation unworkable. Throughout April, IV Corps advanced some 250 miles to a point 40 miles north of Rangoon. In doing so, the British accounted for 6,742 Japanese dead, 273 taken prisoner, 15 tanks, 127 guns and 434 trucks. In return, IV Corps suffered 2,166 casualties including 446 dead.[23] This added to a further 12,912 Japanese and 10,624 British casualties suffered during the earlier fighting around Mandalay and Meiktila of which 6,513 and 2,307 were fatalities respectively.[24] Beyond these known losses, many additional Japanese simply disappeared into the countryside and were never seen again.

The British augmented their conquest of central Burma and subsequent race towards Rangoon with concurrent operations in the Arakan. Beginning on 10 December 1944, XV Corps, commanded by Lieutenant-General Philip Christison, commenced its third Arakan campaign, which included a series of naval landings along Burma's northern coast. Over a five-month period the British employed substantial naval forces to support these operations including the battleship *Queen Elizabeth*, the escort carrier *Ameer*, the headquarters ship *Haitan*, four cruisers, 11 destroyers, nine sloops/frigates, two corvettes, two landing ships, four transports, eight merchant ships/auxiliaries, 22 flotillas of assorted landing craft, six flotillas of motor launches and two flotillas of motor minesweepers.[25] During this time these ships participated in numerous landings and supply operations, conducted dozens of fire support missions and generally interdicted Japanese troop and supply traffic along the coast and waterways of western Burma. British motor torpedo boats and motor launches were predominant in this latter mission. For the loss of one of their number, these boats destroyed six Japanese motor gunboats, 31 armed landing craft and 66 smaller vessels from October 1944 to May 1945.[26] Other British ships, including destroyers and sloops, also participated in this interdiction effort.

With this support, the army made steady progress into the Arakan. At the end of December West African forces from the 81st and 82nd Divisions converged on Myohaung thus cutting the Japanese supply line to the Mayu Peninsula. This action prompted the Japanese to abandon the strategically important island of Akyab, which the 74th Indian Infantry Brigade occupied on 4 January. The British immediately developed the island's airfield and put the harbour back into service. Soon Spitfires were operating from Akyab, and these made their presents felt on the 9th when they intercepted and destroyed five out of six Japanese Oscar fighters attempting to attack Allied shipping in the harbour. By February Akyab was handling the seaborne delivery of 1,050 tons of dry stores per day and this average increased to 1,328 tons in April.[27] Meanwhile, on 21 January the British moved to their next major objective and landed the 26th Indian Division on Ramree Island. With gunfire and air support from the battleship *Queen Elizabeth*, the cruiser *Phoebe* and the escort carrier *Ameer*, these landings were completely successful, and the British had 7,000 troops, 171 vehicles and 90 tons of supplies ashore by midnight. This increased to 23,091 troops, 679 vehicles and 9,233 tons of supplies ashore by 12 February.[28]

Using these vast forces, the British captured Ramree town on 9 February and drove the remains of the 1,000-strong Japanese garrison (estimated to be between 500 and 600 men) to the eastern portion of the island. Then, as efforts were underway to restore the island's airfield and port facilities, the British conducted mopping up operations to cut off and destroy the retreating Japanese forces. Under the designation of Operation *Block*, the British placed the destroyers *Paladin* and *Pathfinder*, eight motor launches, five motor minesweepers and roughly 30 assorted landing craft to the north and east of Ramree to block Japanese escape routes. During the next two weeks these vessels destroyed nearly 100 small boats and rafts and killed a reported 283 Japanese soldiers attempting to escape from the island while 14 more were taken prisoner. Most of the remaining Japanese were believed to have died in the harsh mangrove swamps with only a relative few, perhaps 100, making good their escape.[29]

While this fighting was underway, the British continued their offensive with the 82nd West African Division advancing down the coastal plain while elements of the 25th Indian Division carried out additional amphibious landings further south to entrap retreating Japanese formations. On 22 January the 3rd Commando Brigade landed near Kangaw and engaged 3,000 Japanese defenders in the bloodiest fighting of the campaign. The critical point of this battle occurred on 31 January when the Japanese counterattacked British positions on Hill 170. The British commandos held their ground but suffered 340 casualties including 66 fatalities and 15 missing. Against this, they counted 340 Japanese dead in an area 100 yards square thus attesting to the ferocity and close proximity of the fighting. It took nearly a month and 600 casualties for the British to finally clear the Kangaw area. This, in turn, cost the Japanese an estimated 2,500 casualties including 1,008 confirmed dead along with the loss of sixteen guns and fourteen large motor craft.[30] Meanwhile, on 26 January, 16 February, and 13 March the British conducted similar landings on Cheduba Island, Ruywa and Letpan respectively to expand and solidify their hold over the strategically important area.

Through the execution of these various landings and corresponding ground operations, the British mauled and eventually expelled two severely depleted Japanese divisions from the Arakan and captured important airfields and logistical bases that would help support their continued re-conquest of central and southern Burma. This latter point was critically important because by this time Fourteenth Army had largely advanced beyond the operative reach of its main logistical bases back in eastern India. Even air resupply was quickly reaching the limit of its effective range. A sampling of the logistical benefit incurred through this enterprise included the delivery of 202,053 tons of seaborne supplies, excluding bulk petrol, through Akyab and the port of Kyaukpyu on Ramree Island from January through April of which 70,405 tons were delivered in the final month.[31] The cost in attaining this useful outcome consisted of 5,089 casualties for XV Corps including 1,138 fatalities. The navy's overall contribution to the successful campaign included the landing of 54,000 men, 800 animals, 1,000 vehicles and 14,000 tons of supplies and the firing of some 23,000 shells in support of the ground operations.[32]

The navy's close support role was a major factor in these successes, but it was by no means the navy's only contribution to the regional conflict. Despite the departure of most of the heavy ships to the Pacific, the East Indies Fleet, commanded by Vice-Admiral Power, still maintained a sizeable force for offensive actions in the

Indian Ocean. In March 1945 this force included the battleships *Queen Elizabeth* and *Richelieu*, four escort carriers, nine cruisers, two dozen destroyers and a similar number of submarines and escort vessels. To counter this, the Japanese could only muster a handful of cruisers and destroyers stationed in Singapore. This Japanese force, designated the Tenth Area Fleet, could do little more than maintain a defensive posture and constrict Japanese lines of communication. This latter stance was clearly demonstrated in February when the Japanese began operations to withdraw their garrisons from the Andaman and Nicobar Island Groups.

In light of these weaknesses, the East Indies Fleet quickly moved to extend its offensive efforts throughout the theatre. From February through April the fleet conducted a series of photo-reconnaissance missions, fired a naval bombardment against Sabang and launched carrier air strikes that damaged a 4,000-ton merchant ship at Emmahaven and destroyed or damaged a number of Japanese aircraft on the ground. Opposition to these operations was limited, but British naval fighters still shot down seven Japanese aircraft during individual aerial encounters for no loss to themselves. Meanwhile, on 21 February the fleet also began a series of offensive destroyer sweeps that accounted for a number of minor vessels and coasters in the Andaman Sea. Paramount amongst these successes was the destruction of a small Japanese convoy by the destroyers *Saumarez*, *Volage*, *Virago* and *Vigilant* on 26 March. This engagement, supported by RAF Liberator bombers, cost the Japanese the merchant ships *Risui Maru* and *Teshio Maru* (1,500 and 398 tons respectively) and the sub-chasers *CH34* and *CH63*. One month later the British scored a similar success when the destroyers *Roebuck*, *Racehorse* and *Redoubt* destroyed a second convoy consisting of ten small vessels transporting 750 Japanese soldiers from Rangoon to Moulmein. Finally, on 12 June the destroyer *Penn* sank a Japanese landing craft while the destroyers *Tartar*, *Eskimo* and *Nubian* sank the 950-ton cargo ship *Kuroshiyo Maru No. 2* and the sub-chaser *CH57* off Sabang.

The navy was not alone in these interdiction efforts. During the same period the Royal Air Force significantly expanded its offensive operations in the Indian Ocean. The best example of this was No. 222 Group (RAF), which increased in size and moved from a predominately defensive role to that of anti-shipping strikes. In the first four months of 1945 this group destroyed some 50 Japanese vessels of varying sizes along the Arakan coast. The group then moved its operations further east and, in conjunction with RAF Liberators from the Strategic Air Force, destroyed another 20 ships in the Gulf of Siam.[33] These latter successes included the 2,760-ton depot ship *Angthong* and the 10,238-ton tanker *Toho Maru*, which were sunk by RAF Liberators on 1 and 15 June respectively.[34] Finally, RAF Beaufighters of No. 224 Group continued to conduct offensive sweeps against Japanese coastal and river traffic moving along the waterways of Tenasserim and across the Gulf of Mataban to Rangoon. Their targets were almost exclusively commandeered native craft and purpose-built wooden coasters of up to 100 feet in length. From January through April 1945 the group claimed 447 such vessels destroyed with another 5,569 damaged.[35]

Meanwhile, the RAF continued its mine laying campaign against an ever-increasing list of ports and shipping routes throughout the region. By 1945 British and American long-range aircraft ventured out as far a Singapore, Bangkok, Saigon and Cam Ranh Bay to deliver their deadly loads of aerial mines. These mining operations continued until 10 July 1945 when the British finally suspended them

Table 9.1. Results from the Aerial Mining Campaign in the SEAC Area of Operations.

Target location	RAF-laid mines	USAAF-laid mines	Ships sunk		Ships damaged	
Bangkok, Thailand	268	45	16	7,764 tons	1	1,000 tons
Belawan Deli, Sumatra	123	0	5	5,318 tons	1	1,945 tons
Chumphorn, Malaya	202	0	1	2,165 tons	–	–
Koh Sichang, Thailand	129	52	1	2,500 tons	–	–
Malacca, Malaya	64	0	1	5,457 tons	–	–
Mergui, Burma	292	31	1	500 tons	1	100 tons
Moulmein, Burma	329	90	12	2,141 tons	–	–
Packchan River, Burma	260	15	–	–	1	20 tons
Palembang, Sumatra	0	14	3	1,768 tons	4	6,560 tons
Penang, Malaya	298	12	3	1,928 tons	5	6,290 tons
Phan Rang Bay, Indochina	0	6	1	1,200 tons	–	–
Port Blair, Andamans	40	0	1	50 tons	–	–
Rangoon, Burma	248	277	9	7,881 tons	2	4,325 tons
Saigon, Indochina	0	255	1	1,200 tons	3	7,000 tons
Satahib Bay, Thailand	15	7	1	1,799 tons	1	1,000 tons
Singapore	49	366	7	12,011 tons	19	130,620 tons
Singora, Thailand	46	0	–	–	1	3,000 tons
Sittang River, Burma	18	18	1	30 tons	–	–
Tavoy, Burma	222	20	1	100 tons	–	–
Sixteen other target areas*	632	137	–	–	–	–
TOTAL	3,235	1,345	65	53,812 tons	39	161,860 tons

Source: Naval Analysis Division, *The United States Strategic Bombing Survey, The Offensive Mine Laying Campaign against Japan* (Washington D.C.: Department of the Navy, 1969).

Note: Mine totals include 106 dummies. Some of the results and tonnage figures are estimates. Ships sunk or damaged by submarine-laid mines are not included.

* Other regional areas mined by the RAF/USAAF: Aru Bay, Sumatra – 143/0; Bandon, Malaya – 12/0; Camranh Bay, Indochina – 0/54; Chindwin River, Burma – 0/51; Fell Passage, Malaya – 52/0; Heinze Bay, Burma – 75/0; Irrawaddy River, Burma – 0/32; Kesseraing Is., Malaya – 64/0; Klang, Malaya – 53/0; Meklong, Thailand – 26/0; Padang, Sumatra – 8/0; Puket Harbour, Malaya – 12/0; Prachuab Girikan, Thailand – 31/0; Tachin River, Thailand – 9/0; Tanjung Balai, Malaya – 36/0 and Ye River, Burma – 111/0.

due to a lack of worthwhile Japanese shipping remaining in the area. During the course of the war the RAF flew a total of 697 mining sorties and laid 3,235 mines against 29 separate targets in Southeast Asia. For the loss of a mere seven British aircraft, these mines, along with another 1,345 mines laid by the USAAF over the same area, sank an estimated 65 ships totalling 53,812 tons and damaged another 39 ships worth an estimated 161,860 tons.[36] Equally important, this mining campaign had a disruptive effect on Japanese shipping that far outweighed its materiel results. On many occasions, the presence of even a few Allied mines forced the Japanese to shut down major ports and disperse their shipping thus causing severe disruptions to an already overstretched logistical system.

Beyond their triumphs in the maritime realm, the Allied air forces made other significant contributions to the local war effort using a variety of aircraft including the recently-arrived American-built Republic P-47 Thunderbolt fighter-bomber, which began re-equipping some of the long-serving Hurricane squadrons. Amongst these inputs were the infliction of numerous interdiction successes against Japanese ground transportation and tactical targets in Burma and the surrounding region. From 1 June 1944 through 2 May 1945, Eastern Air Command claimed the destruction or damage of 3,846 motor vehicles, 432 locomotives, 364 Japanese aircraft and some 300 bridges. In regard to the latter, 112 were railway bridges and from January through April 1945 the average number of bridges out of service at any given time on the rail line between Bangkok and Pegu was 9.2. This disruption helped reduce applicable rail traffic during this period from 700–800 tons to just 100–200 tons per day. In addition to this, in March and April an estimated 524 Japanese supply dumps, predominately in the Rangoon area, were wholly or partially destroyed by Allied bombing.[37] Meanwhile, in direct support of the army, the RAF flew 4,360 sorties during the fighting around Mandalay and Meiktila. This included an acclaimed engagement on 19 February when rocket-firing Hurricanes destroyed 13 Japanese tanks preparing to counter-attack British forces in the Myinmu bridgehead thus stopping the counter-attack in its tracks.[38] Finally, Allied transport aircraft flew thousands of sorties that logistically supported Fourteenth Army's advance and evacuated wounded and sick personnel.

Table 9.2. Allied Aerial Resupply Effort in Burma December 1944–April 1945.

	Stores landed and dropped (long tons)	Personnel delivered	Casualties and sick evacuated
Dec 44	19,782	5,110	9,349
Jan 45	20,412	4,565	5,823
Feb 45	45,842	7,989	7,680
Mar 45	53,701	11,200	8,859
Apr 45	54,054	11,184	9,566

Source: WO 203/5849, Some Facts about the Burma Campaign, p. 8.

Yet, despite these many interdiction successes and the best efforts of the Fourteenth Army, time was quickly running out for the British to reach Rangoon before the expected beginning of the monsoon season and the imminent withdrawal of USAAF transport aircraft from Burma to China. As such, the British decided to launch a seaborne assault to accelerate this process. Using Akyab and Ramree as staging areas, the British assembled a force of 233 assorted naval vessels split into five elements consisting of an assault force, minesweeping force, carrier force, covering force and diversionary force. The vessels involved consisted of the battleships *Queen Elizabeth* and *Richelieu*, the escort carriers *Hunter, Stalker, Khedive, Emperor, Shah* and *Empress*, three headquarters ships, six cruisers, 12 destroyers, nine sloops/frigates, eight landing ships and 187 assorted landing craft, minesweepers and support vessels.[39] Together, these forces were assigned to perform two primary missions. The first of these was Operation *Dracula*, the actual seaborne landings targeting Rangoon. The second was Operation *Bishop*, a concurrent diversionary action designed to screen the landings and inflict peripheral damage against the Japanese. Other Allied forces allocated to these operations included the 26th Indian Division, the primary assault force earmarked to capture Rangoon, 224 Group of the RAF and 12 assorted heavy and medium bomber squadrons from the USAAF.

At the end of April the British put their plans into motion. From 27 to 30 April six convoys departed Akyab and Ramree and began their 480-mile trek to Rangoon. On 1 May an Indian parachute battalion landed at Elephant Point and seized the gun batteries protecting the mouth of the Rangoon River. Following mine clearing operations, units of the 26th Division landed on both banks of the river the next day and began their advance towards Rangoon. While this was underway, elements of the covering force carried out Operation *Bishop* by executing a series of diversionary actions from 30 April through 7 May including naval bombardments and/or air strikes against airfields, military installations and coastal shipping on and around Car Nicobar, Port Blair, the Andaman Islands and Malacca. Among the results attain by these actions, the British destroyed or seriously damaged 22 Japanese coastal vessels. This included the aforementioned ten vessels sunk by *Roebuck, Racehorse* and *Redoubt* on 30 April while aircraft from the escort carriers accounted for the rest destroying five barges and driving ashore or setting ablaze one coaster, two 100-foot ships, one tug and three junks. Yet, despite this great outlay of effort, Operation *Dracula* proved to be anticlimactic as the Japanese had already abandoned Rangoon leaving behind some 5,000 INA troops who promptly surrendered when the British entered the city on the 3rd. The only significant loss for the operation was a tank landing craft sunk by mines and a second landing ship damaged.

With the capture of Rangoon, the British attained the first significant milestone in their quest to regain their lost imperial possessions in the Far East. Most of Burma was now under British control, and the remaining Japanese forces in the eastern part of the country were in no position to alter this situation. Soon, the British would

An essential factor in Britain's eventual success in Southeast Asia was the effective use of air power. Pictured here are two RAF Thunderbolt fighter-bombers in India with an American B-29 Superfortress in the background. (Moss, Royal Air Force official photographer, public domain)

complete their conquest of Burma, and planning was already underway to carry out similar operations in Malaya and Singapore. Of course, this was just part of the onslaught constricting the Japanese Empire, but it reflected the fact that despite its long absence, Britain was now becoming fully integrated in the war against Japan. In this, it joined the Commonwealth nations of Australia and New Zealand, which had never left this conflict. Whether in Burma, the Indian Ocean, the Southwest Pacific or off the coast of Japan itself, Britain and its Imperial and Commonwealth partners were making major contributions to the overall war effort, and soon they would help facilitate the final destruction of the Japanese Empire and its militaristic regime.

CHAPTER 10

Victory over Japan

By the beginning of May 1945, the war in Europe was almost over. In the Mediterranean theatre, the Allies controlled most of Italy, Greece and southern France. In terms of the former, as referenced in Chapter 7, the Italians abandoned the Axis cause in September 1943. However, at the time of their departure, the Germans had forces stationed in Italy as part of its defensive arrangement. Once Italy's intentions became clear, the Germans promptly seized control over the northern two-thirds of the country against minimal Italian opposition. With the arrival of reinforcements, the Germans quickly rendered their former Axis partner into just another occupied nation in the German empire. Over the next twenty months two Allied armies, the British Eighth and the Anglo-American-Franco Fifth, progressively battled their way up the 620-mile length of the Italian peninsula. This was a hard-fought campaign against heavy German resistance, but at the end of April 1945 the Allies finally attained decisive victory. On the 29th of that month local German authorities signed a document of unconditional surrender for all German forces still present in northern Italy and southern Austria. With this, upwards of a million men laid down their arms, and the war in the Mediterranean came to an end.[1]

The situation was much the same in Northern Europe where Allied armies from both the east and the west were in the process of overrunning Germany. Included in this was the capture of Berlin by Soviet forces and the concurrent suicide of Hitler on 30 April. Britain's contribution to this onslaught centred upon the British 21st Army Group, which at the end of April consisted of 1,053,147 men posted in two armies containing 19 divisions and a number of independent brigades.[2] Under the command of Field Marshal Bernard Montgomery, this force liberated much of the Netherlands and drove deep into northern Germany capturing the major German cities of Bremen, Lübeck and Hamburg from 26 April through 3 May. Then on 4 May a German delegation arrived at Montgomery's headquarters at Lüneburg Heath and agreed to surrender all German forces and naval ships in Holland, Northwest Germany, Schleswig-Holstein, Denmark and their associated islands. Becoming effective the next day, this surrender ended major combat operations on the British front as 1.4 million Germans became prisoners in the impacted areas.[3] When added to the 509,325 prisoners already taken by British and Canadian forces during earlier operations, this brought the 21st Army Group's total prisoner haul to almost two million men during the course of the 11-month Northwest Europe campaign.[4]

While the mass German surrenders in Italy and at Lüneburg Heath clearly constituted monumental accomplishments, they were soon overshadowed by an even greater event. On 6 May a delegation led by General Alfred Jodl, the Chief of Staff to the German High Command, arrived at the headquarters of the Supreme Allied Commander, General Dwight Eisenhower, at Reims and offered the surrender of all German forces confronting the Western Allies. General Eisenhower, through his Chief of Staff, Lieutenant-General Walter Smith, refused this offer and instead threatened to break off all negotiations unless the Germans agreed to a complete unconditional surrender. In doing so, he also threatened to close off the Allied lines thus forcing the Germans to surrender to the Soviets. Given this ultimatum, the Germans were compelled to accept, and at 0241 hours on 7 May Jodl signed the document of unconditional surrender. The next day the Germans conducted a similar signing ceremony for the Russians in Berlin. With this, German forces all across Europe, including Norway, laid down their arms, and the war in Europe came to an abrupt end effective at 2301 hours on 8 May.

For the Allied forces engaged in the conflict in the Pacific and Southeast Asia, no such peace was yet at hand. Indeed, while there was little doubt regarding the attainment of an ultimate Allied victory, many forecasters predicted it might still take years of heavy and costly fighting to secure this outcome. For the American and British naval units operating off Okinawa in the midst of the Kamikaze onslaught or the British and Australian forces fighting their ways across Burma and the Southwest Pacific, the prospect of these forecasts was daunting. Nevertheless, news of the Allied victory in Europe still provided a welcome indicator that peace would eventually reign in the Pacific as well. In a more practical sense, it also meant that a flood of additional resources would soon be available to hasten this effort. For the British, this included the dispatch of additional naval forces including a substantial expansion in aircraft carriers. Already, the large fleet aircraft carrier *Implacable* was en route to the Pacific, and it would soon be joined by the new light carriers *Colossus*, *Glory*, *Venerable* and *Vengeance*. These latter vessels had been designed and built from 1942 through the beginning of 1945 and displaced 13,190 tons with a capacity to operate 40 aircraft. Their anticipated arrival would substantially expand the striking power of the British Pacific Fleet thus making them a welcome addition to subsequent naval operations.

In the meantime, the British continued to make do with what they had, and in mid-May the East Indies Fleet scored a significant victory against the Japanese. On 9 May British intelligence learned through radio intercepts that the Japanese heavy cruiser *Haguro* and the destroyer *Kamikaze* were scheduled to arrive at Port Blair on the 12th to evacuate garrison troops. Early the next morning a British force consisting of the battleships *Queen Elizabeth* and *Richelieu*; the escort carriers *Hunter, Khedive, Shah* and *Emperor*; three cruisers and eight destroyers departed Trincomalee with orders to hunt down and destroy these vessels. Over the next few days, the British vainly searched for the Japanese warships as they twice abandoned their attempt to reach Port Blair and turned back towards Singapore. Throughout these manoeuvres, it looked like the British might lose their opportunity to engage the small Japanese force, but on the 15th a British reconnaissance aircraft from the escort carrier *Shah* located *Haguro* and *Kamikaze* at the entrance of the Malacca Strait. After launching an airstrike, that apparently caused minimal damage to the Japanese cruiser, the British closed in with their surface warships led by the 26th destroyer flotilla consisting of the destroyers *Saumarez, Venus, Vigilant, Virago* and *Verulam.*

Shortly after midnight on the 16th these British destroyers intercepted *Haguro* and *Kamikaze* some 45 miles southwest of Penang. Despite being heavily outgunned by the Japanese force, which possessed a combined ten 8-inch, eight 5-inch and four 4.7-inch guns compared to 20 4.7-inch guns to themselves, the British destroyers pressed forward. Using superior radar technology that allowed them to locate and effectively engage the Japanese warships, the British executed a well-coordinated pincer attack firing a series of torpedo salvos at *Haguro* from multiple directions. At least six, and perhaps as many as nine, of these torpedoes struck the hapless *Haguro* causing more damage than the powerful Japanese cruiser could stand. At 0206 hours *Haguro* sank taking with it over 900 members of its crew including two senior officers, Vice-Admiral Shintaro Hashimoto and Rear-Admiral Kaju Sugiura. On the British side, *Saumarez* sustained some damage with two men killed and three wounded, but the remaining British destroyers escaped the battle unscathed. Likewise, the Japanese destroyer *Kamikaze* sustained damage but also survived the battle. Despite the damage to *Saumarez* and having to fight off Japanese air attacks the next day, the British ships were able to successfully withdraw and return to Trincomalee. Although unknown at the time, this would prove to be the last major surface engagement of the war.

A few weeks later the British scored a second major success against Japan's dwindling cruiser force. On 3 June the Japanese dispatched the heavy cruiser *Ashigara* to evacuate soldiers from Batavia. Four days later the American submarines *Blueback* and *Chub* reported the passage of *Ashigara* as it arrived at and then departed Batavia with some 1,200 troops onboard. Based upon these reports and earlier Allied intelligence, the British submarine *Trenchant*, commanded by Commander Arthur Hezlet, patrolled the Banka Strait in expectation of the cruiser's projected return. This was a bold move since the strait contained dangerous shoals, strong tidal currents and a recently laid Dutch minefield. Fortunately, *Trenchant's* audacity paid off when it sighted *Ashigara* approaching from the south at 1148 hours on the 8th. At 1209

The British destroyer *Saumarez*, which led the surface action resulting in the destruction of the Japanese heavy cruiser *Haguro* in May 1945. (Royal Navy official photographer, public domain)

hours *Trenchant* fired a full salvo of eight torpedoes at the unsuspecting cruiser from a range of 4,700 yards. Five of these torpedoes hit with devastating effect, and *Ashigara* sank a half an hour later. Upwards of a thousand army personnel and untold crewmen perished with the ship. Meanwhile, *Trenchant* made good its escape despite a half-hearted intervention from the destroyer *Kamikaze*. For this action, Commander Hezlet received a bar to his DSO and a U.S. Legion of Merit award.

In less than a month the British had destroyed two Japanese heavy cruisers, and at the end of July they completed a hat trick by adding a third cruiser to this tally. In this case, the perpetrators of the success were British XE-class midget submarines. The XE-class was a self-contained submarine displacing 30 tons and staffed by a four-man crew. It had a top underwater speed of 5.5 knots and an armament consisting of two 4,480-pound detachable saddle charges. The British had used similar X-craft midget submarines to cripple the German battleship *Tirpitz* in 1943 (see Chapter 7), and now they hoped to repeat this success in the Pacific. In the closing days of July, the British submarines *Spark* and *Stygian* transported two XE-craft to a position 40 miles off Singapore. On the night of 30/31 July these midget submarines penetrated into Singapore harbour and deployed explosive charges and limpet mines against the non-operational Japanese heavy cruiser *Takao*. The following evening the mines detonated blowing out the bottom of the stationary cruiser thus rendering it a total loss. In concurrent operations, two other XE-craft, transported by the submarines *Spearhead* and *Selene*, disabled the undersea telegraph cables at Saigon and Hong Kong. When these raids were completed, all the XE-craft successfully rendezvoused with their parent submarines and returned safely to base. British authorities later decorated all of the XE-craft crew members with two of them, Lieutenant Ian Fraser RNR and Leading Seaman James Magennis, receiving Victoria Crosses.

These successes represented the pinnacle of Britain's submarine campaign against Japan. Throughout 1945 British submarine flotillas continued to operate out of Ceylon, Australia and later the Philippines against a dwindling number of Japanese military and merchant vessels in the East Indies, South China Sea and Java Sea. These areas were increasingly devoid of sizeable targets, but the British were still able to score a steady number of victories. During the period of 1 January 1945 to 15 August 1945 British and British-controlled Dutch submarines sank the aforementioned cruisers *Ashigara* and *Takao*, the patrol ship (converted destroyer) *P2/Nadakaze*, the captured Dutch submarine *K-XVIII*, a sub-chaser, four auxiliary warships, five sizeable merchant ships worth 4,728 tons and at least 339 minor vessels and coasters worth an estimated 30,810 tons. During the same period mines laid by these submarines sank at least three more merchant ships worth 3,407 tons and an additional auxiliary warship.[5] British losses amounted to a single submarine, *Porpoise*, sunk by Japanese aircraft with a second submarine heavily damaged.

Nor was this necessarily the extent of British successes. The above listed victories only include merchant ships over 500 tons that Japanese records definitely confirmed as sunk. With some Japanese records incomplete or in a state of disarray by the war's end, it is entirely likely that Britain's submarine force sank additional vessels not officially counted. Paramount amongst these was a merchant ship, estimated at 4,000 to 6,000 tons, claimed sunk by the submarines *Trump* and *Tiptoe* on 3 August 1945 in the Java Sea. Both submarine commanders reported seeing the target sink, but Japanese records did not confirm the loss. The vessel in question was likely the 2,716-ton army cargo ship *Tencho Maru*, but the matter remains an open question.[6] What is certain is that British and Dutch submarines did enjoy a degree of success that, while small compared to American results, more than compensated for their own meagre losses. Even assuming the most conservative success assessments, British and British-controlled Dutch submarines sank by all means at least 15 purpose-built warships, nine auxiliary warships, 46 merchant ships and many hundreds of minor vessels worth upwards of 235,000 tons in Asian and Pacific waters throughout the war. This cost them three British and four Dutch submarines in return thus constituting a favourable exchange rate of at least ten Japanese/Axis vessels sunk (excluding minor craft) for every British/Dutch loss.

Returning now to the ground war in Southeast Asia, from May through August 1945 the British conducted major mopping up operations to solidify their control over central Burma and destroy isolated Japanese formations trying to make good their escape. They did this under the authority of a new headquarters as the British

Table 10.1. Results Obtained by British and Dutch Submarines in the Far East.

Category	Number of ships sunk (estimated tonnage)				
	1941–42	1943	1944	1945	Total
Cruisers	–	–	1 (5,100)	2 (26,400)	3 (31,500)
Destroyers and destroyer-types	1 (2,060)	–	–	1 (1,390)	2 (3,450)
Escort destroyers and sub-chasers	–	–	2 (1,250)	1 (291)	3 (1,541)
Minelayers	–	–	1 (2,330)	–	1 (2,330)
Submarines	–	1 (2,198)	4 (5,501)	1 (782)	6 (8,481)
Auxiliary warships	–	–	4 (605)	5 (900)	9 (1,505)
Merchant ships (over 500 tons)	10 (55,737)	4 (15,344)	24 (44,840)	8 (8,135)	46 (124,056)
Minor vessels	–	1 (165)	268 (31,328)	339 (30,810)	608 (62,303)
TOTAL	11 (57,797)	6 (17,707)	304 (90,954)	357 (68,708)	678 (235,166)

Source: Data taken from John D. Alden, *U.S. Submarine Attacks During World War II, Including Allied Submarine Attacks in the Pacific Theater* (Annapolis, Naval Institute Press, 1989) and J. Rohwer and G. Hummelchen, *Chronology of the War at Sea 1939–1945* (Annapolis, Naval Military Press, 1992).

Twelfth Army, under the command of Lieutenant-General Montagu Stopford, assumed responsibility for operations in Burma on 28 May to free-up Fourteenth Army to prepare for the upcoming invasion of Malaya. This command was essentially created by converting XXXIII Corps headquarters to that of an army headquarters and assigning former Fourteenth Army formations to this new army. The main combat formation available to Twelfth Army was IV Corps, which primarily consisted of the 5th, 17th and 19th Divisions and the 255th Tank Brigade. The army also controlled the 7th and 20th Divisions and the 22nd East African Brigade as well as various static and administrative units.

The most immediate task facing Twelfth Army was the destruction of Japanese forces still west of the Sittang River. Despite their recent defeats, the Japanese still had some 100,000 men present in Burma. Most of these were in the eastern part of the country including large numbers of administrative and support personnel. However, the remnants of the Twenty-Eighth Army along with the 105th Independent Mixed Brigade were trapped in the Pegu Yomas uplands between the Irrawaddy and Sittang Rivers. In June and early July, the Japanese devised plans and made preparations to extract these ensnared forces across the Sittang. The British were aware of these general intentions and had already begun blocking and mopping up operations resulting in the killing of an estimated 4,000 Japanese soldiers in the region west of Pegu Yomas with a further 1,000 killed along the Sittang River by XXXIII Corps/Twelfth Army from 1 May through 11 July.[7] Then on 2 July the British gained a major intelligence coup when a patrol retrieved a copy of the Japanese plan detailing the timing and routes for their proposed breakout from the body of a dead Japanese soldier. Armed with this knowledge, the British set up a series of blocks along key portions of the proposed Japanese escape route.

During the latter half of July and first part of August, the Japanese launched their main effort to evacuate their forces across the Sittang River. From their opening moves, the Japanese came under heavy and relentless assault by the British blocking forces. Aided by an abundant use of tanks, artillery and aerial bombardment, the British subjected the Japanese to a blistering series of reversals as they attempted to advance to and cross the Sittang River. During concurrent operations, the British also blunted attempts by the Japanese Thirty-Third Army (now reduced to an equivalent combat strength of only three infantry battalions and one artillery company)[8] and Fifteenth Army to come to the aid of their comrades. Adding to these Japanese woes, by this stage in the war, the Burmese people had largely turned against them, and large contingents of native guerrilla forces, often led and supported by British operatives, rose up and carried out widespread attacks against the retreating Japanese. The result of this combined onslaught was a slaughter of immense proportions. From 21 July through 15 August, British and irregular forces killed 6,551 and 3,939 Japanese soldiers respectively in the Sittang River area while a further 787 were taken prisoner.[9] Through the expanded period including earlier operations, Twelfth Army claimed 9,843 Japanese soldiers killed and 1,474 taken prisoner while guerilla and irregular formations claimed at least as many killed. Other Japanese losses included 35 assorted artillery pieces and six tankettes.[10] Against this, British IV Corps suffered 435 killed, 1,452 wounded and 14 missing from 7 May through 15 August.[11]

The result of these operations rendered the Japanese army in Burma a spent force. Although some 70,000 Japanese soldiers still remained in eastern Burma, their combat effectiveness was severely reduced. Of the main combat formations, Thirty-Third Army was largely destroyed while the remnants of the Twenty-Eighth Army numbered just 7,949 men ready for duty with another 1,919 men in hospital as of 22 September.[12] Even of the men present for duty, most were of limited combat value with many being sick, malnourished and/or lacking in basic materiel needs. Meanwhile, the shattered Fifteenth Army was in the process of withdrawing into Thailand to reinforce the Eighteenth Area Army. Although unbeknown to the players at the time, the fighting in Burma was essentially over. During the entirety of the Burma campaign, the Japanese lost 185,149 men killed or missing out of a total ground force of 303,501 men who saw service there. Total British casualties for the same campaign amounted to 73,909 including 14,326 fatalities.[13]

With the war in Burma winding down, the British increasingly turned their attention to their next major objective, the reconquest of Malaya (Operation *Zipper*) and Singapore (Operation *Mailfist*). Both of these proposed endeavours centred upon seaborne invasions that were tentatively scheduled for October and December respectively. In June and July the East Indies Fleet conducted a series of forays to help prepare the way for these invasions. On 18–20 June the fleet conducted Operation *Balsam* with the escort carriers *Stalker*, *Khedive* and *Ameer*, two cruisers and five destroyers. This sortie consisted of a number of photo-reconnaissance flights over southern Malaya followed by air strikes against airfields and railway yards in northern Sumatra. During these latter strikes the British destroyed ten Japanese aircraft on the ground (with nine others damaged) and two locomotives for the loss of one British aircraft. Operation *Collie* followed this on 5–11 July. During this operation the escort carriers *Ameer* and *Emperor*, one cruiser, three destroyers and nine minesweepers swept 167 mines from around the Nicobar Islands and conducted a series of shore bombardments and air strikes against local airfields and other targets. Among the damage inflicted were two coasters set alight and one Japanese aircraft destroyed in aerial combat. This operation cost the British five aircraft in return.

On 24–26 July the East Indies Fleet conducted Operation *Livery*, its final combat sortie of the war. Participating units included the newly arrived battleship *Nelson*, the escort carriers *Ameer* and *Emperor*, one cruiser, four destroyers and the minesweepers of the 7th Flotilla. During this operation the British swept 24 mines from around Phuket Island and launched a series of air strikes against airfields and transportation targets on the Kra Isthmus. During these strikes the British destroyed three small ships and at least nine Japanese aircraft with a further 11 vessels and two aircraft damaged along with 15 locomotives and other motor transport. Despite these successes, *Livery* proved to be a costly operation. On 24 July the minesweeper *Squirrel* was lost on a mine. Two days later the Japanese launched a small Kamikaze attack against the fleet. British defences shot down three of the Kamikaze aircraft, but a fourth hit the minesweeper *Vestal* and damaged it so severely that it had to be scuttled. This proved to be the last British warship sunk during the war and the only British ship lost to a Kamikaze attack. By comparison, Operation *Livery* culminated a six-month period during which aircraft from the fleet's escort carriers destroyed an estimated one-third of all remaining Japanese operational aircraft in Burma, Malaya and Sumatra and wrecked numerous coastal craft, railway stock and motor transport.[14] While the Japanese still maintained large forces in Southeast Asia, these forces were increasingly isolated, immobile and devoid of support.

The same can be said for the Japanese forces confronting the Australians in the Southwest Pacific. In Bougainville, New Guinea and New Britain the Australians contained and mopped-up large Japanese formations bypassed by the Allied advance. Highlights of this campaign included operations on Bougainville where Australian II Corps, primarily consisting of the 3rd Australian Division, the 11th and 23rd Brigades and the Fiji Infantry Regiment, launched a series of efforts to clear key locations on the island and systematically destroy or sequester the remaining Japanese forces located there. Early on, Australian forces seized the Pearl Ridge thus gaining them control over central Bougainville. In the north the 11th Brigade cleared the Tsimba Ridge and drove the remaining Japanese forces, some 1,800 men strong, to the Bonis Peninsula on the extreme northern end of the island. Meanwhile, the primary fighting took place in the south where the 3rd Division launched an advance against the main Japanese force located around Buin. Through a series of operations, which included the repulsing of several Japanese counterattacks in an area known as Slater's Knoll, the Australians progressively pushed the Japanese back and contained them on the southern end of the island. During the course of its operations on Bougainville, Australian II Corps killed an estimated 8,500 Japanese soldiers while roughly 9,800 more died from illness and malnutrition. This cost the Australians 2,088 casualties in return including 516 dead.[15]

Meanwhile, in western New Guinea the 6th Australian division launched an offensive to drive the Japanese Eighteenth Army away from the coastline. At the time Eighteenth Army still possessed some 30,000 to 35,000 men, but these forces were heavily impacted by disease and desperately short of supplies. Operating from Aitape, which American forces had previously captured in April 1944 through an amphibious landing, the Australians began an eastward advance towards Wewak to isolate and eventually seize the coastal city. After a number of preliminary operations carried out over a period of five months that positioned Australian forces in the area, the Australian 19th Brigade launched a direct assault against Wewak in early May 1945. Supported by naval gunfire from the Australian cruiser *Hobart*, the British cruiser *Newfoundland* and the Australian destroyers *Arunta* and *Warramunga* as well as RAAF aircraft, the Australians secured Wewak and its nearby airfield on 11 and 15 May respectively. Thereafter, the Japanese withdrew inland towards the Prince Alexander Mountains where the Australians continued operations to contain them. Through the duration of this fighting, the Australians killed an estimated 9,000 Japanese and took 269 prisoners for the cost of 1,533 battle casualties to themselves including 422 fatalities.[16] Beyond this, upwards of another 14,000 local Japanese died from starvation and disease during this period.

Operations on New Britain were less intense as the Australian 5th Division contained a substantially larger Japanese force located on the island. At the time of the handover to the Australians, Allied intelligence estimated that the total Japanese garrison remaining on New Britain numbered about 35,000 men. This proved to be a gross underestimation as the actual Japanese strength on the island numbered roughly 70,000 military and naval personnel along with some 20,000 civilian workers.[17] Even before this discrepancy became known, the Australians embarked upon a campaign to simply contain the Japanese and not decisively engage them. Accordingly, both sides observed a tacit truce that avoided major combat operations, although the Australians did carry out minor advances and aggressive patrolling to maintain pressure. The cost in carrying out these operations amounted to 53 Australian combat fatalities, 21 dead from other causes and 140 wounded.[18]

Finally, beyond these theatre-wide containment actions, the Australians also launched a major new offensive to seize Borneo away from the Japanese. On 1 May 1945 the 26th Australian Brigade landed on Tarakan Island and began the reconquest of Borneo. This was followed on 10 June and 1 July when the Australian 9th and 7th Divisions landed at Brunei Bay and Balikpapan respectively. A number of Australian warships including the cruisers *Shropshire* and *Hobart*, the destroyers *Arunta* and *Warramunga*, three landing ships and several smaller vessels supported these landings. During the fighting that followed, the Australians captured two naval bases, seven important airfields, the immensely rich Seria and Miri oil fields, various oil refineries and vast quantities of equipment.[19] This represented the first significant liberation of oil resources seized by the Japanese in 1942, which was their primary reason for going to war. However, this success had little practical impact at this point in the conflict since the poor state of the Japanese merchant fleet rendered them incapable of transporting this oil back to Japan. The cost of these operations were 460 men killed and 1,486 wounded for the Australians while the Japanese lost 4,559 confirmed dead, 625 more presumed dead, 1,194 killed by guerilla forces and 545 taken prisoner.[20]

During the same period the RAAF concluded its aerial mining campaign. From 22 April 1943 through 29 July 1945 the PBY-5 Catalinas of the RAAF flew a total of 1,215 sorties and laid 2,498 mines against 48 separate targets in the Southwest Pacific.[21] This included various harbours and shipping routes off New Britain, New Guinea, the Dutch East Indies and the coast of China. The number of ships sunk by these mines is a matter of debate. At the low end, the American-based Joint Army-Navy Assessment Committee only credited Australian mines with the sinking of nine Japanese ships worth 21,033 tons. However, this assessment is certainly too low since the committee did not consider losses of merchant ships below 500 tons and occasionally exercised a nationalistic tendency to credit legitimate British and Commonwealth claims to American sources. For its part, the RAAF claimed the destruction of 23 Japanese vessels with another 27 damaged due to its mine laying efforts.[22] Finally, on the high end, the United States Strategic Bombing Survey credited Australian-laid mines with the destruction of 33 Japanese vessels worth 57,061 tons and damage to 48 others worth 148,079 tons. The survey further assessed another 18 vessels worth 27,335 tons sunk and 27 vessels worth 87,644 tons damaged in fields laid jointly by Australian and American sources.[23] Whatever the correct number, the Australians achieved this success at a very low cost. In all, only 11 RAAF aircraft were lost during mine laying operations during the entire Pacific conflict.

The summer of 1945 also saw the culmination of the RAAF's conventional bombing campaign. Throughout the war the RAAF flew thousands of conventional

In addition to carrying out large-scale containment actions in the Solomon Islands, Bismarck Archipelago and New Guinea, Australian forces ended the war by launching a new offensive to recapture Borneo. Pictured here are Australian troops landing at Tarakan Island. (Watermann, C. F. (Lt JG), USNR, CPU-8, May 1, 1945, public domain)

anti-shipping strikes and claimed the destruction of at least 66 Japanese vessels with another 155 probably sunk.[24] Most of these vessels were of small tonnage, but as previously discussed; the RAAF occasionally scored against more substantial targets. This occurred again in April 1945 when RAAF aircraft played a role in the destruction of the Japanese light cruiser *Isuzu*. On the evening of 4 April Allied submarines reported the passage of a Japanese convoy consisting of *Isuzu* and four smaller vessels en route to Timor to evacuate troops and equipment. One of the submarines involved was the British *Spark*, which fired four torpedoes at *Isuzu* at long range but missed. Nevertheless, *Spark*'s sighting report helped set in motion a series of Allied actions that eventually led to the cruiser's destruction. The RAAF was unable to organise a strike before the convoy arrived at Kupang, Timor, but they did dispatch Mosquito and Catalina reconnaissance aircraft to track its progress. On the night of 5/6 April, the convoy departed Kupang for its return journey. On the following day 29 RAAF and RAAF-affiliated Dutch Liberator and Mitchell bombers

Table 10.2. Results from the RAAF's Aerial Mining Campaign.

Target Location	RAAF-laid mines	U.S.-laid mines	Ships sunk		Ships damaged	
Babo, New Guinea	17	0	1	2,913 tons	–	–
Balikpapan, Borneo	118	0	5	18,063 tons	6	14,415 tons
Banka Strait, Sumatra	117	0	1	1,200 tons	3	12,729 tons
Cape Seletan, Borneo	28	0	–	–	1	100 tons
Geser, Ceram	9	0	2	1,300 tons	–	–
Kaimana Bay, New Guinea	19	0	1	575 tons	2	4,255 tons
Kau Bay, Halmahera	62	0	5	13,500 tons	7	12,393 tons
Kavieng, New Ireland	104	0	3	6,518 tons	4	14,701 tons
Kolaka-Pomalaa, Celebes	63	0	–		2	10,112 tons
Laikang Bay, Celebes	32	0	1	3,098 tons	–	–
Laut Strait, Borneo	207	0	1	2,219 tons	3	12,416 tons
Manila Bay, Philippines	50	0	–	–	2	4,528 tons
Pare-Pare Bay, Celebes	14	0	–	–	1	6,435 tons
Seeadler, Admiralties Is.	35	0	1	1,200 tons	1	3,000 tons
Sorong, New Guinea	29	0	–	–	2	8,832 tons
Surabaya, Java	375	0	9	4,897 tons	12	39,887 tons
Swatow, China	30	0	–	–	1	96 tons
Tana Keke, Celebes	43	0	1	50 tons	–	–
Tioro Strait, Celebes	76	0	2	1,528 tons	1	4,180 tons
Hong Kong, China	151	195	14	10,336 tons	13	47,587 tons
Palau Atoll	23	78	–	–	3	12,347 tons
Takao, Formosa	18	98	3	12,999 tons	8	15,668 tons
Yulinkan Bay, China	52	16	1	4,000 tons	3	12,042 tons
Twenty-five Other Targets*	826	0	–	–	–	–
TOTAL	2,498	387	51	84,396 tons	75	235,723 tons

Source: Naval Analysis Division, *The United States Strategic Bombing Survey, The Offensive Mine Laying Campaign against Japan* (Washington D.C.: Department of the Navy, 1969).

Note: Some of the results and tonnage figures are estimates. Ships sunk or damaged by submarine-laid mines are not included.

* Other regional areas mined by the RAAF: Amoy, China – 114/0; Balabac Strait, Borneo – 60/0; Banka Strait, Celebes – 28/0; Baoe Baoe, Celebes – 46/0; Bima Bay, Sumbawa – 8/0; Boela, Ceram – 12/0; Brunei Bay, Borneo – 20/0; Hainan Strait – 130/0; Kendari, Celebes – 44/0; Lembeh Strait, Celebes – 4/0; Macassar, Celebes – 142/0; Mako, Pescadores – 10/0; Manokwari, New Guinea – 17/0; Panarukan Road, Java – 10/0; Pasuruan Road, Java – 32/0; Probolinggo Road – 8/0; Samarinda, Borneo – 12/0; Sandakan, Borneo – 12/0; Sekar Bay, New Guinea – 8/0; Tarakan, Borneo – 30/0; Vesuvius, Soela Is. – 8/0; Waingapu Roads, Sumbo – 3/0; Wenchow, China – 8/0; Woleai Atoll – 36/0; Wowoni Strait, Celebes – 24/0.

attacked the convoy and claimed two hits and many near misses on the hapless Japanese cruiser. Then on the 7th the American submarines *Charr* and *Gabilan*, vectored in by Allied tracking reports, torpedoed and sank *Isuzu* thus completing a process that included American, British, Australian and Dutch inputs.

While the Allies were scoring these many victories in the outer regions, the British Pacific Fleet made itself ready for its next operational sortie, a series of strikes directed against the Japanese home islands. On 5 June the fleet returned to Sydney to rejuvenate itself after two months of hard fighting off the Sakishima Gunto. Over the next month the fleet repaired damage, conducted routine maintenance, replenished itself and rested tired personnel. They did this under the new designation of Task Force 37. This redesignation occurred on 27 May when Admiral William Halsey replaced Admiral Spruance as the commander of the American Fast Carrier Fleet. With this, the Fifth Fleet became the Third Fleet, and all subordinate commands underwent similar transformations. In other changes, the British withdrew the battleship *Howe* and the aircraft carrier *Indomitable* for refits and replaced them with the newly arrived aircraft carrier *Implacable* and its contingent of 80 Seafire, Avenger and Firefly aircraft.

To give this new carrier and its aircrews operational experience, Admiral Fraser immediately sent *Implacable* out to conduct a quick series of training strikes against the Japanese-controlled island of Truk in the central Pacific. Earlier in the war, Truk had been an important Japanese naval and military base, but the Allied advance and a series of American carrier strikes had completely bypassed the island and rendered it impotent. As such, Truk was an ideal target for the training operation. On 12 June Task Group 111.2, consisting of the aircraft carrier *Implacable*, the escort carrier *Ruler*, four cruisers and five destroyers, departed Manus to conduct Operation *Inmate*. On the 14th and 15th this force conducted a series of air strikes and a naval bombardment against Truk that damaged airfields, shore defences and other military installations and destroyed at least two Japanese aircraft with three more damaged. Of greater consequence, *Inmate* provided the operational experience sought by Fraser as *Implacable* launched 113 offensive and 103 defensive sorties. The only British combat loss was a single Seafire shot down by anti-aircraft fire.

On 6 July 1945 Task Force 37 departed Manus for Japan. Initially, this force was built around the aircraft carriers *Formidable*, *Victorious* and *Implacable*, the battleship *King George V*, six cruisers and 15 destroyers. The fourth British carrier, *Indefatigable*, was delayed in Sydney due to machinery difficulties and was unable to depart Manus until 10 July. Once together, these carriers would operate a total of 255 aircraft broken down into 88 Seafires, 73 Corsairs, 62 Avengers, 24 Fireflies, six Hellcats and two Walruses. This represented the most powerful force yet deployed by the Fleet Air Arm as the British prepared to strike directly into the heart of the Japanese Empire. On 16 July Task Force 37 rendezvoused with the massive American Task Force 38 some 300 miles east of Japan. This American task force, which had already commenced offensive operations against Japan on 10 July, possessed 16 aircraft carriers and some 1,200 combat aircraft. Now, the British fell in with their American allies to continue these offensive strikes that were designed to soften up Japan for a proposed invasion that was scheduled to begin in October.[25] The primary targets for these attacks included naval warships, aircraft, transportation assets and military infrastructure.

Immediately upon the British fleet's arrival, Admiral Halsey summoned Admirals Rawlings and Vian to his flagship, the battleship *Missouri*, to discuss the command relationship for the upcoming operation. During this meeting, Halsey pointed out that his operating instructions did not give him tactical control over Task Force 37. He suggested three alternatives to clarify this situation. First, he suggested that Task Force 37 operate as another task group within Task Force 38. Under this option, Task Force 37 would manoeuvre with Task Force 38, but would not receive direct orders from the latter. Next, he suggested that Task Force 37 position itself some 60–70 miles away from Task Force 38 and operate semi-independent of the latter. Finally, he suggested that Task Force 37 operate completely independent of Task Force 38 against separate targets in Japan. Without hesitation, Admiral Rawlings accepted the first option and ceded operational control to Admiral Halsey. From this point on, relations between Halsey and Rawlings remained high, and Task Force 37 became an integral part of the U.S. Third Fleet

On 17 July the three aircraft carriers of Task Force 37 began air operations against the Japanese home islands. Air strikes commenced early in the morning from a launch position some 250 miles east-north-east of Tokyo. Severe weather forced the Americans to abort their attacks, but some of the British aircraft got through to attack targets at Sendai, Masuda, Matsushima and the Sea of Japan. During these strikes the British destroyed nine aircraft, three locomotives and a junk while further damaging another nine aircraft, various shore installations and a 4,000-ton tanker. The British lost three aircraft in return. That night the battleship *King George V*, along with the destroyers *Quality* and *Quiberon*, participated in a bombardment of industrial targets around Hitachi and Mito on the east coast of Honshu. Weather conditions were still bad, and the British had to conduct the bombardment by radar. As a result, they only inflicted marginal damage against their assigned targets. Things improved somewhat on the 18th when the British launched another series of air strikes against various airfields and maritime targets around Tokyo and the seaplane base at Kitaura. Weather conditions were better than on the previous day, and the British were able to destroy 12 Japanese aircraft with 18 more damaged and destroy or damage a number of junks and minor vessels. British losses amounted to two Corsairs shot down over their targets and two Seafires forced to ditch.

Due to persistent bad weather, the Allies were not able to continue their operations against Japan until 24 July. Even then, the weather conditions were far from ideal as low clouds obscured many of the target areas. Despite this, Task Force 38 conducted a series of major air attacks against the important Japanese naval bases at Kure and Kobe. These bases contained the remnants of the once formidable Japanese fleet now immobilised due to a lack of fuel. The American attacks were highly successful as their carrier aircraft sank or heavily damaged a large number of Japanese warships including the battleships *Ise*, *Hyūga* and *Haruna* and the aircraft carriers *Amagi* and *Katsuragi*. The Americans excluded the British from participating in these attacks for political reasons. They wanted revenge for Pearl Harbor and sole credit for delivering the final coups de grace against the Imperial Japanese Navy. Despite this, the British refused to accept denial of their own revenge as Task Force 37, now reinforced by the arrival of the carrier *Indefatigable*, launched a maximum effort against targets in and around the Inland Sea. In all, the British conducted 15 strikes against Japan consisting of 227 offensive sorties out of a total of 416 sorties flown for the day.

In the early afternoon one of these strikes, consisting of six Avengers, two Fireflies and two Corsairs from the aircraft carriers *Victorious* and *Implacable*, happened upon and attacked what they described as a Kobe-class escort carrier off Shido Bay in the Inland Sea. For the loss of one Firefly, these aircraft succeeded in hitting the Japanese carrier with two 500-pound bombs. In follow-up strikes, Corsairs from *Formidable* strafed and bombed the stricken carrier, and then a force of Avengers and Seafires from *Indefatigable* bombed it again claiming two more hits and a near miss. These attacks left the Japanese escort carrier fatally damaged with a broken back and a breached hull. It bottomed in shallow water and remained a derelict wreck until 1948 when it was finally scrapped. Interestingly, the identity of this ship remained in dispute for a number of years. Most early historical accounts identified it as the escort carrier *Kaiyo*, but more recent analysis shows it was in fact the 11,800-ton auxiliary escort carrier *Shimane Maru*. In either case, the Fleet Air Arm could take solace in avenging the loss of *Hermes* in what proved to be its only attack against a hostile aircraft carrier during the war.[26] In other attacks, the British destroyed a small freighter (possibly the 873-ton *Komyo Maru*), at least seven other minor vessels and 15 aircraft. They further damaged numerous other vessels, 31 aircraft and various shore installations and transportation centres. British losses in attaining these successes amounted to just four aircraft in return.

On the 25th the British continued their aerial onslaught against Japan, but a deterioration in the weather quickly curtailed offensive operations, and Task Force 37 was only able to launch 155 sorties for the day. Despite this low number, the British still achieved a fair degree of success as their aircraft destroyed two enemy aircraft on the ground with six more damaged and sank or damaged three freighters, a large cargo ship and several junks and coasters in the Inland Sea. That night the

British added to this score when two Hellcats from *Formidable* intercepted and shot down three out of four Grace torpedo-bombers that were attempting to attack the fleet for no loss to themselves. Unlike at Okinawa a few months earlier where the Allied navies had endured heavy Japanese air attacks highlighted by the Kamikaze onslaught, this current series of Allied operations garnered little response from the Japanese other than often heavy anti-aircraft fire as the latter were attempting to conserve their resources for use against the anticipated Allied invasion. Yet, as this event with the Grace torpedo-bombers demonstrated, the Allies had to maintain a heavy vigilance to counter even minor Japanese attempts to attack the fleet.

After two replenishment days, the Allies resumed offensive operations against Japan on the 28th. While the Americans used this day to mount a follow-up attack against Kure, Task Force 37 launched ten individual and four combined strikes totalling 260 offensive sorties against the airfields at Akashi, Fukuyama, Minato and Sato, the shipyards at Harima and Habu and shipping in and around the Inland Sea. During these strikes the British destroyed the Japanese Kaibōkan escort destroyers *CD4* and *CD30* in Ise Bay and the Yura Strait respectively while combining with American aircraft to exact a similar fate on *CD45* at Owase.[27] Likewise, the British also claimed the destruction of at least six other vessels, one of which was likely the 865-ton tanker *Kinyu Maru No. 4*, while several other vessels were damaged including the escort destroyer *CD190* and a second tanker worth an estimated 6,000–8,000 tons. Finally, the British destroyed six aircraft on the ground with a further 14 damaged. British losses in return amounted to eight aircraft during the day's operations.

The British continued this offensive pressure through the remainder of the month. On the evening of the 29th the battleship *King George V* and the destroyers *Urania*, *Ulysses* and *Undine* participated in a bombardment of the industrial town of Hamamatsu. A collision between *Urania* and *Ulysses* marred the beginning of this operation, but neither ship was significantly damaged, and both were able to continue on with the assault. The bombardment was successful with *King George V* firing 265 14-inch shells at an aircraft factory. This was followed on the 30th with another series of strikes as Task Force 37 launched 216 offensive sorties against the naval base at Maizuru, the nearby harbour at Miyazu and other local maritime and military targets. During these attacks the British sank or participated in the destruction of the destroyer *Hatsushimo*, the Kaibōkan escort destroyers *Okinawa* and *CD2*, the coastal minelayer *Toshima*, the 9,877-ton transport *Teiritsu Maru* (which had been previously damaged by a mine), the merchant ships *Shokei Maru* and *Kashi Maru* (3,620 and 884 tons respectively) and numerous lesser vessels. They further damaged other maritime craft including the escort destroyer *Takane*, the submarine depot ship *Chogei* and the submarines *I-153* and *I-202* and destroyed or damaged a total of 14 Japanese aircraft (two of which were shot down in aerial combat). Many of these damaged vessels, including the escort destroyers *CD190* (which was damaged on the 28th) and *Takane* and the submarines *I-153* and *I-202*, were never again made seaworthy and were broken up after the war. British losses amounted to just three aircraft in return.

Replenishments, typhoon warnings and the dropping of the American atomic bomb on Hiroshima delayed further offensive operations until 9 August. On this day the Fleet Air Arm conducted its greatest effort of the war in terms of ordinance expended. In all, Task Force 37 launched 407 sorties of which 258 were offensive. These sorties were organised into 10 individual and four combined strikes against airfields at Matsushima, Shiogama, Kesennuma, Yamada, Hachinohe and Koriyama and shipping at Onagawa, Yamada, Kesennuma and Okotsu. During these strikes the British sank or destroyed the Kaibōkan escort destroyer *Amakusa*, the converted escort destroyer *W33*, the 478-ton tanker *Juko Maru* and over 20 auxiliary and minor vessels and damaged several other ships including the large escort destroyer *Ōhama*, the converted escort destroyer *W1* and the sub-chaser *CH42*. They also destroyed 44 Japanese aircraft on the ground with 22 more damaged while British fighters shot down a Grace torpedo-bomber over the fleet. In other action during the day the British cruiser *Newfoundland* and the New Zealand cruiser *Gambia*, along with the destroyers *Terpsichore*, *Tenacious* and *Termagant*, detached themselves from the fleet and participated in a bombardment of the coastal town of Kamaishi in northern Honshu. This bombardment was highly successful with the two cruisers firing a total of 733 rounds between them. The British ships then successfully withdrew without suffering damage to themselves despite a halfhearted Japanese air attack. Total British combat losses for the day amounted to seven aircraft destroyed including the one piloted by Lieutenant Robert 'Hammy' Gray as detailed in the introduction.

The battle continued on the 10th as Task Force 37 launched yet another 372 sorties, of which 236 were offensive. The British directed much of their effort against Onagawa Bay where they combined with American aircraft to complete the destruction of a number of Japanese warships damaged there the day before. These victims included the large escort destroyer *Ōhama*, the sub-chaser *CH42* and the auxiliary minesweeper *Kongo Maru 2*. In two days of air strikes, the Japanese lost 14 out of an estimated 15 warships and auxiliaries located in Onagawa Bay; the only survivor being the 86-ton auxiliary sub-chaser *CHA 161*.[28] In other attacks during the day the British attacked Japanese shipping at Okachi, Sendai and along the coastal plain where they claimed a 1,500-ton freighter and numerous lesser vessels destroyed or damaged. Likewise, the previously damaged escort destroyer *W1* was finished off in Yamada Bay.[29] Finally, in attacks against airfields at Masuda, Matsushima and Koriyama the British destroyed 16 Japanese aircraft on the ground with 31 more damaged. British combat losses in return amounted to six aircraft destroyed.

By 11 August it was increasingly clear that Japan remained wide open to further assaults, but it was equally apparent that Task Force 37 had reached the limit of its logistical endurance. During the preceding three and a half weeks the British had strained their fragile logistical system to a near breaking point in order to meet Task Force 38's aggressive strike schedule. Aided by the advent of timely weather delays and unofficial American support, the overtaxed British Fleet Train successfully met the fleet's requirements, but it had often been a near run thing. Now in the middle of August, the British were obliged to withdraw the majority of their forces to prepare for the upcoming invasion of Japan. Travelling to Sydney, they would rendezvous with the battleships *Anson* and *Duke of York* and the light carriers *Colossus*, *Glory*, *Venerable* and *Vengeance* that had already arrived or were due to arrive in the next few days thus further expanding the power of the British fleet. Of what remained behind, the British were able to deploy a reduced force to operate with the Americans off Japan. This force, designated Task Group 38.5, consisted of the battleship *King George V*, the aircraft carrier *Indefatigable*, two cruisers and ten destroyers.

On 12 August the bulk of Task Force 37 departed Japanese waters for Sydney. From 16 July through 10 August Task Force 37 had participated in eight days of air strikes and three naval bombardments against Japan. During this period the British flew 2,615 sorties of which 1,595 were offensive.[30] For the cost of 40 aircraft lost in combat and another 51 dispatched through operational causes, the British destroyed 142 Japanese aircraft on the ground and six more in aerial combat while damaging a further 199 aircraft on the ground. Of even greater consequence, the British destroyed or damaged 309 military and commercial vessels worth an estimated 356,760 tons.[31] In fairness, most of this latter toll came from vessels that only sustained minor damage, but it also included at least 12 combatant warships worth 22,533 tons and 25,640 tons of commercial shipping destroyed solely or partially as a result of these British strikes.[32] During roughly the same period Task Force 38 flew a staggering 18,163 sorties and destroyed or damaged an estimated 924,000 tons of shipping and 2,408 aircraft.[33] Thus, considering the sizes of the forces involved, Task Force 37's operational record compared quite favourably to that of its American counterpart.[34]

On 13 August Task Group 38.5 commenced air operations against Japan as part of Task Force 38. During this day *Indefatigable* launched 42 offensive and 36 defensive sorties, hitting a number of targets around Tokyo and north central Honshu including a chemical factory at Onagawa. The Japanese responded to this onslaught by launching a number of Kamikaze attacks against the fleet. *Indefatigable* helped direct Allied fighters to intercept these Japanese aircraft, and 21 were shot down in aerial combat. Following a day of replenishment, Task Group 38.5 resumed operations on the 15th. Early that morning the British launched their first strike of Avengers, Fireflies and Seafires. Twelve Japanese fighters intercepted this force while en route to their target, and a fierce air battle ensued. During this action eight British Seafires shot down eight Japanese fighters for the loss of one of their own numbers. Meanwhile, the Avengers flew on to successfully bomb a chemical factory at Odaki Bay while the Fireflies strafed an airfield.

Table 10.3. Japanese Warships Sunk Solely or Partially as a Result of British Carrier Air Attacks against the Japanese Home Islands in July and August 1945.

Date	Vessel name	Vessel type	Tonnage	Main armament	Location
24 Jul	*Shimane Maru*	Escort carrier	11,800	12 Aircraft, 2 × 4.7in guns	Shido Bay
28 Jul	*CD4*	Escort destroyer	740	2 × 4.7in guns, 120 DCs	Ise Bay
28 Jul	*CD30*	Escort destroyer	740	2 × 4.7in guns, 120 DCs	Yura Straits
28 Jul	*CD45*	Escort destroyer	745	2 × 4.7in guns, 120 DCs	Owase
30 Jul	*Hatsushimo*	Destroyer	1,715	5 × 5in guns, 6 x 24in TT	Miyatsu Bay
30 Jul	*Okinawa*	Escort destroyer	940	3 × 4.7in guns, 120 DCs	Maizuru
30 Jul	*CD2*	Escort destroyer	740	2 × 4.7in guns, 120 DCs	Maizuru
9 Aug	*Amakusa*	Escort destroyer	870	3 × 4.7in guns, 60 DCs	Onagawa Bay
9 Aug	*W33*	Escort destroyer	648	3 × 4.7in guns, 36 DCs	Onagawa Bay
10 Aug	*Ōhama*	Escort destroyer	2,560	2 × 4.7in guns, 36 DCs	Onagawa Bay
10 Aug	*W1*	Escort destroyer	615	1 × 4.7in gun, 36 DCs	Yamada Bay
10 Aug	*CH42*	Sub-chaser	420	1 × 3in gun, 36 DCs	Onagawa Bay

Note: The destroyer *Hatsushimo* sank as a result of a mine strike and Allied air attacks at Miyatsu Bay near Maizuru. British strike reports indicate that their aircraft did attack a destroyer on this date at this location resulting in severe damage from at least one bomb hit and repeated strafing.

Unbeknown to the participants, this would prove to be the last British airstrike against Japan as events were already well underway regarding Japan's surrender. This had not been an easy decision as large segments of the Japanese military were determined to fight on in accordance with their Bushido tradition. To this end, Japanese plans called for the entire population to be utilised in the defence of their homeland. In some cases, military and civilian personnel were armed with spears to confront the massive Allied juggernaut projected to descend upon them. Still, not all Japanese leaders were ready to commit national suicide, and the Japanese war cabinet was split on how to proceed. On 6 and 9 August the United States dropped two atomic bombs on the Japanese cities of Hiroshima and Nagasaki. Also, on the 9th the Soviet Union declared war on Japan and launched a massive invasion into Japanese-occupied Manchuria. Given these events, Emperor Hirohito intervened in the deliberations and ordered his government to accept the Allied surrender terms. Despite considerable opposition including an attempted coup d'état, most government and military officials acquiesced to the emperor's will, and at noon on the 15th a radio broadcast announced the emperor's decision to surrender.

That same day Admiral Halsey ordered Third Fleet, including Task Force 38.5, to cancel all further offensive operations. Over the next two weeks, the fleet maintained a strong presence off Japan as officials made preparations for the formal surrender ceremony. During this time Admiral Fraser joined Task Group 38.5 with his flagship, the battleship *Duke of York*. On 30 August this ship, along with the battleship *King George V*, three destroyers and numerous American ships, entered Tokyo Bay. Three days later a Japanese delegation, led by the Foreign Minister Mamoru Shigemitsu, gathered on board the American battleship *Missouri* and signed the official instrument of surrender. General Douglas MacArthur then signed this document on behalf of the Allied nations. Other signatories included Admiral Chester Nimitz for the United States, Admiral Bruce Fraser for the United Kingdom, General Thomas Blamey for Australia, Air Vice Marshal Leonard Isitt for New Zealand and Colonel Lawrence Moore-Cosgrove for Canada.

In the days and weeks following this ceremony, British and Australian forces reoccupied former Allied territories and accepted the surrender of local Japanese commands. The first such major event occurred on 6 September when the British aircraft carrier *Glory* hosted a proceeding at Rabaul in which Australian Lieutenant-General Vernon Sturdee accepted the surrender of some 138,000 Japanese personnel located in the Solomon Islands, Bismarck Archipelago and New Guinea. A breakdown of these prisoners included 57,368 army and 31,923 naval personnel (including civilian workers) from Rabaul, 12,400 from New Ireland, 23,571 from Bougainville and 13,000 from New Guinea.[35] Even as this was underway, strong British naval forces were already congregating in Hong Kong, which eventually included the battleships *Anson* and *Duke of York* and the aircraft carriers *Indomitable*, *Venerable* and *Vengeance*. Here, the British reclaimed possession of the colony on 30 August and received the formal surrender of 22,194 Japanese military and civilian personnel on 16 September.[36]

Meanwhile, on 9 September the British launched Operation *Zipper*, which had been substantially moved up from its original proposed start date, and landed some 100,000 men on Malaya. Even though the war was technically over, the British conducted these landings in a tactical manner and supported them with a large naval contingent including the battleships *Nelson* and *Richelieu* and six escort carriers. These precautions proved unnecessary as the Japanese did not oppose the landings, and the British were able to enter Singapore on the 10th. Two days later General Seishirō Itagaki surrendered all Japanese forces in Southeast Asia to Admiral Mountbatten. Thereafter, some 350,000 British troops and 120 ships fanned out across the region where they eventually took possession of roughly 730,000 Japanese prisoners including 633,000 military personnel, 93,000 civilians and 10,000 Koreans and Formosans. A general breakdown of these Japanese prisoners included 72,000 from Burma, 20,000 from the Andaman and Nicobar Islands, 118,000 from Thailand, 122,000 from Malaya and Singapore, 72,000 from southern French Indochina, 75,000 from Sumatra, 73,000 from Java, 33,000 from Borneo, 25,000 from the Lesser Sundas and 123,000 from the outer Dutch East Indies and Dutch New Guinea.[37]

By October 1945 the British and Australians had liberated all of their lost territory, and Japan's defeat was complete. Replacing Japan's dream of a vast Asian empire was an eviscerated nation with a prostrate army, shattered navy and collapsed

Major-General W. A. Crowther of the 17th Indian Division accepting the local surrender of the Japanese Thirty-Third Army at Thaton north of Moulmein. (Chris Turner, public domain)

economy. For the British Commonwealth, this development not only signalled an end of the local fighting but constituted the culmination of a momentous struggle stretching back six years to the advent of Germany's invasion of Poland. From this seemingly localised event sprang a conflict of unprecedented proportions that soon engulfed all of the major powers of the world. In the process of this great conflagration, the union of British nations and peoples faced numerous trials and tribulations while confronting Germany, Italy and Japan. In turn, through dogged perseverance and martial prowess, the British played the pivotal role in forging the grand alliance that eventually toppled this immense evil. One by one, the Axis nations crumbled in the face of the Allied onslaught, and now with the defeat of Japan, the British Commonwealth's great and noble crusade was finally over, and the Second World War entered the province of history.

CHAPTER 11

Reflections on the Asia/Pacific War

Unlike the surrender of Nazi Germany, which took place on 7 May 1945 to little fanfare in a French schoolhouse in the middle of the night, the ceremony bringing about the official surrender of Japan, which took place on the American battleship *Missouri* on 2 September 1945, was a spectacular event steeped in pageantry and witnessed by thousands ranging from high-ranking dignitaries to common enlisted servicemen. Among the throng present at this momentous event were British Lieutenant-General Arthur Percival and American Lieutenant-General Jonathan Wainwright. Until very recently, both men had been prisoners of the Japanese, the former having surrendered at Singapore while the latter surrendered at Corregidor in the Philippines. During the ceremony, both men stood directly behind General Douglas MacArthur when he signed the surrender document on behalf of the Allied nations. During this process, MacArthur used six pens, two of which he gave to Wainwright and Percival. The presence of these men and this act had great symbolic significance as it reflected the miraculous and definitive turn of events that had occurred over the previous three and a half years. Early in the war, Japan had inflicted the worst series of military defeats ever to befall the United Kingdom and the United States. Both Generals Percival and Wainwright had been key participants and witnesses to these earlier events in which Japan appeared almost invincible. Now, like a phoenix rising from the ashes, both men emerged from this bleak period and years of horrendous Japanese confinement to witness Japan's downfall as it acknowledged a defeat of far greater magnitude.

Following this same theme, ten days later the British carried out a similar ceremony in the Singapore Municipal Building where General Seishirō Itagaki surrendered all Japanese forces in Southeast Asia to Admiral Louis Mountbatten. Accompanying Mountbatten on this grand occasion were many of the key leaders who had prosecuted Britain's war effort within the region. Amongst these was Lieutenant-General William Slim, the indomitable commander of the Fourteenth Army; Admiral Arthur Power, the commander of the East Indies Fleet; and Air Chief Marshal Keith Park, the Allied Air Commander South-East Asia Command.

The surrender ceremony in Tokyo Bay. Directly behind a seated General MacArthur are Generals Wainwright (left) and Percival (right). Also visible is General Blamey (the first full person on the left). (Cross, W. G. (Sub Lt), Royal Navy official photographer, public domain)

Following this ceremony, the British conducted a celebration and victory parade in Padang. Of course, Singapore had been the scene of Britain's humiliating surrender some three and a half years earlier, which had culminated the disastrous Malaya campaign in which the British gave up some 130,000 prisoners. Now with the culmination of these actions, the British regained control over their lost territory and secured the surrender of some 633,000 Japanese military personnel thus once again seeing events turn full circle.

In reviewing the many factors that brought about these outcomes, a number of irrefutable facts are readily apparent. First, that the Allies were entirely victorious in their war effort against Japan. Second, that the Asia/Pacific contest was just part of a larger global struggle in which the Allies successfully vanquished the forces of the Axis coalition. Similarly, within the context of this overall conflict, the Allied efforts expended against Japan were subordinate to those expended against the European Axis, which was seen as the greater threat. Third, that the United States was the primary perpetrator of the victory over Japan. Fourth, despite the validity of this latter point, the British Empire and Commonwealth still made substantial

Admiral Mountbatten flanked from left to right by Admiral Power, General Slim, American Lieutenant-General Wheeler and Air Chief Marshal Park during the surrender ceremony in Singapore. (Ashley (Fl Off), Royal Air Force official photographer, public domain)

and relevant contributions to this Asia/Pacific victory. Finally, that there were a number of major components facilitating the Allied victory, and in each case the Allies significantly outperformed their Japanese adversaries. The reality of the Allied victory over Japan is self-evident as demonstrated by the events described in this book. The remaining factors will now be discussed in greater detail.

Starting first with its place in the greater global conflict, while involving over 50 countries and as many colonies and territories, the conduct of World War II essentially boiled down to a contest between six major powers divided evenly into two competing coalitions. For the Allies, this consisted of the British Empire and Commonwealth of Nations, the Soviet Union and the United States. Confronting this alliance was the Axis consisting of Germany, Italy and the Japanese Empire. Beyond this breakdown of primary combatants, World War II was further divided into two major theatres of operation: the war in Europe and the war in the Far East. Participants at the time and subsequent historians have substantially agreed that the war in Europe was the more critical of the two contests with Germany posing the greatest threat to the Allied cause. As such, all three of the major Allied powers devoted the bulk of their war efforts into defeating Germany and winning the war in Europe. For the United States and Britain, a key tenet in their grand strategy was the adoption of a 'Europe First' policy in which the two nations agreed to devote the preponderance of their collective military power to subdue Germany first (and by extension Italy) while only using those resources necessary to hold the line against Japan. Once Germany was defeated, the Allies would then turn their concentrated efforts against the Japanese and defeat them in kind.

With some minor deviations, the policy of prioritising the European conflict was generally followed and proved to be justified as it took the combined strength of all three Allied powers to subdue Germany. In breaking down these national contributions, the Soviet Union devoted 100 percent of its immense war effort against the Germans until that nation was defeated. To put this mammoth contribution into perspective, for most of the war the Soviets employed more ground forces against the Germans than the Japanese had in their entire army. For the British Empire and Commonwealth, the breakdown of resources devoted to the European conflict was in the realm of 90 percent for most of the war, although it substantially shifted towards the Asia/Pacific conflict from 1944 on. Nevertheless, even during this latter period, the British still maintained roughly 75 to 80 percent of their overall combat strength in Europe. The situation was the opposite for the United States, which despite the Europe First policy, initially devoted a majority of its engaged resources to contain the Japanese. However, in 1944 this allocation substantially shifted as large contingents of men and resources were sent to Europe to engage Germany. Throughout the duration of the war, the Americans devoted the bulk of their naval strength to confronting Japan while the majority of the American army fought against Germany and Italy. In terms of this latter point, by 1945 almost three out of every four deployed American divisions were engaged in Europe thus highlighting America's commitment to this endeavour.

Conversely, given this massive effort in Europe, the war against Japan did not garner the same level of involvement. Again, of the three main Allied powers, the Soviet Union did not even engage in the effort against Japan until the last few days of the war by which time Japan was already on the brink of defeat. Meanwhile, the British and Americans only devoted a minority of their resources to prosecute the war against Japan ranging from 10 to 20 percent for the former and perhaps 40 percent for the latter. Yet, even with this limited outlay of effort, this still proved to be enough to bring the island nation to its knees. This was particularly impressive considering the stated Allied strategy was only to contain Japan. If there is any doubt regarding the wisdom of the Europe First policy or the notion that Germany represented the greater threat, it is dispelled by the fact that after America's entry into the war in December 1941, it took 41 months of fighting during which the three major Allied powers devoted all or most of their efforts against Germany to bring about that nation's defeat. By comparison, the Japanese, who were only engaged by a small fraction of this combined power, only managed to hold out for another three months following the German collapse.

Yet, despite this reality, one should not lose sight of the fact that the Asia/Pacific conflict represented a major undertaking notwithstanding it subordinate position to the European struggle. In facilitating the victory over Japan, this was overwhelmingly an American endeavour. This was true if for no other reason than the United States provided the bulk of the Allied forces involved, conducted the majority of fighting, suffered the majority of related Allied combat losses and inflicted the majority of losses against the Japanese. Beyond this, it was overwhelmingly the Americans who scored the key victories that progressively diminished Japan to a point of final defeat. While acknowledging this American dominance, it is equally viable to recognise that the United States received substantial help in this overall effort. While this help came from many sources, it was particularly prevalent in terms of the contributions made by British and Commonwealth forces. Even though the British only devoted a small percentage of their combat efforts against Japan, this still eventually amounted to upwards of two million men and the employment of hundreds of ships and thousands of aircraft. In terms of the former, by the end of March 1945 the British portion of the Allied Land Forces South-East Asia numbered 971,828 assigned personnel.[1] Added to this were large numbers of men in the regional naval and air forces as well as hundreds of thousands of Australians and New Zealanders serving in the Southwest Pacific. In fairness, given the immense materiel realities of modern warfare, most of these personnel performed logistical or support functions, but this force also included at least 300,000 men at the sharp end of the conflict.

So how did the Allies execute the defeat of Japan and what was the national breakdown in bringing about this outcome? At its core, the war against Japan was a naval contest in which the key to Japan's demise centred upon the application of naval and air power. As an island nation lacking in many key natural resources, Japan primarily went to war in 1941 to remedy this situation. In doing so, the Japanese were initially successful in seizing large swaths of territory that were rich in natural resources. Still, the seizure of these areas was only meaningful as long as the Japanese could defend their territorial gains and transport the attained resources back to their home islands. This prospect was solely dependent upon the use of maritime power exercised by the Japanese navy and merchant fleet. Unfortunately for them, these forces became dwindling assets as Allied naval and air units took an ever-increasing toll upon their numbers. As Japan's maritime power progressively diminished, so too did its ability to defend its empire and support itself. Likewise, the Allies used their own maritime power to conduct a series of amphibious operations that seized key islands throughout the Pacific thus further isolating Japan and bringing it within range of American strategic bombers. By the end of the war, the Japanese still controlled a sizeable empire with substantial forces spread throughout, but their maritime power was almost completely destroyed thus leaving their home islands fully isolated, under heavy aerial bombardment and in a state of ongoing economic collapse. Eventually this aerial bombardment included the use of atomic weapons. With the threat of invasion looming and with no prospect for reversing these conditions, the Japanese had no choice but to surrender or suffer more pointless loss.

The forces responsible for bringing about this result came overwhelmingly from the United States. It was primarily American ships, submarines, mines and aircraft that decimated the Japanese navy and merchant fleet. In all, the Japanese lost 332 out of the 451 major surface warships and submarines (73.6 percent) in commission during the war. Of what remained, only 37 vessels (8.2 percent) were still operational at the end of the conflict.[2] Included in these losses were 94 percent of their capital ships, 91 percent of their cruisers and 87 percent of their destroyers.[3] Beyond these major combatants, some 354 lesser warships, including escort destroyers, frigates, corvettes and minesweepers, were also lost. Likewise, 144 percent of their originating and 85 percent of their accumulated merchant tonnage was sunk during the conflict.[4] Together, these losses totalled 686 military vessels and 2,346 merchant ships of 500 tons or greater that were sunk during the war.[5] Of what remained, most surviving vessels were still under construction or ended the war in an immobilised state due to damage or a lack of fuel. All of these surviving warships surrendered at the end of hostilities thus putting them under Allied control and bringing Japan's total loss for the war to 773 principal warships, the entirety of their navy. American forces accounted for roughly 90 percent of these military and commercial losses while the portion attributable to British, Commonwealth and Dutch forces (either fully or partially) amounted to about five percent.[6]

This disparity of results was even more pronounced in the strategic air war. This was particularly true regarding the aerial bombardment of Japan, which was almost exclusively an American effort. In fact, Britain's only contribution to this two-year campaign consisted of the carrier air strikes conducted by Task Force 37 against the Japanese home islands in July and August 1945. During these strikes the British dropped a total of 517 tons of bombs against domestic Japanese targets compared to 176,647 and 6,788 tons dropped cumulatively by the USAAF and United States Navy respectively.[7] As such, Britain's portion of this effort constituted little more than one-quarter of one percent. This bombing campaign, coupled with the material shortages brought about by the maritime blockade, caused Japanese arms production to collapse in the last year of the war as output in many key industries declined by 70 percent or better compared to peak year performance. Likewise, large segments of the Japanese population were rendered homeless while food shortages became widespread. Capping off this aerial onslaught was the dropping of two atomic bombs that devastated the cities of Hiroshima and Nagasaki and proved to be a final determinant that helped convince the Japanese to surrender. Thus, given this disparity of effort and outcome in both the naval and aerial campaigns, America's pre-eminence in bringing about Japan's defeat is undeniable.

Conceding this point, what were the British and Commonwealth contributions to this naval and aerial effort. In terms of the former, British and Commonwealth forces

Table 11.1. Decline in Annual Japanese Wartime Production.

Production categories	Key military production by year 1941	1942	1943	1944	1945	Percent decline from peak year to 1945
Crude steal (million metric tons)	–	8.0	8.8	6.5	0.8	90.9%
Aluminum (000 metric tons)	–	103	141	110	7	95.0%
Tanks and self-propelled guns (units)	595	557	558	353	137	77.0%
Artillery pieces (units)	2,250	2,550	3,600	3,300	1,650	54.2%
Military trucks and lorries (units)	46,389	35,386	24,000	20,356	1,758	96.2%
Aircraft (units)	5,088	8,861	16,693	28,180	8,263	70.7%
Merchant shipping (000 gross tons)	210.4	260.1	769.1	1,699.2	599.6	64.7%

Source: John Ellis, *World War II, A Statistical Survey, the Essential Facts and Figures for all the Combatants* (New York: Facts on File, 1993), pp. 276–280.

Note: Some of these figures are estimations.

sank or participated in the destruction of 42 principal Japanese warships during the course of the war. Although comprehensively covered earlier in the book, a quick synopsis of the major British/Commonwealth successes in this area include the limited contributions made by the Australian cruiser *Shropshire* and destroyer *Arunta* in destroying the Japanese battleship *Yamashiro* during the battle of Surigao Strait. During this action, these Australian ships undoubtedly inflicted damage against the Japanese battleship, but this constituted only a small portion of the destruction meted out. Still, these vessels did participate in the engagement and thus contributed to *Yamashiro*'s loss. In other joint actions, British and Commonwealth air and naval units also participated with American forces in destroying the Japanese cruisers *Jintsū* and *Isuzu* in 1943 and 1945 respectively. Meanwhile, British submarines sank the Japanese cruisers *Kuma* and *Ashigara* in conventional attacks in 1944 and 1945 while British XE-craft midget submarines rendered the cruiser *Takao* a total loss in Singapore harbour during this latter year. Likewise, in the last major naval surface action of the war, British destroyers sank the Japanese cruiser *Haguro* off Penang. Finally, in July and August 1945 British aircraft carriers launched a series of air strikes against the Japanese home islands that destroyed some 50,000 tons of Japanese military and commercial shipping including the auxiliary escort carrier *Shimane Maru*.

An accurate accounting of British and Commonwealth successes against the Japanese merchant fleet is more difficult to determine. This is primarily due to the lack of records regarding Japanese merchant losses of less than 500 tons as well as other data shortfalls and contradictions. At a minimum, British and Commonwealth forces were responsible for the loss of at least 56 Japanese merchant ships (of 500 tons or greater) worth 138,529 tons and contributed to the destruction of a further 11 merchant ships worth 56,931 tons.[8] Added to this were several hundred minor

Table 11.2. Japanese Warship Losses Exclusively or Partially due to British/Commonwealth Means.

	Total losses	Losses exclusively due to British/ Com means	Losses partially due to British/ Com means	Percent of losses due solely or partially to British/Com means
Battleships	12	–	1	8.3%
Aircraft carriers	24	1	–	4.2%
Cruisers	43	4	2	14.0%
Destroyers	143	–	9	6.3%
Escort destroyers/escorts*	305	8	4	3.9%
Submarines	232	9	2	4.7%
Minelayers	5	1	–	20.0%
Fleet minesweepers	9	1	–	11.1%
TOTAL	773	24	18	5.4%

* Many of the escort destroyers/escorts were conversions from other warship types. In particular, large numbers of minesweepers were converted to serve as escorts and are thus counted as such here.

craft worth at least 100,000 tons that were destroyed by British or Commonwealth means. Finally, it is almost certain that the British were solely or partially responsible for further Japanese losses ranging from at least 25,000 tons to perhaps as high as an additional 100,000 tons, but it is difficult to determine an exact number given the lack of Japanese confirmation and conflicting claims in the Allied records. Thus, when combined together, total Japanese commercial losses that were solely or partially attributable to British/Commonwealth means numbered 70 plus primary merchant ships and upwards of 1,000 minor vessels worth somewhere between 300,000 and 400,000 tons. Dutch forces, which usually operated under British or Australian control, added at least another 16 Japanese merchant ships worth 62,594 tons to this total.[9] When added together, these British, Commonwealth and Dutch successes accounted for about 4 percent of Japan's total merchant shipping losses of vessels of 500 tons or greater accrued during the war.

Britain's impact on the air war was roughly equivalent to that of its naval effort. In terms of the strategic air offensive, British and Commonwealth aircraft (both naval and ground-based) made limited, but meaningful, contributions to the interdiction actions targeting Japanese fuel production and distribution. Of particular impact was the FAA's successful series of attacks against the Palembang oil refineries in southern Sumatra that halved Japan's aviation fuel production during the final year of the war. Augmenting this were similar raids carried out by the FAA against other regional refineries that caused further damage to Japan's oil producing capabilities. Meanwhile, British and Commonwealth aircraft carried out both mining and direct attacks that sank a number of Japanese merchant ships (as discussed in the previous paragraph) and caused disruptions to Japanese seaborne lines of communication that impeded the transport of oil and other important commodities back to Japan

While the United States was clearly the dominant player in the maritime contest against Japan, British and Commonwealth forces also made notable contributions. Pictured here (postwar) is the British submarine *Thorough*, which sank some 40 Japanese minor vessels during the war. (Sam Hood, public domain)

for subsequent industrial and military use. A primary example of the latter was the RAAF's mining campaign against Balikpapan harbour in Borneo that proved to be a persistent obstacle to this critical trade.

While clearly garnering some successes at the strategic level, most British and Commonwealth air activities were focused on tactical or regional operations. I will review these tactical contributions in greater detail later, but one area to address now is the direct impact that British and Commonwealth air operations had in causing attrition to Japanese air units. While a precise accounting of Japanese aircraft losses is difficult to ascertain given variations in competing records and the universal tendency for all parties to overclaim their successes, a reasonable estimate is that about 1,000 Japanese aircraft were destroyed due to British or Commonwealth actions during the war. By comparison, the Japanese lost an estimated 38,105 aircraft during operational use with their total aircraft losses from all causes, including training and ferrying mishaps, numbering perhaps as high as 50,000. In terms of this latter number, 40 percent were believed lost in combat while 60 percent were lost due to accidents, mechanical failures and other non-combat related factors.[10] Given these figures, roughly five percent of all Japanese aircraft combat losses and 2 to 2.5 percent of their total losses were likely attributable to British or Commonwealth means, which would make these results roughly equivalent to the British successes attained against Japan's maritime forces.

Turning now to the ground war, unlike the limited, but tangible, results attained by their naval and air force counterparts, the contributions made by British and Commonwealth ground forces were actually quite substantial within the overall framework of the Allied war effort. In fact, during the fighting in Southeast Asia and the South Pacific, the British Commonwealth employed as many divisions in active combat against the Japanese as did the United States. To be specific, a total of 27 British and Commonwealth divisions (consisting of four British, twelve Indian, seven Australian, three African and one New Zealand) saw service at one point or another during the war against Japan compared to an identical number of American divisions that saw similar service during the conflict. The results attained by these British/Commonwealth forces were substantial. In 1949 the Japanese government did an analysis of Japanese casualties sustained during the war. This analysis was far from complete as it did not account for 240,000 army personnel who went missing during the conflict and only counted wounded personnel who received pensions. Still, this examination documented a total of 1,140,429 Japanese army personnel killed with a further 295,247 wounded. Of these, 407,537 of the ground fatalities and 154,225 of the wounded were determined to have occurred in operations confronting British, Australian or Dutch forces thus equating to 35.7 and 52.2 percent of the total losses respectively. By comparison, the study assigned the figures killed and wounded by American forces at 485,717 and 34,679 respectively thus constituting 42.6 and 11.7 percent of the total losses. In combining the killed and wounded together, the analysis put the overall casualties incurred against British, Australian and Dutch forces at 561,762 while those explicitly incurred against American forces amounted to 520,396.[11]

While again stipulating that these figures are incomplete, this data clearly shows that British and Commonwealth forces played a substantially greater role in the theatre's ground combat than in other aspects of their regional war effort. In doing so, they tended to engage in a different kind of fighting than their American counterparts. In particular, British and Commonwealth forces tended to engage in more traditional ground campaigns that were fought over wide areas for extended periods of time. The most prevalent examples of this were the campaigns in Burma and Papua New Guinea, which were protracted undertakings lasting years over contested areas stretching for hundreds of thousands of square miles. Given this reality, these were often battles of manoeuvre as both sides had ample territory in which to advance or retreat. Likewise, much of this took place over extremely harsh terrain that taxed the logistical capabilities of the competing forces. By comparison, most of the American fighting consisted of island warfare in which the forces involved fought intense battles of relatively short durations in geographically limited locations

Table 11.3. Breakdown of Known Japanese Army Casualties from December 1941 to December 1946.

	Killed*	Wounded**
Versus China after Pearl Harbor	202,958	88,920
Versus the United States	485,717	34,679
Versus the United Kingdom and Netherlands	208,026	139,225
Versus Australia	199,511	15,000
Versus the Soviet Union	7,483	4,641
French Indochina	2,803	6,000
Other overseas locations	23,388	–
On the Japanese home islands	10,543	6,782
Total Japanese army losses	1,140,429	295,247

Source: Executive Office of the Statistics Commission (Editor), *Japan Statistical Year-Book, 1949* (Tokyo: Statistics Bureau of the Prime Minister's Office, 1949) p. 1,058.

*These figures do not include an additional 240,000 missing army personnel.

**Wounded figures only apply to personnel receiving pensions.

against isolated Japanese garrisons that had minimal opportunities to manoeuvre, disengage or receive reinforcements. Accordingly, these American operations were often battles of annihilation against a set enemy in a confined location. The differing natures of these campaigns explain why the Japanese suffered a larger percentage of wounded facing British and Australian units than they did facing the Americans. Likewise, it is safe to assume that a far larger percentage of Japanese fatalities incurred in the British/Commonwealth areas were the result of disease and starvation as opposed to direct combat action.

In closing out this topic, there were two major indirect contributions that Britain and the Commonwealth made in prosecuting the war against Japan. The first of these dealt with Britain's dominant position in the overall maritime conflict. As discussed earlier in the chapter, the United States was able to employ most of its naval power against Japan. A key dynamic in allowing the Americans to do this was the fact that the British shouldered most of the burden in the naval contests in the Atlantic and Mediterranean against Germany and Italy. This was no minor undertaking as the struggle in the Atlantic constituted the war's premier maritime contest in terms of its size, duration and relevance and was the most important military campaign waged by the Western Allies. Although not normally viewed as a great naval power, the German Kriegsmarine actually attained a strength that was twice the size of the Imperial Japanese Navy in terms of accumulated principal warships during the war (1,640 to 773).[12] While almost three-fourths of these German combatants were U-boats, this force also included 450 surface warships ranging in size from battleships down to fleet minesweepers. Emphasising the scale of this conflict, the Germans lost more principal warships in the Atlantic theatre alone than did all of the combatants in the Asia/Pacific war combined. Of these German losses, British and Commonwealth forces solely or partially accounted for 100 percent of their capital ships, 75 percent of their cruisers, 86 percent of their destroyers, 75 percent of their torpedo boats and escort destroyers, 86 percent of their fleet minesweepers, 77 percent of their U-boats and 73 percent of their merchant and commercial vessels. The British enjoyed similar success against the Italians accounting for 86 percent of Italy's principal warship losses during their time as an Axis partner.[13]

Another example of Britain's immense naval contribution was the role that British maritime forces played in carrying out a series of amphibious landings that changed the shape of the European war. In nine out of ten such landings, British and Commonwealth ships provided the sole or dominant naval contributions to these undertakings. This was certainly the case in the war's two largest amphibious assaults. The first of these was Operation *Husky*, the invasion of Sicily, in which 1,614 (62.3 percent) of the 2,590 assorted vessels used were British or British-affiliated. The Royal Navy's contribution to this massive force included six battleships, two aircraft carriers, 13 cruisers, three monitors, 71 destroyers, 35 escorts, 34 mine-sweepers and 23 submarines compared to just five cruisers, 48 destroyers and eight minesweepers provided by the United States Navy.[14] This was followed up a year later with Operation *Overlord*, the invasion of Normandy. The naval component of this invasion was Operation *Neptune*, which involved some 7,000 vessels. Included in this were 1,213 combatant warships and 4,126 assorted landing ships and craft.[15] In terms of the former, 79 percent of the assigned warships, ranging from battleships to coastal craft, came from British or Canadian sources while a further 4.5 percent came from affiliated Allied navies.[16] Likewise, the British provided at least 60 percent of the assigned landing ships and associated craft for the invasion.[17] Thus, when viewed in a global context, Britain's maritime contribution to the overall war effort was at least equivalent to that of the United States, and this British predominance against Germany and Italy allowed the Americans to dedicate most of their naval forces against Japan.

The second indirect contribution made by the British Empire and Commonwealth was the role that British-affiliated territory played in facilitating the war against Japan. A substantial portion of America's regional war effort was staged out of British or Commonwealth territory such as India, Burma, Australia and New Zealand. These territories served as bases of operation for direct attacks as well as important logistical hubs. As an example of the latter, the use of India provided the United States with the means to send logistical support to China thus helping to keep that nation in the war. Similarly, by using India as an intermediary, the Americans were able to establish bases within China itself that allowed them to carry out bombing and mining operations against the Japanese home islands from a different quarter. Beyond their geographical benefits, some of these same areas provided the Allies with important materiel support in the form of food and industrial production. So important was this support that the Allied governments collectively decided to scale back the direct military efforts of Australia and New Zealand to better accommodate this agricultural and industrial output during the latter years of the war.

Now that we know the magnitude of Japan's defeat, what were the critical factors that facilitated this outcome? While there were undoubtedly many, I will review two major strategic and five tactical dynamics that brought about Japan's demise. Starting with the former, a key contributor to Japan's defeat was the flawed premise guiding its entire war effort regarding the moral character of the Western nations and particularly that of the United States. Japanese authorities surmised that the Allied nations were too preoccupied and/or morally weak to engage in a protracted war if dealt a chain of early defeats. Therefore, they sought to deliver a series of quick, decisive victories that would demoralize the Allied nations and compel them to sue for peace. Ideally, this peace would be advantageous to Japan and secure their acquisition of a regional empire. Unfortunately for the Japanese, if the United States did not act in the way predicted, it was Japan that would find itself ensnared in an all-out protracted war that it was ill suited to wage. In fact, against the combined military and industrial power of the United States and British Empire, Japan had virtually no prospect of success in such a contest. Therefore, by gambling and opting for war, the Japanese ceased to be masters of their own destinies as success or failure entirely depended upon the reactions of their enemies. In this case, the United States responded to Japan's aggression by embarking upon a total war that sealed Japan's fate.

Similarly, by pursuing a flawed strategy of attaining decisive naval victories as a means to secure an early resolution to the war, the Japanese failed to adequately prepare for the prospects of a protracted contest. Once again, this strategy depended upon America's acquiescence to Japanese designs. Even had the Japanese destroyed the entire American Pacific fleet in the opening months of the war, this would not have ensured a Japanese victory. If choosing to do so, the United States would have simply built a new Pacific fleet (which is essentially what it did by the close of 1943) and eventually overwhelmed Japan with its superior strength. Arguably, there is little the Japanese could have done to prevent this outcome, but there are a number of things they should have done that would have at least made this process more difficult. A prime example of this was their gross neglect in building adequate escorts and putting prudent measures in place to secure their maritime lines of communication. Another example was not having a robust infrastructure in place to train the large numbers of replacement pilots and aircrews that would invariably be needed in an extended war. By gambling for a short, decisive victory, Japan neglected many of these judicious measures. Finally, in another example of flawed strategic thinking, the Japanese hoped that the vast expanses of the Pacific Ocean would provide both a practical and psychological barrier to protect their newly acquired empire and dissuade the Americans from taking action against them. As events would quickly demonstrate, this belief was entirely misplaced.

The practical result of Japan's flawed strategies and the second major component of its defeat was the severe materiel disparity it suffered compared to the Western Allies. During the course of the war, the Allies attained an immense materiel abundance that progressively overwhelmed Japan. From warships to aircraft and tanks to artillery pieces along with the vast amounts of ammunition, fuel and components needed to operate them, both the United States and Britain produced and deployed massive stockpiles of weapons that were well beyond Japan's ability to emulate. Even though much of this production was used in Europe to confront Germany and Italy, the Allies still had an abundance of resources available for use against the Japanese. Beyond their vast numbers, the Allies also benefitted from a growing qualitative advantage as the war progressed. Not only did Allied technology increasingly outperform that of the Japanese, but as the Japanese struggled to keep up, the quality of their manufacturing declined. This was particularly true regarding aircraft production, which resulted in high rates of crashes due to engine failures and other technical issues during the latter half of the war. Key factors in these losses were shotty practices and materials used during the production process.

Nor was this materiel and qualitative abundance limited to the acquisition of major weapon systems and equipment. The Allies also produced large contingents of well-trained personnel in all branches of their respective armed services to carry out comprehensive and effective military operations against Japan. Similarly, logistics played an important part in this Allied onslaught as a critical factor was not only having the human and materiel resources available in the theatre, but exercising the ability to effectively deploy and maintain those assets over vast areas and in a variety of conditions. As such, the Allies had to ensure that their deployed units had the food, fuel, ammunition, repair parts, medical supplies and all other implements of modern warfare necessary to succeed. In general, the Allies were able to maintain

Table 11.4. Comparative Wartime Production.

	British Empire	United States	Japan
Tanks and self-propelled guns	33,574	88,410	2,515
Assorted artillery pieces	140,644	257,390	13,350
Military trucks and lorries	480,943	2,382,311	165,945
Assorted aircraft	151,061	324,750	76,320
Selected principal warships*	458	749	257
Merchant shipping (tons)	9,081,842	33,993,230	4,152,361

Source: John Ellis, *World War II, A Statistical Survey, the Essential Facts and Figures for all the Combatants* (New York: Facts on File, 1993), pp. 277, 278, 280.

Note: These figures are for general comparison purposes only as the measurement timeframes differ for certain countries in certain categories. Notwithstanding minor errors that likely exist, the overall data clearly shows the overwhelming materiel ascendancy attained by the Allies over Japan.

*The compared warships consist of aircraft carriers, battleships, cruisers, destroyers and submarines.

an effective logistical network that kept their units and operations adequately, and often lavishly, supplied. The same cannot be said for the Japanese, who even under ideal conditions, generally operated with far less materiel abundance than their Allied counterparts.

Given these factors, the Japanese increasingly found themselves unable to compete with the growing materiel surge progressively overwhelming them. A prime example of this centred on the air war. In January 1943 the United States and Japan had relative parity regarding frontline aircraft available in the Pacific contest with the former possessing 3,537 to the latter's 3,200. However, by January 1945 American air strength had grown to 17,976 aircraft compared to just 4,600 for the Japanese, an almost four to one advantage, and by July 1945 this imbalance increased to 21,908 aircraft for the United States compared to 4,100 for Japan, a better than five to one ratio.[18] If British and Commonwealth aircraft were included, this disparity was even greater. Likewise, of the aircraft available to the Japanese towards the end of the war, a high percentage were unserviceable due to maintenance issues, and all were severely restricted due to chronic fuel shortages. Finally, the vast bulk of Japanese pilots by this time were insufficiently trained compared to their Allied counterparts thus further reducing the combat effectiveness of this outnumbered force. When all of these factors were combined, the strength disparity between the two sides increased exponentially.

Turning now to the main tactical factors contributing to Japan's defeat, I will limit my evaluation to issues impacting British and Commonwealth ground operations within the theatre. Given that these represented the British Empire's greatest combat contributions to this contest, what were the key factors that helped facilitate British and Commonwealth successes on the battlefield? The first of these was the effective use of maritime power, which was the essential foundation for the entire Allied war effort. Nothing else would have been remotely possible within the theatre without success in the maritime realm. This was particularly true regarding the maintenance of logistical support. From India and Burma in Southeast Asia to Papua New Guinea and the Bismarck Archipelago in the Southwest Pacific, a large percentage of the men and nearly all of the supplies and equipment had to come in either directly or indirectly by sea. Of course, much of this was carried out by the United States, but a substantial portion was also accomplished by British and Commonwealth assets. For the British, this represented an enormous undertaking as their maritime forces had to support major and sustained combat operations on what was literally the other side of the world. Other than the United States, no other major power during World War II could have possibly pulled off such a massive task. Still, given the extensive size of the Royal Navy and the British merchant fleet as well as their vast global maritime network, the British were successful in this endeavour. Beyond this, British and Allied naval forces carried out numerous amphibious landings, conducted innumerable fire support missions and interdicted Japanese logistical operations within the theatre. These contributions were indispensable to the overall effort and directly helped facilitate success on the battlefields.

Concurrent with this, a second major contributor to British and Commonwealth ground operations was the successful use of air power. First and foremost, the exploitation of air power provided a viable means to logistically support forward deployed British and Commonwealth formations in the vast and difficult terrain of the contested battle areas. The ability to do this substantially reduced Allied dependency on ground-based logistical infrastructure and negated the effectiveness of Japanese infiltration tactics that had worked so well for them earlier in the conflict. By using aerial transport and resupply, British and Commonwealth forces gained a degree of enhanced mobility and improved logistical support that allowed them to exploit their materiel advantage over the Japanese. A second major component of this aerial contribution was the provision of close air support in which Allied aircraft carried out tens of thousands of sorties in direct support of Allied ground formations. Beyond the materiel results these attacks attained, they also injected an important psychological impact on the forces involved boosting Allied resolve and demoralizing the Japanese. Third, the Allies used both strategic and tactical air power to attack Japanese logistical assets and lines of communication on both land and sea thus further weakening Japan's already tenuous logistical situation in the contested battle areas. Finally, the Allies used their air power to substantially prevent the Japanese from providing similar support to their own ground forces. With few exceptions, British and Commonwealth ground forces generally enjoyed impunity from Japanese aerial interference during the latter half of the war thus enhancing their ability to mass and manoeuvre.

The third major component in the Allies ground success was their superior use of fire power and mechanisation. Although certainly less prevalent than in the European conflict and often hampered by harsh terrain, both British and Commonwealth formations were able to utilise combined arms operations to a far greater degree than their Japanese opponents. This had major impacts on the battlefield as time and again British and Commonwealth forces used artillery and tanks to repulse Japanese attacks or ease the execution of their own assaults against hardened Japanese positions. As part of this, Allied ground units were often able to augment their internal artillery assets with the aforementioned naval gunfire and direct air support thus further enhancing their striking power. Against this, while it is certainly true that the Japanese possessed artillery and tank units of their own, these were far less numerous and capable and generally had minimal impact during the latter half of the war. Accordingly, the typical opposition encountered by British and Commonwealth formations consisted of light infantry only armed with the weapons they could carry or transport on pack animals. While this often enhanced Japanese ability to move through jungle and mountain territory deemed impassable by the British, it put them at a distinct disadvantage when it came to direct fighting.

The fourth contributing factor dealt with the superior logistical and support structures available to the Allied armies. Much of this has been touched upon already, but the simple fact remains that all the tanks and artillery pieces in the world meant nothing without the fuel and ammunition available to utilise them. Accordingly, the Allies made great efforts to ensure that their forward-deployed formations received the resources necessary to attain victory. This support went beyond the equipment and munitions used to wage war, but also comprised essential activities to maintain the health and wellbeing of the soldiers involved. This included ensuring that the soldiers were adequately fed and received the best medical care reasonably available. Both sides had to operate under difficult conditions in extremely inhospitable terrain, but as the conflict developed, the British and Commonwealth forces did a much better job overcoming these conditions than did their Japanese counterparts. By the end of the fighting in both Burma and the Southwest Pacific, the surviving Japanese forces were reduced to half-starved and disease-ravaged formations cut off from external support. Within these areas, Japanese deaths from starvation and disease were at least as prevalent as those resulting from combat actions. This was not the case with the Allied forces, which still had to deal with disease and other privations, but had far fewer fatalities given their superior medical care and provisioning to their troops.

While the British and Commonwealth armies benefitted from these many factors, the men at the sharp end still had to perform their duties and come to grips with the enemy. Accordingly, the final major facet of this Allied success was the prowess and determination of the soldiers involved. At the beginning of the conflict, poor leadership and training contributed to some of the early Allied defeats, but things substantially improved as the war progressed. This recovery ranged from the effectiveness of the commanding generals down to the skill and bravery of the men wielding the bayonets and all those supporting their activities. In terms of the former, the Allies were fortunate to eventually field competent and conscientious commanders such as Thomas Blamey, William Slim, Vernon Sturdee, Montagu Stopford, Geoffry Scoones, Frank Messervy and Philip Christison to lead their armies and major formations. In terms of the latter, the officers and men of the British and Commonwealth armies progressively learned and successfully executed their functions in an effective manner. Given the many materiel advantages they had, it was not necessary for these British and Commonwealth forces to match the degree of fanaticism and tenacity exhibited by their Japanese foes, but they still had to attain a certain level of proficiency and perseverance in order to attain victory, and in this, they were entirely successful. Finally, while there were substantial British contributions to this effort including dedicated British units and the British portions of the Indian and African divisions, it is appropriate to acknowledge that most of this fighting was done by Imperial and Commonwealth troops. Regardless of their origins, whether British, Indian, African, Australian, or New Zealander, the soldiers

The Asia/Pacific war involved men from across the British Empire and Commonwealth. Pictured here are troops of the 17th Indian Division. (Chris Turner, public domain)

involved performed with distinction in overcoming numerous adversities and beating the tenacious Japanese army.

In closing out the chapter, I will now provide a brief analysis regarding the overall effectiveness of the competing sides. Starting first with the naval forces, the Imperial Japanese Navy emerged from World War II with a fairly positive reputation in terms of its formidability and performance. The view regarding its formidability is valid, although as pointed out earlier, the German Kriegsmarine was actually twice its size in terms of total numbers. In fairness, the Imperial Japanese Navy had more battleships, aircraft carriers and cruisers than the Kriegsmarine, and it may have been larger in terms of total tonnage, but this does not change the fact that it was only half the size in terms of total hulls. Beyond this, the Germans were responsible for the destruction of far more Allied ships than were the Japanese. Still, notwithstanding these realities, the Imperial Japanese Navy clearly constituted a formidable force that was a major player in the Asia/Pacific war. With that acknowledged, did it perform well? When looking at the totality of its performance, the answer is no. While certain aspects of Japanese naval performance were good for a limited period of time, that was not the case overall.

Exploring this matter further, at the beginning of the Asia/Pacific war, the Japanese touted the strongest naval air arm in the world. Among its attributes, the Imperial Japanese Navy possessed more aircraft carriers than did the American or British navies, their naval aircraft were generally as good, if not superior, to that of their Allied counterparts and the training and proficiency of their pilots and aircrews were second to none. This air arm was the premier striking force within the Japanese navy, and the Japanese used it early in the war to secure a number of victories against the Allies. Unfortunately for them, this superiority was short lived lasting only about six months before the United States scored a resounding victory at Midway that altered this status. By the end of 1942, any advantages the Japanese had in naval air power was now negated and increasingly the United States Navy and eventually the Fleet Air Arm would surpass the Japanese in this regard. The situation became so bad that in the summer of 1944 the Japanese suffered a terrible defeat in the Marianas during the battle of the Philippine Sea that effectively destroyed their naval air arm as a decisive weapon. A few months later, the Japanese were reduced to using their remaining aircraft carriers, which were largely devoid of aircraft, as decoys to the American fleet during the battle of Leyte Gulf. Thereafter, the Japanese were forced to adopt Kamikaze tactics as their only viable means to engage the Allies, but this too failed to attain decisive results. Given this devolution, a Japanese strength at the beginning of the war was entirely reversed to a point of irrelevance by the end of the conflict.

The situation was much the same regarding a second major component of Japanese naval performance, the prowess of their surface forces in ship-to-ship combat. Early in the war the Japanese gained a fearsome reputation in this area as their warships won a string of victories over the Allies. This positive standing was particularly true regarding their night fighting capabilities. Whether this reputation was fully justified is open to debate as the Japanese enjoyed many advantages during these early engagements. Still, whatever pre-eminence they had in this area dissipated as the war went on. It perhaps took a little longer than in the air war, but by the end of 1943 the Allies had clearly gained the ascendancy in this area as well. While there were many examples of this change in fortunes, the British destroyer action resulting in the destruction of the heavy cruiser *Haguro* in May 1945 serves as an ample testament to this Japanese decline. Thus, once again, what was initially a strength for the Imperial Japanese Navy was eventually turned against them to become a weakness.

Against these areas of temporary positive performance, there were two major elements of Japanese naval execution that performed poorly during the duration of the war. The first of these was the Japanese submarine force, which attained a mediocre exchange rate of little better than 1.5 Allied ships sunk for every Japanese submarine lost. A contributing factor to this poor performance was a flawed strategy in which Japanese submarines were extensively used to support fleet operations as opposed to the execution of general mercantile warfare. As points of comparison, the American and British submarine arms attained exchange rates of 24.6 and 9.3 to one respectively in their own naval operations.[19] Almost the entirety of this American exchange rate was attained against the Japanese, which brings me to my next major area of poor Japanese performance, their inability to defend their maritime lines of communication. I have already addressed this shortfall in earlier sections of the book, so I won't elaborate further, but this constituted a failure of the highest strategic consequence. Again, as a point of comparison, the British faced a similar challenge in the Atlantic in defending their own critical lines of communication against a German and Italian onslaught that was arguably more powerful than that employed against the Japanese. Fortunately for the Allied cause, the British and their Allied partners took the necessary actions to successfully secure these vital lines of communication, and this served as the catalyst for the entire Allied victory. The Japanese failed to do the same, and this was the greatest instrument of their defeat.

While there are certainly additional areas worth evaluating, the totality of the performance already discussed clearly indicates that Japanese naval execution during the war was at best mediocre. On an overall basis, the Imperial Japanese Navy failed to attain any of its strategic objectives, and in the process of doing so, lost the entirety of its strength either sunk during the conflict or surrendered at the end of hostilities. In fairness, against the vast materiel might of the United States, this outcome was arguably inevitable, but this realisation does not mitigate the poor performance put forth by the Japanese. Once again, the Kriegsmarine also lost, but it put forth a much better showing against the Allies in terms of damage inflicted. How much of this outcome was the result of superior American and Allied prowess versus inferior Japanese performance is a matter worth further discussion, but the totality of this Japanese defeat was substantial thus validating my assessment.

Compared to this, the Allied navies attained much better performance. Starting first with the Americans, at the beginning of the conflict, the United States Navy was stung by a number of costly reversals. This obviously included the Pearl Harbor attack, but the navy's greatest failure during this period was its initial poor response to the German U-boat offensive that ravaged America's eastern seaboard. Fortunately, the Americans were quick to turn this around, and in June 1942 they scored a stunning victory against heavy odds at Midway that immediately reversed the tide of war. From there, American naval forces held their own during the extended fighting around Guadalcanal that finally secured an Allied victory. The conclusion of this fighting also signalled an end to the period in which there was some degree of parity between the two sides. From the beginning of 1943 on, America's immense materiel and qualitative superiority increasingly came into play until the United States Navy attained an irreversible advantage by the middle of 1944. Japan's demise quickly followed, and even the adoption of Kamikaze tactics could not stem the overwhelming tide engulfing them. At the conclusion of hostilities, the Americans possessed a fleet of unprecedented size and capabilities, and this force was overwhelmingly responsible for the destruction of the Imperial Japanese Navy. The Americans achieved these many accomplishments for the relative minor cost of 189 principal warships sunk during the war including those sunk in the European conflict thus serving as an ample testament to the substantial effectiveness of their overall naval effort.

This laudatory appraisal is similarly applicable to the Royal Navy and its Commonwealth counterparts. In evaluating this performance, there is little benefit in directly comparing the British and Japanese as direct competitors since the former was not a dominant player in the Asia/Pacific war. However, a review of these direct engagements shows a series of near-complete Japanese successes at the beginning of the war followed by a similar set of uninterrupted British victories at the end of the conflict. A more viable way in evaluating British naval performance is to do so against the major strategic tasks assigned to it. In this regard, while there were certainly some reversals, overall British naval performance was exemplary. During World War II Britain's maritime services fulfilled five major roles. These were to defend the United Kingdom from invasion and direct assault, secure vital seaborne lines of communication, place a maritime blockade against Germany, provide logistical support to the Soviet Union and support the needs of the British army. The British were successful in carrying out all five of these major endeavours thus directly contributing to the overall Allied victory. In the process of doing so, the British were the primary architects of the maritime defeats of both Germany and Italy while playing a minor, but meaningful, role in the war against Japan. The cost in attaining these many successes consisted of 377 British and Commonwealth principal warships that were sunk during the war, which was a highly economical result given the sheer impact of their accomplishments.

In regards to the competing ground forces, I have already address many of the factors impacting the ground war, so I will limit my comments to a few overriding themes. At the beginning of the war, the Imperial Japanese Army possessed a number of positive attributes in terms of its combat effectiveness. Paramount amongst these was the toughness and marshal spirit of its soldiers. The Japanese also benefitted from being adept jungle fighters and masters of small unit and infiltration tactics. Finally, the Japanese exhibited substantial confidence and an aggressive outlook in pursuit of their objectives. Together, these qualities served the Japanese well during the opening campaigns of the Asia/Pacific war when they won a number of stunning victories over their European and American adversaries. This earned the Japanese a fierce reputation of near invincibility. However, as events were to show, the Imperial Japanese Army was not invincible. The Allied armies just had to learn how to effectively fight against it. First, they had to learn how to operate in the inhospitable environments making up the battle areas, and then they had to learn how to utilise their own strengths to neutralise those of the Japanese. This was no simple process, but as discussed earlier in the chapter, the Allies made decisive inroads in accomplishing these various tasks. Instead of trying to emulate the Japanese, the Allies adopted and mastered their own methods of warfare to overcome their formidable foes. While the Japanese maintained their tough marshal qualities through the duration of the war, they were unable to effectively adapt to these Allied innovations. Accordingly, by the end of the conflict, the Allies had entirely turned the tables against the Japanese and proven themselves the superior fighting force.

And so it was throughout the theatre. Whether on land, sea or in the air, the American, British and other Allied forces emerged victorious over the Japanese Empire. In turn, this brought about the end of World War II, which for Britain had started six years earlier almost to the day. As mentioned in the introduction, during the time of its existence, the men of the Fourteenth Army regularly referred to themselves as the Forgotten Army. If this was a forgotten army, then by extension, the conflict it waged might have been a forgotten war. In fairness, these notions are obvious hyperbole as neither the army nor the war were ever truly forgotten. Still, if not forgotten, the conflict has also not garnered as much attention as it deserves. In the United Kingdom, the war in Europe attains far more notice than that in the Far East while people in the United States tend to view the Pacific contest as an American affair thus overlooking or undervaluing the contributions made by the other Allied participants. Similarly, while the Asia/Pacific conflict might retain more awareness in Australia, India and New Zealand, the sad reality is that the contributions made by these nations have largely gone unnoticed by much of the rest of the world. Complicating the matter further, at the conclusion of hostilities, the British Empire underwent a period of devolution that saw many of the areas featured in the fighting subsequently attain their independence including India and Burma in 1947, Malaya in 1957 and Hong Kong in 1997.

Still, notwithstanding this post-war history and lack of general popular awareness, the fact remains that during a period of desperate trial and tribulation, men from all across the British Empire and Commonwealth came together in their millions to collectively confront a common enemy bent upon regional conquest and social subjugation. Overcoming innumerable hardships, these men turned back and eventually helped destroy the Japanese Empire, which in turn, helped form the democratic world now prevalent throughout much of Asia including in Japan itself. In doing so, their actions not only warrant our awareness, but also our thoughtful recognition and genuine gratitude. This latter point echoes the epitaph of the British 2nd Division memorial in the Kohima War Cemetery that states, 'When you go home, tell them of us and say, for your tomorrow, we gave our today.' May we never forget.

Timeline of Significant Global Events during World War II

	Northwest Europe & Atlantic/Arctic	Africa/Southern Europe & Mediterranean	Eastern Europe	Southern Asia & Indian Ocean	Pacific
1939	Britain & France declare war on Germany.		Germany & USSR invade Poland.		Australia and New Zealand declare war on Germany.
	Britain imposes naval blockade against Germany. Germany begins U-boat war against Britain.				
			USSR attacks Finland.		
1940	Germany attacks the West. British Expeditionary Force withdraws from France.				
	Fall of France.	Italy declares war on Britain and France.			

Northwest Europe & Atlantic/Arctic	Africa/Southern Europe & Mediterranean	Eastern Europe	Southern Asia & Indian Ocean	Pacific
British conduct Operation *Catapult.*	Attack on Mers-el-Kébir. Naval actions off Calabria & Cape Spada.		British temporarily close Burma Road.	
Battle of Britain.	Italians invade British Somaliland.			
Seelöwe postponed. Dakar Expedition.	Italians invade Egypt.			French cede control of Indochina to Japan.
			Convoy naval action in Red Sea.	
First U-boat Happy Time.	Italy invades Greece. FAA strike against Taranto.			
The Blitz.	British launch Operation *Compass.*			
1941	British destroy Italian Tenth Army & begin conquest of East Africa.		British blockade Axis shipping in Red Sea & around East Africa.	
Five U-boats sunk. End of Happy Time.	British reinforce Greece. Battle of Cape Matapan.			

Northwest Europe & Atlantic/Arctic	Africa/Southern Europe & Mediterranean	Eastern Europe	Southern Asia & Indian Ocean	Pacific
	Germans attack Cyrenaica, Yugoslavia & Greece.		British capture Massawa securing the Red Sea. Heavy Axis naval losses.	
Bismarck sunk.	Invasion of Crete.		British suppress rebellion in Iraq.	
Beginning of full convoy coverage in the Atlantic.	Operation *Battleaxe*.	Germany invades USSR.	British secure Syria.	
British break U-boat Home Waters key.	Malta becomes offensive base.			USA imposes embargo against Japan.
Beginning of Arctic convoys to USSR.		Battle of Kiev.	British & Soviets invade Iran.	
	Germans send U-boats to assist Italians.	Siege of Leningrad begins.		
British attain temporary respite in the battle of the Atlantic.	British finish conquest of East Africa. Begin Operation *Crusader*.	Germans arrive on outskirts of Moscow.		

	Northwest Europe & Atlantic/Arctic	Africa/Southern Europe & Mediterranean	Eastern Europe	Southern Asia & Indian Ocean	Pacific
	USA enters war.	British relieve Tobruk. Alexandria attacked.	Soviets launch counter-attack.		Japan attacks British and American interests in Pacific. *Prince of Wales* & *Repulse* sunk. Fall of Hong Kong.
1942	U-boats attack America. Beginning of Second Happy Time.	Rommel regains western Cyrenaica. Renewed aerial assault against Malta.	The battles of Rzhev.	Burma invaded.	Malaya, the Philippines & Dutch East Indies invaded.
					Fall of Malaya. Battle of Java Sea.
	Raid on St Nazaire.	Convoy MW.10. Second battle of Sirte.	Battle of the Demyansk Pocket.	Fall of Rangoon.	
	U-boat assault shifts to Caribbean & Gulf of Mexico.	Height of Malta blitz.		Japanese raid against Ceylon.	Fall of Philippines. Doolittle Raid.
	First 1,000-bomber raid against Cologne.		Second battle of Kharkov.	Operation *Ironclad*.	Battle of the Coral Sea.
	.	Battle of Gazala. Fall of Tobruk.			Battle of Midway.
	Assault against Convoy PQ.17 in Arctic.	First battle of El Alamein.	Battle of Voronezh.		

	Northwest Europe & Atlantic/Arctic	Africa/Southern Europe & Mediterranean	Eastern Europe	Southern Asia & Indian Ocean	Pacific
	Raid on Dieppe.	Pedestal convoy.	Germans attack Caucasus.		Americans land on Guadalcanal. Battle of Savo Island.
	U-boats switch back to North Atlantic convoy routes.	Battle of Alam Halfa.	Germans begin assault on Stalingrad.		Battles of Milne Bay and Kokoda Trail.
		Second battle of El Alamein.			Battle of Santa Cruz Island.
	USN landings in French Morocco.	Invasion of North Africa.	Soviets counter-attack at Stalingrad.		Naval battles off Guadalcanal.
	British break Triton U-boat key. Battle of the Barents Sea.	Race to Tunisia.		Start of the first Arakan campaign.	
1943		British capture Libya.			Capture of Buna-Gona.
		Battle of Kasserine Pass.	German Sixth Army surrenders at Stalingrad.	First Chindit raid.	Battle of Wau. End of Guadalcanal campaign.
	Convoy battles SC.121 & SC.122/ HX.229.	Battles of Mareth and Wadi Akarit.	Third battle of Kharkov.		Battle of the Bismarck Sea.
	Germans lose 40 U-boats in May. Withdraw from North Atlantic.	Operation *Strike*. Surrender of all Axis forces in Tunisia.			Landing on Attu.

Northwest Europe & Atlantic/Arctic	Africa/Southern Europe & Mediterranean	Eastern Europe	Southern Asia & Indian Ocean	Pacific
Allies launch Bay of Biscay and mid-Atlantic offensives.	Operation *Corkscrew*. Capture of Pantelleria.			Landing on Rendova Island.
RAF bombs Hamburg.	Invasion of Sicily. Mussolini deposed.	Battle of Kursk.		Naval actions at Kula Gulf and Kolombangara.
USAAF Schweinfurt-Regensburg raids.	Capture of Sicily.	Soviets launch counteroffensive.		Landing on Vella Lavella.
	Italy signs armistice. Surrender of Italian fleet.	Battle of Smolensk.		Capture of Salamaua and Lae.
Renewed U-boat offensive in the North Atlantic fails.	Capture of Naples. Failed British Aegean expedition.	Battle of the Dnieper.		
	Activation of U.S. 15th Air Force in Italy.	Second battle of Kiev.	SEAC activated.	Naval action in Empress Augusta Bay. Landing on the Gilbert Islands.
Battle of North Cape. *Scharnhorst* sunk.		Dnieper-Carpathian offensive begins.		Landings on Arawe and Cape Gloucester.

	Northwest Europe & Atlantic/Arctic	Africa/Southern Europe & Mediterranean	Eastern Europe	Southern Asia & Indian Ocean	Pacific
1944		Landing at Anzio. Assault on Gustav Line.		Sinking of *Kuma*.	Landing on Kwajalein. Clearing of Huon Peninsula.
	Big Week bomber raids.	Assault on Cassino.		Battle of Ngakyedauk Pass.	Raid on Truk.
	Transportation Plan implemented.			Japanese invasion of India. Second Chindit operation begins.	
		Mining of Danube River begins.	Crimean offensive.	Eastern Fleet begins offensive operations. Kohima relieved.	Capture of Mandang.
		Operation *Diadem*. Anzio breakout.			Landings on Wakde and Biak.
	Invasion of Normandy.	Capture of Rome.	Soviets launch Operation *Bagration*.	Imphal siege lifted.	Landing on Saipan. Battle of the Philippine Sea.
	Breakout from the Normandy lodgment.		German Army Group Centre routed.	Battle of Imphal and Kohima ends.	

	Northwest Europe & Atlantic/Arctic	Africa/Southern Europe & Mediterranean	Eastern Europe	Southern Asia & Indian Ocean	Pacific
	Battle of Falaise. Bay of Biscay evacuated.	Invasion of Southern France.	Romania leaves Axis. Warsaw uprising.	Capture of Myitkyina.	
	Liberation of France & Belgium.	Operation *Olive*. Gothic Line breached.	Bulgaria & Finland leave Axis.		Landing on the Palau Islands.
		Greece Liberated. High German naval losses.		Advance to the Chindwin River.	Landing on Leyte & battle of Leyte Gulf.
	Assault on Walcheren. Antwerp opened. Battleship *Tirpitz* sunk.	Naval action off Pag Island.	Budapest Offensive.		Mariana-based USAAF bombers begin aerial offensive against Japan.
	Battle of the Bulge.			Beginning of third Arakan campaign.	
1945			Vistula-Oder Offensive.	FAA strikes against Palembang oil refineries.	Landing on Luzon.
	Battle of the Rhineland.				Landing on Iwo Jima.
	Rhine crossed. Advance into Germany.		Operation *Spring Awakening*.	Battle of Meiktila & Mandalay.	

Northwest Europe & Atlantic/Arctic	Africa/Southern Europe & Mediterranean	Eastern Europe	Southern Asia & Indian Ocean	Pacific
Battle of the Ruhr pocket. Advance to the Elbe River & Baltic.	Operation *Grapeshot*. Conquest of N. Italy. Death of Mussolini.	Battle of Berlin. Death of Hitler.		Landing on Okinawa. Kamikaze onslaught against USN and RN.
Surrender of Germany.			Landing in Rangoon. Naval action off Penang.	
				Landings in Borneo. Sinking of *Ashigara*.
			Mopping up in Burma.	USN & RN strike Japanese home islands. XE-craft raid on Singapore.
				Atomic bombs dropped. USSR invades Manchuria. Japan surrenders.
			Surrender of Japanese forces in Singapore.	Surrender of Japanese forces in SW Pacific & Hong Kong.

Note: This timeline reflects general timeframes and the corresponding proximities of events to each other. It is not meant to be an exact representation of event dates.

Wartime Biographies of Selected Senior British/Commonwealth Leaders in the Asia/Pacific Theatre

Navy

Admiral Sir Victor Alexander Charles Crutchley, VC, KCB, DSC, DL. Born on 2 November 1893 in London, England. Died on 24 January 1986 in Nettlecombe, England. Served in the Royal Navy from 1906 to 1947. Started the war as the commander of the battleship HMS *Warspite* and Flag Captain to the Commander-in-Chief, Mediterranean Fleet. In April 1940 commanded *Warspite* during the second battle of Narvik during which eight German destroyers and a U-boat were sunk for no British loss. Thereafter, served as Commodore-in-Charge of the Royal Naval Barracks, Devonport, for almost two years. In March 1942 was lent to the Royal Australian Navy for service in the Southwest Pacific. From June 1942 through June 1944 commanded the Allied Task Force 44/74. Among his actions, was commander of the Allied cruiser squadron during the battle of Savo Island, although was personally not present at the time of the battle. Ended the war in the Mediterranean as Flag Officer, Gibraltar.

Admiral of the Fleet Bruce Austin Fraser, 1st Baron Fraser of North Cape, GCB, KBE. Born on 5 February 1888 in Acton, England. Died on 12 February 1981 in London, England. Served in the Royal Navy from 1904 to 1951. Started the war as Third Sea Lord and Controller of the Navy. In June 1942 appointed Vice-Admiral Commanding 2nd Battle Squadron and Second-in-Command, Home Fleet. From May 1943 through June 1944 served as the Commander-in-Chief, Home Fleet during which he oversaw the sinking of the battlecruiser *Scharnhorst* during the battle of North Cape and executed numerous Arctic convoys and carrier air strikes against Norway. In August 1944 appointed Commander-in-Chief, Eastern Fleet followed three months later by Commander-in-Chief, British Pacific Fleet. Maintained this latter position through the end of the war and was the British signatory to the Japanese surrender.

Admiral of the Fleet Louis Francis Albert Victor Nicholas Mountbatten, 1st Earl Mountbatten of Burma, KG, GCB, OM, GCSI, GCIE, GCVO, DSO, PC, ADC, FRS. Born on 25 June 1900 in Windsor, England. Died on 27 August 1979 in Mullaghmore, Ireland. Served in the Royal Navy from 1913 to 1965. Served as Captain (D) of the 5th Destroyer Flotilla for the first 19 months of the war. After the loss of his flagship, HMS *Kelly*, to Luftwaffe aircraft off Crete in May 1941, briefly commanded the aircraft carrier HMS *Illustrious* and then became Chief Advisor (and later Chief) of Combined Operations Headquarters in October 1941. In August 1943 appointed as Supreme Allied Commander South East Asia and held this position for the remainder of the war

Admiral Sir Tom Spencer Vaughan Phillips, KCB. Born on 19 February 1888 in Falmouth, England. Died on 10 December 1941 in the South China Sea off Kuantan, Malaya. Served in the Royal Navy from 1903 to 1941. Spent the first two years of the war as a Lord Commissioner of the Admiralty and Deputy (later Vice) Chief of the Naval Staff. In October 1941 appointed Commander-in-Chief, China Station. Killed in action on 10 December 1941 during the destruction of Force Z.

Admiral of the Fleet Sir Arthur John Power, GCB, GBE, CVO, KStJ. Born on 12 April 1889 in London, England. Died on 28 January 1960 in Gosport, England. Served in the Royal Navy from 1904 to 1953. Started the war as the commander of the aircraft carrier HMS *Ark Royal*. From December 1939 through May 1942 served as Naval ADC to the King and a Lord Commissioner of the Admiralty and Assistant Chief of the Naval Staff. In August 1942 became the commander of the 15th Cruiser Squadron of the British Mediterranean Fleet. In 1943 briefly served as the Flag Officer in charge of Malta where he participated in the planning for the invasion of Sicily and oversaw the landings at Taranto in July and September respectively. In December 1943 appointed Vice-Admiral Commanding 1st Battle Squadron and Second-in-Command of the Eastern Fleet. Became Commander-in-Chief of the East Indies Fleet in November 1944 and held this position for the remainder of the war.

Admiral Sir Henry Bernard Hughes Rawlings, GBE, KCB. Born on 21 May 1889 in St Erth, England. Died on 30 September 1962 in Bodmin, England. Served in the Royal Navy from 1904 to 1946. Started the war as the commander of the battleship HMS *Valiant* and participated in the bombardment of the French fleet at Mers-el-Kébir. Later commanded the 1st Battle Squadron and 7th Cruiser Squadron and participated in evacuation operations from Crete. In 1943 and 1944 served as Flag Officer, West Africa and then later Flag Officer, Eastern Mediterranean. Ended the war as Second-in-Command of the British Pacific Fleet and the commander of Task Force 57/37 during strike operations against the Palembang oil refineries, Sakishima Gunto and the Japanese home islands.

Admiral of the Fleet Sir James Fownes Somerville, GCB, GBE, DSO, DL. Born on 17 July 1882 in Weybridge, England. Died on 19 March 1949 in Somerset, England. Served in the Royal Navy from 1897 to 1946. Started the war on special service to the Admiralty where he performed important work on naval radar development and helped organise the Dunkirk evacuation. From June 1940 through January 1942 served as Flag Officer Commanding Force H at Gibraltar where he led the attack against the French fleet at Mers-el-Kébir, the bombardment of Genoa and the conduct of multiple Malta convoys. Thereafter, spent the next two and a half years as Commander-in-Chief of the Eastern Fleet where he shepherded the fleet through a period of great danger and revitalized it to begin offensive operations against the Japanese. Ended the war as the head of the British naval delegation in Washington.

Admiral Sir Edward Neville Syfret, GCB, KBE. Born on 20 June 1889 in Newlands, South Africa. Died on 10 December 1972 in Highgate, England. Served in the Royal Navy from 1904 to 1948. Started the war as the commander of the battleship HMS *Rodney* and then became Naval Secretary to the First Sea Lord and commander of the 18th Cruiser Squadron. In January 1942 became Flag Officer Commanding Force H where he oversaw Operation *Ironclad*, the Pedestal convoy and the covering force for the invasion of North Africa. Spent the last two years of the war as a Lord Commissioner of the Admiralty and Vice-Chief of the Naval Staff.

Admiral of the Fleet Sir Philip Louis Vian, GCB, KBE, DSO & Two Bars. Born on 14 June 1894 in London, England. Died on 27 May 1968 in Ashford Hill, England. Served in the Royal Navy from 1907 to 1952. Spent the first two years of the war as the commander of the 11th and 4th Destroyer Flotillas where he led the rescue of British seaman from the German merchant ship *Altmark* and participated in the destruction of the battleship *Bismarck*. In mid-1941 briefly commanded Force A in the Arctic where he oversaw the destruction of the German gunnery training ship *Bremse*. In 1942 commanded the 15th Cruiser Squadron in the Mediterranean earning distinction during the second battle of Sirte. After holding various administrative positions, commanded an assault group and Task Force 88 during the invasions of Sicily and Salerno. In 1944 served as Commander, Eastern Task Force during the Normandy invasion. Ended the war as Flag Officer Commanding, 1st Aircraft Carrier Squadron, British Pacific Fleet during strike operations against the Palembang oil refineries, Sakishima Gunto and the Japanese home islands.

Army

Field Marshal Sir Thomas Albert Blamey, GBE, KCB, CMG, DSO, CStJ, ED. Born on 24 January 1884 in Wagga Wagga, New South Wales. Died on 27 May 1951 in Heidelberg, Victoria, Australia. Served in the Australian army in either an active

262 • FORGOTTEN WAR

or reserve status from 1906 to 1946. Appointed to command the 6th Australian Division at the beginning of the war followed shortly thereafter by command of the 2nd Australian Imperial Force. Arrived in the Middle East in June 1940 where he directly or indirectly oversaw Australian operations in North Africa, Greece and Syria. Returned to Australia in March 1942 to become Commander-in-Chief of the Australian Military Forces and the commander of Allied Land Forces South West Pacific Area. Served in this capacity for the remainder of the war and was the Australian signatory to the Japanese surrender.

General Sir Alexander Frank Philip Christison, 4th Baronet, GBE, CB, DSO, MC & Bar. Born on 17 November 1893 in Edinburgh, Scotland. Died on 21 December 1993, Melrose, Scotland. Served in the British army from 1914 to 1949. Began the war in India as the commander of the Quetta Brigade and then appointed Commandant of the Staff College, Quetta, in March 1940. After a yearlong stint as commander of the 15th Scottish Division in the United Kingdom, returned to India in June 1942 and was appointed commander of XXXIII Corps in November. Served in this position for a year and then became commander of XV Corps in November 1943 where he oversaw the second and third Arakan campaigns and the capture of Rangoon.

General Sir Frank Walter Messervy, KCSI, KBE, CB, DSO & Bar. Born on 9 December 1893 in Trinidad. Died on 2 February 1974 in Heyshott, England. Served in the British Indian Army from 1913 to 1947. Promoted to colonel and became a general staff officer for the 5th Indian Division at the beginning of the war. From 1940 through 1942 served in the Middle East where he held a number of high-level command positions including that of Gazelle Force, 9th Indian Brigade, 4th Indian Division, 1st Armoured Division and 7th Armoured Division during the East and North Africa campaigns. Returned to India in late 1942 and assumed command of the 7th Indian Division in July 1943. Commanded the division during the battles of Ngakyedauk Pass and Kohima. Appointed commander of IV Corps in December of 1944 and oversaw the capture of Meiktila and subsequent advance towards Rangoon.

Lieutenant-General Arthur Ernest Percival, CB, DSO & Bar, OBE, MC, OStJ, DL. Born on 26 December 1887 in Aspenden, England. Died on 31 January 1966 in London, England. Served in the British army from 1914 to 1946. During the first year and a half of the war, served in various staff positions and briefly commanded the home-based 43rd and 44th Divisions. In April 1941 appointed as General Officer Commanding Malaya. Oversaw British forces during the battle of Malaya and surrendered to the Japanese in February 1942. Spent the remainder of the conflict as a prisoner of war.

General Sir Geoffry Allen Percival Scoones, KCB, KBE, CSI, DSO, MC. Born on 25 January 1893 in Karachi, India. Died on 19 September 1975 in Cambridge, England. Served in the British Indian Army from 1912 to 1949. Began the war as a general staff officer in the Directorate of Military Operations and Intelligence. In May 1940 became the deputy director of military operations in India followed a year later as director of military operations and intelligence. After briefly serving as the commander of the 19th Division in 1942, became commander of IV Corps in August of that year. Served in this position until December 1944 during which he commanded the British forces at Imphal during the Japanese U-GO offensive. In December 1944 appointed commander of Central Command (India) and remained in this position through the end of the conflict.

Field Marshal William Joseph Slim, 1st Viscount Slim, KG, GCB, GCMG, GCVO, GBE, DSO, MC, KStJ. Born on 6 August 1891 in Bishopston, England. Died on 14 December 1970 in London, England. Served in the British Indian Army from 1914 to 1952. Commanded the 10th Indian Brigade and the 10th Indian Division during the opening years of the war seeing service in East Africa, Iraq, Syria and Iran. In March 1942 assumed command of Burma Corps and oversaw the withdrawal from Burma. Thereafter, commanded XV Corps until selected to command Fourteenth Army in October 1943. Commanded Fourteenth Army through its operational service in Burma and ended the war as Commander-in-Chief, Allied Land Forces South East Asia.

General Sir Montagu George North Stopford, GCB, KBE, DSO, MC, DL. Born on 16 November 1892 in London, England. Died 10 March 1971 in Chipping Norton, England. Served in the British Army from 1911 to 1949. At the onset of the war assigned command of 17th Infantry Brigade, which saw service in France as part of the British Expeditionary Force. From January 1941 through November 1943 commanded the 56th Division, served as Commandant of the Staff College, Camberley and commanded XII Corps all in the United Kingdom. Thereafter, went to India and took command of XXXIII Corps. Served in this capacity for the next year and a half where he oversaw the effort to relieve Kohima and the capture of Mandalay. In May 1945 assumed command of British Twelfth Army and conducted final mopping up operations in Burma.

Lieutenant-General Sir Vernon Ashton Hobart Sturdee, KBE, CB, DSO. Born on 16 April 1890 in Frankston, Australia. Died on 25 May 1966 in Heidelberg, Australia. Served in the Australian Army from 1908 to 1950. Other than a brief interlude as commander of the 8th Division, spent the first two and a half years of the war as the head of Eastern Command and Chief of the General Staff in Australia. After further service as the Head of the Australian Military Mission to the United

264 • FORGOTTEN WAR

States, appointed commander of the Australian First Army in March 1944 where he directed combat operations in New Guinea and the Bismarck Archipelago through the end of the war.

Major-General Orde Charles Wingate, DSO & two Bars. Born on 26 February 1903 in Nainital, India. Died on 24 March 1944 near Bishnupur, India. Served in the British Army from 1921 to 1944. Started the war as commander of an anti-aircraft unit in the United Kingdom. In 1940 and 1941 commanded Gideon Force in the conduct of irregular operations in East Africa. In March 1942 arrived in India and shortly thereafter formed the Long Range Penetration Groups known as the Chindits. Commanded the Chindits from the summer of 1942 until his death due to a plane crash in March 1944.

Air Force

Air Vice Marshal William Dowling Bostock, CB, DSO OBE. Born on 5 February 1892 in Sydney, Australia. Died on 28 April 1968 in Benalla, Australia. Served in the Australian Army and Royal Air Force from 1914 to 1919 and the Royal Australian Air Force from 1921 to 1946. Started the war as Deputy Chief of the Air Staff. After briefly serving as the Chief of Staff of Allied Air Forces in the South West Pacific Area, became Air Officer Commanding RAAF Command in September 1942 and oversaw the majority of RAAF operational activities within the theatre through the remainder of the war.

Air Chief Marshal Sir Keith Rodney Park, GCB, KBE, MC & Bar, DFC. Born on 15 June 1892 in Thames, New Zealand. Died on 6 February 1975 in Auckland, New Zealand. Served in the New Zealand Military Forces and British Army from 1911 to 1918 and the Royal Air Force from 1918 to 1946. Started the war as the second-in-command of Fighter Command and commanded No. 11 Group during the Battle of Britain. After a year commanding No. 23 Group, Training Command, proceeded to the Middle East in early 1942 and spent the next three years as Air Officer Commanding in Egypt, Malta and Middle East Command respectively. In February 1945 became Allied Air Commander-in-Chief, South East Asia Command and retained this position through the end of the conflict.

Air Chief Marshal Sir Richard Edmund Charles Peirse, KCB, DSO, AFC. Born on 30 September 1892 in London, England. Died on 5 August 1970 in Aylesbury, England. Served in the Royal Navy from 1912 to 1918 and Royal Air Force from 1918 to 1945. Started the war as Deputy and later Vice Chief of the Air Staff. From October 1940 through January 1942 served as Air Officer Commanding, Bomber Command. In March 1943 became Air Officer Commanding, India and then eight months later Allied Air Commander-in-Chief, South East Asia Command.

Maintained this position until November 1944 and retired from active service six months later.

Air Vice Marshal Conway Walter Heath Pulford, CB, OBE, AFC. Born on 26 January 1892 in Agra, India. Died on 10 March 1942 in Chibia, Dutch East Indies. Served in the Royal Navy from 1905 to 1918 and the Royal Air Force from 1918 to 1942. In March 1941 appointed Air Officer Commanding, Far East. Oversaw the Allied air effort during the battle for Malaya and died from malaria and exhaustion after his evacuation vessel was hit and stranded on the island of Chibia.

Air Vice Marshal Donald Fasken Stevenson, CB, CBE, DSO, MC & Bar. Born on 7 April 1895 in Barton upon Irwell, England. Died on 10 July 1964. Served in the British Army from 1915 to 1918 and the Royal Air Force from 1918 to 1948. Started the war as an ADC to the King and later became Director of Home Operations for the Royal Air Force. For most of 1941 served as Air Officer Commanding, No. 2 Group in Bomber Command. In January 1942 became Air Officer Commanding, No. 221 Group and later Air Officer Commanding, Air Headquarters Bengal where he oversaw Allied air operations during the Japanese conquest of Burma. Returned to the United Kingdom in 1943 where he served as Air Officer Commanding RAF in Northern Ireland and No. 9 Group. Ended the war as the Head of the British Military Mission in Romania.

Victoria Cross Recipients in the Asia/Pacific Conflict

The Victoria Cross, which was instituted on 29 January 1856, is the highest military decoration awarded for valour 'in the face of the enemy' for members of the armed forces and civilians under military command for the United Kingdom, certain Commonwealth countries and the previous British Empire. During World War II, a total of 182 Victoria Crosses were awarded to 181 recipients (one serviceman won two). Of these, 49 Victoria Crosses were awarded to servicemen engaged in the Asia/Pacific war. The breakdown of these awards is as follows listed in chronological order:

Squadron Leader Arthur Stewart King Scarf, British, No. 62 Squadron, Royal Air Force. Awarded posthumously for carrying out an air raid against Japanese positions at Singora, Thailand, and successfully bringing his aircraft back despite being severely wounded on 9 December 1941.

Company Sergeant Major John Robert Osborn, Canadian, Winnipeg Grenadiers. Awarded posthumously for throwing himself on a grenade to save the lives of his comrades during the battle for Hong Kong on 19 December 1941.

Lieutenant Colonel Arthur Edward Cumming, British, Frontier Force Regiment. Awarded for leading a counter-attack against Japanese forces near Kuantan, Malaya, on 3 January 1942. Despite being wounded, Cumming restored the situation thus allowing the bulk of his battalion to safely withdraw.

Lieutenant Colonel Charles Groves Wright Anderson, Australian, 2/19th Battalion, Australian Imperial Force. Awarded for actions during the battle of Muar, Malaya, on 18–22 January 1942 when he led a small force through enemy-occupied territory under difficult conditions.

Lieutenant Thomas Wilkinson, British, Royal Naval Reserve. Awarded posthumously for commanding the patrol vessel HMS *Li Wo* during an engagement against a vastly superior Japanese force north of the Banka Strait in the Java Sea on 14 February 1942.

Private Bruce Steel Kingsbury, Australian, 2/14th Battalion, Australian Imperial Force. Awarded posthumously for leading a counter-attack against Japanese forces that helped stabilise a difficult situation at Isurava on 29 August 1942 during the battle of the Kokoda Track.

Corporal John Alexander French, Australian, 2/9th Battalion, Australian Imperial Force. Awarded posthumously for single-handedly taking out three Japanese machine-gun posts that were holding up his section on 4 September 1942 during the battle of Milne Bay.

Havildar (Sergeant) Parkash Singh, Indian, 8th Punjab Regiment. Awarded for rescuing ten stranded comrades while under fire during two separate engagements on 6 and 19 January 1943 near Donbaik on the Mayu Peninsula in Burma.

Flight Lieutenant William Ellis Newton, Australian, No. 22 Squadron, Royal Australian Air Force. Awarded posthumously for successfully carrying out two attacks against Japanese positions at Salamaua, New Guinea, on 16 and 18 March 1943 despite heavy opposition that damaged his aircraft on the first attack and shot it down on the second.

Havildar (Sergeant) Gaje Ghale, Nepalese Gurkha, 5th Gurkha Rifles. Awarded for leading his platoon in a successful assault against Japanese positions in the Chin Hills, Burma, despite suffering wounds to his arm, chest and leg on 24 May 1943.

Private Richard Kelliher, Australian, 2/25th Battalion, Australian Imperial Force. Awarded for taking out a Japanese machine-gun position and rescuing a wounded comrade while under heavy fire on 13 September 1943 during the battle of Lae in New Guinea.

Sergeant Thomas Currie Derrick, Australian, 2/48th Battalion, Australian Imperial Force. Awarded for reducing ten enemy posts thus allowing his unit to capture key terrain on the approach to Sattelberg, New Guinea, on 24 November 1943.

Lieutenant Alec George Horwood, British, Queen's Royal Regiment (West Surrey). Awarded posthumously for actions over a three-day period during which he carried out critical reconnaissance and fire direction while under heavy fire himself and then led an attack (during which he was killed) against Japanese positions at Kyauchaw, Burma on 18–20 January 1944.

Major Charles Ferguson Hoey, Canadian, Lincolnshire Regiment. Awarded posthumously for leading an attack and personally taking out a Japanese strong point despite sustaining multiple wounds including a fatal one during the battle of Ngakyedauk Pass in Burma on 16 February 1944.

Naik (Corporal) Nand Singh, Indian, Sikh Regiment. Awarded for leading an assault against Japanese positions on a steep ridge and capturing three trenches despite sustaining wounds to his thigh, face and shoulder on the Maungdaw–Buthidaung road in Burma on 11–12 March 1944.

Lieutenant George Albert Cairns, British, South Staffordshire Regiment. Awarded posthumously for leading an action against a Japanese force during which he was grievously wounded but continued on killing or wounding a number of Japanese soldiers before succumbing to his own wounds near Henu, Burma, on 13 March 1944.

Naib Subedar (Junior Commissioned Officer) Abdul Hafiz Khan, Indian, 9th Jat Regiment. Awarded posthumously for successfully leading a platoon attack against a Japanese position despite sustaining wounds that eventually proved fatal during the battle of Imphal, India, on 6 April 1944.

Lance Corporal John Pennington Harman, British, Queen's Own Royal West Kent Regiment. Awarded posthumously for personally destroying a Japanese machine-gun position and taking out a section of Japanese soldiers before being fatally hit himself during the battle of Kohima, India, on 8–9 April 1944.

Captain John Niel Randle, British, Royal Norfolk Regiment. Awarded posthumously for successfully leading a company attack, personally recovering a number of wounded comrades and single-handedly silencing a Japanese machine gun firing from a bunker despite being fatally wounded in the process at Kohima, India, on 4–6 May 1944.

Sergeant Hanson Victor Turner, British, West Yorkshire Regiment (The Prince of Wales's Own). Awarded posthumously for leading his section in a successful defensive action and personally carrying out a number of grenade attacks to prevent the Japanese from flanking their position before being killed at Ningthoukhong, India, on the night of 6/7 June 1944.

Captain Michael Allmand, British, 6th Gurkha Rifles. Awarded posthumously for successfully leading a series of attacks from 11 to 23 June 1944 that seized key positions during the advance on Mogaung, Burma, culminating with the silencing of a Japanese machine-gun position at which time he was fatally wounded.

Rifleman Gyamtso Shangdarpa (better known as **Ganju Lama**), Indian, 7th Gurkha Rifles. Awarded for personally disabling two Japanese tanks using a PIAT anti-tank weapon despite sustaining wounds to his right leg and left hand during a Japanese attack on his unit's position near Ningthoukhong, India, on 12 June 1944.

Rifleman Tul Bahadur Pun, Nepalese Gurkha, 6th Gurkha Rifles. Awarded for single-handedly assaulting and capturing a key Japanese position at Mogaung, Burma, on 23 June 1944 despite heavy opposition and then providing covering fire thus assisting the remainder of his platoon in securing their objective.

Corporal Sefanaia Sukanaivalu, Fijian, Fiji Infantry Regiment. Awarded posthumously for going forward to rescue two wounded comrades while under fire and then sustaining fatal wounds when attempting to rescue a third at Bougainville, Solomon Islands, on 23 June 1944.

Acting Subedar (Junior Commissioned Officer) Netrabahadur Thapa Magar, Nepalese Gurkha, 5th Gurkha Rifles. Awarded posthumously for leading a small force that repulsed a Japanese attack on their isolated position and then leading a counter-attack resulting in his death at Bishenpur, India, on 25–26 June 1944.

Naik (Corporal) Agansing Rai, Nepalese Gurkha, 5th Gurkha Rifles. Awarded for leading a small section to take out two Japanese machine-gun positions and a Japanese bunker personally killing several Japanese soldiers in the process at Bishenpur, India, on 26 June 1944.

Major Frank Gerald Blaker, British, 9th Gurkha Rifles. Awarded posthumously for leading a company attack against a Japanese machine-gun position during which time he was mortally wounded but inspired his men to take the position in Taunggyi, Burma, on 9 July 1944.

Acting Subedar (Junior Commissioned Officer) Ram Sarup Singh, Indian, 1st Punjab Regiment. Awarded posthumously for leading his platoon to successfully capture a Japanese position and then repel a series of Japanese counter-attacks despite sustaining several wounds including one that proved fatal at Tiddim, Burma, on 25 October 1944.

Sepoy (Private) Bhandari Ram, Indian, 10th Baluch Regiment. Awarded for single-handedly taking out a Japanese machine-gun position despite sustaining serious wounds to himself in the Arakan, Burma, on 22 November 1944.

Havildar (Sergeant) Umrao Singh Yadav, Indian, Royal Indian Artillery. Awarded for leading his field gun detachment in combatting three Japanese attacks against their position during which he killed several Japanese soldiers, including some in hand-to-hand combat, but was heavily wounded himself in the Kaladan Valley, Burma, on 15–16 December 1944.

Lance Naik (Corporal) Sher Shah Awan, Indian, 16th Punjab Regiment. Awarded posthumously for leading a section of his platoon in repelling three Japanese attacks despite sustaining two wounds including one that proved fatal at Kyeyebyin, Burma, on 19–20 January 1945.

Lieutenant George Arthur Knowland, British, No. 1 Commando. Awarded posthumously for leading his platoon in repelling a series of Japanese attacks against their position during which he personally killed a number of Japanese soldiers before being killed himself at Kangaw, Burma on 31 January 1945.

Jemadar (Junior Commissioned Officer) Prakash Singh Chib, Indian, 13th Frontier Force Rifles. Awarded posthumously for leading his platoon in repelling an attack despite sustaining several wounds to himself including one that proved fatal at Kanlan Ywathit, Burma, on 16–17 February 1945.

Naik (Corporal) Fazal Din, Indian, 10th Baluch Regiment. Awarded posthumously for leading a platoon section in an attack against Japanese positions during which he personally silenced a Japanese bunker and then helped repel a minor counter-attack killing three Japanese soldiers in hand-to-hand combat despite being badly (and ultimately fatally) wounded himself at Meiktila, Burma, on 2 March 1945.

Naik (Corporal) Gian Singh, Indian, 15th Punjab Regiment. Awarded for leading a platoon section during an attack against a Japanese-held village during which he personally cleared a number of Japanese positions and captured an anti-tank gun despite sustaining a wound to himself at Myingyan, Burma, on 2 March 1945.

Lieutenant William Basil Weston, British, Green Howards (Alexandra, Princess of Wales's Own Yorkshire Regiment). Awarded posthumously for leading a platoon attack during which he helped clear a number of bunkers including a final one where he was badly wounded and used a grenade to blow himself up along with the occupants of the bunker at Meiktila, Burma, on 3 March 1945.

Rifleman Bhanbhagta Gurung, Nepalese Gurkha, 2nd Gurkha Rifles. Awarded for single-handedly clearing a number of Japanese positions including a bunker killing several Japanese soldiers in the process and then organising a defence to repel a Japanese counter-attack at Tamandu, Burma, on 5 March 1945.

Lieutenant Karamjeet Singh Judge, Indian, 15th Punjab Regiment. Awarded posthumously for leading a platoon attack in which he repeatedly exposed himself to enemy fire to coordinate with supporting tanks and personally led multiple assaults against a series of Japanese bunkers before being fatally wounded at Meiktila, Burma, on 18 March 1945.

Lieutenant Claud Raymond, British, Corps of Royal Engineers. Awarded posthumously for leading a successful assault against a Japanese position despite receiving repeated wounds and then refusing aid until the other wounded were attended to at Talaku, Burma, on 21 March 1945. He died the next day.

Corporal Reginald Roy Rattey, Australian, 25th Battalion, Australian Militia. Awarded for single-handedly subduing three Japanese bunkers and a gun position at Bougainville, Solomon Islands, on 22 March 1945.

Lieutenant Albert Chowne, Australian, 2/2nd Battalion, Australian Imperial Force. Awarded posthumously for personally taking out two Japanese machine-gun positions and then leading an assault during which he was fatally wounded at Dagua, New Guinea, on 25 March 1945.

Corporal John Bernard "Jack" Mackey, Australian, 2/3rd Pioneer Battalion, Australian Imperial Force. Awarded posthumously for single-handedly eliminating two Japanese machine-gun positions before receiving a fatal wound while assaulting a third at Tarakan Island, Borneo, on 12 May 1945.

Rifleman Lachhiman Gurung, Nepalese Gurkha, 8th Gurkha Rifles. Awarded for holding his position for more than four hours through a series of Japanese attacks despite being grievously wounded at Taungdaw, Burma, on 12–13 May 1945.

Private Edward Kenna, Australian, 2/4th Battalion, Australian Imperial Force. Awarded for engaging Japanese machine gunners and killing two while in an exposed position and under heavy fire and thus helping his platoon capture their objective at Wewak, New Guinea, on 15 May 1945.

Private Leslie Thomas Starcevich, Australian, 2/43rd Battalion, Australian Imperial Force. Awarded for single-handedly subduing four Japanese machine-gun positions during a company advance at Beaufort, Borneo, on 28 June 1945.

Private Frank John Partridge, Australian, 8th Battalion, Australian Militia. Awarded for single-handedly eliminating a Japanese machine-gun position despite sustaining two wounds in Bougainville, Solomon Islands, on 24 July 1945.

Lieutenant Ian Edward Fraser, British, Royal Naval Reserve. Awarded for commanding the midget submarine *XE3* during the attack against the heavy cruiser *Takao* in Singapore harbour on 31 July 1945.

Leading Seaman James Joseph Magennis, British, Royal Navy. Awarded for serving as the diver on the submarine *XE3* during the attack against the heavy cruiser *Takao* in Singapore harbour on 31 July 1945.

Lieutenant Robert Hampton 'Hammy' Gray, Canadian, Royal Canadian Naval Volunteer Reserve, No. 1841 Naval Air Squadron. Awarded posthumously for sinking the Japanese escort destroyer *Amakusa* in the face of heavy anti-aircraft fire that subsequently downed his aircraft in Onagawa Bay, Japan, on 9 August 1945.

Plight of the Prisoners of War

From December 1941 through April 1942 the Japanese took over 300,000 Allied prisoners during their initial onslaught across Southeast Asia and the Southwest Pacific. This was in addition to the multitudes of Chinese prisoners taken earlier in the conflict, most of whom were summarily executed by their Japanese captors. While there were many examples of similar Japanese treatment carried out against Allied prisoners, such as at Parit Sulong, Malaya, in January 1942 where approximately 150 wounded Australian and Indian prisoners were brutally executed by the Japanese, this was not the norm in terms of the overall numbers. Accordingly, a total of about 140,000 European and North American prisoners were eventually taken by the Japanese during the war, of which the vast majority were taken during this initial offensive period. Added to this were another 180,000 Asian prisoners consisting mainly of Filipinos, Indians, Chinese and Indonesians who were affiliated with the Allied forces.[1] In terms of the latter, thousands were initially killed during events such as the Bataan Death March, but most were subsequently released after a few months of captivity. This primarily left the 140,000 European/American prisoners along with about 40,000 Indians who chose to remain loyal to the British Empire forsaking membership in the Indian National Army. These men would remain in Japanese captivity through the end of the war.

To accommodate this, the Japanese eventually established some 600 prisoner of war camps spread throughout the occupied territories from Korea to Java. Then as the war went on, the Japanese increasingly moved prisoners to the Japanese home islands to perform slave labour. Conditions in the camps varied with some providing relatively humane treatment. An example of this was the island of Blakang Mati off southern Singapore, where only four out of some one thousand prisoners perished during the war. Unfortunately, camps like this were the rare exception, and the vast majority of Allied prisoners experienced extremely harsh conditions ranging from gross neglect and callous indifference from their Japanese overlords to criminal brutality and outright murder. Prisoners were routinely subjected to torture, beatings, starvation, denials of medical care and horrendous working conditions as they were forced to work slave labour. The most notorious example of this was the construction of the Burma–Thailand Railway, which became known as the Death Railway. From July 1942 to October 1943, 61,000 Allied prisoners along with some 270,000 conscripted civilians constructed a railway line through 260 miles of mountainous jungle. In the process, some 12,000 prisoners and upwards of 100,000 of the native labourers died from overwork, disease, starvation or Japanese cruelty.[2] Another horrendous example was Sandakan camp in North Borneo where only six Australians out of an estimated 2,500 Australian and British prisoners survived.[3] Many of these died during a forced relocation through the interior of the island in 1945 to prevent their potential liberation while most of the survivors were murdered by their Japanese guards.

Given these grievous privations and blatant atrocities, it is amazing that the majority of Allied prisoners survived their ordeals. Through the duration of the war, roughly 37,800 Western prisoners died while in Japanese captivity thus constituting a 26.9 percent mortality rate.[4] As a point of comparison, the mortality rate for British prisoners under German control during the war was 3.5 percent.[5] In a partial breakdown of these losses, 7,412 of the 21,726 Australian, 12,433 of the 50,016 British and 7,107 of the 21,580 American prisoners held by the Japanese did not survive captivity.[6] Most of the remaining fatalities came from the ranks of Dutch prisoners, but this also included small contingents of Canadians and New Zealanders. Meanwhile, the mortality rate for Indian prisoners was roughly equivalent to that of their Western counterparts with an estimated 11,000 having died during their confinement.[7] Unfortunately, for many Allied prisoners, liberation did not entirely alleviate their suffering as chronic conditions brought about by their wartime afflictions plagued them for the rest of their lives. Studies later revealed that rates of premature death for these former prisoners of war far exceeded those of other veterans or prisoners from the European theatre with doctors in Canada determining that the life expectancy for former prisoners captured in Hong Kong was ten to 15 years below that of the national average. Meanwhile, in 1987 a major study revealed that former prisoners suffered from elevated levels of blindness, heart disease, hypertension, neurological disorders, spinal or paraspinal ailments, psychiatric conditions and gastrointestinal ailments.[8] Still, in at least one respect they were fortunate compared to their Chinese counterparts as virtually none of the Chinese prisoners taken in China survived the war.

Turning now to the Japanese, given their Bushido honour code, relatively few Japanese servicemen surrendered during the course of the war. By October 1944 the total number of Japanese prisoners in Allied custody was only about 6,000. In some cases, as Allied personnel became increasingly aware of the atrocities being meted out against their own prisoners, they were less inclined to accept the surrender of Japanese personnel. However, this was not official policy, and the Allies generally made concerted efforts to convince wavering Japanese forces to surrender. Similarly,

Allied authorities generally treated Japanese prisoners humanely and regularly communicated this point to the Japanese government in the hope that this treatment might induce the Japanese to do the same towards Allied prisoners. Unfortunately, for most of the war the Japanese refused to even acknowledge the existence of Japanese prisoners, and they showed an utter disregard for their wellbeing. The Allies established prisoner of war camps in both Australia and New Zealand where Japanese prisoners received adequate food and medical treatment. At Camp Featherston in New Zealand, Japanese prisoners enjoyed a prescribed diet of 2,700 calories per day, which was three to four times the average caloric intake provided to most Allied prisoners under Japanese control. Similarly, the Allies at Camp Featherston paid the Japanese for the work that they performed.[9]

Despite this generally humane treatment, there were incidents of violence that erupted between Japanese prisoners and Allied personnel. In February 1943 some 250 Japanese prisoners refused to work at Camp Featherston. During the resulting standoff, New Zealand officials attempted to arrest two Japanese officers leading this revolt. In the process, violence ensued which immediately escalated to a brief, but bloody, clash in which the guards opened fire while being pelted by rocks and other objects. This resulted in the deaths of 48 Japanese prisoners and one guard (the latter being reportedly hit my friendly fire) while another 74 prisoners and several guards were wounded. A year and a half later a substantially worse event occurred at Cowra prison camp in Australia when several hundred Japanese prisoners, armed with a variety of homemade weapons, attempted a mass escape. Engaged by the Australian guards, order was quickly re-established, but this came at a high price as 234 prisoners were killed, including many who died by their own hands, and 108 were wounded. Australian casualties consisted of three killed and three wounded.[10]

At the conclusion of hostilities, millions of Japanese servicemen surrendered to Allied authorities including roughly three million men who were stationed in overseas locations. Unlike their compatriots who had surrendered earlier in the conflict contrary to the Japanese honour code, these men were granted official sanction to surrender and thus did so in a fairly orderly fashion. Included in these prisoners were almost 800,000 taken in by British and Commonwealth authorities in Southeast Asia and the Southwest Pacific. Of these, most were repatriated back to Japan relatively quickly with the last such troops being returned at the end of 1947. At least another 1.2 million Japanese surrendered in China. Surprisingly given the immense atrocities carried out by the Japanese forces in China, which rivaled the Nazi atrocities in Europe, there were few reprisals against these forces and most were quickly repatriated back to Japan. A major factor in this was the Nationalist governments preoccupation in dealing with the Communist insurrection and thus wanting the Japanese out of the country as quickly as possible. Finally, in the short time the Soviet Union was involved in the war against Japan and in its immediate aftermath, it took possession of at least 594,000 Japanese prisoners (with some estimates being substantially higher). Of these, 71,000 were quickly released, but the rest were sent to Siberia where they performed slave labour under harsh conditions.[11] The Soviets repatriated these prisoners back to Japan over a number of years with the last major group being released in 1956 (11 years after the conclusion of the war).

Contributions made by the Various Elements of the British Empire and Commonwealth during World War II

As repeatedly addressed throughout the book, the British war effort during World War II was a collective endeavour with substantial contributions made by a number of nations and territories. While there is little need to reiterate this point, a brief breakdown of these various contributions to the overall war effort is worthwhile.

At the beginning of World War II, the British Commonwealth of Nations, which was still often referred to as the British Empire, directly or indirectly controlled about 25 percent of the world's land surface and population. While there were a number of different political and social structures that existed within this overarching entity, these could generally be broken down into three major subdivisions. The first of these was the United Kingdom, which was the mother country and the centre of British political, economic, social and military power. The second was Britain's imperial possessions consisting of crown colonies, protectorates and India. While many of these entities practiced some degree of local autonomy, they still fell within the overarching umbrella of British authority. The final major partition consisted of the fully independent nations (former dominion states) of Australia, Canada, New Zealand and South Africa, which along with the United Kingdom, were co-members within the British Commonwealth under the rule of the British sovereign, which at the time was King George VI. Together, these three major elements waged a collective effort against the Axis powers during World War II.

The United Kingdom

As the centre of British political, economic, social and military power, the United Kingdom served as the leader of the British war effort, provided the bulk of the combat forces used in this endeavour and suffered the highest corresponding combat casualties in terms of numbers. With a population of roughly 47.5 million citizens, the United Kingdom eventually mobilised 5.9 million men and women to serve in its armed forces. Utilising this strength, the British army formed a total of

48 field divisions of which 34 saw active combat at one point or another during the war.[1] Beyond this, British forces staffed numerous brigades and other lesser units as well as provided staffing for portions of Indian and Imperial formations. Similarly, they provided most of the staffing to the Royal Navy and Royal Air Force, which attained peak strengths of almost 10,000 assorted vessels including over 1,000 principal warships and 9,200 aircraft respectively. In viewing the totality of this effort, British forces engaged in substantial combat operations against all three major Axis powers and provided extensive or meaningful service in the Atlantic, Mediterranean, Northwest Europe, Southern Europe, Africa, Indian Ocean, Southeast Asia and Pacific Ocean.

India

Outside of the United Kingdom, the next largest contributor to the collective war effort, at least in terms of personnel, was India. Depending entirely upon volunteers, the Indian Army attained a roughly ten-fold expansion as 2,499,909 men joined its ranks from the outbreak of the war through August 1945 of which 2,038,001 were classified as combatants.[2] This constituted the largest solely volunteer army in the world and allowed British authorities to eventually create 23 Indian field divisions (excluding the 36th Division which was redesignated a British formation) of which 15 saw combat. Of the latter, three saw service against the European Axis in Africa and/or Southern Europe, 11 saw service against the Japanese and one saw service against both the European Axis and the Japanese. Two other divisions performed garrison duties in the Middle East but saw no meaningful combat. Beyond these major formations, the Indian Army also produced large numbers of lesser formations including some that saw combat. Finally, the substantially smaller Royal Indian Navy and Royal Indian Air Force augmented these efforts primarily confining their activities to supporting operations around India, but some naval units also saw service in the European conflict.

African Colonies

While India was the greatest colonial contributor to the British war effort, it was by no means the only contributor. Of particular consequence were Britain's east and west African colonies, which produced enough troops to staff five divisions that saw combat during differing periods of the war. Two of these divisions saw service early in the conflict participating in the East Africa campaign, but were subsequently disbanded at the end of 1941 and in early 1943 respectively. Then in 1943 the British formed three new African divisions, and these all saw service in Burma through the end of hostilities. Thus, the peak strength of this African contribution at any given time was three divisions. Other British colonies made further contributions, but none on a divisional level.

Australia

Of the four independent Commonwealth nations outside of the United Kingdom, Australia made the greatest contribution to the collective war effort in terms of per capita forces employed with almost one million men and women serving in the armed forces out of a total population of 6.9 million. During the war, Australia formed or maintained a total of 15 divisions of which six saw active combat as full units while elements of a seventh also engaged in combat operations. Three of these engaged divisions split their wartime service between confronting the European Axis and the Japanese while the remaining four were entirely used against the latter. Beyond this, both the Royal Australian Navy and the Royal Australian Air Force saw extensive combat in the European and Asia/Pacific conflicts with the former eventually operating more than 350 warships and support vessels while the latter formed or maintained 76 squadrons during the course of the war.

Canada

In terms of population, at 11.1 million, Canada was the largest of the former dominion countries and also made substantial contributions to the Allied war effort eventually providing roughly 1.1 million service men and women to this endeavour. Canada's wartime effort was almost entirely directed towards the European conflict providing five divisions that saw active service in Italy and/or Northwest Europe. Meanwhile, the Royal Canadian Navy grew to a strength of over 1,100 assorted vessels including over 300 principal warships during the course of the war and was a major player in the battle of the Atlantic and other naval operations off Northwest Europe. Similarly, the Royal Canadian Air Force attained a peak deployment of 48 squadrons that served overseas (mostly in Europe) while 11 more performed anti-submarine reconnaissance duties from Canadian territory in conjunction with the battle of the Atlantic.

New Zealand

With a population of only 1.6 million citizens, New Zealand was the smallest of the former dominion countries, and its war effort reflected this point. However, on a per capita basis, this New Zealand effort was quite substantial. Starting with just 2,570 men serving in its armed forces at the beginning of the war, New Zealand's contribution expanded to a peak strength of 157,000 by September 1942.[3] This allowed New Zealand to provide a single division for extended service in the European conflict while elements of a second division briefly served in the Asia/Pacific war. Likewise, throughout the conflict, the New Zealand Division of the Royal Navy and later the Royal New Zealand Navy maintained a small contingent of warships highlighted by two light cruisers, which saw action against both the European Axis and the Japanese. Finally, the Royal New Zealand Air Force operated 28 squadrons during the war plus a further seven squadrons that were directly embedded into the Royal Air Force. Beyond these dedicated units, thousands of additional New Zealanders served in British squadrons in both the Royal Air Force and Fleet Air Arm.

The Union of South Africa

South Africa was the least enthusiastic member of the British Commonwealth during World War II, and its contribution to the war effort reflected this. Out of a total population that was approximately ten million strong, 334,224 South Africans volunteered for wartime service.[4] This allowed South Africa to provide two divisions for wartime service in Africa, a third for service in Southern Europe and elements of a fourth to briefly participate in the invasion of Madagascar. Beyond this, the South African Naval Force ended the war with a strength of 78 mostly minor vessels while the South African Air Force eventually operated 28 squadrons in Africa and Southern Europe. Almost the entirety of the South African war effort was earmarked against the European Axis.

The Cost

As indicated in the tables below, the British Commonwealth of Nations suffered almost 1.26 million military casualties during World War II. As high as this was, it was only about a third of the casualties sustained by the British Empire during World War I and was substantially less than that suffered by many of its wartime contemporaries. Of the six major powers engaged in World War II, only the United States suffered slightly fewer total casualties than the British Commonwealth while Italy suffered moderately more and Germany, Japan and the Soviet Union suffered many millions (or tens of millions) more. Of these British/Commonwealth casualties, roughly 80 percent were incurred in the European war with about 20 percent occurring in the Asia/Pacific conflict. The United Kingdom sustained roughly 60 percent of all personnel casualties while Canada suffered the highest losses (in terms of numbers) of any of the former dominion countries. Meanwhile, with over 12,000 combat fatalities, New Zealand suffered the highest per capita loss in this category of any of the British/Commonwealth participants.

Table E.1. **Personnel Casualties** of the Primary Combatant Powers during World War II.

	Military Killed or Missing	Military Wounded	Military Prisoners of War	Civilian Fatalities
British Commonwealth	453,667	479,764	324,366	60,595
Soviet Union	8.7–13.6 mil	14.7 mil	4.6–5.7 mil	13–18 mil
United States of America	324,053	671,278	237,709	c.2,000
Germany	3.25–5.5 mil	4.9–6 mil	11 mil	0.5–2.5 mil
Italy	279,820	120,000	1.3 mil	60,000–150,000
Japan	1.5–1.8 mil	100–500 thou	2.4–2.9 mil	400,000–1 mil

Source: Compiled from a variety of sources. Paramount amongst these are Spencer C. Tucker (Editor) *Encyclopedia of World War II, A Political, Social and Military History, Volume I: A–C* (Santa Barbara: ABC-CLIO, Inc., 2005), p. 301 and Peter Goralski, *World War II Almanac: 1939–1945, A Political and Military Record* (New York: Bonanza Books, 1981), pp.425–428.

Table E.2. **Breakdown** of British and Commonwealth Casualties during World War II.

	Killed and Missing in Action	Wounded in Action	Prisoners of War	Total
United Kingdom Armed Forces	271,311	277,077	172,592	720,980
British Merchant Marine	34,902	4,707	5,720	45,329
British Colonial Forces	57,897	71,326	87,604	216,827
Australian Armed Forces	29,395	39,803	26,363	95,561
Canadian Armed Forces	39,319	53,174	9,045	101,538
New Zealand Armed Forces	12,162	19,314	8,453	39,929
South African Armed Forces	8,681	14,363	14,589	37,633
TOTAL	453,667	479,764	324,366	1,257,797

Source: Robert Goralski, *World War II Almanac: 1939–1945, A Political and Military Record* (New York: Bonanza Books, 1981), pp.425–428.

Endnotes

Introduction

1   ADM 199/2447, German Ships: Losses and Damage in NW European Waters, 1939–1945.
2   John D. Alden, *U.S. Submarine Attacks During World War II (Including Allied Submarine Attacks in the Pacific Theater)* (Annapolis: Naval Institute Press, 1989), pp. 220–224.
3   Letter from SLT (A) A. Hughes RNVR to Gray family dated 28 December 1945. See Stuart E. Soward, *A Formidable Hero, Lt R.H. Gray, VC, DSC, RCNVR* (Toronto: Canav Books, 1987), p. 182.

Chapter 1: The Long Road to War

1   Randal Gray and Christopher Argyle, *Chronicle of the First World War, Volume II: 1917–1921* (Oxford: Facts on File, 1990), p. 288.
2   Henry Newbolt, *History of the Great War, Naval Operations, Volume V* (London: Longmans, Green and Co., 1931), p. 431.
3   Gray and Argyle, *Chronicle of the First World War, Volume II*, p. 290.
4   Ibid., p. 292.
5   Operations Division, Naval Staff, "Present Naval Policy," 17 September 1917; Admiralty MSS. See Arthur J. Marder, *From the Dreadnought to Scapa Flow, Volume V: Victory and Aftermath (January 1918 – June 1919)* (London: Oxford University Press, 1970), p. 298.
6   C. Ernest Fayle, *History of the Great War, Seaborne Trade, Volume III: The Period of Unrestricted Submarine Warfare* (London: John Murray, 1924), p. 429.
7   Roy Humphreys, *The Dover Patrol 1914–18* (Gloucestershire: Sutton Publishing, 1998), p. 189.
8   The breakdown of total mobilised strength for the various armies in August 1914 was 713,514 for Britain, 2,000,000 for Austria, 4,500,000 for Germany, 3,781,000 for France and 4,500,000 for Russia. See Randal Gray and Christopher Argyle, *Chronicle of the First World War, Volume I: 1914-1916* (Oxford: Facts on File, 1990), p. 281.
9   J. E. Edmonds and R. Maxwell-Hyslop, *Military Operations France and Belgium, 1918, Volume V* (London: His Majesty's Stationery Office, 1947), p. 557.
10 Gray and Argyle, *Chronicle of the First World War, Volume II*, p. 284.
11 Ibid., p. 286.
12 Marder, *From the Dreadnought to Scapa Flow, Volume V*, pp. 202, 224.
13 Ibid., p. 202.
14 S. W. Roskill, *Naval Policy between the Wars, Volume 1: The Period of Anglo-American Antagonism 1919–1929* (New York: Walker and Company, 1968), p. 586.
15 David Fraser, *And We Shall Shock Them, the British Army in the Second World War* (London: Sceptre, 1988), p. 12 and Michael Carver, *Britain's Army in the 20th Century* (London: Pan Books, 1998), p. 157.

16 Gray and Argyle, *Chronicle of the First World War, Volume II: 1917–1921*, p. 288.

17 David Hobbs, *The British Pacific Fleet, the Royal Navy's Most Powerful Strike Force* (Annapolis: Naval Institute Press, 2011), p. 2.

18 Robert W. Love, Jr., *History of the U.S. Navy 1775–1941* (Harrisburg: Stackpole Books, 1992), p. 526.

19 The United States retained the battleships *Colorado, Maryland* and *West Virginia*. The fourth *Maryland*-class battleship, the nearly completed *Washington*, was scrapped under the provisions of the treaty. Likewise, the new 43,000-ton *South Dakota*-class battleships that were under construction were also scrapped. See Love, Jr., *History of the U.S. Navy 1775–1941*, pp. 532, 535.

20 Compiled from Appendix C: Naval Building Programmes as Finally Implemented 1919–1939. See Roskill, *Naval Policy between the Wars, Volume 1*, pp. 580–582.

21 Averages determined from data compiled in Appendix D: British Navy Estimates and Actual Expenditure 1919–1939 and Personnel Numbers. See Roskill, *Naval Policy between the Wars, Volume 1*, pp. 586–587.

22 Ibid., p. 586.

23 David Chandler (Editor) and Ian Beckett (Associate Editor), *The Oxford Illustrated History of the British Army* (Oxford: Oxford University Press, 1994), p. 263 and Carver, *Britain's Army in the 20th Century*, p. 157.

24 John Terraine, *The Right of the Line, The Royal Air Force in the European War 1939–1945* (London: Hodder and Stoughton, Sceptre edition, 1988), pp. 31–32.

25 S. W. Roskill, *Naval Policy between the Wars, Volume II: The Period of Reluctant Rearmament 1930–1939* (London: Collins, 1976), p. 305.

26 Ibid., p. 184.

27 Terraine, *The Right of the Line, The Royal Air Force in the European War 1939–1945*, p. 33.

28 Ibid., pp. 34–35.

29 Compiled from Appendix C: Naval Building Programmes as Finally Implemented 1919–1939 and Appendix D: British Navy Estimates and Actual Expenditure 1919–1939 and Personnel Numbers. See Roskill, *Naval Policy between the Wars, Volume 1*, pp. 584–586.

30 Roskill, *Naval Policy between the Wars, Volume II*, p. 490.

31 S. W. Roskill, *White Ensign, The British Navy at War 1939–1945* (Annapolis: United States Naval Institute, 1960), p. 20.

32 David French, *Raising Churchill's Army, the British Army and the War against Germany 1919–1945* (Oxford: Oxford University Press, 2000), p. 82.

33 Fraser, *And We Shall Shock Them, the British Army in the Second World War*, p. 15.

34 Stanley Sandler (Editor), *World War II in the Pacific, an Encyclopedia* (New York: Garland Publishing, Inc., 2001), p. 405.

35 Winston Churchill, *The Second World War, Volume I: The Gathering Storm* (Boston: Houghton Mifflin Company, 1948), p. 336.

36 F. W. Perry, *The Commonwealth Armies: Manpower and Organisation in Two World Wars* (Oxford Road: Manchester University Press, 1988), pp. 45, 47.

Chapter 2: The Storm in Europe

1 This includes some ships held in reserve or under refit, but does not include ships held in the Commonwealth navies. Cruisers with 8-inch guns are classified as heavy cruisers. See S. W. Roskill, *The War at Sea 1939–1945, Volume I: The Defensive* (London: Her Majesty's Stationery Office, 1954), pp. 31, 577–582 and David Brown, *Warship Losses of World War Two* (London: Arms and Armour Press, 1990), pp. 161, 170–176.

2   Roskill, *The War at Sea 1939–1945, Volume I*, pp. 49, 586.
3   John Keegan, *The Rand McNally Encyclopedia of World War II* (Chicago: Rand McNally & Company, 1977), p. 95 and John Ellis, *World War II, A Statistical Survey, the Essential Facts and Figures for all the Combatants* (New York: Facts on File, 1993), p. 245.
4   Cajus Bekker, *Hitler's Naval War* (New York: Kensington Publishing Corp., 1977), pp. 369–371.
5   French, *Raising Churchill's Army, the British Army and the War against Germany 1919–1945*, p. 63.
6   I. C. B. Dear and M. R. D. Foot, *The Oxford Companion to World War II* (Oxford: Oxford University Press, 1995), pp. 468, 471.
7   Perry, *The Commonwealth Armies: Manpower and Organisation in Two World Wars*, p. 102.
8   Ibid., p. 161.
9   Dear and Foot, *The Oxford Companion to World War II*, p. 186.
10 Fraser, *And We Shall Shock Them, the British Army in the Second World War*, p. 22.
11 Dear and Foot, *The Oxford Companion to World War II*, pp. 468, 474.
12 Terraine, *The Right of the Line, The Royal Air Force in the European War 1939–1945*, p. 701 and Ellis, *World War II, A Statistical Survey, the Essential Facts and Figures for all the Combatants*, pp. 231, 241.
13 Denis Richards, *Royal Air Force 1939–1945, Volume I: The Fight at Odds* (London: Her Majesty's Stationery Office, 1953), p. 41 and Terraine, *The Right of the Line, The Royal Air Force in the European War 1939–1945*, p. 97.
14 Richards, *Royal Air Force 1939–1945, Volume I*, pp. 56, 65.
15 Roskill, *The War at Sea 1939–1945, Volume 1*, p. 615 and The Central Statistical Office, *Statistical Digest of the War* (London: Her Majesty's Stationery Office, 1975), p. 180.
16 The Central Statistical Office, *Statistical Digest of the War*, p. 174.
17 Ibid., p. 184.
18 ADM 199/2447, German Ships: Losses and Damage in NW European Waters, 1939–1945; J. Rohwer and G. Hummelchen, *Chronology of the War at Sea 1939–1945* (Annapolis: Naval Institute Press, 1992), pp. 1–14 and Rodger Jordan, *The World's Merchant Fleets 1939, The Particulars and Wartime Fates of 6,000 Ships* (Annapolis: Naval Institute Press, 1999), pp. 465–480.
19 P. K. Kemp, *Key to Victory, The Triumph of British Sea Power in World War II* (Boston: Little, Brown and Company, 1957), p. 37.
20 Roskill, *The War at Sea 1939–1945, Volume 1*, p. 63.
21 Ibid., p. 64.
22 The count of British divisions only includes those deployed to France and designated for combat operations. It does not include three Territorial Army divisions that were deployed in France to provide logistical and service support. Sources differ on the exact number of forces available to the competing sides during Germany's assault against France and the Low Countries. However, it is generally acknowledged that the combined Allied nations maintained at least parity if not numerical superiority in most force categories. The strength figures presented here come from Basil Liddell Hart (Editor In Chief), *World War II, An Illustrated History* (London: Purnell Reference Books, 1977), p. 96.
23 ADM 234/360, Battle Summaries, No. 41: Evacuation from Dunkirk (Operation *Dynamo*) 26 May–4 June 1940, Table 3(b).
24 Ibid., p. 209.
25 Roskill, *The War at Sea 1939–1945, Volume 1*, p. 603.
26 Terraine, *The Right of the Line, The Royal Air Force in the European War 1939–1945*, p. 157.
27 Roskill, *The War at Sea 1939–1945, Volume 1*, p. 239.
28 Terraine, *The Right of the Line, The Royal Air Force in the European War 1939–1945*, pp. 174, 181.
29 Roskill, *The War at Sea 1939–1945, Volume 1*, pp. 593–597.

30 I. S. O. Playfair, *The Mediterranean and Middle East, Volume I: The Early Success against Italy* (London: Her Majesty's Stationery Office, 1954), pp. 93–94.

31 Ibid., pp. 178–179.

32 Ibid., p. 273.

33 Ibid., p. 362.

34 Terraine, *The Right of the Line, The Royal Air Force in the European War 1939–1945*, pp. 317–318.

35 Gavin Long, *Australia in the War of 1939–1945, Series 1(Army), Volume II: Greece, Crete and Syria* (Canberra: Australian War Memorial, 1953), p. 183 and I. S. O. Playfair, *The Mediterranean and Middle East, Volume II, The Germans come to the Help of their Ally* (London: Her Majesty's Stationery Office, 1956), p. 147.

36 Playfair, *The Mediterranean and Middle East, Volume I*, p. 439.

37 The fatality figure comes from the Italian Ministry of Defence. See Angelo Del Boca, *The Ethiopian War 1935–1941* (Chicago: University of Chicago Press, 1969), p. 261. The prisoner figures are an author estimate based upon the culmination of multiple inputs from various sources.

38 Based upon equipment totals present at the beginning of the campaign as well as additional aircraft flown in as the campaign progressed. See Michael Glover, *An Improvised War, the Ethiopian Campaign 1940–1941* (London: Leo Cooper, 1987), p. 21.

39 Culmination of multiple inputs from Rohwer and Hummelchen, *Chronology of the War at Sea 1939–1945*.

40 The British casualty figures are an author estimate based upon the culmination of multiple events throughout the campaign as documented by multiple sources.

41 The Central Statistical Office, *Statistical Digest of the War*, pp. 173–174.

42 Ibid., p. 184. Figure contains minor adjustments from monthly totals.

43 I. S. O. Playfair, *The Mediterranean and Middle East, Volume III: British Fortunes Reach their Lowest Ebb* (London: Her Majesty's Stationery Office, 1960), p. 97.

44 James J. Sadkovich, *The Italian Navy in World War II* (London: Greenwood Press, 1994), p. 344.

45 Christina J. M. Goulter, *A Forgotten Offensive, Royal Air Force Coastal Command's Anti-Shipping Campaign, 1940–1945* (London: Frank Cass, 1995), p. 284.

Chapter 3: On the Brink in Asia

1 S. W. Roskill, *The War at Sea 1939–1945, Volume II: The Period of Balance* (London: Her Majesty's Stationery Office, 1956), pp. 476, 480.

2 Ibid., p. 480.

3 Elizabeth Anne Wheal, Stephen Pope and James Taylor, *A Dictionary of the Second World War* (London: Grafton Books, 1989), p. 244.

4 Ellis, *World War II, A Statistical Survey, the Essential Facts and Figures for all the Combatants*, p. 239.

5 Kent Roberts Greenfield (Editor), *Command Decisions* (Washington D.C.: Office of the Chief of Military History, United States Army, 1960), p. 111.

6 Spencer C. Tucker (Editor), *Encyclopedia of World War II, A Political, Social and Military History, Volume II: D–K* (Santa Barbara: ABC-CLIO, Inc., 2005), p. 770.

7 Lend-Lease was a programme adopted by the United States government in March 1941 to provide materiel aid to the United Kingdom, and later other Allied nations, in recognition of the threat that Germany and the Axis posed to American security.

8 French, *Raising Churchill's Army, The British Army and the War against Germany, 1919–1945*, pp. 187–188.

9 Perry, *The Commonwealth Armies: Manpower and Organisation in Two World Wars*, pp. 103–104.

10 Ibid., p. 107.

11 Dear and Foot, *The Oxford Companion to World War II*, p. 798.

12 Ellis, *World War II, A Statistical Survey, the Essential Facts and Figures for all the Combatants*, p. 277.

13 Henry Probert, *The Forgotten Air Force: The Royal Air Force in the War Against Japan 1941–1945* (London: Brassey's Ltd., 1995), p. 311.

14 Dennis Richards and Hilary St. George Saunders, *Royal Air Force 1939–1945, Volume II: The Fight Avails* (London: Her Majesty's Stationery Office, 1954), pp. 7–10.

Chapter 4: Japan Unleashed

1 Rohwer and Hummelchen, *Chronology of the War at Sea 1939–1945*, p. 104.

2 Edwyn Gray, *Operation Pacific, The Royal Navy's War against Japan 1941–1945* (London: Leo Cooper, 1990), p. 63.

3 ADM 234/330 Battle Summaries, No. 14: Loss of HM Ships *Prince of Wales* and *Repulse*, 10 December 1941, pp. 17–18.

4 Winston S. Churchill, *The Second World War, Volume 3: The Grand Alliance* (Boston: Houghton Mifflin Company, 1950), p. 620.

5 It is interesting to note that the Tripartite Pact did not technically obligate Germany and Italy to declare war on the United States. The Pact only stipulated that the signatories would provide political, economic and military support to each other in the event of an attack by a power not already involved in the European war or Sino-Japanese conflict. Since Japan attacked the United States, the above stated condition was not met.

6 Churchill, *The Second World War, Volume 3*, p. 607.

7 S. Woodburn Kirby, *The War Against Japan, Volume I: The Loss of Singapore* (London: Her Majesty's Stationery Office, 1957), p. 150.

8 Rohwer and Hummelchen, *Chronology of the War At Sea 1939–1945*, p. 110.

9 Roskill, *The War at Sea 1939-1945, Volume II*, pp. 7–8.

10 Alden, *U.S. Submarine Attacks During World War II (Including Allied Submarine Attacks in the Pacific Theater)*, pp. 1–3 and Rohwer and Hummelchen, *Chronology of the War at Sea 1939–1945*, pp. 108, 115, 118.

11 On 13 December 1941 the Dutch submarine *K-XII* claimed the destruction of a 3,500-ton tanker off Kota Bharu. Some researchers believe the impacted vessel was the 3,525-ton *Taizan Maru* lost near Cape Camau, but this assessment remains in question since the cited locations do not match. On 24 January 1942 *K-XVIII* claimed the destruction of a warship, later identified as the 935-ton escort destroyer *P37*, off Balikpapan. The validity of this claim remains in dispute since many sources credit the destruction of *P37*, along with other vessels, to an American destroyer attack that was carried out at approximately the same time as that of *K-XVIII*. Post-war analysis confirms damage to five merchant ships worth 41,702 tons. Two additional ships worth an estimated 12,114 tons may have been damaged, but Japanese records do not confirm this. See Alden, *U.S. Submarine Attacks During World War II (Including Allied Submarine Attacks in the Pacific Theater)*, pp. 1–3 and Rohwer and Hummelchen, *Chronology of the War at Sea 1939–1945*, pp. 108, 118.

12 Alden, *U.S. Submarine Attacks During World War II (Including Allied Submarine Attacks in the Pacific Theater)*, p. 7.

13 Bruce T. Swain, *A Chronology of Australian Armed Forces at War, 1939–45* (Sydney: Allen & Unwin, 2001), p. 120.

14 Chris Shores, Brian Cull, and Yashuo Izawa, *Bloody Shambles, Volume 2: The Defence of Sumatra to the Fall of Burma* (London: Grub Street, 1993), pp. 86–87.

15 Kirby, *The War Against Japan, Volume I*, p. 473.

16   Gray, *Operation Pacific, The Royal Navy's War against Japan 1941–1945*, p. 94.

17   Richards and Saunders, *Royal Air Force 1939–1945, Volume II*, pp. 58–61.

18   ADM 186/797, Battle Summaries, Nos. 1, 6, 7 and 19: Operations against French Fleet at Mersel-Kebir (Oran) 3–6 July 1940, the bombardments of Bardia June 1940–Jan 1941, Genoa 9 Feb 1941 and Tripoli 21 Apr 1941, Appendix B.

19   Ibid., p. 33.

20   ADM 234/331 Battle Summaries, No. 15: Naval Operations off Ceylon, 29th March to 10th April, 1942, Appendixes E and E(1).

21   Louis Allen, *Burma, The Longest War 1941–1945* (London: J. M. Dent & Sons Ltd, 1984), p. 638.

22   S. Woodburn Kirby, *The War against Japan, Volume V: The Surrender of Japan* (London: Her Majesty's Stationery Office, 1969), p. 542.

Chapter 5: Turning the Tide

1   Doolittle survived the raid and received fast promotion to general-grade rank. He later went on to command the American Twelfth, Fifteenth and Eighth Air Forces in the Mediterranean and European theatres.

2   John Winton, *The Forgotten Fleet, The British Navy in the Pacific War 1944–1945* (New York: Coward-McCann, Inc., 1970), p. 22.

3   For Britain's portion of these losses (including those sustained by Commonwealth forces) see Chapter 4.

4   During the battle and subsequent retreat Eighth Army suffered some 60,000 casualties which constituted about half of its strength. Most of these casualties were prisoners. See (CS/1405 20/7) Personal and Most Secret for CIGS from General Corbert. Great Britain, War Cabinet, *Cabinet History Series, Principle War Telegrams and Memoranda, 1940–1943, Middle East III* (Nendeln, Liechtenstein: KTO Press, 1976).

5   Roskill, *The War at Sea 1939–1945, Volume II*, pp. 467, 486.

6   Niklas Zetterling, *Normandy 1944, German Military Organization, Combat Power and Organizational Effectiveness* (Winnipeg: J. J. Fedorowicz Publishing, Inc., 2000), p. 91.

7   ADM 234/331 Battle Summaries, No. 16: Naval Operations at the Capture of Diego Suarez (Operation *Ironclad*), May 1942, Appendix A.

8   Ibid., Appendix F.

9   Ibid., Appendix G.

10   Evan Mawdsley, *The War for the Seas, A Maritime History of World War II* (New Haven: Yale University Press, 2019), pp. 289–290.

11   For personnel losses see Warren Tute, *The Reluctant Enemies, The Story of the last War between Britain and France 1940–1942* (London: Collins, 1990), p. 206. For naval losses see David Brown, *Carrier Operations in World War II, Volume One: The Royal Navy* (Annapolis: Naval Institute Press, 1968), pp. 101–102 and Rohwer and Hummelchen, *Chronology of the War at Sea 1939–1945*, p. 136.

12   ADM 199/1277, Madagascar and Jordan, *The World's Merchant Fleets 1939, The particulars and Wartime Fates of 6,000 ships*, pp. 480, 526 and 532.

13   ADM 234/331 Battle Summaries, No. 16: Naval Operations at the Capture of Diego Suarez (Operation *Ironclad*), May 1942, Appendix E.

14   The former was taken as a prize; the latter was scuttled on 30 September. See Swain, *A Chronology of Australian Armed Forces at War, 1939–45*, pp. 197–198.

15   Christopher Buckley, *Five Ventures: Iraq–Syria–Persia–Madagascar–Dodecanese* (London: Her Majesty's Stationery Office, 1954), pp. 206–207.

16 Gray, *Operation Pacific, The Royal Navy's War against Japan 1941–1945*, pp. 134, 136.

17 *O-23*'s claim against *Ohio Maru* remains in dispute. While some post-war analysis, including the British Staff Study and the Dutch Naval History, support this claim, a number of other sources credit *Ohio Maru's* destruction to the American submarine *Tautog* on 5 or 6 August 1942. For results from Allied submarine attacks see Alden, *U.S. Submarine Attacks During World War II (Including Allied Submarine Attacks in the Pacific Theater)*, pp. 11, 12, 14, 21, 23 and Rohwer and Hummelchen, *Chronology of the War at See 1939–1945*, pp. 142, 149, 152, 170, 178.

18 The Joint Army-Navy Assessment Committee, *Japanese Naval and Merchant Losses During World War II By all Causes* (Washington D.C.: US Government Printing Office, 1947), p. 33.

19 Allen, *Burma, The Longest War 1941–1945*, p. 113.

20 Ibid., p. 147.

21 ADM 234/371 Battle Summaries, No. 45: Battle of Coral Sea, 4–8 May 1942, Appendix C.

22 Ibid., p. 27.

23 ADM 234/371 Battle Summaries, No. 46: Battle of Midway, 3–6 June 1942, p. 119.

24 Richard B. Frank, *Guadalcanal, The Definitive Account of the Landmark Battle* (New York: Penguin Books, 1990), pp. 601, 611, 614.

25 G. Hermon Gill, *Royal Australian Navy 1942–1945* (Canberra: Australian War Memorial, 1968), p. 183.

26 Samuel Milner, *The United States Army in World War II: Victory in Papua* (Washington D.C.: Office of the Chief of Military History, Department of the Army, 1957), p. 87.

27 Swain, *A Chronology of Australian Armed Forces at War, 1939–45*, p. 215.

28 Milner, *United States Army in World War II: Victory in Papua*, pp. 370, 372.

Chapter 6: Commonwealth Contributions in the South Pacific

1 Zetterling, *Normandy 1944, German Military Organization, Combat Power and Organizational Effectiveness*, p. 91.

2 This breakdown in Axis prisoners included 7,287 at First El Alamein in July 1942, 32,205 at Second El Alamein and its follow up from 23 October through 31 December, some 30,000 in Tunisia in March and April 1943 and 238,243 during the final mass surrender in May 1943. See Brian E. Walter, *Blue Water War, the Maritime Struggle in the Mediterranean and Middle East, 1940–1945* (Oxford: Casemate Publishers, 2022), pp. 118, 151, 156, 157, 160.

3 Thomas Parrish (Editor), *The Simon and Schuster Encyclopedia of World War II* (New York: Simon and Schuster, 1978), p. 446.

4 Roskill, *The War at Sea 1939–1945, Volume II*, p. 486.

5 The American total is taken from Clay Blair, *Hitler's U-boat War, the Hunted, 1942–1945* (New York: Random House, 1998), p. 161 and the British total is taken from The Central Statistical Office, *Statistical Digest of the War*, p. 135.

6 Roskill, *The War at Sea 1939–1945, Volume II*, p. 486.

7 ADM 199/2447, German Ships: Losses and Damage in NW European Waters, 1939–1945.

8 Percentages based upon declines in average monthly output as reported in Imperial War Museum, Speer Collection, Interrogation Reports, 3063/49. File 4, Report 35, Supplement II, 21 November 1945, p. 3.

9 Phillips Payson O'Brien, *How the War was Won, Air-Sea Power and Allied Victory in World War II* (Cambridge: Cambridge University Press, 2015), p. 306.

10 Douglas Gillison, *Royal Australian Air Force 1939–42* (Canberra: Australian War Memorial, 1962), p. 566 and The Joint Army-Navy Assessment Committee, *Japanese Naval and Merchant Losses During World War II By all Causes*, p. 32.

11 Robert J. Cressman, *The Official Chronology of the U.S. Navy in World War II* (Annapolis: Naval Institute Press, 2000), p. 118.

12 Cressman, *The Official Chronology of the U.S. Navy in World War II*, pp.133–134 and Gillison, *Royal Australian Air Force 1939–42*, p. 641.

13 Gillison, *Royal Australian Air Force 1939–42*, p. 674.

14 Lex McAulay, *Battle of the Bismarck Sea* (New York: St. Martin's Press, 1991), pp. 73, 179.

15 Ibid., p. 117.

16 There is some disagreement as to the total tonnage of the merchant ships destroyed. This is primarily based upon differing displacements allotted to the Japanese naval supply ship *Nojima*. Some early American sources including the Joint Army-Navy Assessment Committee and the Official History of United States Naval Operations in World War II put *Nojima*'s estimated tonnage at 4,500 tons. More recent sources indicate that *Nojima*'s tonnage was actually 8,125 tons. I used this latter figure in calculating Japan's overall tonnage loss. The other seven merchant ships lost were the *Aiyo Maru* (2,746 tons), *Kembu Maru* (953 tons), *Kyokusei Maru* (5,493 tons), *Oigawa Maru* (6,493 tons), *Taimei Maru* (2,883 tons), *Teiyo Maru* (6,869 tons) and *Shin-Ai Maru* (3,793 tons). See McAulay, *Battle of the Bismarck Sea*, pp. 178–180.

17 Gillison, *Royal Australian Air Force 1939–42*, p. 696.

18 Naval Analysis Division, *The United States Strategic Bombing Survey, The Offensive Mine Laying Campaign Against Japan* (Washington D.C.: Department of the Navy, 1969), pp. 35, 74, 77.

19 The Joint Army-Navy Assessment Committee, *Japanese Naval and Merchant Losses During World War II By all Causes*, pp. 8, 44, 46.

20 Ibid., pp. 7, 43.

21 George Odgers, *Air War against Japan 1943–45* (Canberra: Australian War Memorial, 1957), p. 105.

22 Oliver A. Gillespie, *Official History of New Zealand in the Second World War 1939–45: The Pacific* (Wellington: War History Branch, Department of Internal Affairs, 1952), p. 248.

23 Michael Apps, *Send Her Victorious* (London: William Kimber, 1971), p. 123.

24 Dudley McCarthy, *Australia in the War of 1939–1945: Series 1, Volume V: South-West Pacific Area – First Year, Kokoda to Wau* (Canberra: Australian War Memorial, 1959), p. 558.

25 Ibid., pp. 572, 576.

26 David Dexter, *Australia in the War of 1939–1945: Series I, Volume VI: The New Guinea Offensive* (Canberra: Australian War Memorial, 1961), pp. 324, 392.

27 Ibid., pp. 466, 467.

28 Ibid., p. 560.

29 Ibid., pp. 736, 737.

30 Ibid., p. 770.

31 Ibid., p. 817.

32 Gillespie, *Official History of New Zealand in the Second World War 1939–45: The Pacific*, pp. 138, 158, 188.

33 Odgers, *Air War against Japan 1943–45*, p. 133.

34 Ibid., p. 193.

35 Naval Analysis Division, *The United States Strategic Bombing Survey, The Offensive Mine Laying Campaign against Japan*, pp. 35, 74, 77, 110.

36 Odgers, *Air War against Japan 1943–45*, p. 119.

37 Cressman, *The Official Chronology of the U.S. Navy in World War II*, pp. 219, 242, 246, 282.

38 Eric M. Bergerud, *Fire in the Sky, the Air War in the South Pacific* (Boulder: Westview Press, 2000), p. 597.
39 Odgers, *Air War against Japan 1943–45*, pp. 83, 303, 389, 403.
40 Cressman, *The Official Chronology of the U.S. Navy in World War II*, p. 239.
41 For these merchant losses see Helmut Pemsel, *A History of War at Sea, An Atlas and Chronology of Conflict at Sea from Earliest Times to the Present* (Annapolis: Naval Institute Press, 1979), p. 164.
42 S. W. Roskill, *The War at Sea 1939–1945, Volume III, Part I: The Offensive, 1st June 1943 – 31st May 1944* (London: Her Majesty's Stationery Office, 1960), pp. 231–232.
43 S. W. Roskill, *The War at Sea 1939–1945, Volume III, Part II: The Offensive, 1st June 1944 – 14th August 1945* (London: Her Majesty's Stationery Office, 1961), p. 229.
44 Ibid., p. 287.
45 An exact count is impossible to ascertain since several submarines were lost to presumed or unknown causes.
46 AIR 41/79, RAF in the Maritime War, Volume VIII: Statistics, Table 32.
47 Pemsel, *A History of War at Sea, An Atlas and Chronology of Conflict at Sea from Earliest Times to the Present*, p. 164.
48 Rohwer and Hummelchen, *Chronology of the War at Sea 1939–1945*, pp. 301, 309.

Chapter 7: Return to the Indian Ocean

1 S. Woodburn Kirby, *The War against Japan, Volume III: The Decisive Battles* (London: Her Majesty's Stationery Office, 1961), p. 376.
2 Alden, *U.S. Submarine Attacks During World War II (Including Allied Submarine Attacks in the Pacific Theater)*, pp. 33, 35, 40, 54.
3 ADM 234/382 Submarines, Volume III: Operations in Far Eastern Waters including operations of Allied Submarines, p. 28.
4 AIR 41/77, RAF in the Maritime War, Volume VII, Part III: The Indian Ocean and South-East Asia; Operations, November 1943–August 1945, p. 504.
5 The men involved were Major Ivan Lyon (Mission Commander), Lieutenant Hubert Carse, Lieutenant Donald Davidson, Lieutenant Robert Page, Corporal Andrew Crilly, Corporal Ronald Morris, Leading Seaman Kevin Cain, Leading Stoker James McDowell, Leading Telegraphist Horace Young, Able Seaman Walter Falls, Able Seaman Mostyn Berryman, Able Seaman Frederick Marsh, Able Seaman Arthur Jones and Able Seaman Andrew Huston.
6 The Joint Army-Navy Assessment Committee, *Japanese Naval and Merchant Losses During World War II By all Causes*, p. 44.
7 Roskill, *The War at Sea 1939–1945, Volume III, Part I*, p. 378.
8 Lt-Col. G. W. L Nicholson, *Official History of the Canadian Army in the Second World War, Volume II: The Canadians in Italy 1943–1944* (Ottawa: Roger Duhamel, F.R.S.C., 1966), p. 7 and Douglas Porch, *The Path to Victory, The Mediterranean Theater in World War II* (New York: Farrar, Straus and Giroux, 2004), p. 417.
9 ADM 199/2519, World War II Mediterranean Statistics.
10 Kirby, *The War against Japan, Volume III*, pp. 468–470.
11 Roskill, *The War at Sea 1939–1945, Volume III, Part II*, p. 479.
12 Roskill, *The War at Sea 1939–1945, Volume III, Part I*, p. 350.
13 For the stated monthly Allied shipping losses in the Indian Ocean, see H. P. Willmott, *Grave of a Dozen Schemes, British Naval Planning and the War Against Japan, 1943–1945* (Annapolis: Naval Institute Press, 1995), pp. 160–175.

14 Details regarding the results of this raid are vague and contradictory. For the account referenced here see David Brown, *HMS Illustrious, Pt. 2, Warships in Profile No. 11* (Leatherhead, Surrey: Profile Publications Ltd., 1971), p. 257. Some other accounts indicate more damage inflicted but give no definitive details.

15 Roskill, *The War at Sea 1939–1945, Volume III, Part II*, p. 200.

16 ADM 199/2447, German Ships: Losses and Damage in NW European Waters, 1939–1945.

17 This listing of British submarine successes includes a number of victories previously mentioned in the chapter. See Alden, *U.S. Submarine Attacks during World War II, Including Allied Submarine Attacks in the Pacific Theater*, pp. 67–167, 232.

18 AIR 41/77, RAF in the Maritime War, Volume VII, Part III: The Indian Ocean and South-East Asia; Operations, November 1943 – August 1945, p. 504.

19 Dispatch on air Operations in South East Asia, 16th November, 1943 to 31st May, 1944, by Air Chief Marshal Sir R. E. C. Peirse as reported in the London Gazette on 13 March 1951, p. 1,390.

Chapter 8: The Battle for India and the Opening of the Burma Offensive

1   Allen, *Burma, The Longest War 1941–1945*, p. 662.

2   Kirby, *The War against Japan, Volume III*, p. 144.

3   Dear and Foot, *The Oxford Companion to World War II*, p. 4.

4   Kirby, *The War against Japan, Volume III*, p. 327.

5   Hilary St. George Saunders, *Royal Air Force 1939–1945, Volume III: The Fight is Won* (London: Her Majesty's Stationery Office, 1954), p. 328.

6   John Colvin, *Not Ordinary Men, The Story of the Battle of Kohima* (London: Leo Cooper, 1994), p. 126.

7   Kirby, *The War against Japan, Volume III*, p. 372.

8   E. D. Smith, *Battle for Burma* (New York: Holmes & Meier Publishers, Inc., 1979), pp. 113–114.

9   Kirby, *The War against Japan, Volume III*, pp. 526–527.

10 Saunders, *Royal Air Force 1939–1945, Volume III*, pp. 335, 337.

11 Allen, *Burma, the Longest War 1941–45*, p. 638.

12 Despatch on Operations in Assam and Burma, 1944 June 23 – Nov 12, by General Sir George J. Giffard, Commander-in-Chief, 11th Army Group, South East Asia Command as reported in the London Gazette on 2 April 1951, p. 1,729.

13 James Luto, *Fighting with the Fourteenth Army in Burma, Original War Summaries of the Battle Against Japan, 1943–1945* (Barnsley: Pen & Sword Military, 2013), p. 54.

14 Ibid., p. 150.

15 Despatch on Operations in Assam and Burma, 1944 June 23 – Nov 12, by General Sir George J. Giffard, Commander-in-Chief, 11th Army Group, South East Asia Command as reported in the London Gazette on 2 April 1951, p. 1,729.

16 Saunders, *Royal Air Force 1939–1945, Volume III*, p. 312.

17 Probert, *The Forgotten Air Force: The Royal Air Force in the War Against Japan 1941–1945*, p. 194.

18 Of the 740 aircraft present in the theatre at the end of 1943, about half were in Burma with the remainder located in Thailand, French Indochina, Malaya and Sumatra. See Saunders, *Royal Air Force 1939-1945, Volume III*, p. 312.

19   Norman Franks, *Spitfires Over the Arakan* (London: William Kimber & Co., 1988), pp. 219–222 and Probert, *The Forgotten Air Force: The Royal Air Force in the War Against Japan 1941–1945*, p. 192.

20   Probert, *The Forgotten Air Force: The Royal Air Force in the War Against Japan 1941–1945*, p. 164.

21   Ibid.

22   Ibid., p. 194.

23   These two formations consisted of the British Second and Canadian First Armies. In terms of the latter, although designated a Canadian army, the First Army was better described as a Canadian/British army. Although Canadian led and predominately staffed, a sizeable portion of the First Army's combat strength came from British units. In fact, there were times during the Northwest Europe campaign when there were more British soldiers in the First Army than there were Canadians.

24   Per a SHAEF G1 Report of Enemy Prisoners of War Dated 1 October 1944, this breakdown of prisoners consisted of 156,951 taken by the British 21st Army Group through 26 September, 322,718 taken by the American 12th Army Group through 25 September and 87,705 taken by the Franco-American 6th Army Group as of 20 September. See WO 229/47/4, Prisoners of War: Allied Prisoner of War Responsibilities.

Chapter 9: Tightening the Noose

1   Gill, *Royal Australian Navy 1942–1945*, pp. 525–526.

2   Peter C. Smith, *Task Force 57, The British Pacific Fleet, 1944–45* (Manchester: Crecy Publishing Limited, 2001), p. 78.

3   Gray, *Operation Pacific, The Royal Navy's War against Japan 1941–1945*, p. 189.

4   Ibid.

5   AIR 41/77, RAF in the Maritime War, Volume VII, Part III: The Indian Ocean and South-East Asia; Operations, November 1943–August 1945, p. 398.

6   Brown, *Carrier Operations in World War II, Volume One: The Royal Navy*, p. 123.

7   Roskill, *The War at Sea 1939–1945, Volume III, Part II*, p. 367.

8   Ibid.

9   Tucker (Editor), *Encyclopedia of World War II, A Political, Social and Military History, Volume IV*, p. 1,572.

10   John Ellis, *Brute force, Allied Strategy and Tactics in the Second World War* (New York: Viking, 1990), p. 476.

11   Ibid., pp. 469–470.

12   Ellis, *World War II, A Statistical Survey, the Essential Facts and Figures for all the Combatants*, p. 278.

13   Ellis, *Brute force, Allied Strategy and Tactics in the Second World War*, p. 486.

14   Kenneth Poolman, *Allied Escort Carriers of World War Two in Action* (Annapolis: Naval Institute Press, 1988), p. 249.

15   Gray, *Operation Pacific, The Royal Navy's War against Japan 1941–1945*, p. 182.

16   Ibid., p. 209.

17   ADM 234/368 Battle Summaries, No. 47: Naval Operations in Assault and Capture of Okinawa (Operation *ICEBERG*) Mar.–June 1945, p. 115 and Brown, *Carrier Operations in World War II, Volume One: The Royal Navy*, p. 130.

18   Dear and Foot, *The Oxford Companion to World War II*, p. 836.

19   Ibid.

20   S. Woodburn Kirby, *The War against Japan, Volume IV: The Reconquest of Burma* (London: Her Majesty's Stationery Office, 1965), p. 401.

21 Ibid., p. 402.
22 Ibid., p. 313.
23 Ibid., p. 398.
24 Kirby, *The War against Japan, Volume IV*, p. 311 and Allen, *Burma, The Longest War 1941–1945*, p. 638.
25 ADM 234/361 Battle Summaries, No. 42: Burma 1941–1945 Naval Operations, Appendix A.
26 Bryan Cooper, *The Battle of the Torpedo Boats* (New York: Stein and Day Publishers, 1970), p. 283.
27 WO 203/5849, Some Facts about the Burma Campaign, pp. 9–10.
28 ADM 234/361 Battle Summaries, No. 42: Burma 1941–1945 Naval Operations, pp. 75–76.
29 Ibid., pp. 82–85.
30 WO 203/2692, History of the Arakan Campaign, 1944–1945, p. 52 and Winton, *The Forgotten Fleet, The British Navy in the Pacific 1944–1945*, pp. 182–184.
31 WO 203/5849, Some Facts about the Burma Campaign, p. 10.
32 Kirby, *The War against Japan, Volume IV*, p. 350.
33 Saunders, *Royal Air Force 1939–1945, Volume III*, p. 347.
34 AIR 41/77, RAF in the Maritime War, Volume VII, Part III: The Indian Ocean and South-East Asia; Operations, November 1943 – August 1945, pp. 519–520.
35 Ibid., p. 504.
36 Naval Analysis Division, *The United States Strategic Bombing Survey, The Offensive Mine Laying Campaign against Japan*, pp. 35, 72, 79.
37 Despatch on air operations in South-East Asia 1944 June 1–1945 May 2, by Air Chief Marshal Sir Keith Park, Allied Air Commander-in-Chief, Air Command, South-East Asia as reported in the London Gazette on 12 April 1951, pp. 1,970, 1,978, 1,981, 1,982.
38 Kirby, *The War against Japan, Volume IV*, pp. 261, 311.
39 ADM 234/361 Battle Summaries, No. 42: Burma 1941–1945 Naval Operations, pp. 118–119.

Chapter 10: Victory over Japan

1 By 17 May 1945 the Allies had more than 1.4 million Axis prisoners held in Italy and Austria of which 1,134,000 were under British control. See Field Marshal Alexander to SHAEF Fwd dated 9 June 1945 REF No. 383.7/4. NARS, Washington.
2 L. F. Ellis, *Victory in the West, Volume II: The Defeat of Germany* (London: Her Majesty's Stationery Office, 1968), p. 406.
3 The breakdown of German prisoners collected in these areas as of the middle of May was: the Wilhelmshaven-Emden peninsula – 60,000, Western Holland – 120,000, the Cuxhaven peninsula – 260,000, Denmark – 160,000, north Schleswig-Holstein – 250,000, south Schleswig-Holstein – 134,000, east Prussia – 75,000, Wismar Cushion – 360,000. See Francis De Guingand, *Operation Victory* (New York: Charles Scribner's Son, 1947), p. 458.
4 Per daily prisoner returns, 21st Army Group reported a total of at least 521,343 prisoners taken from 6 June 1944 through the morning of 5 May 1945. This included 12,018 prisoners taken by American units temporarily assigned to 21st Army Group. When these American prisoners are subtracted, this leaves 509,325 prisoners that were taken by British, Canadian and affiliated forces. See WO 219/1545 and WO 219/1547, Casualty Reports: 21 Army Group Daily Reports, including Reinforcements and Enemy Prisoners Taken.
5 Alden, *U.S. Submarine Attacks During World War II (Including Allied Submarine Attacks in the Pacific Theater)*, pp. 168–226, 232.
6 Cressman, *The Official Chronology of the U.S. Navy in World War II*, p. 340.
7 WO 203/2212, History of the 12th Army from its Formation on 28 May 1945 to the End of Operations Sept. 1945, p. 15.

8 Allen, *Burma, The Longest War 1941–1945*, p. 494.
9 WO 203/2212, History of the 12th Army from its Formation on 28 May 1945 to the End of Operations Sept. 1945, p. 19.
10 Ibid., p. 62.
11 Kirby, *The War against Japan, Volume V*, p. 443.
12 Ibid.
13 Allen, *Burma, The Longest War 1941–1945*, pp. 640–642.
14 Brown, *Carrier Operations in World War II, Volume One: The Royal Navy*, p. 120.
15 Kirby, *The War against Japan, Volume V*, p. 133.
16 Ibid., p. 134.
17 Galvin Long, *Australia in the War of 1939–1945: Series I, Volume VII: The Final Campaigns* (Canberra: Australian War Memorial, 1963), p. 242, 268.
18 Ibid., p. 269.
19 Hugh Buggy, *Pacific Victory, A Short History of Australia's Part in the War against Japan* (North Melbourne: Victorian Railway Printing Works, 1945), p. 296.
20 WO 203/2690, 1 Australian Corps: Report on Operations during Borneo Campaign May – Aug. 1945, pp. 34, 101, 146, 173.
21 Naval Analysis Division, *The United States Strategic Bombing Survey, The Offensive Mine Laying Campaign against Japan*, pp. 74, 77.
22 Odgers, *Air War Against Japan 1943–45*, p. 372.
23 Naval Analysis Division, *The United States Strategic Bombing Survey, The Offensive Mine Laying Campaign against Japan*, pp. 35, 36, 74, 77.
24 Buggy, *Pacific Victory, A Short History of Australia's Part in the War against Japan*, p. 301.
25 This proposed invasion had two primary parts. The first, Operation *Olympic*, was scheduled to begin in late October and called for the capture of the southern third of the southernmost main island of Kyūshū. Using this territory to provide airfields and staging areas, the Allies would then launch the second portion of their plan, Operation *Coronet*, to capture the main Japanese island of Honshu beginning in the spring of 1946. Although primarily an American-run affair, British and Commonwealth naval and air assets were slotted to support the entire undertaking while a Commonwealth Corps, consisting of at least three divisions (one each British, Australian and Canadian) was tentatively earmarked for inclusion in Operation *Coronet*.
26 Japanese naval aircraft sank the British carrier *Hermes* off Ceylon on 9 April 1942. *Hermes* displaced 10,850 tons and carried a maximum complement of 15 aircraft. By comparison, *Shimane Maru* displaced 11,800 tons and was designed to carry 12 aircraft.
27 There remains some minor disagreement regarding the destruction of *CD4* and *CD30*. A number of British sources indicate that the vessels were sunk on 24 July 1945. However, Japanese and American sources generally indicate that the vessels were lost on the 28th. Fleet communiqués and strike reports from the period clearly bolster this latter claim. As such, it is likely that post-war historians simply made a mistake (which was then repeated) regarding the earlier date sometimes associated with these losses.
28 Soward, *A Formidable Hero, Lt R.H. Gray, VC, DSC, RCNVR*, p. 141.
29 There is a degree of uncertainty regarding the dates and details associated with the destruction of *Ōhama*, *W1* and *CH42*. While most sources assign 10 August as the date on which these ships were sunk, other accounts indicate that the 9th was the actual date of their demise. When exploring the matter further, all three warships were hit and severely damaged on the 9th but may have been further damaged on the 10th. Since all three bottomed in shallow water, it could be a matter of interpretation as to when this damage became fatal. Likewise, while most sources indicate that *W1* was sunk in Yamada Bay, some of these same sources provide latitude and longitude coordinates that actually place the vessel's location in Onagawa Bay. Finally, while it

is clear that British aircraft played a definite role in destroying each of these vessels based upon strike reports and photographic evidence (see ADM 199/1478, Operations Against Japan: British Pacific Fleet Narrative of Events including 22 Pictures), it is unknown to what degree American aircraft also contributed to these losses. This latter point is complicated by the fact that both navies conducted a series of strikes against Onagawa during this period thus making a precise attribution of the damage inflicted difficult to ascertain.

30   ADM 199/118, The British Pacific Fleet in Operations against Japan, Table II.

31   Enclosure No. 1 to A.C.1's letter No. 0109/16/923 of 23rd August, 1945. See ADM 199/1478, Operations Against Japan: British Pacific Fleet Narrative of Events including 22 Pictures.

32   The warship losses come from a variety of sources. The tonnage of commercial ships lost comes from ADM 199/118, The British Pacific Fleet in Operations against Japan, Tables XXIV and XXV.

33   Winton, The Forgotten Fleet, The British Navy in the Pacific 1944–1945, p. 342.

34   While these figures represent the official British and American results for the campaign, it is entirely likely that a degree of inaccuracy or over-claiming is present in these numbers. In just viewing the British claims, some inconsistencies are plainly apparent. For instance, the claim of 347 Japanese aircraft destroyed or damaged is clearly stated in British after-action reports following the operation, but a computation of the claims made on the daily strike reports (as used in the text of this book) only brings this number to 253. Complicating the matter further, a series of CINCPOA communiques from 18 July through 11 August 1945 indicates that the British destroyed or damaged a total of 343 Japanese aircraft and 24 gliders during this period. How British authorities settled upon the official number of 347 is unclear. There are similar questions regarding the British claims made against Japanese shipping. In particular, of the 356,760 tons of Japanese shipping claimed sunk or damaged, a full 131,727 tons comes from vessels claimed damaged by Firefly aircraft. The notion that these Fireflies, which only made up nine percent of the British air group and conducted 11 percent of the total offensive sorties, were responsible for 37 percent of the total tonnage claims seems dubious. At best, it would indicate that the vast bulk of this Firefly tonnage only received minor or superficial damage. While a similar review of the American claims is beyond the scope of this book, it is highly likely that similar inaccuracies and/or over-claiming also exist in their numbers given the well-established tendency for all combatants to overestimate the results of their actions. At a minimum, it is known that the Americans made claims against certain Japanese warships that were definitely sunk by British action.

35   Swain, A Chronology of Australian Armed Forces at War, 1939–45, p. 412 and Kirby, The War against Japan, Volume V, pp. 133–134.

36   WO 203/6076, Report on British Military Administration in Hong Kong 1945 Aug.–1946 Apr., p. 49.

37   Vice-Admiral The Earl Mountbatten of Burma, Post Surrender Tasks, Section E of the Report to the Combined Chiefs of Staff by the Supreme Allied Commander South East Asia, 1943–1945 (London: Her Majesty's Stationery Office, 1969), p. 282.

Chapter 11: Reflections on the Asia/Pacific War

1   Kirby, The War against Japan, Volume IV, p. 202.

2   Dear and Foot, The Oxford Companion to World War II, p. 626.

3   Brown, Warship Losses of World War Two, pp. 184–189.

4   Roskill, The War at Sea 1939–1945, Volume III, Part II, p. 367.

5   The Joint Army-Navy Assessment Committee, Japanese Naval and Merchant Losses During World War II By all Causes, p. vi.

6   Ibid.
7   ADM 199/1478, Operations Against Japan: British Pacific Fleet Narrative of Events including 22 Pictures and Ellis, *World War II, A Statistical Survey, the Essential Facts and Figures for all the Combatants*, p. 235.
8   These loss figures come primarily from The Joint Army-Navy Assessment Committee, *Japanese Naval and Merchant Losses During World War II By all Causes* with some additions or adjustments taken from other sources.
9   Ibid.
10   Ellis, *World War II, A Statistical Survey, the Essential Facts and Figures for all the Combatants*, p. 259.
11   Executive Office of the Statistics Commission (Editor), *Japan Statistical Year-Book, 1949* (Tokyo: Statistics Bureau of the Prime Minister's Office, 1949) pp. 1,056–1,058.
12   Brian E. Walter, *The Longest Campaign, Britain's Maritime Struggle in the Atlantic and Northwest Europe, 1939–1945* (Oxford: Casemate, 2020) pp. 263, 274. Table 11.1 shows 1,634 German principal warships lost during the war. Added to this were six U-boats seized by the Japanese upon Germany's surrender thus bringing this total to 1,640.
13   Ibid., p. 269.
14   ADM 234/356, Battle Summaries, No. 35: Invasion of Sicily (Operation Husky), pp. 12, 14.
15   L. F. Ellis, *Victory in the West, Volume I: The Battle of Normandy* (London: Her Majesty's Stationery Office, 1962), pp. 508–509.
16   ADM 234/367, Battle Summaries, No. 39, Volume II: Landings in Normandy (Operation *Neptune*) June 1944: Appendices, Appendixes A (1) and C.
17   Ibid., Appendixes A2 and B2.
18   Ellis, *Brute Force, Allied Strategy and Tactics in the Second World War*, p. 486.
19   Erminio Bognasco, *Submarines of World War Two* (Annapolis: Naval Institute Press, 1977), p. 102.

Appendix D: Plight of the Prisoners of War

1   Sandler (Editor), *World War II in the Pacific, an Encyclopedia*, p. 487.
2   Ibid., p, 489.
3   Ibid.
4   Tucker (Editor), *Encyclopedia of World War II, A Political, Social and Military History*, p. 1,217.
5   Ibid., p. 1,215.
6   Sandler (Editor), *World War II in the Pacific, an Encyclopedia*, p. 491.
7   Dear and Foot, *The Oxford Companion to World War II*, p. 566.
8   Sandler (Editor), *World War II in the Pacific, an Encyclopedia*, p. 491.
9   Ibid., p. 490.
10   Dear and Foot, *The Oxford Companion to World War II*, p. 275.
11   Tucker (Editor), *Encyclopedia of World War II, A Political, Social and Military History*, p. 1,218.

Appendix E: Contributions made by the Various Elements of the British Empire and Commonwealth during World War II

1   Fraser, *And We Shall Shock Them, The British Army in the Second World War*, pp. 399–409.
2   Perry, *The Commonwealth Armies: Manpower and Organisation in Two World Wars*, p. 117.
3   Dear and Foot, *The Oxford Companion to World War II*, p. 798.
4   Ibid., p. 1,027.

Selected Bibliography

Primary Sources and Official Histories

ADM 199/118, The British Pacific Fleet in Operations against Japan.

ADM 234/330 Battle Summaries, No. 14: Loss of HM Ships *Prince of Wales* and *Repulse*, 10 December 1941.

ADM 234/331 Battle Summaries, No. 15: Naval Operations off Ceylon, 29th March to 10th April, 1942.

ADM 234/331 Battle Summaries, No. 16: Naval Operations at the Capture of Diego Suarez (Operation *Ironclad*), May 1942.

ADM 234/339 Battle Summaries, No. 21: Naval Operations in Campaign for Guadalcanal, Aug 42–Feb 43.

ADM 234/344 Battle Summaries, No. 25: Naval Strategy in Pacific, Dec. 1941–Feb. 1943.

ADM 234/346 Battle Summaries, No. 28: Battle of Java Sea, 27 February 1942.

ADM 234/357 Battle Summaries, No. 34: Naval Strategy in Pacific, Feb. 1943 to Aug. 1945.

ADM 234/361 Battle Summaries, No. 42: Burma 1941–1945 Naval Operations.

ADM 234/365 Battle Summaries, No. 40: Battle for Leyte Gulf, 23–26 Oct 1944.

ADM 234/368 Battle Summaries, No. 47: Naval Operations in Assault and Capture of Okinawa (Operation *ICEBERG*) Mar.–June 1945.

ADM 234/371 Battle Summaries, No. 45: Battle of Coral Sea, 4–8 May 1942.

ADM 234/371 Battle Summaries, No. 46: Battle of Midway, 3–6 June 1942.

ADM 234/382 Submarines, Volume III: Operations in Far Eastern Waters including operations of Allied Submarines.

AIR 41/77, RAF in the Maritime War, Volume VII, Part III: The Indian Ocean and South-East Asia; Operations, November 1943–August 1945.

Dexter, David. *Australia in the War of 1939–1945: Series I, Volume VI: The New Guinea Offensive* (Canberra: Australian War Memorial, 1961).

Gill, G. Hermon. *Royal Australian Navy 1942–1945* (Canberra: Australian War Memorial, 1968).

Gillespie, Oliver A. *Official History of New Zealand in the Second World War 1939–1945: The Pacific* (Wellington: War History Branch, Department of Internal Affairs, 1952).

Gillison, Douglas. *Royal Australian Air Force 1939–42* (Canberra: Australian War Memorial, 1962).

Kirby, S. Woodburn. *The War Against Japan, Volume I: The Loss of Singapore* (London: Her Majesty's Stationery Office, 1957).

——. *The War Against Japan, Volume II: India's Most Dangerous Hour* (London: Her Majesty's Stationery Office, 1958).

——. *The War against Japan, Volume III: The Decisive Battles* (London: Her Majesty's Stationery Office, 1961).

——. *The War against Japan, Volume IV: The Reconquest of Burma* (London: Her Majesty's Stationery Office, 1965).

———. *The War against Japan, Volume V: The Surrender of Japan* (London: Her Majesty's Stationery Office, 1969).

Long, Galvin. *Australia in the War of 1939–1945: Series I, Volume VII: The Final Campaigns* (Canberra: Australian War Memorial, 1963).

McCarthy, Dudley. *Australia in the War of 1939–1945: Series 1, Volume V: South-West Pacific Area – First Year, Kokoda to Wau* (Canberra: Australian War Memorial, 1959).

Naval Analysis Division, *The United States Strategic Bombing Survey, The Offensive Mine Laying Campaign Against Japan* (Washington D.C.: Department of the Navy, 1969).

Odgers, George. *Air War against Japan 1943–45* (Canberra: Australian War Memorial, 1957).

Richards, Dennis and Saunders, Hilary St. George. *Royal Air Force 1939–1945, Volume II: The Fight Avails* (London: Her Majesty's Stationery Office, 1954).

Roskill, S. W. *The War at Sea, 1939–1945, Volume I: The Defensive* (London: Her Majesty's Stationery Office, 1954).

———. *The War at Sea, 1939–1945, Volume II: The Period of Balance* (London: Her Majesty's Stationery Office, 1956).

———. *The War at Sea, 1939–1945, Volume III, Part I: The Offensive, 1st June 1943–31 May 1944* (London: Her Majesty's Stationery Office, 1960).

———. *The War at Sea, 1939–1945, Volume III, Part II: The Offensive, 1st June 1944–14 August 1945* (London: Her Majesty's Stationery Office, 1961).

Saunders, Hilary St. George. *Royal Air Force 1939–1945, Volume III: The Fight is Won* (London: Her Majesty's Stationery Office, 1954).

The Joint Army-Navy Assessment Committee, *Japanese Naval and Merchant Losses During World War II By all Causes* (Washington D.C.: US Government Printing Office, 1947).

WO 203/2212, History of the 12th Army from its Formation on 28 May 1945 to the End of Operations Sept. 1945.

WO 203/2690, 1 Australian Corps: Report on Operations during Borneo Campaign May – Aug. 1945.

WO 203/2692, History of the Arakan Campaign, 1944–1945.

WO 203/5849, Some Facts about the Burma Campaign.

Secondary Sources

Alden, John D. *U.S. Submarine Attacks During World War II (Including Allied Submarine Attacks in the Pacific Theater)* (Annapolis: Naval Institute Press, 1989).

Allen, Louis. *Burma, The Longest War 1941–1945* (London: J. M. Dent & Sons Ltd, 1984).

Brown, David. *Carrier Operations in World War II, Volume One: The Royal Navy* (Annapolis: Naval Institute Press, 1968).

———. *The Seafire, The Spitfire that went to Sea* (Annapolis: Naval Institute Press, 1989).

———. *Warship Losses of World War Two* (London: Arms and Armour Press, 1990).

Buggy, Hugh. *Pacific Victory, A Short History of Australia's Part in the War against Japan* (North Melbourne: Victorian Railway Printing Works, 1945).

Cressman, Robert J. *The Official Chronology of the U.S. Navy in World War II* (Annapolis: Naval Institute Press, 2000).

Ellis, John. *Brute force, Allied Strategy and Tactics in the Second World War* (New York: Viking, 1990),

Ferguson, Ted. *Desperate Siege: The Battle of Hong Kong* (Garden City: Doubleday & Company, Inc., 1980).

Fraser, David. *And We Shall Shock Them, the British Army in the Second World War* (London: Sceptre, 1988).

Gray, Edwyn. *Operation Pacific, The Royal Navy's War against Japan 1941–1945* (London: Leo Cooper, 1990).

Hobbs, David. *The British Pacific Fleet, the Royal Navy's Most Powerful Strike Force* (Annapolis: Naval Institute Press, 2011).

Luto, James. *Fighting with the Fourteenth Army in Burma, Original War Summaries of the Battle Against Japan, 1943–1945* (Barnsley: Pen & Sword Military, 2013).

Mawdsley, Evan. *The War for the Seas, A Maritime History of World War II* (New Haven: Yale University Press, 2019).

McLynn, Frank. *The Burma Campaign: Disaster into Triumph, 1942–45* (New Haven: Yale University Press, 2011).

O'Brien, Phillips Payson. *How the War was Won, Air – Sea Power and Allied Victory in World War II* (Cambridge: Cambridge University Press, 2015).

Probert, Henry. *The Forgotten Air Force: The Royal Air Force in the War Against Japan 1941–1945* (London: Brassey's Ltd., 1995).

Raghavan, Srinath. *India's War: World War II and the Making of Modern South Asia* (New York: Basic Books, 2016).

Ready, J. Lee. *Forgotten Allies: The Military Contributions of the Colonies, Exiled Governments, and Lesser Powers to the Allied Victory in World War II, Volume II: The Asian Theater* (Jefferson: McFarland & Company, Incorporated Publishers, 1985).

Rohwer, J. and Hummelchen, G. *Chronology of the War at Sea 1939–1945* (Annapolis: Naval Institute Press, 1992).

Smith, E. D. *Battle for Burma* (New York: Holmes & Meier Publishers, Inc., 1979).

Smith, Peter C. *Task Force 57, The British Pacific Fleet, 1944–45* (Manchester: Crecy Publishing Limited, 2001).

Swain, Bruce T. *A Chronology of Australian Armed Forces at War, 1939–45* (Sydney: Allen & Unwin, 2001).

Willmott, H. P. *Grave of a Dozen Schemes, British Naval Planning and the War Against Japan, 1943–1945* (Annapolis: Naval Institute Press, 1995).

Winton, John. *The Forgotten Fleet, The British Navy in the Pacific 1944–1945* (New York: Coward-McCann, Inc., 1970).

Index

Vessels

Army and Air Formations

African Army Formations

American Army Formations

American Air Formations

Personalities

General Index